Mike Meyers'
CompTIA A+® Guide to Managing and Troubleshooting PCs Lab Manual

Fourth Edition

(Exams 220-801 & 220-802)

About the Authors

Mike Meyers, lovingly called the "AlphaGeek" by those who know him, is the industry's leading authority on CompTIA A+ certification. He is the president and cofounder of Total Seminars, LLC, a provider of PC and network repair seminars, books, videos, and courseware for thousands of organizations throughout the world. Mike has been involved in the computer and network repair industry since 1977 as a technician, instructor, author, consultant, and speaker. Author of numerous popular PC books and videos, Mike is also the series editor for the highly successful Mike Meyers' Certification Passport series, the Mike Meyers' Computer Skills series, and the Mike Meyers' Guide To series, all published by McGraw-Hill.

Scott Strubberg is a master teacher in computer maintenance and networking. He began his career in IT as a consultant and technician, earning the CompTIA A+, CompTIA Network+, and CompTIA Security+ certifications along the way. Scott taught in the public school system for over half a decade and, after joining Total Seminars, has led computer training courses all over the United States. Scott has worked as a mentor to countless teachers and enjoys inventing labs that make learning computer and networking subjects entertaining as well as productive.

Aaron Verber graduated from the University of Wisconsin, Eau Claire, with a focus on the spoken and sung word, and turned a passion for computers and a love of English into a career in computer training. Aaron has edited numerous books on computer maintenance, troubleshooting, and networking, including the best-selling *CompTIA A+ Certification All-in-One Exam Guide*, by Mike Meyers. Aaron puts his CompTIA A+ certification to good use crafting informative and creative labs suitable for all learners.

About the Technical Editor

Christopher A. Crayton (CompTIA A+, CompTIA Network+, MCSE) is an author, editor, technical consultant, and trainer. Chris has worked as a computer and networking instructor at Keiser University, as network administrator for Protocol, an eCRM company, and as a computer and network specialist at Eastman Kodak. Chris has authored several print and online books on PC Repair, CompTIA A+, CompTIA Security+, and Microsoft Windows. Chris has served as technical editor on numerous professional technical titles for leading publishing companies, including the *CompTIA A+ All-in-One Exam Guide*, the *CompTIA A+ Certification Study Guide*, and the *Mike Meyers' CompTIA A+ Certification Passport*.

Mike Meyers' CompTIA A+® Guide to Managing and Troubleshooting PCs Lab Manual

Fourth Edition

(Exams 220-801 & 220-802)

Mike Meyers
Scott Strubberg
Aaron Verber

New York   Chicago   San Francisco
Lisbon   London   Madrid   Mexico City
Milan   New Delhi   San Juan
Seoul   Singapore   Sydney   Toronto

The *McGraw·Hill* Companies

Cataloging-in-Publication Data is on file with the Library of Congress

**Mike Meyers' CompTIA A+® Guide to Managing and Troubleshooting PCs Lab Manual,
Fourth Edition (Exams 220-801 & 220-802)**

34567890   QVS QVS   10987654

ISBN   978-0-07-179555-5
MHID   0-07-179555-3

Sponsoring Editor
Tim Green

Editorial Supervisor
Jody McKenzie

Project Manager
Vastavikta Sharma,
Cenveo Publisher Services

Acquisitions Coordinator
Stephanie Evans

Technical Editor
Christopher Crayton

Copy Editor
William McManus

Proofreader
Linda Manis Leggio

Indexer
Jack Lewis

Production Supervisor
Jean Bodeaux

Composition
Cenveo Publisher Services

Illustration
Cenveo Publisher Services

Art Director, Cover
Jeff Weeks

To students young and old who keep the faith, that with hard work and diligence you will succeed.

Contents at a Glance

Contents

Acknowledgments

The crew at Total Seminars contributed mightily to this edition. Our Editor in Chief, Scott Jernigan, helped manage the flow of the textbook and provided direction for the accompanying lab manual. Michael Smyer and Ford Pierson provided stellar art, editing, and help with labs. Doug Jones and Dave Rush, fellow instructors at Total Seminars, added great feedback and support on the many labs in this book.

Our acquisitions editor, Tim Green, and his trusty assistant, Stephanie Evans, did a superb job managing priorities and adding tons of encouragement and praise as the book unfolded. Thanks!

Chris Crayton, our technical editor, did a great job on this edition. Thank you for helping make this book happen.

On the McGraw-Hill side, the crew once again demonstrated why McGraw-Hill is the best in show as a publisher. With excellent work and even better attitude, this book went smoothly together.

Our editorial supervisor, Jody McKenzie, rocked it once again, with great direction and follow-up on missing pieces. Our project manager, Vastavikta Sharma, and her excellent team were wonderful to work with (*again*, for Mike and Aaron, and *for the first time*, for Scott). Quiet competence is totally *not* overrated and you and your team have it to spare. Thank you!

To the copy editor, page proofer, and indexer—Bill McManus, Linda Leggio, Jack Lewis—superb work in every facet. Thank you for being the best.

Additional Resources for Teachers

This lab manual supplements *Mike Meyers' CompTIA A+ Guide to Managing and Troubleshooting PCs, Fourth Edition (Exams 220-801 & 220-802)*. The textbook includes an instructor and student Web site available online:

www.MHAplusOLC4e.com

McGraw-Hill Connect, a Web-based learning platform, connects instructors with their support materials, including lab solutions, and students with chapter assessments from the textbook. The Connect Online Learning Center provides resources for instructors in a format that follows the organization of the textbook and lab manual.

This site includes the following:

- Answer keys to the Mike Meyers' Lab Manual activities.

- Answer keys to the end-of-chapter activities in the textbook.

- Access to test bank files and software that allows you to generate a wide array of paper- or network-based tests, and that features automatic grading. The test bank includes:

  - Hundreds of practice questions and a wide variety of question types categorized by exam objective, enabling you to customize each test to maximize student progress.

  - Blackboard cartridges and other formats may also be available upon request; contact your McGraw-Hill sales representative.

- Engaging PowerPoint slides on the lecture topics that include full-color artwork from the book.

- An Instructor's Manual that contains learning objectives, classroom preparation notes, instructor tips, and a lecture outline for each chapter.

Please contact your McGraw-Hill sales representative for details.

Chapter 1
The Path of the PC Tech

Lab Exercises

Well, now you've really done it. The fact that you hold this lab manual in your hands says one thing loud and clear—you're deadly serious about getting that CompTIA A+ certification! Good. Even though the CompTIA A+ certification exams are considered entry level, you need to take them seriously if you want to pass.

Because you're serious, I'm going to let you in on a secret: The key to passing these exams is preparation. When I say "preparation," I'm not talking about studying, although studying is important! I'm talking about *preparing to study*. You need to know exactly how to study for these exams, and you need to have the right tools to get that studying done. Sure, you have a textbook and a lab manual, but you're not ready to hit the books just yet.

In this chapter, you'll learn how to start studying for the CompTIA A+ exams. First, you'll organize what you need to study. Second, you'll explore how the CompTIA A+ certification helps move you toward more advanced certifications. Finally, you'll get some ideas on how to gather equipment so that you can reinforce what you read with real hardware and software. So stay serious, roll up your sleeves, and start preparing to study for the CompTIA A+ exams!

 60 MINUTES

Lab Exercise 1.01: Preparing to Study

Back in the 1980s, there was a popular TV show called *The A-Team*, starring George Peppard and Mr. T. It wasn't the greatest TV show, but I always remember one repeated line: "I love it when a plan comes together!" I want you to feel like that while you prepare for your CompTIA A+ certification. In fact, just for fun, let's call ourselves the "A+ Team" as we get ready to knock those exams right into next week's episode!

Learning Objectives

This lab helps you lay out a logical path for your studies. To do this, you need to deal with three issues: determining your weak points, checking your study habits, and scheduling the exam.

At the end of this lab, you'll be able to

- Identify the CompTIA A+ topics you need to learn
- Develop a good study plan
- Schedule the CompTIA A+ exams

Lab Materials and Setup

The materials you need for this lab are

- A PC with Internet access
- A phone

Getting Down to Business

Total Seminars has been teaching CompTIA A+ certification for years. We've developed a handy template that will show you what you need to study and how much time you need to devote to preparing for the CompTIA A+ exams. These tables are shown in the *Mike Meyers' CompTIA A+ Guide to Managing and Troubleshooting PCs* textbook, but with extra steps added to help you determine the topics you need to study.

Step 1   For each skill listed in the table that follows, circle the number that corresponds to the amount of experience you have: None, Once or Twice, Every Now and Then, or Quite a Bit. You'll use that number to calculate the total number of hours you need to study for the exams.

Tech Task	Amount of Experience			
	None	Once or Twice	Every Now and Then	Quite a Bit
Installing an adapter card	6	4	2	1
Installing and configuring hard drives	12	10	8	2
Installing modems and NICs	8	6	6	3
Connecting a computer to the Internet	16	10	8	4
Installing printers and scanners	16	8	4	2
Installing RAM	8	6	4	2
Installing CPUs	8	7	5	3
Repairing printers	6	5	4	3
Repairing boot problems	8	7	7	5
Repairing portable computers	8	6	4	2

Tech Task	Amount of Experience			
	None	Once or Twice	Every Now and Then	Quite a Bit
Configuring mobile devices	4	3	2	I
Building complete systems	12	10	8	6
Using the command line	8	8	6	4
Installing and optimizing Windows	10	8	6	4
Using Windows XP	6	6	4	2
Using Windows Vista	8	6	4	2
Using Windows 7	8	6	4	2
Configuring NTFS, Users, and Groups	6	4	3	2
Configuring a wireless network	6	5	3	2
Configuring a software firewall	6	4	2	I
Configuring sound	2	2	I	0
Removing malware	4	3	2	0
Using OS diagnostic tools	8	8	6	4
Using a volt-ohm meter	4	3	2	I

Great! You now have a good feel for the topics you need to study. Now you need to determine the total study time. First, add up the numbers you've circled. Then add the result to the number from the following table that corresponds to your experience. The grand total is the number of hours you should study to be ready for the exams.

Months of Direct, Professional Experience...	Hours to Add to Your Study Time...
0	50
Up to 6	30
6 to 12	10
Over 12	0

A total neophyte usually needs around 240 hours of study time. An experienced tech shouldn't need more than 60 hours.

You'll need to spend _____ hours studying for the CompTIA A+ certification exams.

Step 2 Go to the Computing Technology Industry Association (CompTIA) Web site and download a copy of the exam objectives for both the CompTIA A+ 220-801 exam and the CompTIA A+ 220-802 exam. As of this writing, you can find them here:

http://certification.comptia.org/Training/testingcenters/examobjectives.aspx

You have to fill out a short form (requiring your name, e-mail address, and country of residence) before you can view the objectives. Bear in mind, however, that CompTIA changes its Web site more often than TV networks invent new reality shows, so be prepared to poke around if necessary! Compare what you circled in the tables to the CompTIA A+ exam objectives. Note that any single tech task in the table covers more than one exam objective on the CompTIA A+ exams. In the table that follows, list the top five exam objectives that you think will challenge you the most as you begin your journey toward CompTIA A+ certification.

Exam	Objective
Example: 220-801	*5.3 Given a scenario, demonstrate proper communication and professionalism.*

Step 3 If you are taking this course at your high school, career center, or community college, ask your instructor about the most effective ways to learn and study. If you're studying on your own, think about your favorite teachers from the past and list which methods they used that helped you best learn the material.

1. _____

2. _____

3. _____

Step 4 Now that you know which topics are most important to you and how much time you need to devote to studying them, you need to develop your study plan. Take the amount of time you've set aside and determine how many days you have to prepare. Consider work, holidays, weekends, and anything else that will affect your study time.

Ask your instructor when he or she plans to have you take the certification exams. Every school handles the exam differently. It's important that you know how getting certified at your school works so that you'll know what to expect down the road.

If you aren't taking a course, you need to pick a day to take the exams. Keep in mind how much time you'll need to study, but don't put it off so long that you get lazy. Challenge yourself to take the exams as soon as you feel comfortable.

Enter the number of days you have to prepare for the CompTIA A+ certification exams: _____. You now have your deadline—the day you'll say, "I'm ready to take the exams!"

Step 5   You should also investigate how much it will cost you to take the exams. Several vendors sell vouchers that enable you to take the exams at a discounted price. This step introduces you to a few vendors and their pricing options.

    a.   Visit the following link to begin searching for pricing information:

        www.vue.com/vouchers/pricelist/comptia.asp

    b.   In the Pricing section, click the Pricing Spreadsheet link to download a file containing Pearson VUE's voucher pricing information. Open the downloaded file using Microsoft Excel and record the current cost for a single CompTIA A+ exam voucher for your region.

        Price: _____

    c.   On the same Web site, click the Academic/E2C Member Pricing Spreadsheet link to download another file. Open the file, and then find and record the cost for a single CompTIA A+ exam.

        Price: _____

    d.   Now visit this Web site:

        www.totalsem.com/vouchers/index.php

    e.   At the Total Seminars Web site, listed under Step 1, click the CompTIA A+ certification logo. Find and record the price for a CompTIA A+ Exam Voucher.

        Price: _____

Some vouchers require you to be a member of an academic or technology organization. Check to see which voucher applies to you. You may be eligible for one, two, or even all three pricing options!

Step 6   Go online and schedule your exams with Pearson VUE (www.vue.com). You'll almost certainly need to make a phone call to do this. Make sure you have both a method of payment (credit cards are preferred) and some form of identification when you call. In the United States you need your Social Security number to schedule CompTIA exams. It's very important that you schedule your exams *now*—setting a test date early in the process will help motivate you to study, and keep you from procrastinating!

✔ Cross-Reference

For details about taking the CompTIA A+ exams, go to the CompTIA Web site (www.comptia.org).

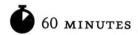 60 MINUTES

Lab Exercise 1.02: Considering Other Certifications

CompTIA A+ certification may be your first certification, but it certainly should not be your last! The information technology (IT) industry considers obtaining certifications an ongoing process, one that continues as long as you're working in the IT field. You need to appreciate how the CompTIA A+ certification leads into other certifications.

Learning Objectives

This lab helps you learn about the various IT certifications that are available, and how they fit with both your skills and aptitude.

At the end of this lab, you'll be able to

- Understand some of the more common certifications that follow the CompTIA A+ certification

- Plan in what order you might attain those certifications

Lab Materials and Setup

The materials you need for this lab are

- A PC with Internet access

Getting Down to Business

It's time to jump onto the Internet and do a little research! You'll tour some of the more popular IT certifications and see how CompTIA A+ helps you gain these more advanced certifications.

✔ **Cross-Reference**

To review the domains of each CompTIA A+ exam, refer to "The Basic Exam Structure" in Chapter 1 of *Mike Meyers' CompTIA A+ Guide to Managing and Troubleshooting PCs*.

Step 1   Fire up a Web browser and go to this Web address:

http://certification.comptia.org/ExploreCareers/careerpaths.aspx

CompTIA offers many other certifications related to the IT field. Research their certification offerings by clicking the Launch IT Certification Roadmap button. From here, list three careers that most interest you.

1. _____

2. _____

3. _____

Of the three career paths you listed, choose the one that appeals to you the most. You can always change your mind later if you don't like it! List three CompTIA certifications you'll need to become an expert in that field.

1. _____

2. _____

3. _____

List three certifications that CompTIA recommends you take that are *not* CompTIA certifications.

1. _____

2. _____

3. _____

Step 2   CompTIA strongly recommends pursuing CompTIA A+ certification as the starting point to your career in information technology. Why do you think they do that?

_____

_____

_____

Step 3   Now that you've seen some common certifications and career paths that follow the CompTIA A+ certification, write a short paragraph explaining why you chose the career path and certifications that you did.

_____

_____

_____

_____

_____

 TIMES WILL VARY

Lab Exercise 1.03: Gathering Equipment

Although it's theoretically possible to obtain CompTIA A+ certification by doing nothing but reading books, you'll be far better prepared for the real world if you can practice with real equipment. You also need some tools so you can take things apart and put them back together. Finally, you need some operating system software, in particular Windows XP, Windows Vista, and Windows 7. If you're taking a course, all of this equipment should be provided to you. If you are not taking a course, you could find yourself spending some serious cash trying to buy everything you need!

Learning Objectives

In this lab, you'll discover some rather interesting ways to get inexpensive or free hardware and software. None of these ideas will work every time, but with a little patience, you'll be amazed how much you can get for very little!

At the end of this lab, you'll be able to

- Acquire inexpensive or free hardware and software

- Acquire a standard PC technician toolkit

Lab Materials and Setup

The materials you need for this lab are

- A phone

- Transportation

- A PC with Internet access

Getting Down to Business

Most of the objectives on the CompTIA A+ exams don't require state-of-the-art hardware. If you're willing to use systems that are a few years old, you can get plenty of good hands-on practice with the techniques you need to know to pass the CompTIA A+ exams.

Step 1 Go on a scavenger hunt. Get a list of the smaller "mom and pop" PC repair companies and small PC parts suppliers in your town. Drive to these companies (don't call them) and ask them, "What do you guys do with your broken or obsolete parts?" The vast majority of these stores simply throw the parts away! Ask when they toss stuff and if you can have what they throw away. Most of these companies pay to get rid of equipment and will be glad to give it to you. Oh, and you can forget the big chain stores—they almost never let folks have equipment.

Step 2   Shop the sale bins at the local computer parts stores. You'll always find one or two pieces of equipment at outrageously low prices. Granted, you may end up using a bright pink Barbie keyboard, but if it only costs $3, who cares? Don't forget about rebates—you can often get parts for free after rebate! Really!

Step 3   Tell everyone you know that you're looking for PC hardware. Almost every organization will have occasional in-house sales where they sell older (but still good) PCs, printers, and so on, to employees. If you can get in on some of these sales, you'll have some amazing deals come your way!

✔ **Hint**

You'll often find that older machines still have the Windows 98 or Windows 2000 operating system software installed. If you come across one of these systems, see if you can work with the seller or donor to get the licensed disc. Working with an older operating system (even DOS) will introduce you to the installation and configuration process. Having an operating system installed will also enable you to verify that the hardware is working.

Step 4   Take one weekend to check out local garage sales. People often sell older PCs at a tiny fraction of their original cost. If you're not afraid to barter a bit, you'll get incredible deals—just watch out for equipment that's simply too old to be worthwhile.

✔ **Hint**

I avoid PC flea markets. The problem is that these folks know the value of their computer equipment, so it's often hard to find excellent deals.

Step 5   Locate the local PC user groups in your town—almost every town has at least one. Explain your situation to them; you'll usually find someone who's willing to give you a part or two, and you may also find others who are studying for the CompTIA A+ exams. You may even be able to start or join a study group!

Step 6   Check out the Craigslist page for your area (www.craigslist.org) and look in the For Sale/Computer category. Craigslist is like a big online garage sale, and you can almost always find someone trying to get rid of old PC equipment for next to nothing. Failing that, you can check out their forums, or even place an ad yourself saying that you're looking for old PC parts.

Step 7   Speaking of study groups, try teaming up with as many fellow students as you can to pool cash for parts and to work as a study group. If you're in a course, this is easy—your fellow students are your study group! Have everyone go equipment hunting, using the different methods described to get equipment, and pool the items you find for everyone to use. You might even hold a drawing after you all get certified, to choose who gets to keep the equipment.

Step 8   After searching your area, online and off, for the best deals on tools and equipment, record what you think are the three best deals you found. If you can, find out what the full price is for each product so you can see how much money you saved.

1. _____

2. _____

3. _____

Chapter 2

Operational Procedures

Lab Exercises

Achieving CompTIA A+ certification is a great way to demonstrate to prospective employers that you have the appropriate technical skills to make you a worthy candidate for their workplace. But you have to demonstrate more than just technical skills to get hired by and succeed in an organization. You also need to demonstrate that you have the appropriate interpersonal skills to interact effectively with fellow employees and with clients. CompTIA recognizes the importance of interpersonal skills in the workplace and thus includes related questions on its CompTIA A+ certification exams to make sure you are prepared to show that you have the people skills to work well with others.

Face it: You're great at fixing computers and extremely interested in the latest gadgets, but do you have the people skills to land a job, keep a job, and climb the ladder of success? I've seen many talented young individuals who can fix just about anything, struggle in the area of how to communicate professionally with others; their impressive resume allows them to walk in the front door to a promising future...only to slink out the back door in disappointment after failing due to lack of people skills.

Whether you like it or not, people evaluate you based on how they perceive you. Developing and maintaining personal and professional workplace habits ensures that people perceive you as the IT professional that you are. This set of labs applies the information you learned in Chapter 2 of *Mike Meyers' CompTIA A+ Guide to Managing and Troubleshooting PCs*, with a focus on communicating properly, presenting yourself professionally at all times, and demonstrating your technical knowledge regarding safety. These labs will help you not only to pass the CompTIA A+ exam but also to develop skills that will serve you well throughout your career, whether in IT or another field.

The CompTIA objectives challenge you to conduct yourself in a professional manner while on the job. Objective 5.3 (Exam 220-801) goes into detail to clarify how you should act on the job. Let's review some of the major points:

5.3   GIVEN A SCENARIO, DEMONSTRATE PROPER COMMUNICATION AND PROFESSIONALISM

- Use proper language—avoid jargon, acronyms, slang when applicable
- Maintain a positive attitude

- Listen and do not interrupt the customer

- Be culturally sensitive

- Be on time (if late contact the customer)

- Avoid distractions

  - Personal calls

  - Talking to coworkers while interacting with customers

  - Personal interruptions

- Dealing with difficult customer or situation

  - Avoid arguing with customers and/or being defensive

  - Do not minimize customer's problems

  - Avoid being judgmental

  - Clarify customer statements (ask open-ended questions to narrow the scope of the problem, restate the issue or question to verify understanding)

- Set and meet expectations/timeline and communicate status with the customer

  - Offer different repair/replacement options if applicable

  - Provide proper documentation on the services provided

  - Follow up with customer/user at a later date to verify satisfaction

- Deal appropriately with customers' confidential materials

  - Located on a computer, desktop, printer, etc.

Many of the following labs will require you to have a partner, and your instructor will actually lead the classroom through a few of them, so buddy up.

 30 MINUTES

Lab Exercise 2.01: The Rude Computer Technician

Everyone is familiar with the stereotype of the rude technician so wrapped up in technology that he is unable to relate to the people around him. Sneering technobabble, a condescending attitude, and rude remarks have become traits that people expect to find in techs, and, all too often, the techs don't disappoint. In this exercise, you'll work with a partner first to role-play the part of the stereotypical rude tech and then to role-play a professional, well-behaved tech. In this way, you'll learn how you should and should not behave as a technician.

Learning Objectives

The plan is to have a classmate play the role of the client, and to have you play the role of the PC tech. Work through the scenario in a live person-to-person role-playing of the situation, just as if it were real.

At the end of this lab, you'll be able to

- Demonstrate proper communication skills
- Avoid distractions in the workplace

Lab Materials and Setup

The materials you need for this lab are

- Blank drawing paper and pencil
- A clock with a second hand, or a timer
- A space to place chairs so that you can face your partner
- The *Mike Meyers' CompTIA A+ Guide to Managing and Troubleshooting PCs* textbook, for reference
- A PC with Internet access

Getting Down to Business

In this exercise, one person will act as the PC technician while the other acts as a customer sitting in a cubicle. As the PC tech, you will first try to emulate as many bad communication habits as possible while your partner, the customer, identifies and writes down those bad habits. Then, repeat the process, this time using proper communication skills. You will then trade roles and repeat the scenario.

Step 1   Create a scenario in which a customer would ask for technical support. For example, try "My computer is running slowly and all these Web pages keep popping up!"—a classic case of malware infection. The person playing the customer should act as if he or she is *not* technically savvy and is unable to answer any technical questions or understand any terms outside of what might be considered "common." What is considered "common" is up to the person playing the customer, so have fun!

Step 2   Between 1999 and 2001, the popular television show *Saturday Night Live* put on a series of comedy sketches called "Nick Burns, Your Company's Computer Guy." Many of these sketches are available online. Do a search for and watch a few of these humorous sketches to see actor Jimmy Fallon portray how insensitive a technician can be in his personal communications. Why are these sketches so funny? What does their popularity tell you about how techs are perceived by our society? Use these videos to get an idea of how to behave during the next step, and how never, ever to behave in real life.

Step 3   It's now time for the technician to do his thing in a timed scenario. Pretend the customer is sitting in a cubicle. Every computer has an "asset tag number," and the tech must confirm that number to make sure he is working on the right computer. After that, it's up to the tech! Be as rude as possible (but not so rude that a person normally would get fired), concentrating on the issues listed in Step 1 of this lab. Your goal is to try to get started working on the PC within three minutes.

As the customer, your job is to describe the problem and answer the tech's questions to the best of your ability. You want your computer fixed, but you won't get up until you have confidence in the tech. As the tech talks, jot down how he is rude or inconsiderate to you.

The scenario ends when either the tech is sitting at the customer's computer or three minutes have elapsed, whichever happens first.

Step 4   Discuss the issues that the customer wrote down. After a quick discussion, repeat the process, this time using good communication techniques. In most cases, the customer will quickly relinquish his or her seat and let you get to work.

The scenario ends when the tech is sitting at the customer's computer or three minutes have elapsed, whichever happens first.

Step 5   Repeat the entire process, this time trading roles. The person now playing the tech should attempt to come up with different ways to be inappropriate, within reason.

 15–40 MINUTES DEPENDING ON CLASS SIZE

Lab Exercise 2.02: Communicating Effectively

So, you want to be a successful IT technician but you have trouble communicating? One of the keys to professional communication is being able to listen well as duties are being assigned to you so that you can produce the results expected.

Learning Objectives

At the end of this lab, you'll be able to

- Communicate more effectively

- Help discern when it's best to talk and when it's best to listen

Lab Materials and Setup

The materials you need for this lab are

- Blank drawing paper and pencil

- A clock with a second hand, or a timer

- A sufficient number of folding chairs for all the students involved in the exercise

- The *Mike Meyers' CompTIA A+ Guide to Managing and Troubleshooting PCs* textbook, for reference

For the setup, arrange the chairs back to back in pairs around the room, with about five feet between each set of chairs.

Getting Down to Business

In this exercise, you'll listen as your partner speaks to you and you'll write down whatever he or she tells you under a tight timeline. The goal is to help you work under pressure while remaining professional at all times.

Step 1   Students should pair up. Each pair of students should designate one person to be the PC tech and the other to be the customer and then write their respective titles on the top of their papers.

Step 2   The instructor should start the timer and ask the designated customers to say the first five technology-related problems that come to mind; they have 20 seconds to do this. As the customers speak, their respective partner techs should write down what they say in the order stated. *An example might be "system fails to boot, no wireless connection, printer not printing properly, no picture on the monitor,"* and so on.

Stop the timer at 20 seconds.

Step 3   The PC techs write a brief solution to the five problems just mentioned by the customers. They have three minutes to complete this and must address the problems in the order received.

Stop the timer at three minutes.

Step 4   The PC tech and customer groups face each other for one minute and share their information. Then, each pair presents their problems and solutions to the class, in turn. They have two minutes to present their solutions. The other groups should sit quietly and listen. After all groups finish, the instructor will give feedback to each group as to how they could communicate better. Students should be allowed to participate in the feedback as well.

 30 MINUTES

Lab Exercise 2.03: Integrating Safety into the Workplace

Demonstrating safety precautions at all times is one of the most important things you can do to protect yourself and your customers...and impress your employer. This mostly involves using common sense, but you should also make sure to carefully read and put into practice the safety guidelines provided in Chapter 2 of *Mike Meyers' CompTIA A+ Guide to Managing and Troubleshooting PCs.*

Many techs go into the field with the mind-set that safety is not that important, but it can save your life and the lives of others. The U.S. Department of Labor Occupational Safety and Health Administration's Web site at www.osha.gov is loaded with information for employers and employees to help them understand the importance of safety. It offers guidelines for electronics and computers/peripherals that we'll explore in this lab exercise.

Learning Objectives

In this lab, you will identify the safety hazards in the workplace and become more aware of guidelines that are useful in a PC environment.

At the end of this lab, you will be able to

- Explain ESD

- Explain MSDSs and various hazards

- Explain proper equipment disposal procedures

Lab Materials and Setup

The materials you need for this lab are

- A PC with Internet access

- A notepad

- Presentation software, if possible, to present your findings

Getting Down to Business

In Chapter 2 of *Mike Meyers' CompTIA A+ Guide to Managing and Troubleshooting PCs*, you read that electrostatic discharge (ESD) can cause permanent damage to some components and erase data on some storage devices. If you take this to heart and practice ESD safety measures as a PC tech early on, you will gain respect in the workplace and demonstrate that you care about your employer's investment.

Step 1   Research ESD, material safety data sheets (MSDSs), and how to dispose of old computer equipment properly, while typing results. You can use the Internet, magazines, tech articles, manuals, and so forth, but make sure you properly document where you find your information.

Step 2   Compile the data into a presentation. Include the following:

1. Pages that describe and define ESD, MSDSs, and proper disposal

2. Pictures of the following:

    a.   Various anti-static devices

    b.   Samples of MSDSs

    c.   Disposing of old, outdated computer devices

3. A short video clip of either:

    a. A student wearing an anti-static wrist strap and installing components into a PC

    b. How to fill out an MSDS

    c. How to properly dispose of computer components

4. A bibliography page listing the sources used for your research

Step 3 (If Time Permits) Students take turns presenting their report to the class to demonstrate their knowledge.

 30 MINUTES

Lab Exercise 2.04: Safeguarding Your IT Future—Becoming a Professional

To safeguard your IT future, it is extremely important that you know how to carry yourself as a professional and keep your customers satisfied. As discussed in *Mike Meyers' CompTIA A+ Guide to Managing and Troubleshooting PCs*, good techs demonstrate professionalism in the workplace at all times.

Learning Objectives

In this lab, you will learn the proper way to dress and present yourself in the workplace.

After completing this lab, you'll be able to

- Properly dress and present yourself on the job
- Understand the do's and don'ts about cell phone usage on the job

Lab Materials and Setup

- A PC with Internet access

Getting Down to Business

Choosing the proper way to dress and present yourself is extremely important in securing and maintaining a good job. Did you know that within the first 15 seconds of meeting someone, they form opinions of you based entirely on your appearance—your body language, your demeanor, your mannerisms, and how you are dressed? Once you have made that first impression, it is virtually irreversible, so you must be aware at all times how you are being perceived and maintain a positive and clean self-image.

Step 1 Based on your current knowledge of what it means to be a professional in the workplace, list three characteristics that show these qualities.

1. _____

2. _____

3. _____

Step 2 Go to www.mindtools.com/CommSkll/FirstImpressions.htm and read the article "Making a Great First Impression." Notice some of the characteristics you might have missed in Step 1. List three of them.

1. _____

2. _____

3. _____

Step 3 Read the article "Top 6 Rules for Using Cell Phones at Work," by Dawn Rosenberg McKay, at http://careerplanning.about.com/od/workplacesurvival/tp/cell_phone.htm. Then, read the following scenarios and write a short explanation of what you would do next.

    A. Your boss has specifically stated that you cannot use your cell phone on the job unless you are on break (away from your work space) or at lunch. You found out before you left for work that your father will be having outpatient surgery today, and you want to be informed right away about his status. What should you do?

    _____

    _____

    _____

    B. You're on the company phone with a client, attempting to walk her through various trouble-shooting steps so that you don't have to travel to the client's location to fix the problem. Your personal cell phone suddenly rings (because you forgot to turn it off) and you can see on the caller ID that it's an old friend you have not talked to in a while. What should you do?

    _____

    _____

    _____

C. Your boss just came in the office from a meeting with his boss and is extremely frustrated about issues that do not involve you. He speaks to you rather harshly and then abruptly leaves. The moment he leaves, you receive a phone call from a client who demands that you return his PC to him today and a text message you've been waiting for about a part for the client's computer that's due in. How should you react?

_____

_____

_____

Lab Analysis Test

1. Your coworker Sara constantly takes personal calls on her cell phone even though she knows your employer has a rule banning personal use of the cell phone while in the workplace. Whenever she's on her cell phone, she does not answer her regular work phone, thus adding more work for you and others. How do you think you should handle this situation?

2. You just got a phone call from a PC repair company that wants to interview you today. It is dress-down day at your workplace, so you're wearing jeans and a T-shirt. Should you accept the offer to interview today or decline? Explain your answer.

3. You're the lead PC technician for a company and have been put in charge of two inexperienced technicians who know nothing about ESD and MSDSs. What steps will you take to educate them to ensure they use anti-static devices and dispose of hazardous materials properly?

4. What is EMI and which components are particularly susceptible to it?

5. What is RFI? Write down three examples of RFI.

Key Term Quiz

Use the following terms to complete the following sentences. Not all terms will be used.

cell phones

electromagnetic interference (EMI)

electrostatic discharge (ESD)

honesty

integrity

professional

radio frequency interference (RFI)

responsibility

1. A(n) _____ technician is one who not only possesses great technical expertise but also has good communication and people skills.

2. Interference produced by microwaves and cell phones is an example of _____.

3. Anti-static wrist straps prevent _____.

4. When on the job, it is your _____ to follow the rules and guidelines set by the company regarding the use of _____.

5. _____ can disrupt wireless network communication.

Chapter 3

The Visible PC

Lab Exercises

Every competent tech knows the PC inside and out. Nothing destroys your credibility in the eyes of a client as quickly as not knowing the basics, like the difference between a graceful shutdown and a forced power down. The word "Oops!" doesn't go over well in the real world! In this chapter, you'll be poking and prodding a real PC. You'll begin by exploring the functions of a PC: input, processing, output, and storage. Then you'll examine the typical user-accessible components—for example, what happens when you press the power button? The final lab takes you on a tour of common connectors.

 30 MINUTES

Lab Exercise 3.01: Exploring the Functions and Components of a PC

Everything a computer does falls into one of four categories: input, processing, output, and storage. To troubleshoot PC problems successfully, you need a good understanding of these four processes and the components that are involved with each one.

Learning Objectives

At the end of this lab, you'll be able to

- Define the four functions of computer systems

- Detail common components involved in each of these four functions

Lab Materials and Setup

The materials you need for this lab are

- A notepad and pencil, to draw a four-column table

- Optional: Access to a working computer with a word processing or spreadsheet application installed to aid in drawing the table

- The *Mike Meyers' CompTIA A+ Guide to Managing and Troubleshooting PCs* textbook, for reference

✔ **Hint**

Get used to taking notes and drawing pictures. Even after many years of repairing computers, from mainframes to PCs, I still use a notepad to keep track of what I see and what I change. I recommend that you save your drawings and notes, as you'll find them useful in subsequent labs.

Getting Down to Business

In this exercise, you'll review, list, and define the various components involved in the PC's vital functions.

Step 1 Reread the "How the PC Works" section in Chapter 3 of *Mike Meyers' CompTIA A+ Guide to Managing and Troubleshooting PCs*, paying particular attention to the sections on input, processing, output, and storage.

Step 2 For each of the following functions, write a definition and give a brief example:

Input:

_____

_____

Processing:

_____

_____

Output:

_____

_____

Storage:

_____

_____

Step 3 Using the following table, list the components that operate in each of the four functional categories. Try to include as many components as you can; you might take a peek at some of the later chapters in the textbook to see if you can add any other components. Think about how each of the components contributes to the overall workings of the PC, and include as much detail about the component as possible.

Input	Processing	Output	Storage

Step 4 If you completed the table right here in the lab book, you can review it later while finishing the rest of the lessons. If you made a table in your notebook or created an electronic version, make sure you keep it nearby. As you work on later chapters, you'll want to update the table with additional components and extra details. The information in the table (and in your head) will expand as you develop a better understanding of how the components relate to the PC's "big picture."

 30 MINUTES

Lab Exercise 3.02: Examining User-Accessible Components

It's been one of those days. You walked into what should have been a simple job interview only to meet a very frantic IT manager dealing with a crisis of epic proportions. She doesn't even bother to interview you. Instead, she shuttles you out of her office, points down the hall, and says, "Go check Jane's PC—fourth cubicle on the left. Her PC's locked up and rebooting itself! I told her to turn it off until you get there. Don't change anything, and don't open it up. Find out if it will shut down, boot properly, and access the drives." Then the IT manager leaves to deal with her crisis, and you're on the spot.

This exercise looks at the many PC components that you can access without removing the case. Scanning the outside of your PC can help you track down any basic issues. Take your time, and jot down notes when you feel the need. Practice each step until you're confident you can do it on the job as a PC tech.

Learning Objectives

In this lab exercise, you will locate and describe the various user controls and built-in user-accessible devices of a PC system. You *will not* be opening the system case during this lab.

At the end of this lab, you'll be able to

- Recognize and manipulate user controls

- Describe the use of built-in user-accessible devices

Lab Materials and Setup

The materials you need for this lab are

- One fully functioning desktop computer system unit, with monitor

- A working *optical drive* (any drive that reads or records CD, DVD, or Blu-ray Discs)

- One readable data CD with files

- One keyboard

- One mouse

- A paper clip

Getting Down to Business

As a technician, you need to know how everything works on a PC. Let's start with the externally accessible functions. Make sure the computer is turned off.

Step 1 Before you can do much work with a PC, you need a functioning output device, such as a monitor. Check the monitor to see if it has power. If the monitor is not on, find the power button on the monitor and press it. You'll notice a small *light-emitting diode* (*LED*) on or near the monitor's power button. Record the color of the LED when the PC is turned off.

Color of the LED when the system is off: _____

Later in this exercise, we'll check the color of the LED when the PC is turned on. Stay tuned!

Step 2 Look at the front of your system unit. Locate the power button. Compare your button to the one shown in Figure 3-1.

Figure 3-1 Recognizing the power and reset buttons on the front of a PC.

Once you have located the power button on your system, make a note of its appearance. Is it in plain sight, or hidden behind a door or lid? Is it round, square, or some odd shape? Pressing the power button to start a PC when the electricity is off is known as a *cold boot* or sometimes a *hard boot*. Many systems also have a reset button, which you can use to restart a PC that is already on. This is also called a *warm boot*.

Describe your power and reset buttons here:

_____

_____

Sometimes software will lock up your system, in which case the only way to shut the system down is to force a *power down*. This requires that you press and hold the power button for four to six seconds.

Notice the two LEDs on the front panel near the power button. These LEDs will become important later in this exercise.

✔ **Hint**

Most systems have a power switch located on the back of the case that controls the flow of electricity to the power supply, and a power button on the front that boots and shuts down the PC.

Step 3 Locate the floppy drive. You can recognize it by its 3½-inch horizontal slot. How many visible 3½-inch slots does your PC have?

    a.   _____

Do you see the eject button below the slot on the right side of the drive? Below the slot on the left side is an LED that lights up when the drive is actively reading or writing information on a floppy diskette.

✔ **Hint**

Because floppy disks can store only a relatively tiny amount of data, floppy drives are disappearing from PCs. In fact, most new computer systems ship without floppy drives. As a computer tech, however, you will most likely still have to deal with floppy drives for a few more years. If your system doesn't have a floppy drive, you may want to explore an older machine to see one in action. Just remember to clear the dust and cobwebs out of the way first.

On the front of your system, you should also see the external face of your system's optical drive. It fits comfortably inside an available 5¼-inch slot (or drive bay). How many 5¼-inch drive bays does your PC have?

    b.   _____

You'll see either the front edge of the tray that opens to accept an optical disc, or a small door that protects the tray when it's retracted. Once you've located this drive, notice that it also has a button in the lower-right corner. When the system is on, you can press that button to open the tray door (if there is one) and slide the tray out to receive your disc (see Figure 3-2). Pressing the button while the tray is out retracts the tray so that the drive can read the disc.

Don't be tempted to force the disc tray to close by pushing it in. Always press the button on the front of the drive to close the tray or to eject a disc. Forcing the tray to close can cause the gears inside to become misaligned, so that the tray no longer closes properly.

Your system may have other devices installed, such as a USB flash drive, a tape drive, a Blu-ray Disc drive, or a Secure Digital (SD) memory card slot. Each of these uses removable media; take care when inserting or removing the media.

→ **Note**

With USB flash drives—or *thumb drives*, as they're often called—the drive *is* the removable media.

FIGURE 3-2 Can you locate the floppy drive and optical drive on this system unit?

Step 4 Now it's time to prepare your system for the scenario outlined in the opening text.

Earlier, this exercise mentioned many different kinds of LEDs. It referred to the monitor and floppy drive LEDs, as well as to the two LEDs next to your power button. Now, let's watch them in action. Turn on your PC.

    a.   Color of monitor LED: _____

    b.   Color of floppy drive LED: _____

    c.   What is the status of the green LED next to the power button? Is it steady, flashing, or intermittent?

                _____

    d.   What is the status of the red (or amber) LED next to the power button? Is it steady, flashing, or intermittent?

                _____

→ Note

The power LED generally lights up green to indicate that the power is on, and the hard drive LED lights up red when the internal hard drive is active.

    e.   Press the eject button on the front of the optical drive. When the tray opens, carefully insert a disc. Press the eject button again to close the tray. If you haven't done this a lot, practice inserting and removing a disc until you feel comfortable with the process. When the optical drive closes, what is the status of its LED? Is it steady, flashing, or intermittent?

_____

✖ Warning

Don't start any applications yet! Close any open applications or open windows before performing Step 5. You're going to force a "power down," and you do not want to damage any of the software or data.

Step 5   Now you're going to simulate a PC that has become nonresponsive and "locked up." Perform a forced power down as follows:

    a.   Press *and hold* the power button.

    b.   While continuing to hold the power button in, count out loud (one–one thousand, two–one thousand, three–one thousand...) until the system powers down and the screen goes blank.

        According to your count, how many seconds did it take for the screen to go blank?

_____

Step 6   After the system has been powered down for approximately one minute, do the following:

    a.   Press the power button and allow the system to boot.

    b.   Log on in a normal fashion so that you are viewing the operating system desktop.

    c.   Select Start | My Computer or Computer and double-click the icon that represents the optical drive. This should enable you to view the contents of the disc that was inserted prior to the forced power down.

        List some of the contents of the disc:

_____

_____

_____

d.   Select Start | Shut Down. If you're using Windows Vista or 7, it goes straight to a shutdown routine. Windows XP opens the Shut Down Windows dialog box, in which you select Shut Down from the drop-down list. This performs a graceful shutdown of the system.

✔ Hint

If all the actions in Step 6 were successful, the system likely is stable and you can report to the IT manager that Jane's machine is back up and running. If any of the actions failed, you should select Start | Restart in Windows Vista/7 or Start | Shut Down in Windows XP. In the Shut Down Windows dialog box, select Restart from the drop-down list. After the system reboots, complete substeps b, c, and d once more. Sometimes, the forced power down leaves some of the files in a state of flux; restarting shuts the computer down "gracefully," properly closing all open files before powering down. This should clear everything up and enable the computer to function properly.

Step 7   While the computer is turned off, take a paper clip and straighten it out, giving yourself a small handle to hold. Find the small hole on the front of your optical drive and insert the end of your paper clip. What happens?

_____

 30 MINUTES

Lab Exercise 3.03: Recognizing External Connections

Just as you finish working with Jane's PC, her intercom buzzes. It's the head of IT, and she has a new assignment for you: The new satellite office in Albuquerque has received a delivery of new PCs, but the machines are all in boxes and none of the salespeople there knows a mouse from a monkey wrench. Your job is to call him up and walk him through the process of connecting a PC, describing each cable and connector, and explaining how they connect to the PC.

Learning Objectives

In this lab, you will identify, describe, and explain the function of the external connections on a standard PC.

At the end of this lab, you will be able to

- Identify the external connectors on a PC and the related cables

- Explain the function of each external connection

Lab Materials and Setup

The materials you need for this lab are

- At least one fully functioning PC that's less than two years old (two or more systems is ideal, with one older than and one newer than two years old)

✔ **Cross-Reference**

Before you begin this lab, read the sections "External Connections" and "Devices and Their Connectors" in Chapter 3 of *Mike Meyers' CompTIA A+ Guide to Managing and Troubleshooting PCs*.

Getting Down to Business

Now it's time to learn about all the external things that can be attached to a PC. This lab exercise steps you through identifying and understanding the function of the various connectors.

✖ **Warning**

Shut off the power to your system and *unplug your PC* from the wall socket before you start the following exercise.

Step 1 Look at all those wires coming from the back of your PC! There's a power cable, a telephone or network cable, a keyboard cable, a mouse cable, and maybe a few others, depending on your system. Looking at the back of my current system (the one I'm using to write this manual), I count 15 cables coming out the back. Yowza!

The great thing about PCs is that it's difficult to connect the cables incorrectly. Each one has a unique connector; some are male (connectors with pins), and some are female (connectors with holes). Each connector has a particular shape and a specific number of pins or holes that match those of a specific device connected to the system unit.

✔ **Hint**

Cables have conductors. A *conductor* is a wire that can carry electrical signals. You may see a cable described by the number of conductors it has; for example, a telephone cable can be a two- or four-conductor cable. A power cable is a three-conductor cable. A network cable is an eight-conductor cable.

Step 2   Unplug each of your PC's cables one at a time and practice plugging them back in until you get a feel for how each fits. You should not have to force any of the cables, though they may be firm. How is each cable held in place and prevented from coming loose? Is there a screw, clip, or some other fastener that holds the cable connector tight to the system? Is the connector keyed? What does it connect to? What is the shape of the connector on each end? Is it round, rectangular, D-shaped? How many pins or holes does it have? How many rows of pins or holes?

Step 3   Is it possible to plug any cable into the wrong connector? If so, which one(s)? What do you think would happen if you plugged something into the wrong connector?

_____

_____

Step 4   Disconnect the following cables from the back of your PC and record some information about each in the following table. Keep in mind that the table was created for average PCs. I threw in three additional blank spaces for any custom devices in your system. If you don't have a particular connector, don't feel bad. Just write "N/A."

	Number of Conductors/Pins	Cable Gender	Name of the Port	Port Gender	Port Color
Mouse					
Keyboard					
Monitor					
Printer					
Network					
Modem/phone					
Speaker					
Power					

Once you complete this table, know it, live it, and love it. Every great technician should be able to identify these connectors at a glance.

Step 5   If you're working with someone else, play "Flash Cords." Have your partner hold up various cables, and try to guess what they connect to by looking at the connectors on the ends. Then switch roles and quiz your partner. Another really good way to learn the connector names is to have your partner sit behind the computer, while you reach around from the front, feel the various ports with your fingers, and call them out by name. Switch back and forth with each other until you both can easily identify all the ports by touch.

Step 6   Properly reconnect all the cables that you removed and prepare to turn on the system. If you have an On/Off button on the back of the system, be sure it is set to the On position. Make sure the monitor is turned on as well.

Step 7   Identify the connectors pictured next. What is the name of each connector and what does it connect to?

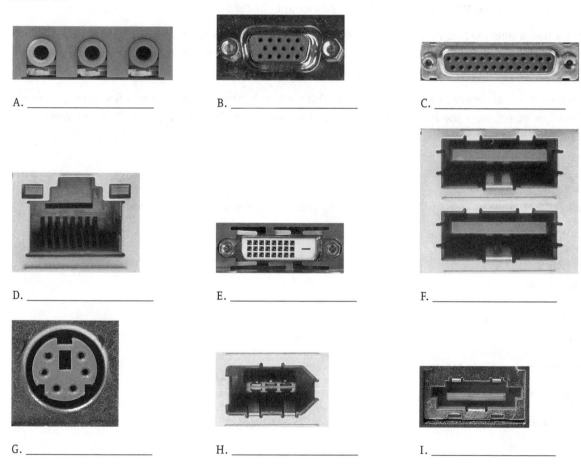

A. _____

B. _____

C. _____

D. _____

E. _____

F. _____

G. _____

H. _____

I. _____

Use the following list of connector names to correctly identify the ports. You will not use every name listed.

PS/2	Parallel	USB	Serial	FireWire	eSATA
RJ-45	RJ-11	1/8-inch audio	DVI	VGA	S/PDIF

Lab Analysis Test

1. Joe has just moved his PC to his new office. After hooking up all the cables, he turns on the system, and when it asks for his password, the keyboard will not respond. What could possibly be wrong?

2. Theresa has just finished the production of a PowerPoint presentation detailing the design of a new office building. She has included some cool 3-D animations in the presentation to show off the design. When she attempts to save the presentation to a floppy disk, an error occurs. What might have caused the error? Do you have any suggestions that may solve the problem?

3. Cal has purchased a new set of speakers for his PC. The old ones worked just fine, but he wanted more power and a subwoofer. When he plugged in the new speakers, they would not work. Power is on to the speakers. What is the first thing you would check?

4. John had a new modem installed in his computer at a local computer shop where he watched as the system successfully connected to his AOL account. When he got home and tried, however, he couldn't get a dial tone. He calls you to ask for help. What should you suggest that he check first?

5. Audrey has just returned to her desk after taking a break. She was only gone a few minutes, so she kept her PC on. Now the monitor is blank and the monitor LED is blinking a different color than usual. What might have happened?

Key Term Quiz

Use the following terms to complete the following sentences. Not all of the terms will be used.

cold boot

data cable

female connector

FireWire

hard boot

light-emitting diode (LED)

male connector

optical drive

parallel port

power cable

power down

thumb drive

USB flash drive

1. Before USB was a common connector standard, printers used the _____ to connect to PCs.

2. A(n) _____ is a visible indicator to tell you that your PC is on or that your hard drive is active.

3. Remember to use the eject button on your _____ when closing the tray so you don't damage anything.

4. A USB flash drive (also known as a(n) _____) is a form of removable storage that plugs directly into a USB port.

5. When the computer is off, pressing the power button begins a(n) _____ (also known as a(n) _____).

Chapter 4

Visible Windows

Lab Exercises

Every good PC technician should know the Windows environment inside and out. This is vital to any troubleshooting scenario, and it won't happen automatically—it takes some practice and discovery on the technician's part. You need to be fluent in navigating the PC from a user's perspective. If there's anything magical about Windows, it's that there's almost always more than one way to get a desired result, and your preferred way might not be the same as your client's. As a good customer-oriented tech, you need to be flexible in your thinking, and this comes only through practice and more practice. As you study and work through these labs, always look for more than one way to access the files or programs you need. Many of the short-cuts and hot keys you'll discover can be invaluable aids for a busy tech!

✔ **Hint**

Windows enables right-click menus for most of its buttons, icons, and other screen elements. Be sure to right-click everything you see in Windows to explore the many context menus and options.

In the field, the PC tech is perceived as the Master of All Things Technical. This might not be a fair assessment—for example, why should a PC hardware technician need to know how to open and close the user's programs?—but that's the way it is. You need to be comfortable and confident with the Windows interface, or you'll lose all credibility as a PC technician. If you show up to service a PC and have trouble moving or resizing a window or locating the information you seek, it won't instill a lot of confidence in your client. There's nothing more embarrassing to a tech than having to ask the user how to find or use a Windows feature!

The creators of the CompTIA A+ certification exams understand this, so they test you on Windows user-level information, such as using power saving settings, changing the appearance of the interface, manipulating files and folders, locating information stored on drives, and using Windows' built-in OS tools. You must also know how to navigate to the basic Windows features—the CompTIA A+ exams are big on identifying paths to features. Although you may already know much of the information about to be covered, the labs in this chapter will help you review and catch any bits and pieces you missed along the way.

 30 MINUTES

Lab Exercise 4.01: The Windows XP Interface

Microsoft Windows XP debuted back in August 24, 2001, succeeding the more business-minded Windows 2000 and the more consumer-driven Windows Me. Windows XP features a slick new interface aimed at both professionals and consumers. Microsoft created four editions of the operating system: Windows XP Home Edition, Windows XP Professional Edition, Windows XP Media Center Edition, and Windows XP 64-bit Edition. Windows XP is Microsoft's longest reigning and supported operating system. People around the world still use it 10 years after it was released.

You can think of Windows XP Home Edition as an abridged version of Windows XP Professional. Media Center Edition is based on the Home Edition, plus some added functionality to simplify access to music, videos, and photos. The major advantages of XP Professional include remote access, tighter security, and the ability to network in domains. If possible, try going through this lab exercise with different editions of Windows XP so that you can see what changes and what stays the same.

Learning Objectives

The main objective of this exercise is to familiarize you with the interface of Windows XP.

At the end of this lab, you'll be able to

- Manipulate and use the taskbar, Quick Launch toolbar, notification area, Start menu, and Recycle Bin

Lab Materials and Setup

The materials you need for this lab are

- A fully functioning PC with Windows XP installed

Getting Down to Business

This lab exercise takes you on a tour of the Windows XP interface. You'll see in detail how the Start menu, taskbar, Quick Launch toolbar, notification area, and Recycle Bin work.

Step 1 Let's begin with the Start menu and the Start button, both located in the lower-left corner of the desktop. The Start menu provides you with easy access to the applications and tools on your computer.

a. Click on the Start button to open the Start menu. Record five of the clickable items in this menu.

_____

b. How many columns does this menu have?

_____

c. Close the Start menu by clicking on an unused part of the desktop. Then right-click on the Start button to open the context menu. (Remember that you can right-click on just about anything in Windows to find additional options.) Select Properties to open the Taskbar and Start Menu Properties dialog box. The Start Menu tab should be selected already. You should see two options. List them below.

_____ and _____

FIGURE 4-1 Customize Start Menu dialog box in Windows XP

d. Click the Customize button to open the Customize Start Menu dialog box (see Figure 4-1). From here, you can control what appears on the Start menu. How many programs are shown by default in the Start menu?

_____

e. Click OK or Cancel to close the Customize Start Menu dialog box. Click the Classic Start menu radio button, and then click Apply. Close the Taskbar and Start Menu Properties dialog box by clicking OK. Click the Start button and notice the changes that were made. Just like you did for Step 1a, record five of the clickable items in this menu.

_____

f. Write down how many columns wide this menu system is:

_____

g. When you are finished recording the information, restore the Start menu to the classic style using the radio buttons.

Step 2 The taskbar displays the applications you are running, such as Microsoft Word, Firefox, or League of Legends. Like the Start menu, the taskbar can be customized to your satisfaction.

a. Right-click on the taskbar and select Properties. A familiar dialog box should appear. It's the Taskbar and Start Menu Properties dialog box! This time, the Taskbar tab should be selected, displaying the appearance settings for your taskbar. Record the names of the options and their default settings for the Taskbar appearance section:

Option	Default Setting

b. Uncheck the *Lock the taskbar* checkbox and click Apply. Now click and drag your taskbar to a different corner of the screen (see Figure 4-2). Record what happens when you release the left mouse button.

FIGURE 4-2 Moving the taskbar

c.   The *Group similar taskbar buttons* option does exactly what it sounds like—condenses a lot of
taskbar buttons into a single button—but let's find out just how many buttons it takes to make
that happen. Close all other applications, and then open Internet Explorer multiple times
until the taskbar groups multiple taskbar icons together. How many instances of Internet
Explorer did you need to open to group the buttons?

_____

d.   Uncheck the Show Quick Launch checkbox. The Quick Launch toolbar next to the Start button
enables you to launch applications with a single click. Record which icons disappear.

_____

→ **Note**

You can add icons to the Quick Launch toolbar by dragging and dropping an icon from your
desktop or Windows Explorer into that area.

---

e.   Using the chart you created earlier, reset the taskbar to its default settings.

Step 3   The lower-right corner of the desktop houses the notification area (see Figure 4-3). Some techs
still call it the "systray" or "system tray," but these were never official names. The notification area
usually displays icons for applications running in the background. Clicking the left arrow button next
to the notification area will expand the area and reveal more icons.

a.   Record a few of the icons from your notification area.

_____

b.   Right-click on the taskbar and click Properties to open the Taskbar and Start Menu Properties
dialog box with the Taskbar tab selected. In the Notification area section, click the Customize
button. From the Customize Notifications dialog box, you can choose to show or not show the
clock, hide inactive icons, and more.

c.   Choose an item you like and click the drop-down box. List the three options you can choose
from.

_____, _____, _____

Figure 4-3 The Windows XP notification area

Step 4 When you delete files on your computer, their remains go to the Recycle Bin—unless you want to change how the Recycle Bin operates. Let's try customizing the Recycle Bin:

    a.   Right-click the Recycle Bin, select Properties, and investigate each tab. Record the maximum size for Recycle Bin storage on a Windows XP system.

           _____

    b.   Does Windows give you the option to delete a file without using the Recycle Bin?

           _____

    c.   Try changing the available options. Test your changes by deleting files you don't need. To create a new file, right-click on your desktop and select New. From there, choose any file type you want and name the file. Now delete it.

→ **Note**

While using the default settings, you can permanently delete a file or folder in Windows by selecting the file and pressing SHIFT-DELETE. Be careful! Files deleted in this manner aren't recoverable without a third-party program.

 30 MINUTES

Lab Exercise 4.02: The Windows Vista Interface

On January 30, 2007, Microsoft released Windows Vista. Windows Vista included many improvements to security and big changes to the graphical user interface (GUI). Microsoft created six editions of Vista: Vista Starter, for developing nations; Vista Home Basic and Home Premium, for consumers; and Vista Business, Enterprise, and Ultimate, for businesses and power users. You can get each edition in both 32-bit and 64-bit varieties (except for the Vista Starter edition). Pay close attention to which versions of Vista support which features. This will help you pass your CompTIA A+ exams and be a more knowledgeable technician.

Learning Objectives

The main objective of this exercise is to familiarize you with the interface of Windows Vista.

At the end of this lab, you'll be able to

- Manipulate and use the Start menu, taskbar, Quick Launch toolbar, notification area, Sidebar, and Recycle Bin

Lab Materials and Setup

The materials you need for this lab are

- A fully functioning PC with Windows Vista installed

Getting Down to Business

In this lab exercise, you'll take a tour of the Windows Vista interface. You'll see in detail how the Start menu, taskbar, Quick Launch toolbar, notification area, and Recycle Bin work. You'll also look at how the Sidebar works.

Step 1 Modern versions of Windows revolve around the Start button, and Vista is no different. Windows Vista, however, no longer labels the button "Start." The Start button is now just the Windows logo icon. Don't worry, though—it's still the Start button and still opens the Start menu.

a.   Click on the Start button to open the Start menu. Record five of the clickable items in this menu.

_____

b.   How many columns does this menu have?

_____

c.   Windows Vista removed the Run command found in previous versions of the Windows Start menu. What replaced it in Windows Vista?

_____

d.   You can still restore the Run command to the Start menu in Windows Vista. Right-click on the Start menu and select Properties to open the Taskbar and Start Menu Properties dialog box (remember this?). The Start menu radio button should be selected by default. Click the Customize button to open the Customize Start Menu dialog box (see Figure 4-4). You can use this dialog box to change the appearance of the Start menu. Look at the options for Computer.

e.   What are the three options available for customizing Computer?

_____

_____

_____

Figure 4-4 Customize Start Menu dialog box in Windows Vista

f. Scroll down the list. Find and check the box for the Run command and click OK. Click OK in the Taskbar and Start Menu Properties dialog box. Click the Start button. You should see the Run command in the Start menu.

g. You can also revert the entire Start menu to a more classic style. Right-click on the Start button and select Properties. Change to Classic Start menu and click OK. Record the changes to the desktop and the Start menu.

_____

h. After finishing, return the settings to their original configuration.

Step 2   The Windows Vista taskbar remains similar to the Windows XP taskbar but with a new glossy finish and a few new features.

a.   Right-click on the taskbar and select Properties to open the Taskbar and Start Menu Properties dialog box. The Taskbar tab should be selected by default. From here you can adjust the appearance settings for your taskbar. Record the names of the options and their default settings for the Taskbar appearance section.

Option	Default Setting

b.   Try changing some settings. Uncheck the *Lock the taskbar* checkbox and click Apply. Now click and drag your taskbar to a different corner of the screen. What happens when you release the left mouse button?

_____

c.   Open an application—a Web browser will do. The application should appear on the taskbar. Hover your cursor over the application icon in the taskbar. What happens?

_____

d.   Uncheck the Show Quick Launch checkbox. Remember from Windows XP that the Quick Launch toolbar next to the Start button enables you to launch applications with a single click. Record what icons disappear.

_____

➜ **Note**

You can add icons to the Quick Launch toolbar by dragging and dropping an icon from the desktop or Windows Explorer into that area.

e.   Using the chart you created earlier, reset the taskbar to its default settings once you are finished.

FIGURE 4-5 The Windows Vista notification area

Step 3   The notification area doesn't change much from Windows XP to Windows Vista, though Microsoft did add some new customization options (see Figure 4-5).

    a.   Right-click on the taskbar and select Properties to open the Taskbar and Start Menu Properties dialog box. Then click the Notification Area tab. List the four system icons you have available to choose from.

        _____, _____, _____, _____

    b.   One of the options, Power, is grayed out when using a desktop PC. Why do you think that is?

        _____

Step 4   The Recycle Bin still handles all of your deleted files in Windows Vista, just like it did in Windows XP.

    a.   Right-click on the Recycle Bin and select Properties to view the options you have available. Record the default custom size for Recycle Bin storage on your Windows Vista system.

        _____

➜ Note

If you are in a classroom environment with other students doing this lab, check with them and see if their Recycle Bin size is the same as yours. Depending on the size of the hard drives, you may see different results.

    b.   Windows usually asks for confirmation when you choose to delete a file. Is there a way you can turn off that feature in this area? What would be a benefit to a feature like that?

        _____

        _____

    c.   What is the maximum size of the Recycle Bin on your computer?

        _____

    d.   When finished, return the Recycle Bin to its default settings.

Step 5   One of Windows Vista's new features is the Windows Sidebar. The Sidebar sits on one side of your desktop and holds little programs called Gadgets. There are thousands of Gadgets on Microsoft's Web site that provide such things as weather reports, puzzles, or your *World of Warcraft* stats. You may notice a large analog clock in the upper-right corner of your screen—that's a Gadget. Hovering your cursor over the clock or Sidebar area will highlight it.

Right-click on an empty portion of the Sidebar and click Properties. In the Windows Sidebar Properties dialog box, you can select whether the Sidebar appears on the right side or left side of your screen, as well as which monitor it appears on (if you are using multiple monitors). Click the *View list of running gadgets* button.

a.   Record the list of running Gadgets.

_____

_____

b.   Return to your desktop. Right-click on the Sidebar and click Add Gadgets. Add as many Gadgets as you like. How many Gadgets can fit on your screen at once?

_____

 30 MINUTES

Lab Exercise 4.03: The Windows 7 Interface

As of the first half of 2012, Windows 7 is Microsoft's current flagship operating system. It debuted on October 22, 2009 as a replacement to Windows Vista. Windows 7 comes in several editions for consumers and businesses. For consumers, these include Starter, Home Basic, and Home Premium. Out of those three choices, the only one that you can buy in the store is Home Premium. The Starter edition is sold exclusively on portable devices like netbooks, while Home Basic is only available in "emerging markets." For the business and power users, Microsoft created Professional, Enterprise, and Ultimate. Windows 7 comes in 32-bit and 64-bit flavors.

Learning Objectives

The main objective of this exercise is to familiarize you with the interface of Windows 7.

At the end of this lab, you'll be able to

- Manipulate and use the Start menu, taskbar, Quick Launch toolbar, notification area, and Gadgets

Lab Materials and Setup

The materials you need for this lab are

- A fully functioning PC with Windows 7 installed

Getting Down to Business

In this lab exercise, you will take a tour of the Windows 7 interface. You'll see in detail how the Start menu, taskbar, Quick Launch toolbar, and notification area work—you should be pretty familiar with these by now. You'll also see how Gadgets have changed from Windows Vista to Windows 7.

Step 1 Let's begin once again with the Start menu. Windows 7 only uses the Windows logo icon to label the Start button, though if you hover your mouse cursor over the logo, a tooltip labeled "Start" appears.

a. Click on the Start button to open the Start menu. Record five of the clickable items in this menu.

_____

b. Write down how many columns wide this menu system is:

_____

c. You can get help about your Microsoft operating system by opening the Start menu and clicking Help and Support. If you're like me, you probably use Google instead to search for PC troubleshooting solutions, so you may we want to remove this button from the Start menu. Right-click on the Start button and select Properties. This opens the Taskbar and Start Menu Properties dialog box. From here, you can change how your power button works and change the Start menu's privacy settings.

d. Record the different ways you can customize the power button.

_____   _____   _____

_____   _____   _____

e. Click the Customize button to open the Customize Start Menu dialog box (see Figure 4-6). List four Start menu options that can be displayed as a link, as a menu, or not at all.

_____

_____

_____

_____

f. Scroll down the list and uncheck the Help checkbox, and then click OK. Click OK in the Taskbar and Start Menu Properties dialog box. View the changes to your Start menu.

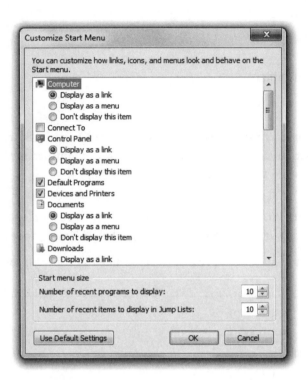

FIGURE 4-6 Customize Start Menu dialog box in Windows 7

Step 2   The Windows 7 taskbar includes a new feature called *pinning*. Pinning enables you to attach any application to the taskbar for later use (see Figure 4-7). I like to think of pinning as what would happen if the taskbar and the Quick Launch toolbar had a baby.

    a.   Select any item that is currently on your desktop or in your Start menu. Click and drag the icon onto your taskbar and let go. To truly enjoy this lab, pin at least five icons to the taskbar.

→ Note

Don't worry if you make a mistake and accidently pin something to the taskbar that you didn't want pinned to the taskbar. Right-click on the pinned icon and select *Unpin this program from taskbar* to remove it.

---

    b.   Right-click on the taskbar and select Properties, as usual. You'll see the same Taskbar and Start Menu Properties dialog box you saw in Windows XP and Windows Vista.

FIGURE 4-7 Pinning objects to the taskbar

FIGURE 4-8 Opening multiple instances of Internet Explorer

c. List the four choices for the location of the taskbar on the screen.

_____

d. Leave the Taskbar and Start Menu Properties dialog box open. Open multiple instances of a program. Try using Internet Explorer. To open multiple instances of the same program, right-click on the program's icon in the taskbar. This opens a new type of menu called a Jump List. Click the title of the application, as shown in Figure 4-8. Repeat this about three or four times. Now, move your mouse cursor over the program's taskbar icon (Internet Explorer or whatever program you chose). It should look something like Figure 4-9.

FIGURE 4-9 Viewing taskbar thumbnails

e.   Return to the Taskbar and Start Menu Properties dialog box. In the *Taskbar buttons* drop-down menu, select *Never combine*. Click Apply. Record the results of selecting and applying this option.

_____

f.   Continue to manipulate and change the settings in this area to get accustomed to how you can affect the taskbar settings. When finished, return the taskbar to the default settings by undoing the changes you made.

Step 3   The Windows 7 notification area remains largely unchanged from previous versions of Windows (see Figure 4-10). There are, however, a few new customization options to learn about.

a.   Right-click on the taskbar and select Properties to open the Taskbar and Start Menu Properties dialog box. Click the Customize button. Record the different Behavior options available in the drop-down menus.

_____

_____

_____

b.   Click the link that says *Turn system icons on or off*. List the five system icons you have available to choose from.

_____ , _____ , _____ , _____ , _____

c.   Change some of these settings to manipulate how your notification area looks and acts on your Windows 7 computer. When you are done, click the link *Restore default icon behaviors*. Close the Taskbar and Start Menu Properties dialog box.

d.   Open each of the applications you pinned to your taskbar. Holy cow! That's a lot of applications loaded! You won't be able to see much of your desktop with all of those applications loaded.

e.   Move your cursor to the bottom-right corner of the screen. There is a small rectangular shape to the right of the clock. This is the Show desktop button.

f.   Hover your cursor over this area and record what happens.

_____

FIGURE 4-10 The Windows 7 notification area

g. Right-click the taskbar and select Properties to reopen the Taskbar and Start Menu Properties dialog box. Using your knowledge from the previous steps in this lab exercise, which feature in Windows 7 allowed you to view the desktop?

_____

h. Click Cancel when you are ready to return to the Windows desktop. Return your taskbar to normal by unpinning applications from it.

Step 4 Windows 7 includes an altered version of Windows Vista's Gadgets and Sidebar. While Vista's Gadgets were forced to live a life of servitude on a small strip of screen known as the Sidebar, Windows 7 Gadgets are free to roam the entire desktop. The Sidebar is no more. By default, Windows 7 won't display any Gadgets on your desktop. You have to choose to add them.

a. To add a Gadget, simply right-click anywhere on your desktop and select Gadgets.

b. List three examples of the default Gadgets.

_____

c. Click and drag a few Gadgets to your desktop to get a feel for how they work in Windows 7. Right-click on one of the Gadgets on your desktop. Set the opacity to 20%. Record what happens to the Gadget after you change the opacity.

_____

➜ Note

If you're an advanced user, open the Windows Task Manager and click on the Processes tab. Look for sidebar.exe. It seems as though the application that runs your Gadgets is still known as sidebar.exe even in Windows 7. Don't worry, though: from a CompTIA A+ certification standpoint, the Sidebar existed only in Windows Vista.

 30 MINUTES

Lab Exercise 4.04: Discovering Aero in Windows 7

When Microsoft released Windows Vista, they updated the desktop interface with a new feature called Windows Aero. Aero is the default theme in Windows Vista and Windows 7. To take advantage of this enhanced desktop, you need to have a compatible Windows operating system and a DirectX 9 compatible graphics card with a minimum of 128 MB of video memory, among other requirements.

Learning Objectives

The main objective of this exercise is to familiarize you with the features of Windows Aero and tools to troubleshoot it.

At the end of this lab, you'll be able to

- Understand and explain the different features provided by Windows Aero

- Troubleshoot a PC with problems related to Windows Aero

Lab Materials and Setup

The materials you need for this lab are

- A fully functioning PC with Windows 7 Home Premium, Professional, Enterprise, or Ultimate installed

- Optional: A fully functioning PC with Windows Vista Home Premium, Business, Enterprise, or Ultimate installed

Getting Down to Business

In this lab exercise, we will be exploring the features of Window Aero from the perspective of Windows 7. Aero takes advantage of modern graphics card technologies to create a more appealing user interface. In Lab Exercise 4.03, you explored the Windows 7 interface and found Aero Peek and Jump Lists. These features are a part of Windows Aero, along with a host of others like Shake, Snap, Flip3D, and Transparency (sometimes called Glass). This lab also looks at how to troubleshoot Aero-related problems. In order to use Windows Aero, you need to have Windows 7 Home Premium, Professional, Enterprise, or Ultimate. Windows 7 Starter and Home Basic do not include Aero.

→ **Note**

This lab was designed using Windows 7. Many of the steps will also work for Windows Vista, but there are minor changes between the two. You might try following the steps with both Windows 7 and Windows Vista to see where Microsoft changed things.

Step 1

a. Before you can see the features of Windows Aero, you must select an Aero theme. Right-click on your desktop and select Personalize to open the Personalization applet.

b. You should see at least three different categories of themes by default. List them here.

_____

_____

_____

c.   Choose a theme from the Aero Themes category. Next, click on the Window Color link at the bottom of the applet. This opens the Window Color and Appearance window. From here you can change the colors and intensity of your window borders. Find a color that suits you and select it.

d.   Uncheck the Enable transparency checkbox. Record what happens to your taskbar and window panes as a result.

_____

e.   Check the box again to reenable transparency. Save your changes and exit to your desktop.

Step 2   To make Aero Shake work, we need to create a little chaos and open some applications. Open as many applications as you would like, but at least three. Your desktop should look something like mine, shown in Figure 4-11.

FIGURE 4-11   The chaotic desktop, pre-Shake

Once you have three or more applications open, go to whichever application is active (or in the foreground) and then click and hold on the top of the foreground window. Now, while holding down the mouse button quickly shake your mouse side to side.

Record what happens.

_____

Step 3   To see Snap in action, open any application. Click and hold the top of the window pane and then drag it to the far-right side of your screen until you can't make your mouse go any further. Release the mouse button and record what happens.

_____

Try snapping the application to the left side of the screen. When might a feature like this be useful?

_____

Step 4   Finally, let's take a look at task switching and Flip3D. Open a few more applications. At least three will do nicely. On your keyboard, press and hold ALT and then press TAB. While holding the ALT key, continue to tap the TAB key. Record the results.

_____

That shortcut key combination has been with us since Windows 3.0. It's older than some of you who are reading this lab manual!

Now, while holding the WINDOWS key, press the TAB key. Record the results.

_____

➜   **Note**

Did you know that Aero is a backronym (an acronym created after the word itself)? It stands for Authentic, Energetic, Reflective, and Open.

Step 5   Troubleshooting Windows Aero is actually a fairly simple process. Aero will either work or it won't. The following steps showcase the Aero troubleshooting tool.

   a.   Right-click on the desktop and select Screen Resolution. Click on the *Advanced settings* link to open the Properties dialog box of your graphics card. Click the Monitor tab. In the Colors drop-down list, switch to High Color (16-bit) and record the results.

_____

We have officially made a settings change with how Windows 7 displays colors onscreen, and Aero has a major issue with that, as the following steps reveal.

b.   Click OK in the dialog box and the applet you opened to return to the desktop.

→ **Note**

While Aero is having problems, try some of the features showcased earlier such as Snap, Shake, and Flip3D. Which features still work and which ones don't?

c.   With your graphics card set to 16-bit color depth, right-click on the desktop and click Personalize. At the bottom of the Personalization window is a troubleshooting tool. Record the title of the link to the troubleshooting tool.

d.   Click the link to open the Aero troubleshooting tool, shown in Figure 4-12.

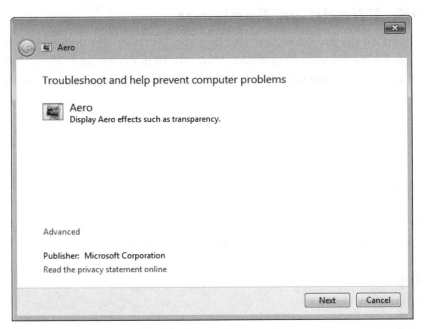

FIGURE 4-12 Aero troubleshooting tool

e. At the bottom of the Aero troubleshooting tool's window is the Advanced link. Click on the link and uncheck the *Apply repairs automatically* checkbox. Click Next to run the troubleshooting tool. Once the tool has been run, a results screen will be presented. List the problems that the Aero troubleshooting tool wants to fix.

_____

f. Click Next to apply the fixes. Your screen will flash a couple of times as it fixes itself. You will then see a summary window. Notice the results of the troubleshooting tool. Click Close.

→ **Note**

You can also access the Aero troubleshooting tool by clicking the Start button and typing **Aero** into the Start search box. Select *Find and fix problems with transparency and other visual effects.*

 30 MINUTES

Lab Exercise 4.05: Windows Explorer

Windows Explorer enables you to see all the programs and data files on a given storage device. Explorer works with hard drives and removable media such as optical media, USB flash drives, and floppy disks. Both users and techs use this program more than any other when they need to locate and manipulate files and folders.

Learning Objectives

In this lab, you'll explore the Windows file structure.

At the end of this lab, you'll be able to

- Use Windows Explorer

- Understand and use the contents of the Windows and Program Files folders

Lab Materials and Setup

The materials you need for this lab are

- A working computer running Windows XP, Windows Vista, or Windows 7

✔ **Hint**

You can perform these steps on any Windows system, but some of them may involve functionality that's available only in Windows XP.

Getting Down to Business

When you open a folder icon to view what's inside, you're seeing Windows Explorer in action. It enables you to see and manipulate files, folders, and their organizational structures quickly and easily without memorizing a bunch of commands. Becoming familiar with its ins and outs is vital to becoming an effective PC technician.

Step 1 Begin by looking at the internal directory structure of Windows. Start Windows Explorer by selecting Start | All Programs | Accessories | Windows Explorer. The first place to go exploring in the Windows directory structure is the root directory:

    a.   Locate the My Computer/Computer icon in the left pane of Windows Explorer and click the plus sign (+) or arrow.

    b.   Locate the C: drive icon, and click it once to highlight it. You should not need to click the plus sign or arrow, as clicking the drive's icon automatically expands its contents. The right pane now displays the contents of the root directory of your C: drive (see Figure 4-13).

    c.   List a few examples of folders stored on your C: drive.

_____

You can choose from several different views, or ways of displaying folder contents.

    d.   At the top of the Explorer window, click the icon called Views. (In Windows 7, the icon isn't labeled, but it looks like a set of icons.) You can also access the different views by clicking on the View drop-down menu (located on the left side of the toolbar in Windows XP, and on the right side of the toolbar in Windows Vista and Windows 7).

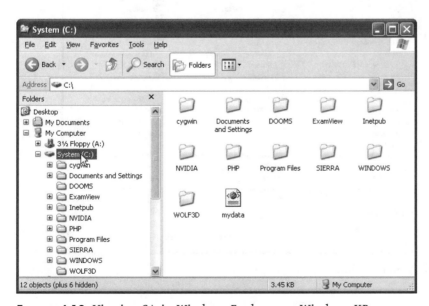

Figure 4-13 Viewing C:\ in Windows Explorer on Windows XP

e.   List the different views available in your operating system.

_____

_____

When you open the menu, the current view is marked with a large dot or slider icon. You can switch views as often as you like, simply by selecting another view from the list.

f.   Find the folders named Windows and Program Files. If you have a 64-bit operating system, you will see Program Files and Program Files (x86). These folders contain the majority of your operating system and program files.

g.   Click the Windows folder icon. Look at Figure 4-14 for a sample of what you should see at this point if you're running Windows XP.

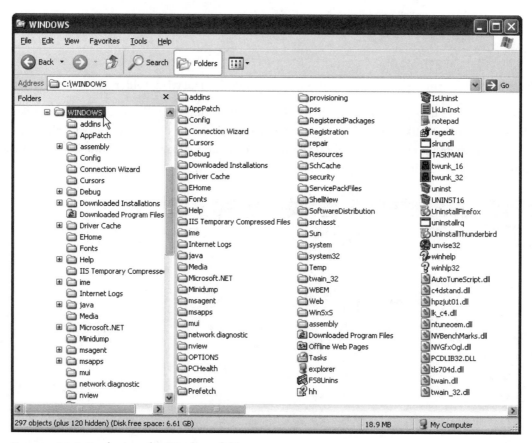

FIGURE 4-14 Exploring the Windows folder

✖ **Warning**

Some system administrators may have changed the names of these folders, but in general this is not the best practice. If you need to contact Microsoft for assistance, they always start by directing you to the default folder names, so changing them can increase your troubleshooting time.

Step 2 In the next few substeps, you'll configure your folder options to provide the maximum information about your files and folders. Techs usually find that the more information they have about a component, the easier it is to troubleshoot or configure. Take a moment and explore the different folders and files in the Windows folder. A typical Windows folder has tens of thousands of files and folders (see Figure 4-15). To view the number of files and folders in your Windows folder, right-click the Windows folder icon and select Properties from the drop-down menu.

a. List the number of files and folders in the Windows folder on your computer.

_____

b. Return to the root of your C: drive by navigating to it in the left pane or clicking the Back button at the top of Windows Explorer.

c. Like you did with the Windows folder above, record the total number of files and folders in the root of the C: drive.

_____

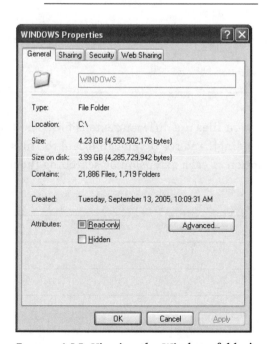

Figure 4-15 Viewing the Windows folder's properties

d.   Maximize your Explorer window (if it isn't already) by clicking the small box button next to the × button in the upper-right corner of the window. Then change the view mode to Details.

e.   Notice the column headings across the right pane. List the default column headings.

_____

f.   Click each of the headings to sort by that value. Click any heading again to sort in reverse order. You can also right-click on any column heading to see additional values for sorting.

g.   In Windows XP, select Tools | Folder Options. In Windows Vista/7, select Organize | Folder and search options. Click the View tab of the Folder Options dialog box.

h.   In the Advanced settings area, click the radio button *Show hidden files and folders, and drives*, in Windows 7. This displays all files and folders, even those for which the Hidden attribute has been set.

i.   Remove the checkmark next to *Hide extensions for known file types*. This directs Windows Explorer to display the filename extensions in all views. This is useful for a tech, and these days it also helps users with such things as identifying e-mail viruses hiding as (for instance) FILE.MP3.SCR.

j.   Remove the checkmark next to *Hide protected operating system files (Recommended)*. This will enable you to examine critical system files when you're troubleshooting problems.

k.   Click Apply to commit these changes to the folder view. Before you close the Folder Options dialog box, click Apply to All Folders (Apply to Folders in Windows 7) in the Folder views section. This will apply the Details view to every folder on the system, and enable you to see file extensions, hidden files, and system files in all folders as well.

l.   List the examples of new files or folders that are present on the root of the C: drive after making the preceding changes.

_____

m.   Click on the Windows folder in the left pane. Different files use different extensions. Sort the folders and files by Type (click the Type column heading), and see if you can locate the files with the following extensions. Give a brief description of each extension by searching them on the Internet.

- .INI   _____
- .BMP   _____
- .EXE   _____
- .TXT   _____

n. Sort the list by Name, and locate these files:

- **Explorer.exe** This is the Windows Explorer application you're using for these exercises.

- **Desktop.ini** This contains the configuration data for your desktop.

✖ **Warning**

Do not alter these files in *any* way! You won't like the results.

Step 3 When working with Windows, it's important to know the key system files that are involved with your operating system and to know how to find them. In Windows XP, use the *Search for files and folders* tool to locate and record the absolute path of any file on your system. If you are using Windows Vista or Windows 7, open the Start menu and type your search terms into the Search bar. Microsoft's more recent operating systems have much more advanced search options. If Windows doesn't find the file you are looking for, click *See more results* and you will be presented with additional search options.

a. In Windows XP, you'll first need to click Start | Search | For Files or Folders, then click *All files and folders*, and finally click *More advanced options*. Select the following checkboxes (see Figure 4-16):

- Search system folders

- Search hidden files and folders

- Search subfolders

b. Search for Notepad.exe Record its absolute path.

_____

Step 4 The following are some of the other important folders you'll find in the Windows folder. Select each one to gain more experience using Windows Explorer.

- **Cursors** Windows stores the many different cursors you can use here.

- **Fonts** Windows stores all its fonts in this folder. Note that fonts usually have one of two extensions, .FON or .TTF. The .FON files are the old-style screen fonts, and the .TTF files are modern TrueType fonts. You can double-click a font icon to see what the font looks like. Some users even print their favorite fonts and keep them in a three-ring binder for later reference.

- **Help** This folder is the default location for all .HLP and .CHM (help) files. Open one to see what program uses it.

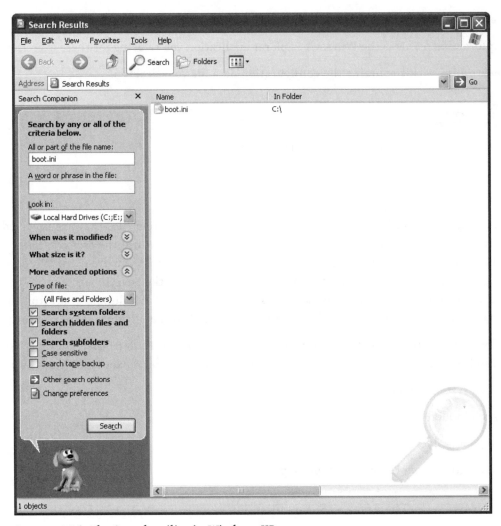

FIGURE 4-16 The Search utility in Windows XP

- **Media**   This folder is the default location for sounds and audio clips. Double-click a file with a .WAV or .MID extension to hear sounds.

- **System32**   This folder is the heart of Windows. Here you can see the core operating system files. This folder also stores almost all of the .DLL files used by Windows.

Step 5   Collapse the Windows folder, and expand the Program Files folder (see Figure 4-17). This is the default location for applications installed on your system.

Follow these steps:

a.   Open the Windows Media Player subfolder and find the application. Remember to look for the .EXE extension.

b.   Click the .EXE file's icon to start the program.

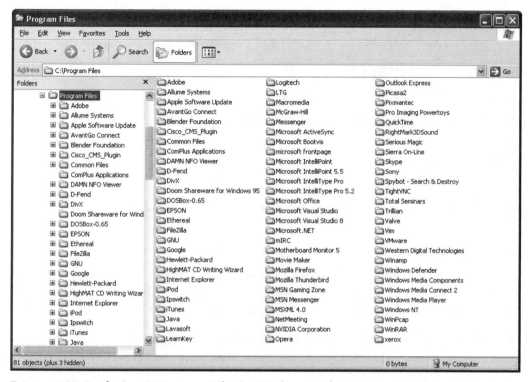

FIGURE 4-17 Exploring C:\Program Files in Windows Explorer

c.   Close the program you just opened.

d.   Exit Windows Explorer.

30 MINUTES

Lab Exercise 4.06: The Windows Control Panel

The Windows Control Panel is the technician's toolbox. It contains the tools you need to do everything from changing the mouse settings to installing new device drivers. This lab exercise won't attempt to examine every tool in the Control Panel, but it will help you become familiar with many of them. Some Control Panel programs—known as *applets*—are specific to particular hardware, while others are used for software configuration. Windows initially sets up defaults that work for most installations, but as a technician, you may need to tweak some of the settings. Also, not all Windows features are enabled in a normal installation, so you may need to enable or disable features according to the needs of a particular user.

✔ **Cross-Reference**

For a refresher on the Windows Control Panel, refer to the "Control Panel" section in Chapter 4 of *Mike Meyers' CompTIA A+ Guide to Managing and Troubleshooting PCs*.

Learning Objectives

In this lab, you'll practice accessing the Control Panel and making configuration adjustments.

At the end of this lab, you'll be able to

- Navigate to the Control Panel
- Explain the use of some common Control Panel applets

Lab Materials and Setup

The materials you need for this lab are

- A working computer running Windows XP, Windows Vista, or Windows 7

Getting Down to Business

The Control Panel is the toolbox, and one of the key tools in the Control Panel is the Device Manager. Device Manager lists all your system hardware. From there, you can load drivers, set resources, and configure other aspects of your hardware devices. You'll now get familiar with both.

Step 1   As a technician, you'll access the Control Panel and Device Manager often. You really do need to know the path to these important tools in each version of Windows. The CompTIA A+ exams have numerous questions about paths to these tools.

→ **Note**

Throughout the rest of this manual, when a lab involves changing settings located in the Control Panel or Device Manager, the directions will assume you know how to get that far, and the steps will begin with the Control Panel or Device Manager already open. Refer to this exercise if you need a refresher on opening the Control Panel.

a.   To open the Control Panel, click on the Start button, then select Control Panel. The Control Panel window opens, as shown in Figures 4.18 and 4.19.

b.   Practice switching between the different views in Control Panel. For Windows XP, on the left pane it says *Switch to Category View*. For Windows Vista, on the left pane it says *Classic View*. For Windows 7, in the upper-right corner of the window it says *View by: Category*. Experiment with each view to see which one fits you the best.

→ **Note**

CompTIA A+ expects you to know both ways of viewing a Windows Control Panel, no matter the operating system. For the rest of this lab, we will operate out of Classic View (also called Icon View).

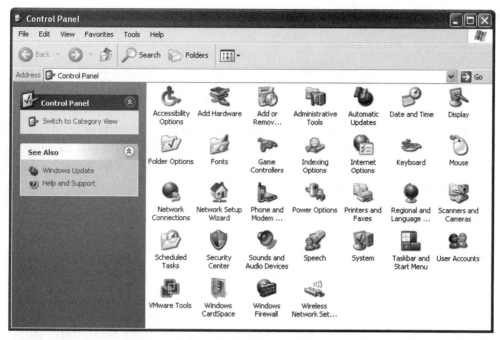

FIGURE 4-18 The Control Panel (Classic View) in Windows XP

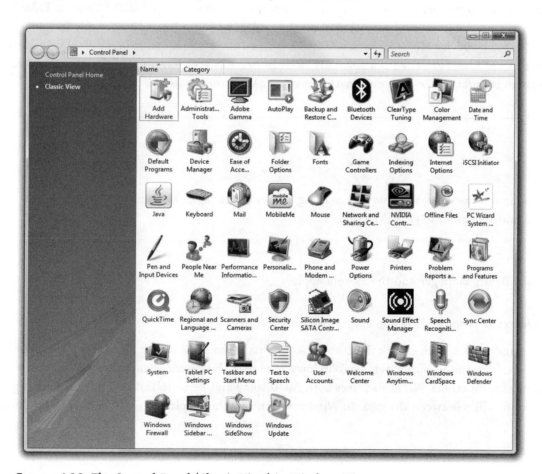

FIGURE 4-19 The Control Panel (Classic View) in Windows Vista

c. List six Control Panel applets that you think are vital to troubleshooting a PC.

_____   _____

_____   _____

_____   _____

d. Open the System applet. The System applet is the gateway to many important tools and utilities you will use as a PC technician. You will also notice that the System applet in Windows XP is very different from the Windows Vista/7 System applet. What kind of information do you see when looking at the System applet?

_____

e. Is your operating system type 32-bit or 64-bit?

_____

f. If you are on a Windows Vista/7 computer, click on Device Manager in the left pane. If you are on a Windows XP computer, click the Hardware tab, and then click the Device Manager button.

g. Device Manager is arguably one of the most important utilities in Microsoft Windows. From here you can see the status and condition of all the devices in your system. Record any irregularities indicated by Device Manager, such as devices with an exclamation point in a yellow field, devices with a red ×, or devices with a down arrow. If Device Manager has none of these symbols, your system is working like a champ; write "devmgmt.msc is the greatest!"

_____

→ **Note**

Devmgmt.msc is the command-line tool to bring up Device Manager. Remember, it's always good to know multiple paths to get to the same thing.

h. Close Device Manager and the System applet.

Step 2 Now examine some other applets in the Control Panel.

a. In Windows XP, double-click the Display icon. This is the same applet you see if you right-click the desktop and select Properties. Windows Vista uses the Personalization applet for many of the same functions. Windows 7 uses both the Display and Personalization applets, splitting the responsibility between the two. In Windows 7, the Display applet adjusts your video resolution and monitor settings, and the Personalization applet changes the look and feel of your desktop interface. According to your OS, find the appropriate Control Panel applet to change your system's video resolution. What is your current resolution?

_____

b.   In Windows XP/Vista, use the slider bar to lower the resolution to the lowest value. In Windows 7, open the drop-down menu and use the slider to lower the resolution to the lowest value. What is the lowest resolution that can be set?

_____

c.   Click Apply. What happens to your desktop interface?

_____

d.   Either let the timer expire to change back to the previous setting, or manually change the setting back to its defaults when you are finished.

✖   **Warning**

Clicking an Advanced button in the Display applet can give you access to many special features of your particular monitor/video card, including the refresh rate. Be sure you know what you're doing before you change these settings!

✔   **Hint**

If you click the Apply button instead of the OK button after making a change, the Display applet will remain open after the change takes effect; this can be useful when you need to experiment a bit.

e.   Return to the Control Panel and double-click the Sounds and Audio Devices icon in Windows XP or the Sound icon in Windows Vista/7 to open the applet.

f.   Tabs line the top of the applet. Explore each one, and become familiar with what each does. In Windows Vista/7, click on the Playback tab. In Windows XP, click on the Audio tab, and then click the drop-down menu for Sound playback. List the devices your PC has for playing sound.

_____

g.   Reset all of your changes, if you made any, and close the applet.

Step 3   Keyboard and mouse settings are a matter of personal preference. Be careful to tell the user if you make any changes to these settings. If you need to speed up the mouse while you use someone else's PC, for example, remember to slow it down again when you finish.

To adjust the keyboard settings:

a.   Double-click the Keyboard icon in the Control Panel. In Windows 7, make sure you are on the Speed tab.

b.   Change the Repeat delay and Repeat rate settings and click Apply. Keep the Keyboard applet open and open Notepad or WordPad. Test your changes by pressing and holding individual keys on the keyboard. Based on your finding, explain repeat rate and repeat delay.

Repeat rate: _____

Repeat delay: _____

✔ **Hint**

The Mouse applet can have many different looks, depending on whether the system uses a default Windows driver or special drivers for the particular mouse. You may have to explore your applet to find these settings.

---

c.   Double-click the Mouse icon to open the Mouse applet.

d.   Look through the tabs of the mouse applet. Find the settings for left-handed mode. Set your mouse to left-handed mode. Try it out. Does that make your brain hurt? Well, then, change it back. (Ahhh, that's better!)

e.   Change the double-click speed. Slow it down a bit. Is that easier? Slow it down more. Do you find that annoying? Now speed it up. Can you click fast enough?

f.   Change the mini-icons that represent your mouse pointer, such as the arrow, hourglass, and so on. Try a couple of different sets. Can you think of situations where some of these alternate icon sets might be useful?

_____

_____

g.   Change the pointer options. Change the speed at which the pointer travels across your screen. Everyone has his or her own sweet spot for this, so experiment to find yours. Turn on pointer trails. Do you find them cool or annoying? If you have a Snap To option, turn that on. Now open a dialog box and watch the pointer jump to the active button. Is this convenient, or too much help? Turn off any features you don't want to keep.

h.   Close the Mouse applet.

Step 4   The CompTIA A+ exams include questions about user accessibility. You need to know which settings you can change to accommodate the hearing and visually impaired, and where to find those settings.

   a.   In Windows XP, open the Accessibility Options applet (see Figure 4-20). In Vista and 7, choose the Ease of Access Center applet (see Figure 4-21). Notice that you have all the previously mentioned options, plus many more!

   b.   Select the Display tab in Windows XP, or click *Make the computer easier to see* in Windows Vista/7.

   c.   In Windows XP, check the Use High Contrast checkbox and click Settings (see Figure 4-22). In Windows Vista/7, check the box to enable the High Contrast key combination and then click *Choose a High Contrast theme*.

   d.   Choose a scheme you like and click OK.

   e.   In Windows XP, click Apply in the Accessibility Options applet to see how it looks. In Windows Vista/7, you have to press LEFT ALT-LEFT SHIFT-PRINT SCREEN to activate High Contrast mode.

   f.   Turn off the Use High Contrast option by repeating the key combination, and then click Apply and click OK.

   g.   Close the Accessibility Options/Ease of Access Center applet.

Step 5   Finally, let's look at the Date and Time applet.

Open the Date and Time applet in the Control Panel. This applet has been around since the dawn of time, more or less, when computers didn't automatically adjust themselves for Daylight Saving Time.

FIGURE 4-20   The Accessibility Options applet in Windows XP

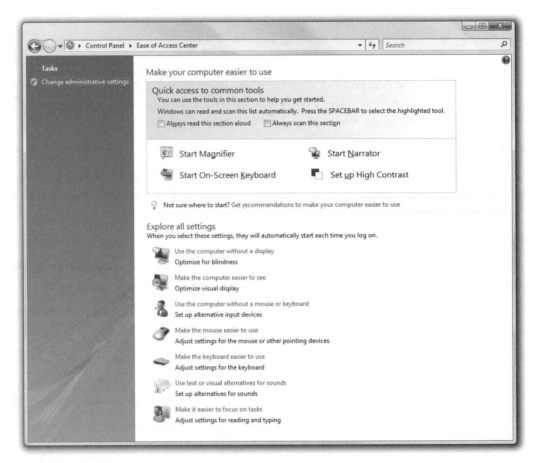

FIGURE 4-21 Ease of Access Center applet in Windows Vista

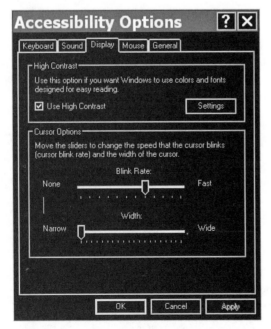

FIGURE 4-22 Setting the High Contrast option for the visually impaired

Adjust the date and time. Notice that you can do this either by scrolling with the arrows or by highlighting the fields and typing in the time on your keyboard. This feature can come in handy if you travel and want to change the time zone on a portable computer.

a. Click on the Internet Time tab. Record the server your PC connects to in order to receive the correct time.

_____

b. If you are using Windows 7, click the Additional Clocks tab. Add more clocks to your notification area. How many total clocks can you have (not including Gadgets)?

_____

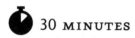 30 MINUTES

Lab Exercise 4.07: The Windows Microsoft Management Console (MMC) Toolbox

You're about to learn how to customize your Windows toolkit! Almost every profession requires a set of tools to get the job done. Some of these tools are necessary, and some are luxuries. If you were a carpenter, you might have a toolbox in which you keep your hammer, saw, screwdrivers, pliers, and so on. You could then buy new tools ("I really needed this pneumatic nail gun, and it was on sale!" is a common excuse) and add them to your toolbox—but you'd need to keep it all organized, or risk not being able to find the tool you need when you need it.

To help organize all of your PC technician's utilities, Microsoft created a handy toolbox: the Microsoft Management Console, or MMC. The MMC not only organizes all of those useful tools, but also provides a consistent look and feel between different systems and even different operating systems, which makes it easier to use them.

✔ **Cross-Reference**

For details on working with the MMC, refer to the "Microsoft Management Console" section in Chapter 4 of *Mike Meyers' CompTIA A+ Guide to Managing and Troubleshooting PCs*.

Learning Objectives

In this exercise, you'll learn how to create an MMC. You'll also create a desktop icon that you can use to access this customized software toolkit whenever you need it.

At the end of this lab, you'll be able to

- Create an MMC

- Add tools (snap-ins) to the MMC

Lab Materials and Setup

The materials you need for this lab are

- A working computer running Windows XP, Windows Vista, or Windows 7

Getting Down to Business

The MMC is a shell program that holds individual utilities called snap-ins. The first time you create an MMC, you get a default blank console. A blank MMC isn't much to look at—like any new toolbox, it starts out empty.

Step 1   To create your MMC, select Start | Run in Windows XP, or use the Start menu Search bar in Windows Vista/7, type **mmc**, and then press ENTER. Voilà! You've created a blank console (see Figure 4-23).

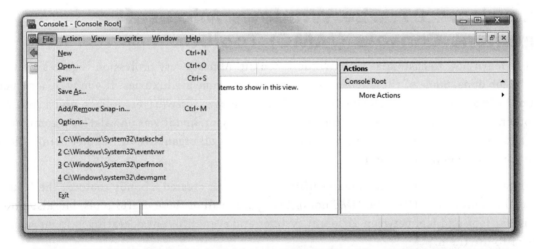

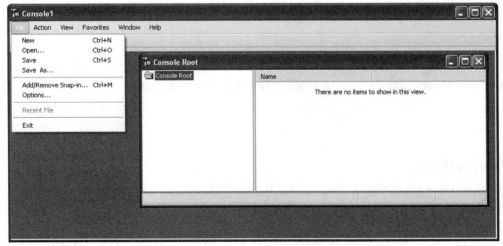

FIGURE 4-23 Blank MMCs in Windows XP (bottom) and Vista (top)

You'll notice that the name in the upper-left corner is Console1. In Vista/7, you'll also notice a panel called Actions, which contains a list of actions that are available to users as you add snap-ins and select them.

Before you actually configure an MMC, you need to understand a few points. First, you can have more than one MMC; successive consoles will be given default names such as Console2, Console3, and so on. Second, you can rename the consoles that you create. Third, you can choose where to save the consoles, so that you can easily find them again. Finally, once you've created an MMC, you can modify it by adding or removing tools—just like your toolbox at home.

Follow these steps to practice working with MMCs:

a. Click File | Save As and fill in the boxes as follows:

   • **Save in**   Desktop

   • **File name**   *Your Name's* MMC

   • **Save as type**   Microsoft Management Console Files (*.msc)

b. Click Save to continue. (Don't exit the MMC!)

c. Notice in the upper-left corner of the open window that the name has changed.

d. Find the new icon that's been created on the desktop. This icon, which bears the same name as your new MMC, enables you to access the MMC in the future with just a double-click of the mouse.

Step 2   When you add snap-ins, they'll show up in the Add/Remove Snap-in dialog box (see Figure 4-24).

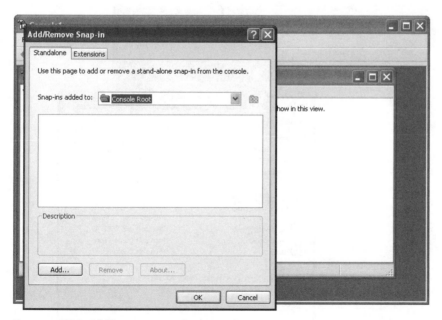

FIGURE 4-24 Adding or removing snap-ins

You'll now add some snap-ins to your MMC:

a.   Click File | Add/Remove Snap-in.

b.   Click Add, and let the fun begin (see Figure 4-25). List five available snap-ins.

_____

_____

_____

_____

_____

c.   Add the Device Manager as your first tool. Select Device Manager from the list and click Add.

✔ **Hint**

When you add a snap-in, you have a choice of adding it for either your local computer or another computer. With the proper access permissions, in other words, you can look at Device Manager on a networked system. More than likely, you don't have the necessary permissions to do this, so stick with the local option for now.

d.   Select Local Computer and click Finish.

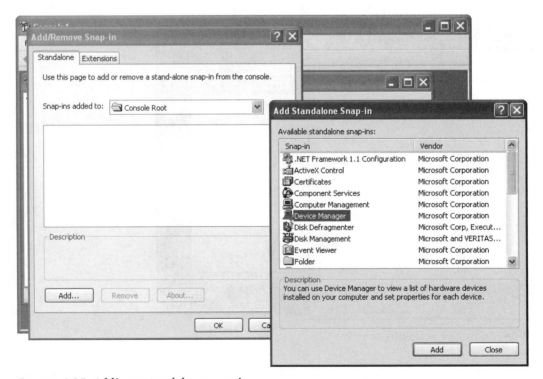

FIGURE 4-25 Adding a standalone snap-in

✖ Warning

I can't emphasize strongly enough that the best way to get a systems administrator mad is to go snooping around on the network. As a technician, your main concern is to do no harm. If you accidentally find your way to an unauthorized area, it's your duty to report it to an administrator.

While you're here, you'll add one more snap-in: Event Viewer. Adding it here will provide an alternate way to access this tool.

    e.   Select Event Viewer from the list.

    f.   Select Local Computer and click Finish to close out the wizard.

    g.   Click Add to close the list window, and click OK to close the Add/Remove window.

    h.   Your MMC should now show two snap-ins.

    i.   Be sure to save your MMC.

    j.   You now have a toolbox with quick access to Device Manager and Event Viewer. You can use these tools in the same way as if you navigated to them through the conventional methods. Have your instructor view your MMC to see if everything works correctly. If you don't have an instructor available, ask a knowledgeable technician that you know to glance at your screen.

        Instructor Check: _____

Step 3   If everything has worked correctly up to now, continue with this step (if you had problems creating your MMC, review the instructions or ask your instructor for assistance):

    a.   Double-click the desktop icon for *Your Name's* MMC.

    b.   Device Manager and Event Viewer are now available directly from your desktop (see Figure 4-26).

✔ Hint

I've only scratched the surface of creating an MMC here. Your customizing options are limited only by the number of snap-ins available and your imagination. Try creating different groupings of tools to organize similar tasks—maybe all the disk management tools together, or all the user, group, and resource tools. Be creative!

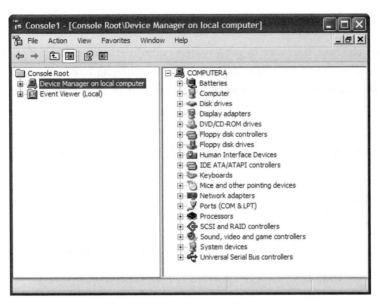

FIGURE 4-26 Accessing Device Manager from a custom MMC

Lab Analysis Test

1. Your friend Brian calls you and asks why his Windows 7 Ultimate desktop interface looks different from other computers he has looked at recently. He elaborates by telling you that he used to be able to see through his window panes, but now they are just solid colors. What is Brian having issues with and how can he go about fixing it?

2. What's the purpose of the MMC? What is the added feature in Windows Vista/7?

3. Your network administrator wants you to set up a lab full of Windows XP computers. He doesn't want the users to mess with important settings, so he wants you to remove the Run command from the Start menu. Give a detailed explanation of how to do that.

4. One of your clients using Windows Vista called your help desk because he's experiencing difficulties using the mouse. He says his mouse moves too fast, and icons don't respond when he double-clicks them. What's wrong? Where would you direct him to go to fix this problem? Give the complete path.

5. A Windows 7 user on your network has just downloaded an important attachment from a colleague, but he is unsure whether the document he downloaded is a .DOCX file or a .DOC file. Give a detailed description of how you can reveal the extensions to known files.

Key Term Quiz

Use the following terms to complete the following sentences. Not all terms will be used.

Aero

Classic View

Control Panel

Device Manager

DirectX 9

Display

Ease of Access Center

Flip3D

Glass

MMC

notification area

Recycle Bin

Shake

Snap

snap-ins

Start button

taskbar

transparency

1. Pressing WINDOWS KEY-TAB in Windows 7 will showcase the _____ feature.

2. The System, Display, and Mouse applets are found in the _____.

3. The various tools in the MMC are known as _____.

4. The area that holds all of your open applications and allows you to pin icons to it in Windows 7 is known as the _____.

5. You can take advantage of Windows _____ as long as you have a _____ compatible video card with 128 MB of video memory installed in your computer running Windows 7.

Chapter 5
Visible Networks

Lab Exercises

There's no doubt about it—a PC technician *will* have networking issues to work through at some point. Whether it's a three-computer, home-based local area network (LAN), a public Wi-Fi access point, a large company with thousands of connected devices, or the Web itself, networks have become as common as PCs. The main consideration is no longer whether you're going to network your computers—it's now what method you're going to use to network your computers.

A competent PC technician is called upon to be a network guru, answering connectivity questions and making recommendations on the best price/performance considerations for homes and businesses. This happens frequently, especially in smaller companies that can't afford to hire multiple people to support both the network *and* the PCs. The CompTIA A+ certification exams reflect these changing roles of the PC technician and include many questions related to computer networking.

In this chapter's lab exercises, you'll imagine that you've been hired to work for a small company that has made the decision to upgrade the network in their office. You'll need to have a working understanding of network hardware and network operating system issues.

 30 MINUTES

Lab Exercise 5.01: Understanding Network Topologies

Networks don't spontaneously come into being—they must be designed and laid out. Choosing the proper layout, or *topology*, is an important decision because each topology has its own advantages and disadvantages. Knowing how a network is put together and organized is an important part of setting one up.

Learning Objectives

In this lab, you'll learn about network topologies.

At the end of this lab, you'll be able to

- Identify different network topologies
- Understand the benefits and drawbacks of each topology

Lab Materials and Setup

The materials you need for this lab are

- A group of four people
- Any small object

Getting Down to Business

This is a group activity that works best in a classroom. If you are working alone or want more practice, you can achieve the same goals with a few more objects—instead of people, use cups or bowls to represent each device and a ball to represent the data going back and forth. For each demonstration, keep in mind the real-world components that would be involved. How many cables would it use? What special devices do you need? What if a component was broken?

Step 1   First, you'll look at the star topology. A star topology has multiple computers connecting to a single, central wiring point (a switch). This is probably the one you are most familiar with, since most home networks are set up this way.

Have your group stand up and form a circle. Designate someone to stand in the middle and be the "switch." Someone else should then begin by taking an object (the data) and passing it to the switch. The switch then passes the object to someone else, who must first pass it back to the switch before it can move anywhere else—remember that the object cannot pass directly from one computer to the next. It must first move through the switch.

Write down your observations about this topology, including its advantages and disadvantages.

_____

_____

_____

_____

Step 2   Next, you'll look at the ring topology. In this topology, each device attaches to a central ring of cable to form a network. Have your group stand in a circle again. Begin passing the object clockwise around the circle. Remember that it cannot skip any person in the circle, nor can it cross to the other side.

Now have one person leave the circle, breaking the chain. The object cannot pass to the next person if the circle is broken, so the network becomes nonfunctional.

Write down your observations about this topology, including its advantages and disadvantages.

_____

_____

_____

_____

Step 3   Now you'll look at a bus topology, where each device attaches to a single network cable. Instead of a circle, stand in a line with everyone facing the same direction. Have each person pass the object to the next person in the line, and when the object reaches the last person, pass the object back in the other direction.

Have one person step out of the line. The object cannot skip that person's place, so the object now has to bounce back and forth between the people on one side of the missing person.

Write down your observations about this topology, including its advantages and disadvantages.

_____
_____
_____
_____

Step 4   Finally, you'll look at a mesh topology. This topology connects every computer to every other computer, without the use of a bus or switch. Have everyone in the group stand in a circle again, and now pass the object to whomever you wish. Continue to do so, feeling free to pass it to the person next to you or across from you.

Write down your observations about this topology, including its advantages and disadvantages.

_____
_____
_____
_____

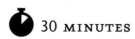 30 MINUTES

Lab Exercise 5.02: Identifying Local Area Network Hardware

Your boss has decided to upgrade the network in your office, which is about five years old. With the changes in networking technology, he wants your ideas about purchasing the right equipment for the upgrade. Your company is a small one, so the task is quite doable, but you need to make sure you know what you're talking about before you give your report.

Learning Objectives

In this lab, you'll familiarize yourself with networking hardware.

At the end of this lab, you'll be able to

- Identify different kinds of network cabling

- Identify different network interface cards (NICs)

- Identify different types of network hubs and switches

- Identify different wireless networking devices

Lab Materials and Setup

The materials you need for this lab are

- Access to a PC running Windows

- Access to a working LAN and the Internet (you may have demonstration devices provided by your instructor)

Getting Down to Business

One of the best ways to find out what a network is made of is to physically look at all of its pieces. Even then, however, it may be necessary to access a manufacturer's Web site to see, for instance, if the "hub" you're using is really a hub or a switch.

Step 1   If you have access to a LAN (the classroom computer lab network, a friend's home network, or your company's network), spend some time exploring the physical hardware connections and devices. If possible, acquire the diagram of the physical layout of the network, or create a simple diagram of the layout to familiarize yourself with the various devices and connections associated with the network you're analyzing.

✖ Warning

Don't disconnect anything, and be careful while probing around. One small mistake, like removing a cable or turning off the wrong device, can disrupt the entire network. If you're using the classroom network, ask the instructor what you can and can't remove while you make closer inspections of the cables and devices.

✔ Cross-Reference

Be sure to check out Chapter 5 of *Mike Meyers' CompTIA A+ Guide to Managing and Troubleshooting PCs* for help identifying network cables and connectors. It's a good idea to have the textbook handy while you progress through this lab.

What sort of cabling does the network use, or is it wireless? Is it twisted-pair cable or older coaxial cable? Are the cable ends RJ-45 connectors? Describe the physical layout of the LAN here.

_____

_____

_____

What sort of NICs do the machines have? Describe the back of the card. Does it have a single connector or a combination of connectors (see Figure 5-1)? Does it have an antenna? Is there a link and/or activity LED? Which of the LEDs is on steady? Which is flashing? Describe the NIC here.

_____

_____

_____

✔ Hint

It is very important to understand the difference between the link light and the activity light. First, these "lights" are really light-emitting diodes (LEDs) and will usually appear in some form of yellow, orange, or green color, depending on the NIC manufacturer. Second, the link light indicates that the NIC and the cable have a valid electrical connection between the PC and the network device, usually a switch. This does not guarantee connectivity—it just means that the electrical connection is intact. The activity light is a better indicator of whether or not the NIC, cable, and hubs or switches are working. When the activity light blinks, it is indicating that data is being transferred between the networking devices. It does not guarantee that the data is usable—it just means that data is making the trip from the NIC to the hub or switch, or from the hub or switch to the NIC. If you are having trouble connecting to a network or communicating to other machines on the network, the link and activity lights are a good place to start your troubleshooting.

Step 2   Switches (and hubs, to an extent) are a part of the majority of networks. (Remember that modern networks almost exclusively use switches.)

Are the PCs connected with a single cable (crossover cable limited to two PCs), or are they connected to a hub/switch (see Figure 5-2)? Is part of the network wireless? What is the model number

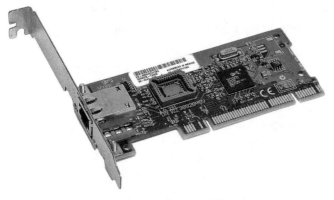

FIGURE 5-1 A network interface card (NIC)

FIGURE 5-2 A LAN hub with multiple cables/devices attached

of the network hub/switch? Who manufactures the hub/switch? How many devices can be attached? Record your findings here.

_____
_____
_____

Is the hub or switch a standard single-speed (10BaseT, for instance) device, or can it handle multiple speeds (10/100/1000 Mbps)? Does it have wireless capabilities? Record your findings here. If this information isn't apparent or printed on the device, ask the instructor or the network administrator.

_____
_____
_____

Step 3 Are you going to have a wireless network or wireless devices in your network? Do you plan on installing a wireless network sometime in the near future? In the current world of networking, the terms _hub_, _switch_, and _router_ are often used interchangeably, but they really are very different devices with very different functions. Conduct an Internet search on the definition of each device.

Compare and contrast each type of device. How do they achieve their functionality? Where or for what purpose does it makes sense to use each device?

Hub _____

_____

Switch _____

_____

Router _____

_____

 30 MINUTES

Lab Exercise 5.03: Exploring Local Area Network Configuration Options

You've made your recommendation, and you've installed the network. The hardware side of installing a basic LAN is really simple these days, so you managed to get that put together in a flash. Now it's time to configure the PCs that connect to the network.

To prepare for the CompTIA A+ exams and to build your toolbox of skills as a PC technician, you need to be able to set up, configure, and troubleshoot networks that use Windows clients. From a network configuration standpoint, each version of Windows is very similar. The CompTIA A+ exams will test your configuration knowledge for all three versions of Windows, including the paths you use to locate configuration settings.

Learning Objectives

In this lab, you'll explore the network configuration options in a Windows environment.

At the end of this lab, you'll be able to

- Configure network access using the networking applets

Lab Materials and Setup

The materials you need for this lab are

- Access to a PC with Windows installed

- Access to the LAN

✔ **Hint**

I don't want to sound like a broken record, but if possible, you should repeat the exercises in each edition of Windows. If you only have a single operating system, be sure you understand how to configure networks in the other operating system environments. It's also a good idea to have the drivers for your NICs handy just in case you need to reload any of them. Finally, you'll want to determine the relevant settings (in other words, the proper protocol, the name[s] of the workgroup[s] you'll be using, and so on); write them down, and keep them with you as you go from computer to computer.

Getting Down to Business

For a computer to gain access to or share resources on a network, it must have an NIC installed and configured. Microsoft provides configuration wizards to set up your network with mostly default parameters and a lot of assumptions. In other words, you tell the wizard the computer name, and it does the rest. Using the Microsoft wizards will enable you to set up a default configuration for quick access (good for at home), but this may not always work for a LAN in a business environment.

Whether you use the wizards or manually configure the system, the following steps must be accurately programmed into the software or you won't be able to take full advantage of the LAN. For the CompTIA A+ exams, you need to know *where to locate* and *how to modify* the network configuration. Specifically, each computer that will be connected to the LAN must have the following:

- An NIC with correct drivers installed
- Client software, such as Client for Microsoft Networks
- Protocols (what language[s] you'll use on the network and the settings)
- Services, such as File and Printer Sharing for Microsoft Networks
- A computer name
- A workgroup name

Step 1   Go to Device Manager and verify that the correct NIC drivers are installed. Reinstall the driver(s) if necessary.

In Device Manager, expand *Network adapters*. Right-click on your network card and select Properties. Click the Driver tab to see what driver is installed or to update the driver.

Step 2   In this step, you'll verify what network services are installed.

In Windows XP, go to Control Panel | Network Connections. Right-click on Local Area Connection and select Properties. In Windows Vista/7, go to the Control Panel and open the Network and Sharing Center. In the Tasks menu on the left, click *Manage network connections* in Windows Vista and click *Change adapter settings* in Windows 7. Right-click on Local Area Connection and select Properties.

✔ Hint

Nothing is necessarily wrong if you don't see any or all of the following components listed or if you see more than the ones listed previously. It simply means that the network configuration hasn't been completed on your system, or it's in a network supported by more than one server.

You should find the following components listed in a selection window. Your system may have others as well.

- **Client**   Client for Microsoft Networks (default**)**

- **Protocol**   Internet Protocol (TCP/IP); newer systems separate these into Internet Protocol version 6 (TCP/IPv6) and Internet Protocol version 4 (TCP/IPv4)

- **Service**   File and Printer Sharing for Microsoft Networks

    a.   What client(s), other than the default, are listed in your system? _____
    _____

    b.   What protocol(s), other than the default, are listed? _____
    _____

    c.   What services, other than the default, are listed? _____
    _____

Step 3   Now that you've found the network configuration screen, take a look at the various options:

- **Install**   The Install button enables you to add network components. Clicking the Install button gives you three choices:

    - **Client**   Adds a client to the configuration (must have at least one).

    - **Protocol**   TCP/IP is the default (must have a protocol to communicate).

    - **Service**   File and Printer Sharing must be enabled for other computers on the network to access the one on which you're working.

- **Remove/Uninstall**   The Remove or Uninstall button enables you to remove network components.

- **Properties**   The Properties button displays a variety of dialog boxes based on the network component selected.

✔ **Hint**

Each of the preceding options asks questions about what you want to change. If one or more of your required settings are missing, use this screen to add them. When you make changes, you may be asked to reboot the system.

Step 4   Now that your system is configured for networking, it needs an identity and to join a workgroup to be recognized by the network and access network resources.

In Windows XP, go to the Control Panel and open the System applet. Select the Computer Name tab. Go to the same applet in Windows Vista/7, but the information should be displayed in the applet directly. Record your system settings here:

Computer name/description _____

Workgroup name _____

Step 5 Now that you've confirmed and recorded the networking components, your computer name, and your workgroup, the next step is to practice reinstalling your network adapter.

> ✖ **Warning**
>
> This step is optional and can cause you grief if you aren't prepared. Ask the instructor if it's okay for you to proceed with this step. If not (or if you think this may harm your configuration), skip this step.

Access Device Manager and uninstall your network adapter. Yes, this will erase all your network settings. Did you take good notes earlier? Expand the *Network adapters* heading, right-click on your specific adapter, and choose Remove or Uninstall.

> ✖ **Warning**
>
> If your notes are incomplete, ask the instructor to fill in the correct settings you're missing.

Reboot your system, and the adapter will be detected (if it's plug and play) and installed. Access the Network Connections/Network and Sharing Center applet, and verify your network configuration using the information you recorded in Steps 1, 2, and 4 previously. If your system doesn't load the drivers for the network card, you'll need the driver disc to complete your settings.

Test your system by accessing the network. Can you browse the network now? Look in My Network Places/Network.

Lab Analysis Test

1. Jodie wants her Windows 7 computer to join a domain. How does she accomplish this?

2. Sam is having a difficult time describing the difference between a switch and a router to a customer. Help him describe the difference between the two devices.

3. Betty just opened the Firefox Web browser. When she attempts to visit a Web page, it is unable to connect. She knows she hasn't changed any settings on the computer, but she did move the computer from her old office to the new office. List some troubleshooting ideas for Betty.

4. How do you access the Local Area Connection Properties dialog box in Windows 7?

5. You have six computers that need to be networked. Take a moment to draw out how the six computers would look arranged in the four different topologies.

Key Term Quiz

Use the following terms to complete the following sentences. Not all terms will be used.

> bus
>
> client
>
> domain
>
> hub
>
> LED
>
> MAC
>
> mesh
>
> NIC
>
> protocol
>
> ring
>
> RJ-45
>
> router
>
> server
>
> star
>
> switch
>
> topology
>
> workgroup

1. A(n) _____ can effectively place a device on its own collision domain, thereby increasing network bandwidth.

2. A(n) _____ topology is where all the nodes are connected to a central device.

3. Twisted-pair network cabling uses a(n) _____ connector.

4. A set of rules that governs communication on a network is known as a(n) _____.

5. A(n) _____ is a device or computer that requests data from a _____, which holds all of the information.

Chapter 6

Microprocessors

Lab Exercises

Many PC users can perform simple installation and upgrade tasks, such as adding RAM or installing a new sound card. When it comes to the more complicated tasks, however, such as installing or replacing a central processing unit (CPU), wise users turn to the experts—this means you!

As a tech, you will install plenty of CPUs. Whether you're building a new system from scratch or replacing the CPU on an existing computer, it's your job to know the important characteristics of the CPU, match the CPU to compatible motherboards, and confirm that the CPU in the PC is running properly.

In this set of lab exercises, you'll identify current CPU types, form factors, and sockets. You'll then explore the specifications of the microprocessor with a freeware program known as CPU-Z. Finally, you'll learn how to remove and install a CPU.

It's time to find your anti-static wrist strap and get started with your exploration of CPUs!

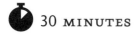 30 MINUTES

Lab Exercise 6.01: Identifying CPU Characteristics

There you are, innocently strolling down the hall at work, following the smell of freshly brewed coffee, when you're ambushed by Joe the accountant, brandishing a CPU/fan unit. He wants to replace the CPU in his machine with this new one he bought on eBay, and he wants you to help him. When you're the resident computer tech geek, your coworkers will expect you to be able to deal competently with a situation like Joe's.

Staying on top of the many developments in CPU technology can be challenging, but it's also a necessary part of your job as a PC technician. By this point, you know that you can't just plug any CPU into any motherboard and expect it to work—you have to match the right CPU to the right motherboard. To accomplish this, you need to identify important CPU characteristics such as form factor, clock speed, and bus speed, as well as things like voltage settings, clock multiplier configurations, and cooling requirements.

Learning Objectives

In this lab, you'll practice identifying CPUs and CPU fan components.

At the end of this lab, you'll be able to

- Recognize the different kinds of CPUs

- Recognize different CPU fan attachments

- Identify the basic specifications of different classes of CPUs

Lab Materials and Setup

The materials you need for this lab are

- A notepad and pencil to document the specifications

- Optional: Access to a working computer with a word processing or spreadsheet application installed and access to the Internet, to facilitate research and documentation of the CPU specifications

Getting Down to Business

In the following steps, you'll review your knowledge of CPU specifications, and then examine the CPU and fan attachment on a PC.

✔ **Cross-Reference**

Use Chapter 6 of *Mike Meyers' CompTIA A+ Guide to Managing and Troubleshooting PCs* to help fill in the specifications for each CPU in the following charts.

Step 1 A good tech not only will learn the specifications of different CPU chips, but also will master the use of reference tools such as the Internet, manufacturers' Web sites, product documentation, and reference books. A quick search of the Web or your motherboard manual will generally yield a full list of specs for a given CPU.

See how many CPU chip features you can fill in given the maker and CPU type:

→ **Note**

CPUs have very short production lives. If some of these CPUs have become obsolete, use the extra rows provided to add more modern processors to the assignment.

Maker	CPU Type	Package	Clock Speed (GHz)	Wattage Consumption	L2 Cache	L3 Cache	Number of Cores
Intel	Core 2 Quad Q9650						
AMD	Phenom II X3 710						
AMD	FX-8150						
Intel	Core i5-2500K						
AMD	Athlon X2 7550 Black Edition						

Maker	CPU Type	Package	Clock Speed (GHz)	Wattage Consumption	L2 Cache	L3 Cache	Number of Cores
Intel	Pentium 4 650						
Intel	Core i7-3960X						
AMD	A8-3850						
Intel	Core i7-960						

Step 2 Look at the CPUs pictured in Figure 6-1, making note of the differences you see. In particular, do the following:

a. Distinguish between pin grid array (PGA) and land grid array (LGA) packages by writing LGA or PGA on top of the processor's picture.

b. Circle the orientation guides in the corner of each CPU.

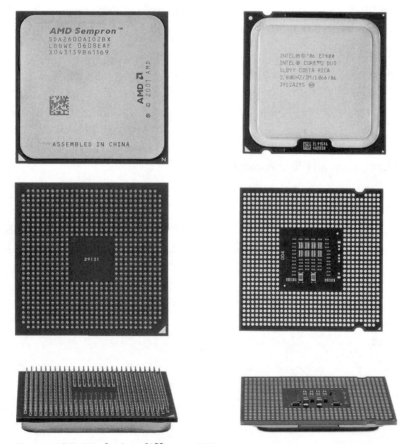

Figure 6-1 Exploring different CPUs

Step 3   Many users argue that Intel is better than AMD or vice versa. What do you think? Do some research and prepare a recommendation for selecting either an Intel processor or an AMD processor. Check multiple Web sites, read different articles online, and then write a short comparison/contrast essay on which CPU manufacturer you think is better. Be sure to cite your sources!

_____

_____

_____

_____

_____

_____

_____

_____

 30 MINUTES

Lab Exercise 6.02: Recognizing CPU Sockets

Now that you've identified Joe's purchase, you explain to him that you can't be sure it will work in his PC until you see his motherboard. CPU compatibility is determined by what the motherboard can support. Most motherboards enable you to upgrade the PC by replacing the existing CPU with a faster model of the same type. As a technician, your job is to make sure that the newer CPU has the same pin configuration as the motherboard. If you do not know where to begin, perform an online search for the maker of the motherboard. In many cases, you must replace the entire motherboard if you want to move up to a faster microprocessor.

Learning Objectives

In this lab, you'll identify various CPU sockets.

At the end of this lab, you'll be able to

- Recognize different kinds of CPU sockets
- Know which CPUs require which sockets

Lab Materials and Setup

The materials you need for this lab are

- A notepad and pencil to document the specifications
- Optional: Access to a working computer with a word processing or spreadsheet application installed and access to the Internet to facilitate research and documentation of the CPU socket specifications

This lab is more effective if you have access to different types of motherboards with different types of CPU sockets.

Getting Down to Business

In the following steps, you'll review your knowledge of CPU socket types.

Step 1 Identify the different socket types in Figure 6-2 by matching the letter with the corresponding socket name.

Socket 1366 _____   Socket AM2 _____

Socket AM3 _____   Socket 775 _____

Socket FM1 _____   Socket 1155 _____

Step 2 Draw a line connecting each CPU to its corresponding socket type. Choose the *best* match.

CPU	Socket Type
Intel Core i5-2500K	Socket 775
AMD Phenom II X3 710	Socket FM1
Intel Pentium 4 661	Socket AM2+
AMD A8-3850	Socket 1366
Intel Core i7-960	Socket AM3
AMD Athlon X2 7550 Black Edition	Socket 1155

A

B

C

D

E

F

FIGURE 6-2 Identifying sockets

Step 3   Using the Internet as your guide, find and list three processor models that fit in the following sockets.

Socket AM3:   _____

_____

_____

Socket 1155:   _____

_____

_____

_____

Step 4   Read the following statements and determine if each is true or false. (Assume that all of the motherboards have the appropriate BIOS flash update.) Circle T or F for each.

a.   Leonard can install his new Intel Core i7-2700K into his socket 1366 motherboard. (T/F)

b.   Rajesh just upgraded his socket AM2 processor to an AM3 processor but retained his socket AM2+ motherboard. After installing the processor and turning the PC on, everything worked fine. (T/F)

c.   Sheldon can upgrade his Pentium 4 631 to a Core 2 Duo 6600 without any issues. (T/F)

d.   Howard's Phenom II X6 1075T running on a socket AM3 motherboard just bit the dust because of an overheating issue. He wants to play *Star Wars: The Old Republic* with his friends, though. He'll have no problem throwing in a replacement Phenom X4 9600 into his machine. (T/F)

e.   Penny just purchased a used AMD Opteron 250 because she heard it was designed for very powerful server computers. She'll have no problem installing it on her socket FM1 motherboard. (T/F)

 30 MINUTES

Lab Exercise 6.03: Cooling Your CPU

Now that Joe has his processor, he needs to keep it cool, and since you've done everything else for him so far, you might as well make sure it's properly cooled, too! Someone new to the CPU cooling business might be tempted to think that CPUs come from the factory with a defined operating temperature. This isn't the case. The operating temperature depends tremendously on the way you cool the CPU. A far more reliable measurement is *power consumption*, the amount of power a CPU needs. CPU power consumption is measured in watts (W), with most desktop CPUs consuming in excess of 100 W. If you've ever tried to touch a 100-W light bulb, you can appreciate that this level of power consumption generates a tremendous amount of heat.

If this heat isn't taken away from the CPU by some form of cooling, the CPU will begin to overheat. If the CPU gets too hot, it will automatically shut itself down to prevent permanent damage. You need to provide Joe's CPU with some form of cooling device.

Learning Objectives

In this lab, you'll identify the strengths and weaknesses of three CPU cooling options: OEM fan assemblies, third-party fan assemblies, and liquid cooling.

At the end of this lab, you'll be able to

- Determine the cooling needs of your CPU
- Decide on which form of cooling to use for your needs

Lab Materials and Setup

The materials you need for this lab are

- Access to a working computer with Internet access
- A notepad and pencil to document the specifications

Getting Down to Business

The three most common types of CPU cooling are original equipment manufacturer (OEM) fans, third-party fans, and liquid cooling. Each of the following steps gives you an opportunity to investigate each of these options for a particular CPU.

Step 1 For the purposes of this exercise, pick out any single modern CPU as a sample CPU—you'll use this to find the proper cooling devices. Any CPU will work, but you'll find more options if you choose one that's readily available on popular online stores. If you're not sure which online store to use, check out www.newegg.com.

Individual CPUs are most commonly sold in what's known as a "retail box." This includes both the CPU and an OEM fan assembly.

Step 2 Many different types of fan assemblies can be attached to CPUs in many different ways. Describe the characteristics of the types of fans shown in Figure 6-3.

a. _____

b. _____

c. _____

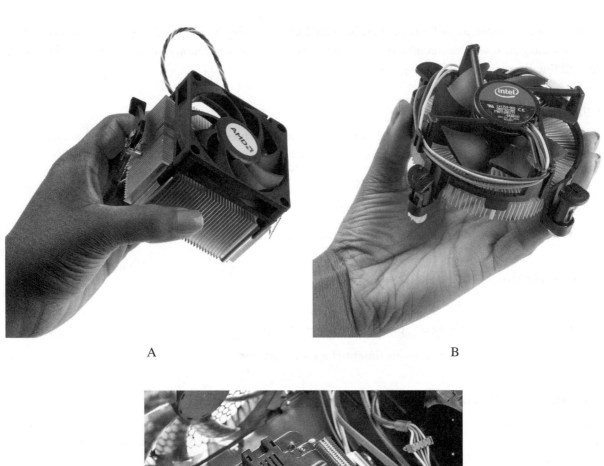

A   B

C

FIGURE 6-3 Comparing different CPU fans

Step 3   Look online for third-party fan assembly solutions for the CPU you've chosen. Look for the following popular brand names and see what third-party fans each of these manufacturers offers for your CPU:

Antec, Arctic Cooling, Cooler Master, Thermaltake, Zalman

Document the name, model number, and price for one of them and list some of the benefits it offers:

Manufacturer _____

Model Number _____

Price _____

Benefits _____

Step 4   Do some research on liquid cooling. What equipment would you need to liquid-cool your PC? (Water doesn't count!)

_____

_____

Why would anyone want to use liquid cooling?

_____

_____

Step 5   Using the same manufacturers listed in Step 3, try to find liquid-cooling options for your chosen CPU. Most liquid-cooling options are either bolt-on (they can be added to an existing case) or case-integrated (they are built into a system case).

Manufacturer _____

Model Number _____

Price _____

Bolt-on or case-integrated? _____

 30 MINUTES

Lab Exercise 6.04: Exploring CPU Specifications with CPU-Z

Joe is very impressed with your knowledge and expertise—and he's relieved that the CPU he purchased on eBay happened to work out. You explain that not only did it work out, but he has really improved the performance of his system with the upgraded CPU. In fact, to further display the characteristics of the CPU Joe has just purchased, you download and run a utility known as CPU-Z from www.cpuid.com. This utility reads the specifications of different PC components from information embedded in those components. You launch the utility to display the parameters of the new CPU for Joe.

Learning Objectives

In this lab, you'll identify various CPU specifications.

At the end of this lab, you'll be able to

- Run the CPU-Z utility

- Recognize key characteristics of CPUs

Lab Materials and Setup

The materials you need for this lab are

- Access to a working computer with Internet access to facilitate downloading and running the CPU-Z utility

- A notepad and pencil to document the specifications

- Optional: A word processor or spreadsheet application to facilitate the documentation

This lab is more informative if you have access to different types of systems with different classifications of CPUs.

Getting Down to Business

In the following steps, you'll download a reference utility known as CPU-Z and use it to further explore the characteristics of the CPU.

Step 1 Log on to a computer with Internet access and point your browser to the following Web site: www.cpuid.com. Follow the directions to download the current version of CPU-Z (the current version at this writing is 1.60). Unzip the file and launch CPU-Z.

Step 2 The CPU-Z utility displays a number of tabs across the top of the window (see Figure 6-4). At this time, you are only concerned with the CPU and Caches tabs.

Using the data gathered by CPU-Z, record some of the pertinent information here:

Name _____

Code Name _____

Package _____

Core Speed _____

Multiplier _____

Bus Speed _____

L2 Cache _____

L3 Cache _____

→ **Note**

The code name is used by the manufactures to refer to different revisions of a chip. For instance, the Core 2 Duo line of CPUs has three main revisions: Conroe, Allendale, and Wolfdale. Core 2 quad-core CPUs include Kentsfield and Yorkfield.

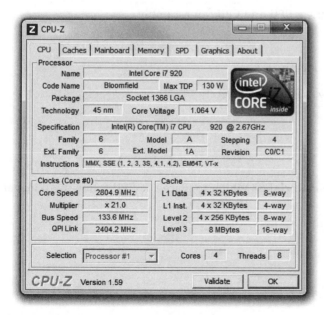

FIGURE 6-4 The CPU-Z utility

✔ **Hint**

Because of variations in CPUs, chipsets, BIOS, and motherboards, CPU-Z may not be able to display all of the information about your CPU. In some cases, the information may actually be erroneous. The CPUID Web site has good documentation on some of the common incompatibilities.

Step 3   If possible, launch CPU-Z on various machines to compare the characteristics of different CPUs. Save the utility for use in future lab exercises.

 30 MINUTES

Lab Exercise 6.05: Removing and Installing a CPU

Luckily for Joe, his motherboard is compatible with his new CPU. Now he expects you to play your "computer expert" role and install the new CPU in his PC. As a PC tech, you must be comfortable with such basic tasks. In this exercise, you'll familiarize yourself with the procedure; using your disassembled PC, you'll practice removing and reinstalling the CPU and fan assembly.

Learning Objectives

In this lab, you'll practice removing and installing a CPU and CPU fan assembly.

At the end of this lab, you'll be able to

- Remove and install a CPU safely and correctly
- Remove and install a CPU fan assembly safely and correctly

Lab Materials and Setup

The materials you need for this lab are

- An anti-static mat, or other static-safe material on which to place the CPU following removal
- An anti-static wrist strap
- Thermal paste
- A small slotted (flat-head) screwdriver

Getting Down to Business

Time to get your hands dirty! Removing and installing CPUs is one of the most nerve-wracking tasks that new PC techs undertake, but there's no need to panic. You'll be fine as long as you take the proper precautions to prevent ESD damage, and handle the CPU and fan assembly with care.

✱ **Warning**

Be careful not to touch any of the exposed metal contacts on either the CPU or the CPU socket.

Step 1   Open your PC's case. If you've never done this before, you might feel a little nervous. That's okay. As long as you don't go unplugging things at random and breaking off bits of the motherboard, you shouldn't have a problem.

Each PC case is built differently, so each will be opened in its own way. Some use screws, and others use latches. Almost all cases have a removable panel on one side that you'll need to take off. Refer to the documentation that came with your PC or case for more information.

How do you open your particular case?

_____

_____

Step 2   Find your motherboard, the largest circuit board in your PC. Everything else should be connected to it. Somewhere in that mess of cables, cards, and drives is your CPU.

Determine whether the process of reinstalling and removing the CPU and fan assembly will be easier with the motherboard on an anti-static mat or installed in its case. You may find that it is easier to work with the stubborn fan assembly clamp if the motherboard is secured in the case. The case may even have a removable motherboard tray to ease the installation process.

Step 3   In most cases, you'll have to remove the heat-sink and fan assembly before you can remove the CPU. (You may also need to unplug any cables in your way.) Screw-down fans are easier to remove than clip fans. Screw-down fans require only that you unscrew the securing hardware. Clip fans, found on many types of CPUs, require you to apply pressure on the clip to release it from the fan mount. Use a small slotted screwdriver to do this, as shown in Figure 6-5. Use caution when prying the clip open, and don't forget to unplug the CPU fan!

✔ **Hint**

You'll discover that releasing a fan clip takes way more force than you want to apply to anything so near a delicate CPU chip. Realizing this in advance, you can be sure to brace yourself and position the screwdriver carefully, to minimize the possibility of it slipping off and gouging something. Always use two hands when attempting this procedure.

Figure 6-5 Using a screwdriver to remove a clip-type CPU fan from its mount

The CPU and fan assembly will have thermal paste residue on the surfaces that were previously touching. You cannot reuse thermal paste, so you'll need to apply a fresh layer when you reinstall the CPU fan. Using a clean, lint-free cloth, carefully wipe the thermal paste residue from the CPU and fan assembly, and then place the fan assembly on an anti-static surface.

Step 4   Before proceeding, notice the CPU's orientation notches. All CPUs have some form of orientation notch (or notches). Remove the CPU. Start by moving the end of the zero insertion force (ZIF) lever a little outward to clear the safety latch; then raise the lever to a vertical position. Next, grasp the chip carefully by its edges and lift it straight up and out of the socket. Be careful not to lift the CPU at an angle—if it's a PGA CPU, you'll bend its tiny pins. LGA CPUs don't have pins, but you can damage the pins on the motherboard, so still be careful! As you lift out the CPU, make sure that the ZIF lever stays in an upright position. Record your socket type in the space provided.

Step 5   Now that you have the CPU chip out, examine it closely. The manufacturer usually prints the chip's brand and type directly on the chip, providing you with some important facts about the chip's design and performance capabilities. Note any markings that denote the processor manufacturer, model, speed, and so forth.

What is the CPU information printed on the chip package?

Step 6 Reinsert the CPU with the correct orientation, lock down the ZIF lever, and reattach the fan. Now remove the fan assembly and the CPU again. Practice this a few times to become comfortable with the process. When you're finished practicing, reinsert the CPU for the last time. Be sure to apply a thin film of fresh thermal paste onto the square in the center of the top of the CPU before you place the fan. Now reattach the fan assembly. Don't forget to plug the fan back in!

Step 7 You may leave your CPU/fan assembly installed on the motherboard and place the motherboard on your anti-static mat. Optionally, if you reinstalled the motherboard in the case, you may leave it assembled.

Lab Analysis Test

1. James has an AMD Phenom CPU installed on his motherboard and has just bought a faster Intel Core i7 from an eBay auction. He asks you to install the new CPU. What is your first reaction?

2. Joanna called you to say that ever since you installed her new CPU, the PC experiences intermittent problems when it runs. Sometimes it just quits or freezes up. What could possibly be wrong?

3. Theresa has an LGA 775 motherboard with an Intel Core 2 Quad 2.83-GHz processor and would like to put in a faster CPU. Can she install an Intel Core i7 2.93-GHz processor? Why or why not?

4. Lindsey runs CPU-Z on her system and notices that the processor's core speed is 2191.2 and the displayed multiplier is ×22. What is the speed of the system clock in Lindsey machine? How would the industry display this system clock speed?

5. David has been reading the trade magazines and keeps seeing all the hype over "quad-core" processors. David decides, since he is a power gamer, that he will upgrade to a quad-core CPU to improve the performance of his system when playing his favorite game. Will a quad-core processor improve the performance in this scenario? Explain.

Key Term Quiz

Use the following terms to complete the following sentences. Not all terms will be used.

code name

CPU

fan assembly

land grid array (LGA)

multicore

package

pin grid array (PGA)

screw-down connector

water block

zero-insertion force (ZIF)

1. The Intel Core 2 Duo CPU uses a package known as a _____.

2. Both Intel and AMD have adopted the use of a _____ to distinguish among revisions of their CPUs.

3. You often need to remove the _____ to get to a system's CPU.

4. To remove a CPU, you'll need to disengage the _____ lever.

5. A _____ is placed directly over the CPU in a liquid-cooled system.

Chapter 7

RAM

Lab Exercises

One of the easiest and most cost-effective upgrades you can make to a PC is to add more memory. As such, you'll perform many RAM installations as a PC tech—get used to it.

RAM installation tasks include determining how much RAM the PC has installed, determining how much RAM the PC can support, determining what type of RAM it uses, and then physically installing the RAM on the motherboard. The following labs are designed to help you practice working with RAM by using visual recognition of the different types and packages and by walking you through the steps of installing RAM.

 15 MINUTES

Lab Exercise 7.01: Determining the Amount of RAM in a PC

While pummeling your fellow PC techs in *Team Fortress 2* over lunch, a coworker named Holly appears, clutching a stick of RAM she got from a guy on the fourth floor. She wants you to install it in her system. You tell her you have to check on some things first, including how much RAM her system can handle and how much it already has, before you can help her.

✔ **Hint**

High-end PCs usually come straight from the factory equipped with hefty amounts of RAM. Lower-cost PCs sometimes cut corners by skimping on RAM.

Before installing any RAM, you'll need to determine how much RAM is already installed in Holly's PC, and then consult the motherboard book to determine how much RAM the system supports.

Learning Objectives

In this lab exercise, you'll use various methods to determine how much memory is currently installed in your system, and how much it is capable of holding.

At the end of this lab, you'll be able to

- Find RAM measurements

- Identify how much RAM is installed in a system

- Determine how much RAM a particular motherboard supports

Lab Materials and Setup

The materials you need for this lab are

- A working Windows PC

- A notepad

✔ **Hint**

> If you're in a computer lab or you have access to multiple PCs, you should practice on as many different PCs as possible.

Getting Down to Business

There are several ways to determine how much RAM is installed in a PC. First, you can check the RAM count during the boot process (some of the newer machines hide the RAM count, even if it's enabled in the BIOS). This tells you how much RAM the system BIOS recognizes during its check of the system. Second, you can check the amount of RAM that Windows recognizes from within the OS. And third, you can remove the PC case cover and physically examine the RAM sticks installed on the motherboard.

Step 1   Turn on your PC, and watch the display as the system goes through its startup routine, otherwise known as a power-on self test (POST). Typically, the RAM count runs near the top-left side of the screen. Figure 7-1 shows an example of a typical RAM count.

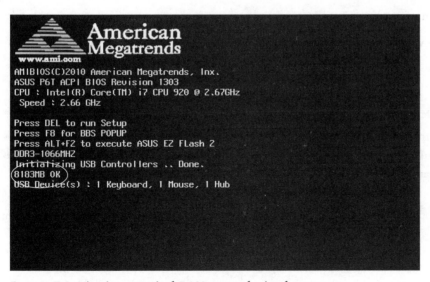

FIGURE 7-1 Viewing a typical RAM count during boot-up

Many systems run through the startup routine quickly, so the RAM count might appear on the screen for only a few seconds. Press the PAUSE/BREAK key to pause the boot process so you have time to write down the number accurately. When you want the boot process to resume, press the ENTER key.

What is the RAM count number displayed on your monitor? _____

✔ **Hint**

If you're starting the PC for the first time that day, the startup routine may run through the RAM count before the monitor has a chance to warm up. If this happens, just reboot the PC and try again.

Step 2   Use the following methods to determine the amount of RAM in a system from within any version of Windows.

a.   In Windows XP, right-click the My Computer icon and select Properties to see the amount of RAM in your system. In Windows Vista and Windows 7, open the Start menu, right-click Computer, and select Properties. The RAM count is under the System area (see Figure 7-2). You can also see other useful information here, like the processor type, Windows edition, the product ID, and more.

Another way to see the amount of memory installed is to follow this procedure:

b.   Click Start | All Programs | Accessories | System Tools | System Information. In the System Summary, look for a value called Installed Physical Memory (see Figure 7-3).

c.   The amount of RAM will be listed in the displayed information.

How much memory is in your system? _____

Does this number agree with what you found in Step 1? _____

Does the amount of RAM shown during the startup routine and that reported by Windows match?

Entry-level PCs and laptops often have onboard display adapters (the display adapter is built into the motherboard). Manufacturers include little to no video RAM on the motherboard, so the display adapter must "steal" some portion of the system RAM to be able to handle today's intense graphic applications.

If the amounts do not add up, and you see a number such as 448 MB or 992 MB, then your system has probably allocated some of the system memory to handle your display adapter's needs.

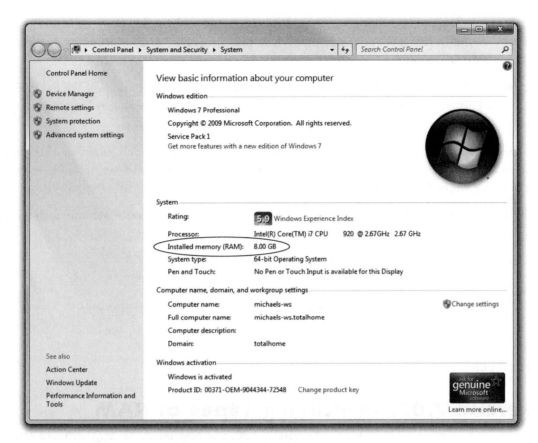

FIGURE 7-2 Viewing the RAM count in Windows 7 via Computer

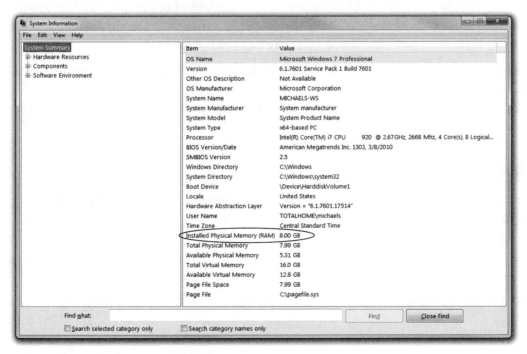

FIGURE 7-3 The System Information dialog box showing Installed Physical Memory

Step 3 We'll save the last method for determining how much RAM is installed (looking inside your PC) for the next exercise in this lab. For the moment, let's talk about how to determine the maximum amount of RAM a system can support.

The amount of RAM you can install on a modern system depends on the limitations of the motherboard hardware. All new CPUs are capable of 64-bit processing, so new chipsets support very large amounts of RAM. How much RAM does your motherboard support?

Neither the CMOS setup utility nor the OS can help you determine how much RAM a motherboard can handle. You can usually find this information in the system's motherboard book, if you have it, or on the PC maker's or motherboard manufacturer's Web site.

Examine the documentation that came with your PC, or visit the manufacturer's Web site, to determine how much RAM you can install on the system.

What is the maximum amount of RAM that your system can support?

_____

 30 MINUTES

Lab Exercise 7.02: Identifying Types of RAM

Once you determine how much RAM is installed on Holly's PC, and how much her motherboard can handle, you conclude that there's room for more. But, you explain to Holly, this doesn't mean you can add that RAM stick she got because not all RAM is the same. Having looked at the specs for her system, you know it takes 240-pin DDR2 SDRAM sticks. Holly thinks the stick she got is the right size, but you know it's 240-pin DDR3 RAM, so it won't fit. This is why they pay you the big bucks.

RAM comes in several standardized form factors, each compatible with specific types of systems. Modern desktop systems use full-sized dual inline memory modules (DIMMs) of various pin configurations (168, 184, and 240). Laptop computers use scaled-down sticks called small outline-DIMMs, or SO-DIMMs.

✔ **Cross-Reference**

For details on the various types of RAM found in modern systems, refer to the "DDR SDRAM," "DDR2," and "DDR3" sections in Chapter 7 of *Mike Meyers' CompTIA A+ Guide to Managing and Troubleshooting PCs*.

The steps for identifying the different types of RAM are presented in this lab exercise.

Learning Objectives

In this lab, you'll examine and compare different RAM packages.

At the end of this lab, you'll be able to

- Recognize and differentiate between different kinds of RAM packages

Lab Materials and Setup

The materials you need for this lab are

- Demonstration units of various RAM packages (optional)

✔ **Hint**

It is helpful to examine the RAM configurations in multiple PCs, if you have them available. Having a laptop with removable RAM is a plus.

Getting Down to Business

Let's do a quick review of the types of RAM packages you'll see in modern PCs. Then you'll check your PC or motherboard documentation to determine the type of RAM it uses.

All modern PCs use some form of DDR memory for their system RAM. As was discussed in the textbook, DDR stands for *double data rate*, which means that for every tick of the clock, two chunks of data are sent across the memory bus. This has the effect of giving you twice the performance without increasing the clock rate.

Step 1   Another performance trick modern systems use to increase memory speed is dual- and triple-channel architectures. This enables the memory controller to access more than one stick of RAM at a time, thus increasing performance. In effect, the 64-bit bus acts like a 128-bit bus (for dual channel) or a 192-bit bus (for triple channel). To use these multichannel architectures, you must install memory in identical pairs or triplets. Check your motherboard manual. Does your system support dual- or triple-channel memory?

_____

What colors represent the different channels?

_____

Step 2   There are many different types of RAM. It's important for you to be able to distinguish the difference between all of them by knowing what they physically look like and what their defining characteristics are. For each of the following descriptions, identify the type of RAM described by entering its name on the blank line preceding the definition.

    a.   _____ This type of RAM comes in 168-pin packages. It uses two notches to help guide the installation of the module: one near the center, and the other near an end. It was the first type of DIMM technology commercially available for PCs and usually had a speed rating of PC100 or PC133.

    b.   _____ The Rambus Corporation developed this type of RAM. It's usually found on a Pentium 4 motherboard. It is a proprietary stick of memory and uses 184 pins. It has two notches in it, both very near each other toward the middle of the stick.

If you are using a typical desktop system and it is relatively new (less than two years old), the motherboard will most likely support one of the following three types of RAM packages:

    c.   _____ This type of RAM doubled the speed by transferring data on both the rising and falling edges of the clock cycle. It uses a 184-pin package and is completely incompatible with the memory developed by Rambus. This style has one notch in it.

    d.   _____ Like its predecessor, it too transfers data on both the rising and falling edges of the clock cycle, but takes it one step further by doubling the clock speed twice. It uses a 240-pin package and has a single notch.

    e.   _____ Well, if doubling the clock speed twice wasn't enough, this type of RAM doubles it three times. Not only is it extremely fast and, as of 2012, the predominant style of RAM, it also uses a 240-pin package. But don't let that fool you: it is completely incompatible with all other types of RAM. Not only is it different electronically, but the notch is in a different place.

Step 3   In your PC or motherboard documentation, or on the manufacturer's Web site, locate the section listing the type of RAM your system uses.

    a.   What type of RAM does your system use? _____

    b.   What speed of RAM does your system need? _____

Step 4   Open your system case and make note of the following:

    a.   How many RAM slots does your motherboard have? _____

    b.   How many RAM slots are filled with RAM sticks? _____

    c.   Is your system set up to use single-channel, dual-channel, or tri-channel RAM? How could you find out?

    _____

 30 MINUTES

Lab Exercise 7.03: Removing and Installing RAM

You've found a stick of RAM for Holly that works with her system, and now you have to install it.

Although RAM installation is one of the simpler PC hardware upgrades, it's still important that you follow the correct steps and take all appropriate safety precautions.

Learning Objectives

In this lab, you'll practice removing and installing RAM.

At the end of this lab, you'll be able to

- Remove RAM safely and correctly
- Install RAM safely and correctly

Lab Materials and Setup

The materials you need for this lab are

- An anti-static mat or other static-safe material on which to place the RAM
- An anti-static wrist strap
- A notepad

✔ **Hint**

If you're in a computer lab or you have access to multiple PCs, you should practice on a variety of systems.

Getting Down to Business

Removal and installation procedures vary depending on the type of RAM your system uses. DIMMs and RIMMs snap into the RAM slots vertically. The following steps describe the removal and installation procedures for DIMMs.

✖ **Warning**

Regardless of the type of RAM in your system, be certain to take measures to prevent ESD damage. Shut down and unplug the PC and place it on an anti-static mat. Strap on an anti-static bracelet and ground yourself. If necessary, remove any cables or components that block access to the system RAM before you begin.

Step 1   Open the PC case. Use whatever methods the case requires: some use screws, some use latches. Once the case is open, look for the RAM sticks on the motherboard. Locate the retention clips on either end of the RAM modules.

Step 2   Press outward on the clips to disengage them from the retention slots on the sides of the RAM sticks (see Figure 7-4).

Step 3   Press down on the clips firmly and evenly. The retention clips act as levers to lift the DIMM sticks up and slightly out of the RAM slots.

Step 4   Remove the DIMM sticks and place them on the anti-static mat, or in an anti-static bag.

Step 5   Make note of the following:

    a.   How many pins does the RAM have? _____

    b.   Where are the guide notches located? _____

    c.   What information is on the RAM's label? _____

Step 6   While you have your system RAM out, this is a good time to check the condition of the metal contacts on both the RAM sticks and the motherboard RAM sockets. Dirty contacts are fairly rare. If you see this problem, use contact cleaner, available at any electronics store.

Are the contacts free of dirt and corrosion? _____

After you've examined your system RAM and inspected the motherboard RAM sockets, reinstall the RAM as described next.

Figure 7-4 Removing a 184-pin DIMM (DDR SDRAM)

To install a DIMM or RIMM:

Step 1 Orient the DIMM or RIMM so that the guide notches on the RAM module match up to the guide ridges on the RAM socket.

Step 2 Press the RAM stick firmly and evenly straight down into the socket until the retention clips engage the retention notches on the ends of the RAM stick.

Step 3 Snap the retention clips firmly into place.

Step 4 Repeat these steps to install other RAM modules as appropriate. If you're using RIMM RAM, don't forget to install the continuity RIMM (CRIMM) sticks into any empty RAM slots.

To finish a RAM installation professionally, specifically if you are on a production-level machine, follow these steps:

Step 1 Once the system RAM is in place, reattach any cables that you may have had to move, and plug in the system power cable. Do not reinstall the PC case cover until after you've confirmed that RAM installation was successful.

Step 2 Boot the system and watch the RAM count to confirm that you correctly installed the RAM.

✔ **Hint**

If the system has any problems when you reboot, remember that you must turn off the power and unplug the computer again before reseating the RAM.

30 MINUTES

Lab Exercise 7.04: Exploring RAM Specifications with CPU-Z

Now that you have Holly's system up and running with double the memory it had before, you can take a moment to analyze the memory. You've already downloaded the utility CPU-Z from the Internet in Lab Exercise 6.04; now you'll need to launch CPU-Z and examine the information on the Memory and SPD tabs.

Learning Objectives

In this lab, you'll identify various RAM specifications.

At the end of this lab, you'll be able to

- Recognize key characteristics of RAM

Lab Materials and Setup

The materials you need for this lab are

- Access to a working computer with the utility CPU-Z installed

- A notepad and pencil to document the specifications

This lab is more informative if you have access to different types of systems with different types of RAM.

Getting Down to Business

In the following steps, you'll explore the different characteristics of RAM.

Step 1   Launch the CPU-Z application.

Step 2   Navigate to the Memory tab. The CPU-Z utility displays the current statistics of the RAM installed, as shown in Figure 7-5.

FIGURE 7-5 CPU-Z showing RAM information

Using the data gathered by CPU-Z, record the following information:

Type _____

Size _____

CAS# Latency (CL) _____

RAS# to CAS# Delay (tRCD) _____

RAS# Precharge (tRP) _____

Step 3   Click the SPD tab in CPU-Z.

Step 4   The SPD tab, shown in Figure 7-6, lists a number of technical bits of information about a particular stick of RAM. This information is contained on every RAM stick in a chip called the serial presence detect (SPD) chip.

Using the data gathered by CPU-Z, record the following information for each of the system's RAM modules:

	Module 1	Module 2	Module 3	Module 4
Slot #				
Module size				
Maximum bandwidth				
Manufacturer				

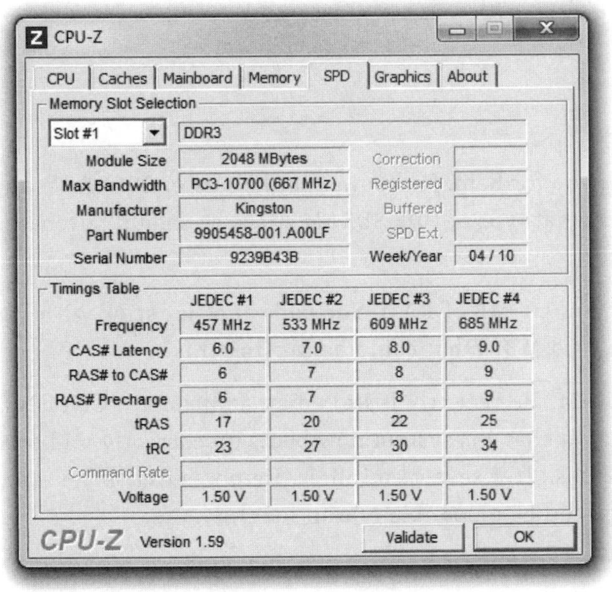

Figure 7-6 CPU-Z showing SPD information

✔ **Cross-Reference**

To review how the SPD chip works with the system, refer to the "Serial Presence Detect (SPD)" section in Chapter 7 of *Mike Meyers' CompTIA A+ Guide to Managing and Troubleshooting PCs*.

Step 5 If possible, launch CPU-Z on various machines to compare the characteristics of different types of RAM. Save the utility for use in future lab exercises.

→ **Try This: PC Wizard**

On a computer with Internet access, point your browser to the following Web site: www.cpuid.com. Follow the onscreen directions and download a copy of PC Wizard.

Extract the files into a folder and launch the PC Wizard application. Once PC Wizard is running, find and click the Mainboard icon in the Hardware area. This brings up a list of components in the right pane of the application window. Click the Physical Memory item and then browse through the information displayed in the lower portion of the window.

Using this information, can you determine the maximum size for individual RAM modules allowed on this system, and the maximum amount of total memory that it supports? Does this correspond to the information you found earlier in the PC or motherboard documentation?

Note that because of variations in chipsets, BIOS, and motherboards, PC Wizard may or may not provide detailed information on the RAM. In some cases, the information may actually be erroneous. The CPUID Web site has good documentation on some of the common incompatibilities.

Lab Analysis Test

1. Jarel wants to upgrade his memory and calls you for help. He knows that he's using DDR RAM and that his system clock is 133 MHz, but he isn't sure what type of DDR SDRAM sticks he should purchase. What DDR RAM would you recommend that he use?

2. Theresa's Windows XP Professional system has 512 MB of RAM. She adds another stick with 512 MB of RAM, but the RAM count still only shows 512 MB. What could be causing this?

3. John's system has 1 GB of PC4200 DDR2 SDRAM. He recently installed an additional 1 GB of DDR2 SDRAM that a coworker gave him. He tells you that his system now boots up correctly and shows the correct amount of RAM, but then it freezes after several minutes. He notes that if he removes the new RAM, the system runs fine. What could be a possible reason for this?

4. Kyle has a system that supports dual-channel architecture (there are two blue DIMM slots on the motherboard). The motherboard has space for three sticks of RAM, so Kyle installs three 2-GB RAM sticks. What will be the result?

5. Joe has recently purchased a pair of 1-GB DDR3 RAM sticks. He's replacing an older pair of DDR2 RAM but can't afford to replace the motherboard. Why won't this work?

Key Term Quiz

Use the following terms to complete the following sentences. Not all terms will be used.

168-pin DIMM

184-pin DIMM

240-pin DIMM

CRIMM

DDR RAM

DDR2 RAM

DDR3 RAM

DIMM

dual channel

megabytes (MB)

RIMM

SDRAM

SO-DIMM

SPD

1. Today's PCs use DDR3 RAM, which comes in a(n) _____ package.

2. A RAM module used in a laptop is called a(n) _____.

3. A component known as a(n) _____ chip provides additional information about an SDRAM module.

4. A stick of _____ looks a lot like a 168-pin DIMM, but it has 184 pins.

5. The technology that uses two sticks of RAM together to increase throughput is known as _____ architecture.

6. When purchasing _____, you must realize that it is not backward compatible with _____ and new hardware must be considered.

Chapter 8

BIOS

Lab Exercises

Basic input/output services (BIOS) provide the primary interface between the operating system's device drivers and most of its hardware. Although a modern BIOS is automated and tolerant of misconfiguration, a good PC technician must be comfortable with situations in which the BIOS may need some maintenance or repair.

A PC needs the BIOS to tell it how each basic component is supposed to communicate with the system. At the beginning of the PC revolution, many different manufacturers developed BIOS for PCs, but over the years the BIOS business has consolidated primarily to only two brands: AMI (American Megatrends, Inc.) and Phoenix Technologies (which absorbed the former third brand, Award Software). Both of these manufacturers provide a utility called the CMOS setup program (CMOS stands for *complementary metal-oxide semiconductor*, which is why everyone says "CMOS") that enables you to reconfigure BIOS settings for boot device order, amount of memory, hard disk drive configuration, and so on. Most of these configurations are automated, but as a PC tech, you're the one who people will call when "automatic" stops working!

As an example for the lab exercises in this chapter, suppose that the company you're working for is planning a mass upgrade from its current OS, Windows Vista, to Windows 7. You've tested the upgrade process on a few lab machines and have found that systems with an out-of-date BIOS are having problems upgrading successfully. In preparation for the Windows 7 installation, besides upgrading any older BIOS versions you find, you'll disable any BIOS-level antivirus functions. You're also aware that the prior IT manager did not use consistent CMOS passwords, so you may need to reset the passwords on a few machines.

The lab exercises in this chapter will teach you to identify, access, and configure system BIOS.

→ **Note**

You might have heard about a replacement for BIOS called the Unified Extensible Firmware Interface (UEFI). Since 2010, the BIOS firmware of PCs started to be replaced by UEFI. Think of UEFI as a super-BIOS, doing the same job as BIOS, but in a 64-bit environment with a lot of added functionality. While UEFI was introduced years ago, you still won't find it on every PC. Because of this, plus the fact that most UEFI setup screens work just like their BIOS counterparts, this chapter only specifically covers BIOS. If you have a UEFI system, you should still be able to complete the lab exercises.

 10 MINUTES

Lab Exercise 8.01: Identifying BIOS ROM

Having received your orders to do the big OS upgrade, your first task is to check the BIOS types and versions on every machine in your office, and then visit each BIOS maker's Web site to determine whether more recent versions are available.

The system BIOS is stored on nonvolatile memory called BIOS ROM. BIOS makers often (but not always) label their BIOS ROM chips prominently on the motherboard. In this exercise, you'll look at two different ways to identify your BIOS ROM chip.

✔ **Cross-Reference**

For details on the two big companies that manufacture BIOS on modern systems, refer to the "Modify CMOS: The Setup Program" section in Chapter 8 of *Mike Meyers' CompTIA A+ Guide to Managing and Troubleshooting PCs*.

Learning Objectives

In this lab, you'll learn two ways to identify your BIOS.

At the end of this lab, you'll be able to

- Locate the BIOS ROM chip on the motherboard

- Identify the BIOS manufacturer

- Determine the BIOS creation date and version

Lab Materials and Setup

The materials you need for this lab are

- A working PC

- An anti-static mat

- A notepad

Getting Down to Business

The first thing you'll do is remove your PC case cover and locate the BIOS ROM chip. Next, you'll make note of the BIOS information displayed during system startup.

✖ **Warning**

Any time you take the cover off your PC, remember to follow all proper safety and ESD avoidance precautions.

Step 1   Remove the case from your PC and locate the system BIOS ROM chip. Some motherboards label their chip with the name of the BIOS manufacturer. Compare your system BIOS ROM chip to the one in Figure 8-1.

Read the manufacturer's label *if you can*, and answer the following questions:

Who made the BIOS? _____

What year was the BIOS written? _____

Are there any other numbers on the label? Record them. _____

Does it look like you could easily remove the system BIOS chip, or does it look soldered to the motherboard? _____

Step 2   Replace the PC case cover and start the system. Be sure the monitor is turned on. When the first data appears on the screen, press the PAUSE/BREAK key on the keyboard. This suspends further operation until you press ENTER. Newer systems actually have instructions somewhere on the screen that indicate which key or keys to press to get into boot options, CMOS setup, and so forth.

FIGURE 8-1 A typical system BIOS ROM chip

Figure 8-2 shows an example of what you may see. At the top of the screen is the BIOS manufacturer's name and version number. At the bottom of the screen is the date of manufacture and the product identification number.

Make note of the following information:

Who made the BIOS? _____

What version is the BIOS? _____

What year was the BIOS written? _____

✔ **Hint**

Not all BIOS display the same type of information. Some BIOS makers modify the BIOS to show nothing more than their logos during the boot process.

FIGURE 8-2 A typical boot screen

Step 3 Press ENTER on the keyboard to continue booting. Once the system is up and running, go online and find out whether a more recent version of the BIOS is available. Your first stop should be the PC maker's Web site. If it does not have this information available, try the motherboard manufacturer's Web site or the BIOS maker's Web site.

> ✖ **Warning**
>
> Do *not* "flash" your system BIOS at this time!

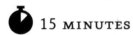 15 MINUTES

Lab Exercise 8.02: Accessing BIOS via the CMOS Setup Program

Once you've assessed the BIOS on each machine, but before you proceed with the Windows 7 installation, make sure the BIOS is properly configured using the special program for this purpose.

You don't access the hundreds of individual programs contained in the system BIOS directly, or from anywhere within the Windows OS. Instead, you use a utility that interfaces with the BIOS programs to enable you to reconfigure settings. This utility is the CMOS setup program.

Learning Objectives

In this lab, you'll go into CMOS and explore your BIOS configuration settings.

At the end of this lab, you'll be able to

- Enter the CMOS setup program
- Navigate the display screens of the system setup utility

Lab Materials and Setup

The materials you need for this lab are

- A working PC whose BIOS settings you have permission to change

Getting Down to Business

In the following steps, you'll reboot your PC and access the boot options or CMOS setup program. Each BIOS maker has its own special way to do this, so how you go about it depends on which BIOS your system has installed. Common methods include the following:

- Press DELETE during the boot process.
- Press F1, F2, F10, or F12 during the boot process.

- Press CTRL-ALT-INSERT during the boot process.

- Press CTRL-A during the boot process.

- Press CTRL-F1 during the boot process.

There are four ways for you to determine which method works for your BIOS:

- Check your motherboard or PC documentation.

- Visit your motherboard or PC maker's Web site.

- Watch the screen display after booting your PC. Most BIOS direct you to press a specific key to enter CMOS.

- Use the trial-and-error method! Boot your system and go down the preceding list, trying each key or key combination until one works. You won't hurt anything if you get it wrong, but if you hold the wrong key down for too long, you may get a keyboard error message. If this happens, just reboot and try again.

Step 1 Determine which method you need to use to enter the CMOS setup program. Then reboot your system and use that method to enter CMOS. Which key or key combination did you use to enter your CMOS setup program?

_____

Step 2 Once you've entered the CMOS setup program, look at the screen and compare it to Figures 8-3 and 8-4. The Phoenix BIOS shown in Figure 8-3 opens up to an initial menu, whereas the Phoenix-Award BIOS in Figure 8-4 opens immediately into the Main screen. Although the screens for different CMOS setup programs may look different, they all contain basically the same functions.

```
       CMOS Setup Utility - Copyright (C) 1984-2009 Award Software
 ┌──────────────────────────────────────┬────────────────────────────────┐
 │                                       │                                │
 │  ▶ MB Intelligent Tweaker(M.I.T.)     │  Load Fail-Safe Defaults       │
 │                                       │                                │
 │  ▶ Standard CMOS Features             │  Load Optimized Defaults       │
 │                                       │                                │
 │  ▶ Advanced BIOS Features             │  Set Supervisor Password       │
 │                                       │                                │
 │  ▶ Advanced Chipset Features          │  Set User Password             │
 │                                       │                                │
 │  ▶ Integrated Peripherals             │  Save & Exit Setup             │
 │                                       │                                │
 │  ▶ Power Management Setup             │  Exit Without Saving           │
 │                                       │                                │
 │  ▶ PC Health Status                   │                                │
 │                                       │                                │
 ├──────────────────────────────────────┴────────────────────────────────┤
 │  Esc : Quit              ↑↓→←: Select Item      F11 : Save CMOS to BIOS │
 │  F8  : Q-Flash           F10 : Save & Exit Setup  F12 : Load CMOS from BIOS│
 ├─────────────────────────────────────────────────────────────────────────┤
 │                 Change CPU's Clock & Voltage                            │
 └─────────────────────────────────────────────────────────────────────────┘
```

FIGURE 8-3 Award CMOS Main screen

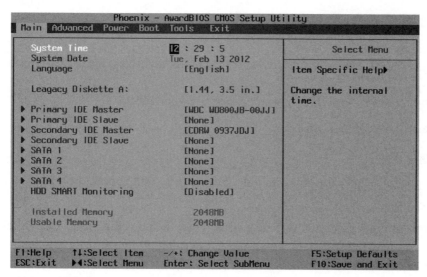

```
              Phoenix - AwardBIOS CMOS Setup Utility
 Main  Advanced  Power  Boot  Tools   Exit

    System Time              12 : 29 : 5            Select Menu
    System Date              Tue, Feb 13 2012
    Language                 [English]           Item Specific Help▶

    Leagacy Diskette A:      [1.44, 3.5 in.]     Change the internal
                                                 time.
  ▶ Primary IDE Master       [WDC WD800JB-00JJ]
  ▶ Primary IDE Slave        [None]
  ▶ Secondary IDE Master     [CDRW 0937JDJ]
  ▶ Secondary IDE Slave      [None]
  ▶ SATA 1                   [None]
  ▶ SATA 2                   [None]
  ▶ SATA 3                   [None]
  ▶ SATA 4                   [None]
    HDD SMART Monitoring     [Disabled]

    Installed Memory         2048MB
    Usable Memory            2048MB


 F1:Help      ↑↓:Select Item   -/+: Change Value      F5:Setup Defaults
 ESC:Exit     ▶◀:Select Menu   Enter: Select SubMenu  F10:Save and Exit
```

FIGURE 8-4   Phoenix-Award BIOS opening screen

✖ **Warning**

Do not make any changes in BIOS settings during this lab exercise. You'll make changes in the next two lab exercises.

The CMOS setup program controls the "changeable" BIOS settings. Many settings depend on what hardware you add to the system. The following are some sample entries on your system that you can change or update (there are more, the specifics of which depend on your BIOS):

- Date

- Time

- Hard drive configuration

- Boot sequence

- RAM

- Serial and parallel port assignments

- Enable/disable onboard controllers

- Enable/disable supervisor and user passwords

Step 3   Explore each screen and make notes about what each setting does. Navigation, like the method to enter the CMOS setup program, varies from maker to maker. Most programs are navigable by keyboard only, but some (AMI, for instance) support a mouse. Look at the bottom of the CMOS setup program screen to see how to navigate in your particular CMOS utility.

✔ **Hint**

Usually the arrow keys and the PAGE UP and PAGE DOWN keys will select and change settings. Sometimes the + and − keys or the SPACEBAR will toggle settings. The CMOS setup program screen usually provides a key to the navigation and selection keys; refer to it as well.

While navigating through the different setup screens, pay particular attention to any password or security menu that enables you to configure administrator/supervisor passwords and user passwords. Do not make any changes at this time; just make a note of where you configure these passwords. You will configure a password in the next lab exercise.

Step 4 Following is a list of common settings found in the CMOS. Know that each BIOS arranges its settings differently. View every screen of your CMOS setup program to locate and record these settings and their location:

- **Drives** Depending on your motherboard configuration, you will either set a primary master/slave drive or, if using SATA, see a list of the different drives attached and their name/type.

  _____

- **Onboard Devices** These settings enable you to configure onboard devices such as your USB ports.

  _____

- **Performance** Only common on better motherboards, this area enables you to tweak system timings for improved performance (also known as overclocking).

  _____

- **Security** This section enables you to set administrator or system passwords.

  _____

- **Boot Sequence** This setting enables you to define the order in which your system looks for boot devices.

  _____

- **Power Management** This section defines when devices shut down and how they awaken.

  _____

Once you're done exploring, press ESC a couple of times until you get the message "Quit Without Saving (Y/N)?" Press Y, and then press ENTER. The system will boot into your operating system.

 30 MINUTES

Lab Exercise 8.03: Configuring and Clearing CMOS Setup Program Passwords

In many professional environments, the IT department doesn't want users to fool with any of the PC's settings, especially detailed items such as the BIOS settings. The IT manager may even devise a password to prevent entry to the CMOS setup program by unauthorized users. Unfortunately, in your organization, the IT manager has resigned and was not very thorough about documenting these passwords.

When a CMOS setup program has been password protected and its password has been subsequently lost, the typical way to clear the password is to shunt a jumper on the motherboard that clears either the password or the entire contents of CMOS.

Learning Objectives

In this lab, you'll learn how to configure CMOS setup program passwords and how to clear the contents of the password and CMOS using the onboard CMOS-clear jumper.

At the end of this lab, you'll be able to

- Set a password using the CMOS setup program
- Locate the CMOS-clear jumper on the motherboard
- Clear passwords and CMOS settings using the CMOS-clear jumper

Lab Materials and Setup

The materials you need for this lab are

- A working PC whose BIOS settings you can change, with access to the CMOS-clear jumper on the motherboard
- An anti-static mat/wrist strap
- A notepad

Getting Down to Business

In the following steps, you'll reboot your PC and access the CMOS setup program using the key combination you verified in Lab Exercise 8.02. You will then navigate to the password or security menu and configure a CMOS setup program password. Then you'll verify the password by rebooting your machine and entering CMOS setup. Finally, you'll open the case and reset the CMOS settings by physically shunting the CMOS-clear jumper.

✖ **Warning**

Any time you remove the cover from your PC, remember to follow all proper safety and ESD avoidance precautions.

Step 1 Reboot your system and use the appropriate key or key combination to enter the CMOS setup program.

Step 2 Once you've entered the CMOS setup program, navigate to the security or password menu (see Figure 8-5). Select the supervisor password and enter a four- to eight-character password. Save changes and exit CMOS setup.

Record your password here: _____

✔ **Hint**

Typically, two types of passwords can be set in CMOS, but a third is now appearing.

The *supervisor* password restricts access to the CMOS setup program so that only authorized personnel can change or modify BIOS settings. Organizations, especially schools, usually configure a supervisor password to keep curious users from causing system errors.

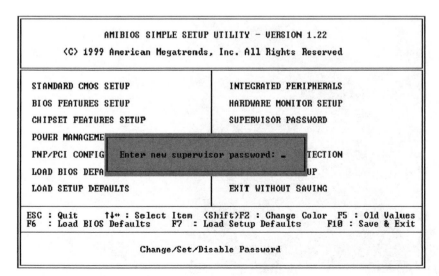

FIGURE 8-5 AMIBIOS supervisor password setup

The *user* or *system* password restricts access to the PC itself, and is required every time the system boots (before an operating system is even loaded). This type of password is often used when an individual's PC is located in a public area.

The *hard drive* password is the third and newest password you'll find on some CMOS setups. Hard drive passwords prevent a user from accessing a hard drive unless they know the password.

Step 3 Reboot the PC and press the key or key combination required to enter the CMOS setup program. If you completed Step 2 correctly, you should be prompted to enter a password. Enter the password you configured in Step 2 and press ENTER. The main menu of the CMOS setup program will appear.

Discard changes and exit the CMOS setup program.

✖ Warning

The next step will erase all CMOS settings! While you are in the CMOS setup program, take the time to write down important settings such as the CPU settings, boot order, which integrated peripherals are enabled/disabled, and the power management setup. Although the system should run fine using the default settings, taking notes now will help you get back to any custom settings that may have been configured.

Step 4 Shut down the PC and unplug the power cord from the wall outlet. Remove the case from the PC and, referring to the PC or motherboard documentation, locate the CMOS-clear jumper. Follow the instructions included with the documentation and move the jumper (see Figure 8-6) to clear the CMOS.

FIGURE 8-6 The CMOS-clear jumper on a motherboard

A less elegant alternative to using the CMOS-clear jumper is to remove the onboard battery for at least 30 seconds. Does your system have an onboard battery? Can it be removed easily?

Step 5   Replace the PC case cover, plug the system back in, and start the system. Press the appropriate key(s) to enter the CMOS setup program.

Were you prompted for a password? _____

Do you need to configure any of the other settings? _____

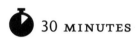 30 MINUTES

Lab Exercise 8.04: Configuring BIOS Settings

If you find any issues when you examine the BIOS settings using the CMOS setup program, you'll need to reconfigure the settings. Remember also that you're preparing the PC for an upgrade to Windows 7. BIOS-level virus checking is known to cause problems with the Windows XP/Vista/7 installation process, so Microsoft advises that you disable it.

Many BIOS functions are unchangeable—such as keyboard and floppy drive recognition—and are therefore inaccessible via the CMOS setup program. Other functions are under your control. These include the boot sequence order and the date/time setting, as mentioned previously, but also some potentially hazardous settings such as BIOS shadowing and memory timing.

✔ **Hint**

If you're not absolutely certain what a particular setting does, the best course of action is to leave it alone! If you have any doubts, you can always exit the CMOS setup program without saving.

Learning Objectives

In this exercise, you'll access the CMOS setup program, navigate to find the various BIOS settings you would commonly need to modify, and practice disabling BIOS-level virus checking.

At the end of this lab, you'll be able to

- Modify the settings in BIOS

Lab Materials and Setup

The materials you need for this lab are

- A working PC whose BIOS settings you have permission to change

- If possible, a BIOS that includes virus checking

Getting Down to Business

In the following steps, you'll learn how to navigate to the CMOS setup program configuration screen that includes the virus-checking option. This example uses the Phoenix-Award BIOS CMOS setup program. Your CMOS setup program may vary, but many BIOS makers and versions should offer the same option.

✔ **Cross-Reference**

> For more details about the features of CMOS setup programs, refer to the section "A Quick Tour Through a Typical CMOS Setup Program" in Chapter 8 of *Mike Meyers' CompTIA A+ Guide to Managing and Troubleshooting PCs*.

Step 1   Enter your CMOS setup program using the steps you learned in Lab Exercise 8.02.

Step 2   Check your notes and navigate to the configuration screen that has the BIOS-level virus-checking option. It's not always obvious where to find this option. For example, the Phoenix BIOS CMOS setup program screen shown in Figure 8-3 doesn't give any hints about where to find the correct screen. As Figure 8-7 shows, virus checking can be disabled in this BIOS from the Advanced BIOS Features screen. Don't hesitate to explore.

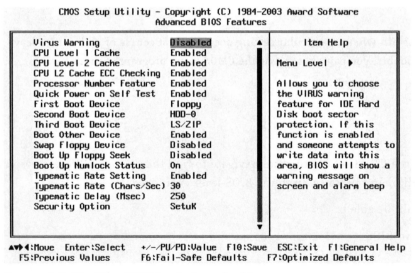

FIGURE 8-7 Disabling BIOS-level virus checking

Step 3 Follow the screen prompts to navigate to the correct configuration screen and find the virus-checking setting. Highlight the option and change it from Enabled to Disabled. Once again, your CMOS setup program's wording or appearance may be different, but the option to control BIOS-level virus checking should be common to most modern types of BIOS.

Step 4 Save and exit the CMOS setup program. After you exit, the system will reboot automatically. You have just made a change to BIOS.

The process you just followed is the same process you'll use for any changes you make to BIOS. Be sure to save the settings before exiting the CMOS setup program.

Step 5 Have your instructor (or a friendly neighborhood technician) check your work to ensure that the settings have been saved correctly.

Lab Analysis Test

1. What can you do in a pinch to clear the CMOS settings if you are unable to find the CMOS-clear jumper?

2. After running Windows XP for a few years, Chris has decided to perform a clean install of Windows Vista. After backing up his important files, he places the Windows Vista DVD in the optical drive and reboots his machine—but it just boots into Windows XP like normal. What setting will he most likely need to configure in the BIOS to correct this situation?

3. Arnold has just installed a new sound card. He boots his system to install the drivers, but his system does not recognize the new card. What BIOS settings might he change using CMOS setup?

4. Alex has just finished making changes to the BIOS-level virus checking and would now like to save these changes. Name two ways to save BIOS settings after making changes in the CMOS setup program.

5. Ryan is working on an older Core 2 Duo system. What key or keys should he press to enter the CMOS setup program?

Key Term Quiz

Use the following terms to complete the following sentences. Not all terms will be used.

AMI

Award Software

BIOS (basic input/output services)

BIOS ROM

CMOS (complementary metal-oxide semiconductor)

CMOS setup program

DELETE key

PAUSE/BREAK key

Phoenix Technologies

1. The system BIOS is stored on nonvolatile memory called _____.

2. Technicians configure the BIOS using the _____.

3. Press the _____ to suspend operation of the POST.

4. _____ provides the primary interface between the operating system's device drivers and most of the system's hardware.

5. A common way to enter CMOS setup is to press the _____ during startup.

Chapter 9
Motherboards

Lab Exercises

While the CPU, system RAM, power supply, hard disk drive, and all the other miscellaneous pieces of a typical PC are important, it is the motherboard that brings them together into a working whole. Every bit and byte of data that moves between devices passes through its sockets and traces. Every component plugs into it, either directly or indirectly—a PC wouldn't be much of a PC without it. Replacing a motherboard is one of the most challenging tasks a PC tech will face.

Luckily, only a couple of circumstances require you to undertake this chore. The first is when the motherboard malfunctions or is damaged; modern motherboards aren't made to be repaired, so when they go bad, they must be replaced as a whole unit. The other is when you want to upgrade the PC to a more powerful CPU than its current motherboard supports. In either of these cases, you've got a bit of work ahead of you! Installing a motherboard requires more effort than any other type of installation— more preparation, more time performing the installation, and more cleanup afterward. Still, you shouldn't be intimidated by the prospect of replacing a motherboard—it's a common and necessary part of PC repair. In this chapter, you'll go through the process from start to finish.

In the following lab exercises, you'll research new motherboards, remove the motherboard from a working PC, and explore the motherboard's features. You'll then install the motherboard again and use CPU-Z to discover all sorts of details. The last three labs of the chapter deal with identifying expansion slots, installing expansion cards, and managing hardware with Device Manager.

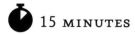 15 MINUTES

Lab Exercise 9.01: Researching New Motherboards

While the motherboard may be the backbone of a PC, all good upgrade efforts should begin with the CPU. Trying to pick out a motherboard and *then* a processor that goes with it is a little like choosing a paint color before you've seen the walls—it can be done, but your walls might end up puce when they should be aquamarine. In other words, it's much less painful to work from CPU to motherboard, especially when your goal is to increase performance. Don't tie yourself down by doing it backward.

You need to make several choices when searching for a new CPU and motherboard. Ensuring compatibility is key. Once you've picked the latest and greatest processor from Intel or AMD, you need to find a motherboard that plays nicely with it: Match the socket type of the processor to the socket type of the motherboard. Make sure the motherboard's form factor fits inside your case. And even after you've narrowed it down to that, you still need to pick a manufacturer and choose which features you want the motherboard to have.

Learning Objectives

In this lab, you'll become familiar with different motherboards and their compatibility with various processors and cases.

At the end of this lab, you'll be able to

- Recognize different motherboard form factors

- Understand considerations for upgrading a system with a newer motherboard

Lab Materials and Setup

The materials you need for this lab are

- A PC with Internet access

✔ **Hint**

As usual, if you have access to multiple systems, take advantage of it. It's most useful to have a variety of motherboards to study.

Getting Down to Business

The following steps will lead you through the process of determining which motherboard you need to obtain to update your client's systems. You'll also see that a motherboard is not an island unto itself, but one piece of the PC archipelago.

Step 1 Go to www.newegg.com (or another online PC component store) and search for a newer, faster processor. When selecting a new processor, be sure to keep track of important specifications so that you can refer to them when you need to pick out a motherboard. Record the following information:

Manufacturer _____

Series _____

CPU socket type _____

Step 2 Search the online PC component store for a new motherboard. Keep in mind that the CPU's socket type must match the motherboard's socket type, otherwise they will be incompatible. You'll find more than one that are compatible, but for now, pick one and record the following information:

Manufacturer _____

CPU socket type _____

Form factor _____

Expansion slots _____

Step 3   The next step to finding a new and compatible motherboard is to make sure that it will work with the form factor of your client's system cases.

Current PC motherboards come in a few different styles, or *form factors*: ATX (Advanced Technology Extended), microATX and FlexATX, ITX, and proprietary form factors from companies such as Dell and Sony. Each motherboard form factor has a corresponding case it is compatible with, but some motherboards will fit in a case with a different form factor. ATX motherboards are what you find in most PCs on the market.

Your client's cases are all ATX. Is the motherboard you picked compatible? _____

Step 4   Look at a few different (but still compatible) motherboards. Compare their features. What makes them different? Does one have more expansion slots than the other? Does one have fewer RAM slots? Are there other features, such as support for NVIDIA's SLI or ATI's CrossFire dual-graphics card technology, that would influence your choice? Using the motherboard you already selected, record the following information:

Number of memory slots _____

Maximum memory supported _____

SATA ports _____

Onboard video chipset _____

Other features _____

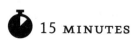 15 minutes

Lab Exercise 9.02: Removing a Motherboard

Techs will tell you that motherboard removal is the exercise that separates the geek from the meek and the true PC tech from the wannabe, but don't let that intimidate you! Motherboard removal is completely straightforward and simple.

Learning Objectives

In this lab, you'll remove your PC's motherboard.

At the end of this lab, you'll be able to

- Remove a motherboard safely and correctly

Lab Materials and Setup

The materials you need for this lab are

- A non-production or lab computer

- A Phillips-head screwdriver

- An anti-static mat and anti-static wrist strap

- A large anti-static bag

Getting Down to Business

Take all precautions to avoid ESD. Remember those tools you learned about back in Chapter 2? Put on an anti-static wrist strap, clip it to your PC case, and dig in.

Start with your PC turned off. Disconnect everything, including the power cable, from the front and back of your PC. If you haven't already, open up your PC case using whatever method your case requires. Because we want to remove the motherboard from the case, we first need to disconnect (almost) everything from the motherboard. You've already learned how to remove RAM and CPUs. I'll quickly outline how to disconnect the remaining cables and expansion cards.

Step 1 If you have any expansion cards installed, first unscrew them from the case. You'll find the screw holding them near the back of the case where the ports are located. After unscrewing the card, gently pull it up and out of the slot without rocking it from side to side. Some PCIe cards use a latch at the opposite end of the card, farthest from the screw. Simply press down on the tab attached to the motherboard and the card should be released.

Step 2 You should also have several power and data cables attached to the motherboard. None of these are difficult to remove, though it may take a bit of force to disconnect them. Disconnect each cable until there are none left.

You can leave your storage devices where they are—they should not get in the way of removing your motherboard.

Step 3 Locate and remove the screws holding the motherboard to the frame of the case. There are most likely six to nine screws, which may also have small washers. Be sure not to lose these washers because they help prevent over tightening the screws during installation. Some systems may use small plastic or metal supports called *standoffs* between the motherboard and the frame. Remove these and store them in a labeled container.

✖ Warning

Remember to handle the motherboard as you would any printed circuit board: gently, by the edges, as if you were holding a delicate old photograph.

Step 4   Carefully remove the motherboard from the PC case and place it on your anti-static mat. You should place the motherboard in a large anti-static bag for the best protection.

 15 MINUTES

Lab Exercise 9.03: Identifying Motherboard Features

At a glance, one motherboard pretty much looks like any other. Of course, as a PC tech, you know that many differences may exist: Two identical-looking motherboards can have completely different feature sets. Chipsets, bus speed, CPU socket type, and clock speed are just some of the important features that separate one motherboard from another. These differences aren't always obvious, but you can turn to your motherboard book to identify your motherboard's features, as described in the following steps.

Learning Objectives

In this lab, you'll become familiar with different motherboard features.

At the end of this lab, you'll be able to

- Recognize different motherboard features
- Identify the location of motherboard features

Lab Materials and Setup

The materials you need for this lab are

- A motherboard, such as the one you removed in Lab Exercise 9.02
- The motherboard book or online documentation for that motherboard

Getting Down to Business

In the following steps, you'll identify the location of key features on your motherboard.

> ✔ **Hint**
>
> If you're using the motherboard you removed in the previous lab, take this opportunity to clean any dust off of it, using canned air, before you begin.

Step 1   Note the location of the make and model information on the motherboards in Figure 9-1. Compare this to your motherboard and locate the manufacturer name and model number.

FIGURE 9-1 Two examples of model number information printed on motherboards

✔ Cross-Reference

For details on chipsets, refer to the "Chipset" section of Chapter 9 of *Mike Meyers' CompTIA A+ Guide to Managing and Troubleshooting PCs.*

What is the name of your motherboard manufacturer? _____

What is the model number of your motherboard? _____

What CPU socket do you have on your motherboard? _____

What type of chipset do you have on your motherboard? _____

Keep this information handy! Having the make and model of your motherboard readily available makes it easy to search the Web for drivers and updated BIOS.

Step 2 Look for any charts or numbers printed on the surface of the motherboard.

Are there any jumper blocks? _____

What are some of the settings that can be configured using jumpers?

_____

_____

_____

Step 3 Find the following on your motherboard and note their locations:

- System clock battery _____
- BIOS _____

- RAM slots (What type? Dual-channel or triple-channel support?) _____

- SATA or RAID (if present) _____

- Graphics adapter support (onboard, PCI, AGP, PCIe?) _____

 30 MINUTES

Lab Exercise 9.04: Installing a Motherboard

Now you get the real test of your tech skills: installing the new motherboard and reconnecting everything so that the computer works again! Don't be intimidated, though. Everything you need to install a motherboard (in your case, probably the motherboard you just removed in Lab Exercise 9.02) is right in front of you.

> When you remove and replace a motherboard in a system, you interact with almost every component of the computer system. In the field, you must not only successfully disassemble/assemble the hardware, but also verify that the system powers up and operates properly afterward. Many competent techs, when installing a new motherboard, will check for proper operation along the way. Here's a good checkpoint: After you've installed the CPU and RAM, configured any jumpers or switches, and installed the motherboard in the case, insert the power connections and test the system. A POST card is a real timesaver here, but you can also connect the PC speaker, a graphics card, monitor, and a keyboard to verify that the system is booting properly.

Learning Objectives

In this lab, you'll install a motherboard. You can use the motherboard and system you disassembled in Lab Exercise 9.02.

At the end of this lab, you'll be able to

- Install a PC motherboard and connect all its associated components

Lab Materials and Setup

The materials you need for this lab are

- A working system from which the motherboard has been removed

- Components and cables previously connected to the removed motherboard

- The motherboard book or online documentation for the motherboard

- An anti-static mat and anti-static wrist strap

- A notepad and pen

Getting Down to Business

Physically installing the motherboard itself is mostly a matter of being careful and methodical. The more complex part of the task is reattaching all the cables and cards in their proper places.

✖ Warning

Motherboards are full of delicate electronics! Remember to follow the proper ESD avoidance and safety procedures.

✔ Hint

When installing a motherboard, it's handy to use your notepad to check off assembly steps as you go along.

Step 1 Carefully line up the motherboard inside the PC case and secure it in place with the mounting screws. Be sure to use the washers and plastic/metal standoffs, if necessary.

Step 2 Insert the front panel control wires in their appropriate places. These should include the power button, reset button, front panel LEDs (power, hard disk activity, and so on), system speaker, and so on. Refer to the labels and your motherboard documentation for the proper connections.

Step 3 Connect all power cables to the hard drive, optical drive, floppy drive (for older systems), CPU fan, main motherboard, and so on.

Step 4 Connect data cables to the hard drive, optical drive, and floppy drive (if applicable), as well as the sound cable and USB connector dongles, if applicable. If you removed the RAM or CPU, reattach them now.

Step 5 Double-check all of your connections and cards to make sure that they're properly seated and connected where they're supposed to be. If something is wrong, it's definitely better to discover it now than to smell smoke after you've hit the power switch!

Step 6 Replace the case cover on your PC, then plug the keyboard, mouse, and monitor back in, plug the power cable back in, and finally turn on the PC. Assuming you've done everything correctly, your system will boot up normally.

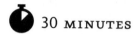 30 MINUTES

Lab Exercise 9.05: Exploring Motherboard Features with CPU-Z

Now that you've completed the analysis and upgrade of your client's systems with new motherboards and CPUs where needed, you can verify some of the characteristics and features the motherboard manufacturer has promoted. You already downloaded the CPU-Z utility, so you can launch that to examine the information on the Mainboard tab.

✔ **Hint**

Over the years, motherboards have been called many names—and not just the bad names you might use when one doesn't work properly! Early motherboards were sometimes called the *planar board*. A motherboard can be referred to as the *system board*, *mainboard*, and sometimes just *board* or *mobo*. Regardless of the name, these terms refer to the large printed circuit board (PCB) used to connect all the components in a computer system.

Learning Objectives

In this lab, you'll identify various motherboard features.

At the end of this lab, you'll be able to

- Verify motherboard features

Lab Materials and Setup

The materials you need for this lab are

- Access to a working computer with the CPU-Z utility installed

- A notepad and pencil to document the specifications

- Optional: A word processor or spreadsheet application to facilitate the documentation

Getting Down to Business

In the following steps, you'll verify the features of your motherboard.

Step 1   Launch CPU-Z and navigate to the Mainboard tab. CPU-Z displays some of the key features of your motherboard, as shown in Figure 9-2.

Step 2   Using the data gathered by CPU-Z, record as much pertinent information as possible:

Manufacturer _____

Model _____

Chipset _____

Southbridge _____

BIOS brand _____

Graphic interface version _____

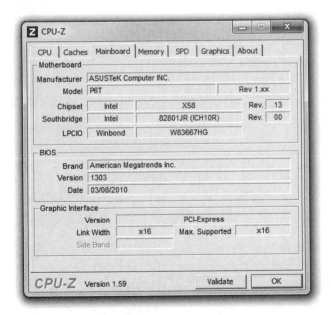

FIGURE 9-2 CPU-Z displaying motherboard information

Step 3 If possible, launch CPU-Z on various machines to compare the features of different motherboards.

→ **Try This: PC Wizard**

Go to http://www.cpuid.com/softwares/pc-wizard.html and download and install PC Wizard. After you've installed it, launch the PC Wizard application. Once PC Wizard is running, click the Mainboard icon. This brings up a number of items (components) in the top-right pane of the window. Click the Mainboard item to display detailed information in the lower-right pane of the window, as shown here:

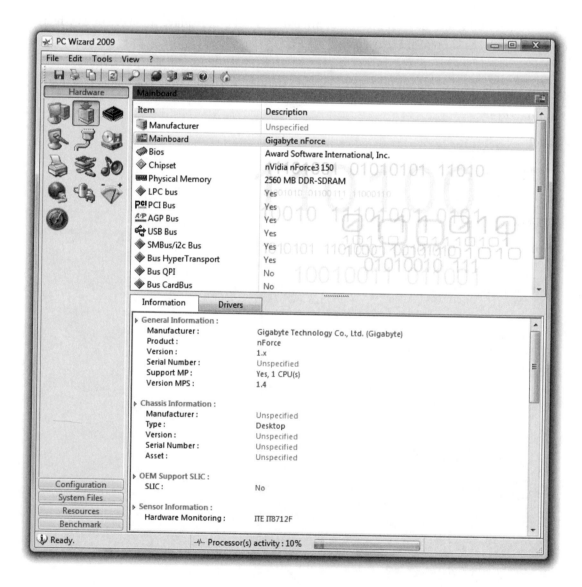

Using this information, can you determine the integrated devices supported by your motherboard? Does this correspond to the information in the PC or motherboard documentation?

 30 MINUTES

Lab Exercise 9.06: Identifying Internal Expansion Slots

Unless you've got X-ray vision, the best way to examine expansion slots is to remove the PC case cover. In this exercise, you'll identify the type of expansion slots on your motherboard. Does your system use a PCIe, AGP, or PCI graphics card, or does it use onboard video? Check to see how many other expansion slots are available for adding a sound card and (if required) upgrading the graphics adapter.

✖ Warning

Remember to use proper safety and electrostatic discharge (ESD) avoidance procedures when working inside the PC case.

Learning Objectives

In this exercise, you'll properly identify expansion slots and the basic features of each type of expansion technology.

At the end of this lab, you'll be able to

- Identify PCI expansion bus slots and component cards

- Identify the AGP expansion bus slot and video card

- Identify PCIe ×1 and PCIe ×16 expansion bus slots and component cards

Lab Materials and Setup

The materials you need for this lab are

- A non-production, disassembled PC

- A working PC (or more than one if possible)

- An anti-static mat

- A notepad

- Optional: Some sample motherboards

Getting Down to Business

Shut down your PC and unplug it from the wall. Place it on your anti-static mat, remove the PC case cover, and take a good look inside. Your aim is to determine what type of expansion slots your motherboard has, and what peripheral card components are currently installed.

Step 1   Here are the physical characteristics of PCI expansion slots:

- About 3 inches long

- Usually white in color (modern motherboards may use bright colors like yellow or green to enhance the visual appeal of the motherboard)

- Offset from the edge of the motherboard by about 1 inch

Figure 9-3 shows PCI slots on a modern motherboard.

Record the following information:

How many PCI slots are on your motherboard? _____

What PCI devices are installed on your system? _____

How many PCI slots are empty? _____

Step 2   See if you can locate a 32-bit AGP slot. As the name suggests, the AGP slot is designed to be used with one type of component only—a graphics adapter. Here are the physical characteristics of the AGP slot:

- One slot per motherboard

- A little less than 3 inches long

- Usually brown in color

- Offset from the edge of the motherboard by about 2 inches

Figure 9-4 shows an AGP slot in its natural habitat. While popular on older motherboards, AGP slots have been all but ousted by PCIe, so your motherboard may not have one.

Figure 9-3 A group of PCI slots

FIGURE 9-4 An AGP slot

Record the following information:

Is there an AGP video card slot on your motherboard? _____

What can you tell about the installed video card without removing it?

Step 3 Take a look at your motherboard and see if there are any PCIe slot connectors. PCIe is very interesting, offering a theoretical throughput of 2.5 Gbps per lane and supporting from 1 to 32 lanes. The first devices to take advantage of PCIe were graphics cards using the 16-lane configuration. The physical characteristics of the PCIe expansion slots depend on the number of lanes.

PCIe ×1 slots have the following characteristics:

- About 1 inch long

- Often brightly colored (blue and white being fairly common)

- Offset from the edge of the motherboard by about 1.25 inches

PCIe ×16 slots have the following characteristics:

- About 3.5 inches long

- Often brightly colored (blue and white being fairly common)

- Offset from the edge of the motherboard by about 1.25 inches

Figure 9-5 shows PCIe slots on a modern motherboard.

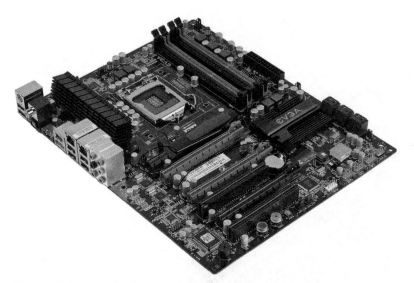

FIGURE 9-5 A motherboard with both PCIe ×1 and PCIe ×16 expansion slots

Record the following information:

Are there any PCIe slots on your motherboard? _____

If yes, how many PCIe ×1 slots are there? _____

How many PCIe ×16 slots are there? _____

Are there any PCIe cards installed in the system? _____

✔ **Cross-Reference**

For more detail about the PCI, AGP, and PCIe buses, refer to the "Expansion Bus" section in Chapter 9 of *Mike Meyers' CompTIA A+ Guide to Managing and Troubleshooting PCs*.

After you've completed your inventory of installed expansion bus devices, put the case cover back on your PC, plug it back in, and turn on the power of the system.

 30 MINUTES

Lab Exercise 9.07: Installing Expansion Cards

There are four steps to installing any expansion card device properly:

1.   Arm yourself with knowledge of the device before you install it. Is the device certified to run on the Windows OS that you're running? Is it compatible with your motherboard and other hardware? If you are running Windows 7, a good place to start is the Windows Compatibility Center Web site, found at www.microsoft.com/windows/compatibility/windows-7/en-us/default.aspx.

2.   Remove the cover from your PC case and install the device. As always, follow all ESD and safety precautions and handle the card with care.

3.   Install device drivers for the component. Windows comes with a large device drivers catalog, so it may try to help you by installing the driver that it thinks the device needs. In most cases, you should visit the card manufacturer's Web site, download the latest drivers for the card and your operating system, and then install the updated drivers. You can also install the card and then use Microsoft/Windows Update, which may find and download a copy of the latest driver from the manufacturer.

4.   Verify that the device is functional.

The following exercise is a somewhat abridged version of this procedure; instead of installing a new device, you'll remove and reinstall devices that are already on your system.

✔   **Cross-Reference**

To review the details of device installation, refer to the "Installing Expansion Cards" section in Chapter 9 of *Mike Meyers' CompTIA A+ Guide to Managing and Troubleshooting PCs*.

Learning Objectives

In this lab, you'll practice removing and installing internal expansion cards.

At the end of this lab, you'll be able to

•   Remove and install expansion cards in a system correctly and safely

Lab Materials and Setup

The materials you need for this lab are

•   At least one working Windows computer with expansion cards installed

•   A Phillips-head screwdriver

•   An anti-static mat and wrist strap

•   Anti-static storage bags

•   A notepad

Getting Down to Business

In this exercise, you'll physically remove expansion card devices from your PC. You'll then make note of any important information you can find on the device's label: device maker, version, and so on. Finally, you'll reassemble and restart the system. In Lab Exercise 9.08, you'll use Device Manager to make sure everything is working properly.

Shut down the system and unplug the power cable, placing it on your anti-static mat. Once you remove the PC case cover and strap on your anti-static wrist strap, you're ready to start.

Step 1   Make a list of the expansion cards installed in your motherboard and note which slot each one uses. You'll want to know this for when you put the cards back in at the end of the lab exercise.

Step 2   Remove the cards one at a time from your system. For each card, follow these procedures:

   a.   Remove the retaining screw and store it safely. Check for any latches on the expansion slot (see Figure 9-6) and release them when removing the video card.

✔ **Hint**

You'll see two main types of screws used in PCs. At first glance, they may look all the same, but while these screws are the same overall size, they have different sizes of threads. Screws with the larger threads, commonly called *coarse-threaded* screws, are generally used to secure expansion cards, hard drives, power supplies, and case covers. Screws with the smaller threads, commonly called *fine-threaded* screws, are typically used to secure storage devices such as floppy disk drives and optical drives into their respective bays.

---

   b.   Taking hold of the card by its edges, carefully and firmly pull it straight up and out of its slot.

FIGURE 9-6 Releasing a latch holding in the video card

✔ Hint

These cards can be difficult to remove. If a card seems stuck, try rocking it back and forth (from front to back in the direction of the slot, not side to side).

c. Holding the card only by the edges and the metal flange, place it in an anti-static bag for safekeeping.

Step 3 Examine each of the cards you removed from your system and record the pertinent information.

Do any of the cards have writing or labels on them? If so, what information do these labels provide?

_____

_____

_____

Can you identify the manufacturers of the cards? If so, list each card and its manufacturer.

_____

_____

_____

Are there any version numbers or codes on the cards? If so, list this information for each card.

_____

_____

_____

What kind of interface does each card use? List whether it is PCI, AGP, or PCIe (or something else).

_____

_____

_____

Step 4   Reinstall into your system the expansion cards you removed. For each card, follow these procedures:

a. Check your notes to confirm where to reinstall the card.

b. Align the card over its motherboard slot, making sure that the metal flange is aligned properly with the case slot. Holding the flange with one hand, place the heel of your hand on the top edge of the card and push the card firmly into the expansion slot.

c. Once the card is in the slot and the flange is flush with the case, replace the screw that holds the card in place. Don't be tempted to skip the screw! It keeps the card from working loose over time.

✖ **Warning**

After you have reinstalled all the expansion cards, take a look at the back of your system (where you can see input/output connections for the cards). Are there any holes where no cards are installed and a slot cover has not been used? It's very important to install slot covers wherever an expansion card is not installed. This ensures that air will flow properly through the computer case, keeping your critical components cool.

 30 MINUTES

Lab Exercise 9.08: Managing Hardware with Device Manager

Windows is capable of utilizing a universe of peripherals and expansion cards—everything from modems to TV tuners. Management of this massive collection of hardware in Windows is handled by Device Manager.

Device Manager provides a centralized location for dealing with all aspects of a computer's hardware. This includes a simple inventory of all installed devices, notification of malfunctioning devices, and the capability to install and update drivers.

This exercise will cover some of the more useful features of Device Manager.

Learning Objectives

In this lab, you'll use Device Manager to examine and update a system.

At the end of this lab, you'll be able to

- Use Device Manager to examine devices on your system, check for problems, and update drivers

Lab Materials and Setup

The materials you need for this lab are

- A working computer running Windows

- Access to the Internet

✔ **Hint**

As usual, if you have access to more than one system, take advantage of it.

Getting Down to Business

In this exercise, you'll use Device Manager to view the system resource settings on your PC.

Step 1   Open the Windows Control Panel. In Windows XP, click the icon for the System applet. Select the Hardware tab and then click the Device Manager button; this brings up Device Manager in a separate window. In Windows Vista, select System and Maintenance, and then choose Device Manager. In Windows 7, select System and Security, then click on Device Manager under System to open Device Manager in a separate window (see Figure 9-7). Note that you can also access Device Manager from

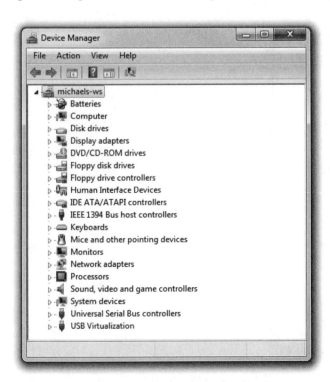

FIGURE 9-7   Device Manager in Windows 7

the System applet. In Windows Vista and Windows 7, press the WINDOWS KEY and the PAUSE/BREAK key at the same time to open the System applet, then click on Device Manager. (In Windows XP, you'll first need to select the Hardware tab.)

Step 2   Check for any missing devices, or devices marked with error icons:

- A device marked with a black "!" on a yellow circle (Windows XP) or triangle (Windows Vista/7) means that the device is missing, Windows does not recognize it, or there is a driver issue.

- In Windows XP, a device marked with a red "X" means the device is disabled. In Windows Vista/7, it is marked with a black downward-pointing arrow.

Step 3   Download and install the latest device drivers for each of your expansion cards. There are many methods you can use to accomplish this task, but the two that follow are the most common.

- If your working PC is connected to the Internet, you can use the Update Driver Wizard from the device's Driver tab in Device Manager to connect to Windows Update. Open Device Manager and select *View device by type*. Locate your expansion cards and right-click one and select Properties. Select the Driver tab, shown in Figure 9-8, and then click Update Driver. This opens a wizard that helps you find new drivers, as shown in Figure 9-9; from here you can manually browse for drivers on your computer or have Windows search for drivers both on your computer and online.

FIGURE 9-8 The Driver tab of the device's Properties dialog box in Windows

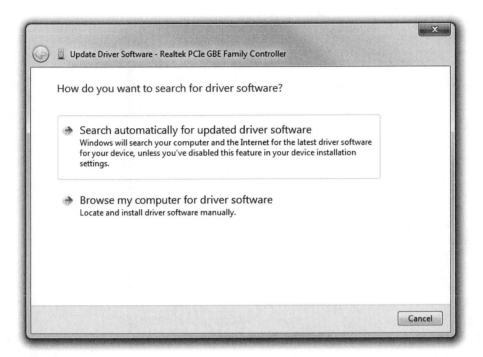

FIGURE 9-9 Updating drivers

- If your working PC is not connected to the Internet, or the device does not have a signed driver available through Windows Update, you will have to follow these instructions before clicking Update Driver. Using a computer with Internet access, find and connect to the manufacturer's Web site. Using the model number of the device, locate and download the correct driver for the operating system on the PC where the device is installed. Save the driver to a USB thumb drive, remove the thumb drive from that system, and insert it into your working PC. Open Device Manager and select *View device by type*. Locate the device that matches the expansion card you have installed, and open its properties. Select the Driver tab, and then click Update Driver. When prompted to connect to the Internet, choose *No, not this time*, and follow the directions to locate and load the new device driver (see Figure 9-10).

✔ **Hint**

Many manufacturers include installation wizards for their devices, so that is yet another method that you can use to update device drivers. Many times, the manufacturer will include related applications along with the drivers to enhance the performance of the device. A good example of this is an inkjet printer that includes the driver and utilities for adjusting print quality, performing printer maintenance, and so on.

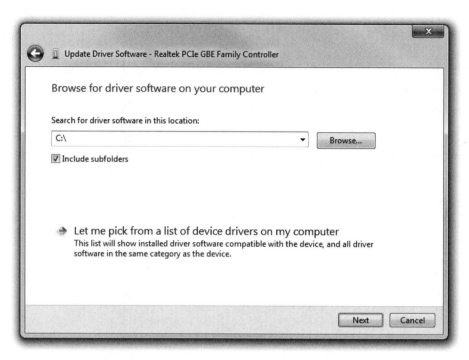

FIGURE 9-10 Manually browsing for new drivers

Lab Analysis Test

1. Jonathan is building a system using an Intel Core i3 processor, and he's purchased a new motherboard from ASUS. He would like to use an old (but working!) ATX power supply he has laying around to power the system. Why might this *not* be a good idea?

2. John has a system that runs at 3.2 GHz and uses a 128-MB AGP video card. He uses Windows XP Professional and wants to try its multiple-monitor support feature. Can he add another AGP video card? Why or why not?

3. Dianne is trying to install an ATX motherboard in a new, empty ATX case. She tries to set it down in the bottom of the case, but it won't fit—the ports on the side are too low to poke out the back of the case, and she can't make the screws work at all. What has she forgotten?

4. After Erik reassembled his PC and turned it on, he noticed that the green LED and the disk active LED never light up, but everything seems to work okay. What is the problem?

5. You've installed an NIC and a PCI FireWire controller card on Susan's Windows Vista Professional system. The system starts up fine, but when you check Device Manager, you see a yellow triangle with a black exclamation mark beside the NIC icon. What is the problem?

Key Term Quiz

Use the following terms to complete the following sentences. Not all terms will be used.

AGP

ATX

device drivers

expansion card

FlexATX

ITX

microATX

motherboard book

PCI

PCIe

sockets or slots

1. Once a standard graphics expansion slot, _____ has been replaced in favor of PCIe video cards.

2. To check the technical specifications of a motherboard, consult its _____.

3. The _____ bus provides for ×1, ×2, ×4, ×8, ×16, and ×32 lanes of bidirectional communication.

4. _____ are the areas where CPUs are installed on motherboards.

5. One motherboard design, known for its lower power-consumption characteristics and small size, is called _____.

Chapter 10
Power Supplies

Lab Exercises

The term "power supply" is somewhat misleading. After all, the power supply in a PC does not actually *supply* power; it just takes the alternating current (AC) supplied by the power company and converts it to the direct current (DC) used by your computer. Local power companies supply AC to the outlet in your home or office, and some conversion must take place to supply the lower operating voltages and DC power required for the PC to function.

As a PC technician, you need to understand the difference between AC and DC power. You should be able to measure the AC power at the wall outlet and determine whether the hot, neutral, and ground wires are properly connected. You must also measure the DC output of the power supply inside the PC case to determine whether the power supply is providing the correct DC voltage.

The power supply in a PC is an electronic device that converts the higher voltage—120 volts of alternating current (VAC) in the United States or 240 VAC outside the United States—into the 12, 5, and 3.3 volts of direct current (VDC) used in today's PC systems. The 12-volt level is traditionally used for devices that have motors to spin, such as hard drives, floppy drives, optical drives, and cooling fans. The 5-volt and 3.3-volt power usually supports all of the onboard electronics. Modern CPUs often use less than 3.3 volts, so there are further step-down regulators and filters to provide core voltages as low as 1.4 volts.

ATX power supplies are, by far, the most common power supplies you will see on desktop PCs. These include ATX (with a 20-pin P1 power connector), ATX 12V 1.3 (which added the AUX 4-pin connector commonly referred to as P4), and the ATX 12V 2.0 (which swapped out the 20-pin P1 connector for a 24-pin P1 connector). Higher-end computers such as servers and gaming systems with multiple high-powered video cards often require much more current, so you may start to see the Server System Infrastructure (SSI)–developed, non-ATX-standard motherboard with a power supply named EPS 12V; it uses a 24-pin P1 connector, a 4-pin P4 connector, and a unique 8-pin connector.

Suppose a client calls you saying that her PC keeps locking up. After walking her through a few simple troubleshooting steps, you rule out a virus or a misbehaving application. This leaves hardware as the likely culprit, and in all likelihood, it's the power supply. In these lab exercises, you'll practice the procedures for measuring power going to the PC, testing the PC's power supply, and replacing a PC power supply.

✔ **Hint**

The CompTIA A+ certification exams show their American roots in the area of electrical power. Watch for power questions that discuss American power standards—especially ones related to household voltage and outlet plug design. The exams will also typically refer to the power supply using the abbreviation PSU (power supply unit) or the acronym FRU (field replaceable unit). FRU can describe any component that would be replaced in the field by a technician.

 30 MINUTES

Lab Exercise 10.01: Electricity

Troubleshooting power-related problems is one of the trickier tasks you'll undertake as a PC tech. Your first step is to go right to the source, so to speak, and make certain that the power being supplied to the PC from the electrical outlet is good.

✔ **Cross-Reference**

> For details on AC power from the power company, refer to the "Supplying AC" section in Chapter 10 of *Mike Meyers' CompTIA A+ Guide to Managing and Troubleshooting PCs*.

Learning Objectives

At the end of this lab, you'll be able to

- Determine if the AC wiring is correct at a wall outlet

- Determine if the AC voltages are correct at a wall outlet

Lab Materials and Setup

The materials you need for this lab are

- An AC electrical outlet tester

- A multimeter

Getting Down to Business

Measuring the voltage coming from an AC outlet is a nerve-wracking task even for experienced techs! Sticking objects into a live power outlet goes against everything you've been taught since infancy, but when done properly, it's completely safe.

Use common sense and appropriate safety procedures. If you're not familiar with using a multimeter, please review the "Supplying AC" section in Chapter 10 of *Mike Meyers' CompTIA A+ Guide to Managing and Troubleshooting PCs*, or ask your instructor for a demonstration.

✔ **Hint**

> If a PC experiences unexplained errors and you suspect the power supply, don't be too hasty in replacing it. First check the wall outlet. In some buildings, especially older ones, the wiring can be improperly connected or otherwise provide poor power.

FIGURE 10-1 A typical AC electrical outlet

Step 1   Look at Figure 10-1, and compare it to your electrical outlet.

A typical electrical socket has three openings: hot, neutral, and ground. The hot wire delivers the juice. The neutral wire acts as a drain and returns electricity to the local source (the breaker panel). The semi-rounded ground socket returns excess electricity to the ground. If your outlet doesn't have a ground socket—and outlets in many older buildings don't—then don't use it! Ungrounded outlets aren't appropriate for PCs.

> **✖ Warning**
>
> Take all appropriate safety precautions before measuring live electrical outlets. In a classroom, you have the benefit of an instructor to show you how to do these exercises the first time. If you're doing these on your own with no experience, seek the advice of a trained technician or instructor.

Step 2   Determine whether or not your electrical socket is "live." Do this with your electrical outlet tester. Plug your outlet tester (see Figure 10-2) into the electrical outlet or power strip where you plug in the PC. Look at the LED indicators. Are they showing good power?

Step 3   Now measure the voltage between the hot and neutral openings of the outlet. Start by setting your multimeter to AC voltage; do not proceed until you're sure you have done this correctly! If you aren't sure, ask your instructor for guidance. Referring to Figure 10-3, take the black probe and place it

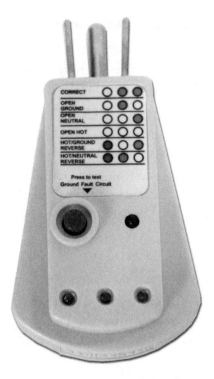

Figure 10-2 A circuit tester for AC electrical outlets

Figure 10-3 Multimeter probe locations when testing an AC outlet's hot-to-neutral circuit

in the neutral opening of the wall socket. Make sure you have good contact inside the outlet. The metal probe tip must contact the metal connector inside the outlet.

Next, place the red probe inside the hot opening. Again, you must make good metal-to-metal contact. You may have to reposition the probes to get a good connection and proper reading for the AC circuit. Your reading should be somewhere between 110 and 120 V.

What is your reading? _____

Step 4 Measure the voltage in the hot-to-ground circuit. Place the black probe into the ground opening of the outlet, as shown in Figure 10-4. Make sure you have good contact. Then place the red probe into the hot opening. Move the probes around until you get a good reading for the AC voltage. Again, your reading should be in the 110- to 120-V range.

What is your reading? _____

Step 5 The last measurement you need to take is the voltage in the neutral-to-ground safety circuit. When the neutral wire is broken or missing, the ground wire is the only way for wayward electrons to depart safely. Any electricity on both the neutral and ground wires should have a direct path back to earth, so there should be no voltage between these wires.

FIGURE 10-4 Multimeter probe locations when testing an AC outlet's hot-to-ground circuit

Figure 10-5 Multimeter probe locations when testing an AC outlet's neutral-to-ground circuit

Place the black probe into the ground opening of the outlet. Make sure you have good contact. Place the red probe into the neutral opening (refer to Figure 10-5). Move the probes around until you get a good reading for the AC voltage. You should get a reading of 0 V.

What is your reading? _____

Step 6 Measure another outlet in the same building, and repeat the previous steps. Are the readings similar? If the readings from your electrical outlets are outside of the ranges described, it's time to call an electrician. Assuming your reading is showing good power, go to the next exercise.

 30 MINUTES

Lab Exercise 10.02: Power Supply Output

Once you've determined that the AC power going to your client's PC is good, you need to test whether the DC power traveling from the power supply to the rest of her system is good.

Learning Objectives

At the end of this lab, you'll be able to

- Identify the connectors of a PC power supply

- Measure the output of a PC power supply

Lab Materials and Setup

The materials you need for this lab are

- An ATX power supply

- A multimeter

- A PC power supply tester

- Optional: A working PC with an ATX power supply

Getting Down to Business

There are two ways to determine whether a power supply is providing the proper voltages to the components of the computer. One is the traditional method, using a multimeter to measure the actual voltages. Another method growing in popularity is the use of a PC power supply tester.

✔ **Cross-Reference**

For details on DC power from the power supply, refer to the "Supplying DC" section in Chapter 10 of *Mike Meyers' CompTIA A+ Guide to Managing and Troubleshooting PCs.*

In the following steps, you'll measure DC voltage coming from the PC power supply. The three places to measure power supply output are at the Molex power connectors, the SATA power connectors, and the motherboard power connectors. Molex power connectors plug into devices that need 5 or 12 volts of power. These include PATA hard drives and PATA optical drives. SATA power connectors connect to SATA hard drives and optical drives. On most recent systems, the power supply will provide two motherboard power connectors: the 20- or 24-pin P1 and the smaller P4 (see Figure 10-6). Both of these power connectors are used on motherboards requiring an additional 12-V power supply.

You'll then plug the P1 power connector into a PC power supply tester and verify that the readings you measured with the multimeter are within tolerance. The power supply tester has LEDs that will glow green for each of the voltages that it passes.

Figure 10-6 Motherboard power connectors: P1 (left) and P4 (right)

✖ **Warning**

Although the power coming out of the PC power supply is considerably less lethal than that coming directly out of the electrical outlet, you should still take all appropriate safety precautions before taking measurements.

Step 1 Set the multimeter to read DC voltage. Find a Molex connector that's not being used for a device. If no Molex connectors are unused, turn the system off and disconnect the one from the optical drive, and then turn the PC back on.

Do you have a free Molex connector? _____

If not, which device did you unplug? _____

Step 2 Referring to Figure 10-7, place the black probe into either one of the holes on the Molex connector that is aligned with a black wire. Now place the red probe into each of the other three holes of the Molex connector in turn, first the other black wire, then the red, then yellow, and record your findings.

Black wire to black wire: _____ V

Black wire to red wire: _____ V

Black wire to yellow wire: _____ V

Step 3 Measuring the voltage from the motherboard connector is a little trickier. Leave the power connector plugged into the motherboard and push the probes into the end of the connector that the wires run into. You must push the probe deep enough to touch the metal contact pins, but be careful not to push too deeply or you might push the pin out of the connector.

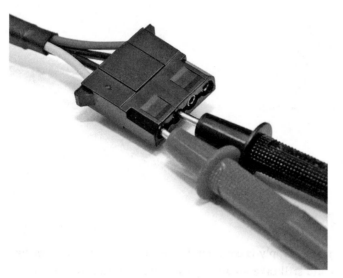

FIGURE 10-7 Measuring the voltage in a Molex connector

Push the black probe into the motherboard connector alongside any black wire, and leave it there. Insert the red probe into each of the other wires, and record your findings. Depending on your motherboard connector, you may not have all of these wires.

Black wire to red wire: _____ V

Black wire to yellow wire: _____ V

Black wire to purple wire: _____ V

Black wire to white wire: _____ V

Black wire to black wire: _____ V

Black wire to blue wire: _____ V

Black wire to green wire: _____ V

The voltages generated by the power supply must be within a tolerance (range) level; readings outside these ranges mean the power supply should be replaced. The 5-V connections have a tolerance of ±2 percent (4.9 to 5.1 V is okay), and 12-V connections have a tolerance of ±6 percent (11.25 to 12.75 V is okay).

✔ Hint

A single reading from a power supply may not be enough to pinpoint a power-related problem. Sometimes a power problem becomes evident only when the power supply is placed under a heavier-than-normal load, such as burning a CD or DVD. Also, some RAM-related errors mimic a failing power supply.

The other method to verify that the power supply is operating properly and supplying all the voltages within tolerance is to use a power supply tester. There are many styles of PSU testers on the market, so make sure you follow the specific directions included with your tester as you complete the steps.

Step 1 Starting with the P1 connector, follow the directions for connecting it to your specific PSU tester. Verify that all of the voltages provided through the P1 connector are acceptable (usually an LED will light to verify voltage present and within tolerance).

Did it light up or display an acceptable voltage? _____

✔ **Hint**

When connecting and disconnecting the power supply connectors, always take care to insert the connector with the proper orientation. Most power connectors are keyed to make it difficult to install the connector backward, but if you use excessive force, you may be able to insert the connector improperly. This applies to powering the motherboard, plugging in devices, and even using the PSU tester.

Step 2 Now, depending on your tester and power supply, plug either the 4-pin, 6-pin, or 8-pin auxiliary connector into the appropriate socket on the PSU tester and verify the voltages provided through this connector. Once they are verified, remove the connector from the socket.

Did it light up or display an acceptable voltage? _____

Step 3 Plug the Molex connector into the PSU tester and verify the voltages provided through this connector. Once they are verified, remove the connector from the socket.

Did it light up or display an acceptable voltage? _____

Step 4 Plug the SATA HDD power connector into the appropriate socket and verify the voltages provided through this connector. Once they are verified, remove the connector from the socket.

Did it light up or display an acceptable voltage? _____

Step 5 Finally, plug the mini floppy drive power connector into the PSU tester and verify the voltages provided through this connector. Once they are verified, remove the connector from the socket and remove the P1 from the socket.

Did it light up or display an acceptable voltage? _____

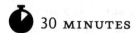 30 MINUTES

Lab Exercise 10.03: Replacing a Power Supply

Let's assume that you've found a variance in the 12-V range that explains your client's system lockups. You know that power supplies aren't user-serviceable components—you don't fix them, you replace them as a unit—so it's time to replace her power supply. Next to the motherboard, the power supply is the most time-consuming component to replace, simply because of all those wires! Nonetheless, replacing the power supply is a simple operation, as described in this exercise.

Learning Objectives

At the end of this lab, you'll be able to

- Determine the total wattage requirements of the system and select the proper power supply

- Replace a power supply

Lab Materials and Setup

The materials you need for this lab are

- A non-production PC with an ATX power supply

- A Phillips-head screwdriver

- A labeled container for holding screws

Getting Down to Business

One of the areas where PC manufacturers cut corners on lower-end systems is power supplies. High-end systems typically come with higher-wattage power supplies, whereas entry-level PCs typically have lower-wattage power supplies. You might not notice it until you add power-hungry components to the system, placing a heavier load on the power supply and causing an early failure.

In the following steps, you'll determine the wattage of the power supply on your system, calculate the power usage of your PC, and then remove and reinstall the power supply.

Step 1   To determine the wattage rating of your power supply, look at the label on the power supply (see Figure 10-8).

Locate the watts rating. If you don't see a clear wattage rating as shown in Figure 10-8, or if you see something less evident, like the smaller "430W" marking on the label, the power supply rating may be hidden in the model number, which in this example is "Neo HE430."

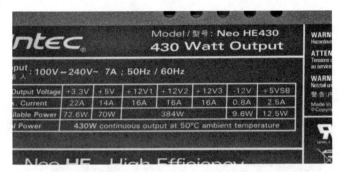

FIGURE 10-8 Typical ATX power supply ratings label

✔ **Hint**

All power supplies have a wattage rating. If it is not apparent on the power supply itself, search the Internet using the model number for reference.

What is the wattage of your power supply? _____

Step 2 When it comes time to replace a power supply, don't skimp on the wattage! As a general rule, get the highest-wattage replacement you can afford while maintaining compatibility with your system. Remember, the system will draw only the current it requires, so you will never damage a system by installing a higher-wattage power supply.

✖ **Warning**

Never replace a PC's power supply with one of lower wattage!

Use the following table to calculate the overall wattage needed for your system. Add the numbers for each component and determine the lowest and highest wattage requirements.

Component	Requirement	Voltage(s) Used
PCIe video card	45–75 W	3.3 V
AGP video card	30–50 W	3.3 V
PCI card	5–10 W	5 V
10/100/1000 NIC	4 W	3.3 V
SCSI controller PCI	20 W	3.3 V and 5 V

Component	Requirement	Voltage(s) Used
Floppy drive	5 W	5 V
7200 rpm PATA hard drive	5–20 W	5 V and 12 V
7200 rpm SATA hard drive	5–20 W	5 V and 12 V
10,000 rpm SATA hard drive	5–20 W	5 V and 12 V
10,000 rpm SCSI drive	10–40 W	5 V and 12 V
15,000 rpm SATA hard drive	5–20 W	5 V and 12 V
CD/DVD/Blu-ray media drive	10–25 W	5 V and 12 V
Case/CPU fans	3 W (each)	12 V
Motherboard (without CPU or RAM)	25–40 W	3.3 V and 5 V
RAM	10 W per 128 MB	3.3 V
Intel Core i7-860	95 W	12 V
Intel Core 2 Duo 3.0GHz	65 W	12 V
AMD Phenom II X4 965	140 W	12 V

If the highest total exceeds the power supply wattage rating, you may run into problems. When selecting a new power supply, you should multiply the load by a factor of 1.5. The multiplier provides a safety factor and allows the power supply to run more efficiently. A power supply is more efficient at 30 to 70 percent of its full capacity rating. Thus, a 450-W PSU works best when only 135 to 315 watts are being used.

What wattage is appropriate for your system? _____

✔ **Hint**

Depending on the design of your PC case, you may have to remove data cables or components before you can get to the power supply. Make certain that you have plenty of room to work inside the case!

Step 3   Shut down the system and remove the power cable from the back of the power supply. Then remove the power supply.

 a.   Disconnect the Molex, SATA, and mini connectors from your drive devices, then unplug the main power connector from the motherboard.

 b.   Disconnect the P4 connector from the motherboard.

 c.   Unscrew the four screws holding the power supply onto the PC case (remembering to support it while you remove the last one), and remove the power supply from the case. Store the screws in the labeled container.

 Was your power supply mounted to the top or bottom of your PC case? _____

Step 4   Take this opportunity to inspect and clean the power supply. Check for any rust or corrosion on the power supply casing or on any of the contacts. Inspect the wires for damage or frayed insulation. Use canned air (outside!) to blow dust and dirt out of the intake and exhaust vents.

Step 5   Reinstall the power supply by performing the preceding steps in reverse order. If you had to remove data cables or other components to get at the power supply, be sure to reattach them.

When you've finished reinstalling the power supply, have your instructor or a knowledgeable tech sign off on it here: _____

 30 MINUTES

Lab Exercise 10.04: Power Protection

You've successfully fixed your client's power-problem-plagued PC (say that five times fast), but now you've noted that she has nothing in the way of power protection for her system, nor do any of her coworkers. None!

When you mention this to her, she tells you that her boss never really saw the point of spending money on surge protectors, uninterruptible power supplies, or any of "that stuff." With a straight face, she asks, "Do those things really do any good?"

Now it's your task to sell the boss on the idea of power protection. To do this, you must explain the types of power problems that lurk in the bushes just waiting to pounce on unwary users without power protection, and suggest precautions that they can take to prevent power-related damage.

Learning Objectives

At the end of this lab, you'll be able to

- Explain the need for power protection
- Explain the types of power protection available for a PC

✔ Cross-Reference

For details on power protection, refer to the "Protecting the PC from Spikes and Sags in AC Power" section in Chapter 10 of *Mike Meyers' CompTIA A+ Guide to Managing and Troubleshooting PCs*.

Lab Materials and Setup

The materials you need for this lab are

- A working PC

Getting Down to Business

Too often, PC users take for granted the electricity that powers their system. After all, there's not much you can do about the electricity, is there? Not so! Armed with the knowledge of the types of power conditions that can affect your PC, you can best determine what precautions to take.

Step 1 Describe the following types of power conditions and the types of damage they can cause.

Power spike: _____

_____

Brownout: _____

_____

Blackout: _____

_____

Step 2 Describe the following types of power protection equipment.

Surge suppressor: _____

_____

Online uninterruptible power supply (UPS): _____

_____

Standby UPS: _____

_____

Lab Analysis Test

1. Your client calls you and says that her PC is unusually quiet and keeps rebooting for no apparent reason. What should you ask her to check?

2. Athena lives in an area where the power is often interrupted. She bought a good surge protector strip, but that does not seem to help. What does she need to prevent her system from shutting down unexpectedly?

3. Your assistant technician calls you and says he suspects a bad power supply in one of your client's systems. He said the multimeter readings are 12.65 volts and 4.15 volts. What should he do?

4. One of your clients has an older Pentium 4 system with a single IDE hard drive and 512 MB of RAM. He had been using this PC as his main workstation, but he's recently purchased a newer system and now wants to redeploy the older system as a file server on his network. He has ordered a PCI SCSI controller board and three SCSI hard drives, so that he can configure a RAID array, and an additional 2 GB of RAM. He also ordered two Y adapters for the power supply connectors. He asks for your advice about any additional hardware he should order. What do you tell him?

5. Approximately how many watts would the power supply for this system need?

- AMD Athlon 64 X2 CPU and 512 MB RAM

- Two SATA hard drives and one floppy drive

- One CD-RW drive and one DVD-ROM drive

- PCIe video

- PCI sound card

- NIC

Key Term Quiz

Use the following terms to complete the following sentences. Not all terms will be used.

3.3 V

5 V

12 V

20-pin P1

24-pin P1

Molex connector

P4

P8/P9

power sags

power spikes

power supply

UPS

1. The ATX 12V 2.0 power supply plugs into the motherboard using the _____ connector(s).

2. PC devices with motors, such as hard drives and optical drives, usually require _____ of DC electricity from the power supply.

3. PATA hard drives and optical drives connect to the power supply with a _____.

4. A surge protector prevents damage from _____ in the voltage.

5. For the best protection against power problems, connect your PC to a _____.

Chapter 11
Hard Drive Technologies

Lab Exercises

As the primary storage area for the operating system, applications, and vital data, the hard drive takes on a level of importance to PC users that borders on reverence. Considering the fact that the death of a drive can mean many hours or days of tediously rebuilding your OS install, reloading applications, and re-creating data, such strong feelings make sense. And that reverence can turn quickly to agony if the user hasn't backed up his or her data in awhile when the hard drive dies!

Every tech must know how to connect, configure, maintain, and troubleshoot hard drives of all types. A fully operational drive requires proper hardware setup and installation, CMOS configuration, and software setup (usually performed by tools that come with the operating system). The first few labs in this chapter cover physical installation and CMOS configuration of the mainstream hard drive technology, namely Integrated Drive Electronics (IDE), in both parallel and serial flavors, and solid-state drives (SSDs). You will then conduct research on the developments of Small Computer Systems Interface (SCSI), primarily used for large, fault-tolerant data storage in network server environments. The next exercise will have you troubleshoot installations, and finally you'll install additional hard drives in preparation for an exercise in the next chapter. You'll work with the software aspects of all hard drives—partitioning, formatting, and running drive utilities—in Chapter 12.

 60 MINUTES

Lab Exercise 11.01: Installing Parallel ATA Hard Drives

The local nonprofit organization where you volunteer has received a donation of 10 used PCs. Most of them have tiny hard drives, so they need an upgrade before you can distribute them to the various workers at the agency. All of the motherboards have built-in parallel ATA (PATA) controllers. Your boss breaks out a stack of donated hard drives and tells you to get to work!

Installing a PATA hard drive successfully requires little more than connecting data and power cables to the drive and plugging the other end of the data cable into the motherboard. Sounds simple enough on the surface, but because all PATA drives give you options to install two on each motherboard controller, unwary techs get tripped up here. This lab walks you through the physical installation of the hard drive.

✔ **Hint**

As you know from Chapter 11 of your textbook, IDE drives have several names that techs use pretty much interchangeably: IDE, EIDE, and ATA. You'll see all three terms in this lab manual and on the CompTIA A+ certification exams. Except for discussions of very old technology, the terms describe the same type of hard drive today.

Learning Objectives

In this lab exercise, you'll identify the different components of PATA hard drives and cables and learn installation procedures.

At the end of this lab, you'll be able to

- Remove a hard drive safely and correctly

- Describe PATA cables and connectors

- Describe jumper settings

- Identify the major parts of a hard drive

- Install a hard drive safely and correctly

Lab Materials and Setup

The materials you need for this lab are

- A working PC with a PATA hard drive installed

- The Windows operating system installed on the PC

- Optional: Access to one or more broken hard drives that have the covers removed for observation of the internal parts

Getting Down to Business

Grab your handy screwdriver and anti-static wrist strap; it's time to remove a hard drive! Make sure you're using a hard drive that doesn't have any mission-critical data on it, just in case.

Step 1 Shut down your system and remove the system cover, following proper electrostatic discharge (ESD) avoidance procedures.

Step 2   Disconnect all the ribbon cables from the hard drives, but first note which device is connected to which cable and where the orientation stripe is located on each device. Be careful but firm. Grasp the cable as closely as possible to the connector on the drive and pull, rocking the connector gently from side to side.

Examine the connector on the end of the ribbon cable. Use Figure 11-1 to help you.

How many holes does your connector have for pins? _____

Are any of the holes in your connector filled in? Does your connector have a raised portion on one side so that it only fits one way? In other words, is it keyed? _____

How many connectors are on your ribbon cable? _____

Do you have a 40-wire or 80-wire ribbon cable? _____

Disconnect the power supply from the PATA hard drives by unplugging the Molex connector from each one.

✖ Warning

Molex plugs can be difficult to remove and brutal on the fingers. Little "bumps" on each side of the plug enable you to rock the plug back and forth to remove it.

Step 3   Now look at the motherboard connections and note the orientation of the cable connectors. Disconnect the ribbon cables from the motherboard. Be careful but firm. Grasp the cable as closely as possible to the connector on the motherboard and pull, rocking the connector gently from side to side. Lay the cables aside for later reinstallation.

FIGURE 11-1 ATA cables: Comparing 40-wire and 80-wire ribbon cable connectors

Step 4   Look at the PATA connections on your motherboard; they may be labeled "IDE" (see Figure 11-2).

How many PATA controllers do you see on your motherboard?

_____

Look closely at your motherboard and see if you can find writing on the board next to the IDE connections. Are the interfaces grouped into pairs? Are any of them dedicated to special configurations such as RAID?

_____

_____

What color are the IDE connections on the motherboard?

_____

Step 5   Remove a hard drive from the system. Be careful to note the type of screws you removed and store them for safekeeping. Also be sure to use proper ESD avoidance procedures when removing the drive from your system.

Because of the variety of cases, caddies, bays, slots, and so on, it's not possible to give detailed instructions on how to remove the drive from your particular system. Look closely for caddy releases or retaining screws. Close inspection and a little logic will usually make it clear how to remove the drive. Make notes of how the drive comes out, as you'll have to reinstall it later.

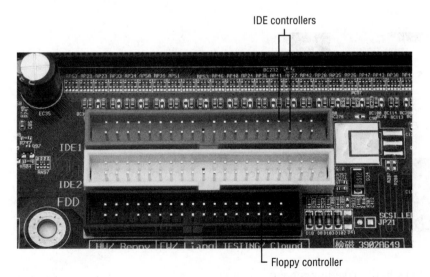

FIGURE 11-2 Viewing the PATA connectors on a motherboard

Step 6 With the hard drive out of the system and on a static-free surface, ground yourself, pick up the drive, and examine it carefully.

Note its dimensions. It should measure about 6" × 3.5" × 1". Some drives are smaller, but those are used mostly in laptops.

Look at the largest surfaces of the drive (the top and bottom). The bottom is where the printed circuit board with a ROM chip is located. This circuitry is the hard drive controller. The top side of the drive normally has a label or another means of listing the specifications for the drive, but this is not always the case.

Write down all the information on the label. Be sure to include the manufacturer and the model number for future reference.

_____

_____

Step 7 Look at the end of the drive where the ribbon cable connects. (Make sure the label is facing up.) Find the markings for where pin 1 of the ribbon cable should go.

a.   Is pin 1 on the left side of the connector or the right side? _____

b.   Does your hard drive have jumpers like the ones in Figure 11-3? _____

c.   Notice that the drive in Figure 11-3 has the jumper set to CS. What does CS stand for?

_____

FIGURE 11-3 Locating the PATA hard drive jumper setting

Each PC system that boots from a PATA hard drive should have the hard drive located on the first PATA interface (IDE1). Normally the jumper must be set to master so that the system can recognize it as the boot drive. A second drive (hard drive or optical drive) can be on the same cable, but must be set to slave.

    d.   How are the jumpers set on your hard drive?

    _____

    e.   How are the jumpers set on your optical drive?

    _____

    f.   Can you have two master drives in the system? Why or why not?

    _____

    _____

    _____

For the purposes of this exercise, make sure you leave your hard drive jumpered as it was when you removed it.

Step 8   Locate a broken hard drive. If you're in a class, ask your instructor for one. Remove its cover.

✖ Warning

Never remove the cover from a functioning hard drive! Hard drives are extremely sensitive, so merely exposing the inside to the air will cause irreparable damage.

Notice the round polished platters that spin in the middle of the drive. This is where the data is stored magnetically.

The actuator arms that move across the platters have tiny coils of wire attached to their ends. These coils hold the read/write heads.

    a.   How many surfaces does your sample drive have (one platter = two surfaces)?

    _____

    b.   How many physical heads does your sample drive have?

    _____

Both of the preceding answers are most likely the same because usually there is a read/write head for each surface.

    c.   Look at Figure 11-4 and identify the following parts by number.

        Read/write heads _____

        Platters _____

        Voice coil motor _____

    d.   Now look at Figure 11-5 and match the numbered components.

        EIDE controller _____

        Molex connector _____

        PATA connector _____

        Master/slave jumper _____

Step 9   Insert the drive back into your system, and secure it with the proper screws. Connect all the ribbon cables to all the drives, and pay attention to the proper alignment of the connectors. Connect the Molex power connectors.

Leave the system case off until you verify that everything works properly.

If you used a working machine for the prior steps, you can verify that you've reinstalled the drives correctly by going to the next major step in the process of hard drive installation: CMOS configuration. Lab Exercise 11.03 in this chapter covers the CMOS details, but if you just can't wait, try Step 10. This bonus step should work on newer motherboard models.

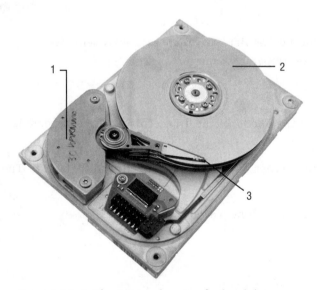

Figure 11-4 The internal parts of a hard drive

FIGURE 11-5 The external parts of a hard drive

Step 10 Turn on the system and wait for it to boot to the desktop. Double-click the My Computer/Computer icon, and confirm that the icons for the reinstalled drives are displayed. The fact that you were able to get to the desktop confirms that you've reinstalled the boot drive correctly, but do the other drives (if you have them) and your optical drive work?

✔ **Hint**

If you cannot boot the system or the optical drive does not work, the first and obvious place to start is to verify all the cable connections. Any kind of disk errors at this time were most likely caused by the technician; after all, it worked before you touched it!

 45 MINUTES

Lab Exercise 11.02: Installing Serial ATA Hard Drives

A wealthy donor has just given your nonprofit organization a dozen brand-new desktop machines. Since these are new machines, their motherboards have built-in serial ATA (SATA) controllers, but the SATA hard drives have yet to be installed or configured. You're asked to do the job!

Installing SATA hard drives is a simple matter of plugging in the data and power cables to the drive and attaching the other end of the data cable to the SATA controller card or motherboard connection. You don't even have to shut down Windows. No, really—it's that simple! Let's go through the steps.

Learning Objectives

This lab is designed to introduce you to the three current flavors of SATA and walk you through the straightforward installation.

At the end of this lab, you'll be able to

- Explain key features of SATA 1.0, SATA 2.0, and SATA 3.0

- Install a SATA hard drive

Lab Materials and Setup

The materials you need for this lab are

- A newer PC system with an onboard SATA controller and Windows installed

- At least one additional SATA hard drive

- Optional: A PCI SATA controller may be installed into an older PC system

Getting Down to Business

To start, you'll review the features and specifications of SATA, and then you'll compare and contrast the technology with PATA. Keep that screwdriver handy, because you'll finish with the installation and hot-swap of a SATA drive.

✔ **Cross-Reference**

To help in answering the following questions, reference the "ATA-7" section in Chapter 11 of *Mike Meyers' CompTIA A+ Guide to Managing and Troubleshooting PCs*.

Step 1 Using your reference materials, review the features and specifications of SATA hard drive technology. Then answer these questions:

   a. What is the speed of data transfer for ATA/133 drives? _____

   b. What is the speed of data transfer for SATA 1.0 drives? _____

   c. What is the speed of data transfer for SATA 2.0 drives? _____

   d. What is the speed of data transfer for SATA 3.0 drives? _____

   e. What is the maximum length of a SATA cable? _____

   f. How many wires are in a SATA cable? _____

   g. What is the maximum length of an 80-wire PATA cable? _____

   h. How many drives can a single SATA cable support? _____

SATA RAID has waltzed into the mainstream today. Motherboards are now being sold with a SATA RAID controller built-in, from Promise or another company, but you can also readily buy a PCIe or PCI SATA RAID controller at your local computer parts store. You'll install additional hard drives in Lab Exercise 11.07, and you'll explore the implementation of a software RAID solution in Chapter 12.

Step 2　It's time to get working with some SATA drives. Shut down your system and remove the system cover, following proper ESD avoidance procedures.

Step 3　Disconnect the data cable(s) from the SATA hard drive(s), as shown in Figure 11-6. Grasp the cable as closely as possible to the connector on the drive and pull, rocking the connector gently from side to side.

Disconnect the power supply from the SATA drive(s) by unplugging the SATA connector from each one. Is the power supply a newer model with SATA connectors directly attached, or is there a Molex-to-SATA power adapter like the one shown in Figure 11-7?

Step 4　Now look at the motherboard connections and note the orientation of the connectors. Disconnect the data cables from the motherboard, being careful but firm. Grasp the cable as closely as possible to the connector on the motherboard and pull, rocking the connector gently from side to side.

Lay the cables aside for later reinstallation.

Step 5　Look at the SATA connections on your motherboard (see Figure 11-8).

How many SATA connectors do you see on your motherboard?

_____

FIGURE 11-6 Removing the SATA data cable

FIGURE 11-7 Molex-to-SATA power adapter

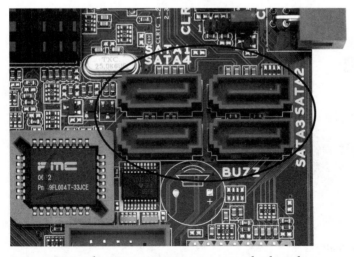

FIGURE 11-8 The SATA connectors on a motherboard

Look closely at your motherboard, and see if you can find writing on the board next to the SATA connectors. Are the interfaces grouped into pairs? Are any of them dedicated to special configurations such as RAID?

_____

_____

Step 6 As in the previous exercise, remove the hard drive from the system, note the type of screws you removed, and store the screws for safekeeping. Be sure to use proper ESD procedures when removing the drive from your system.

Because of the variety of cases, caddies, bays, slots, and so on, it's not possible to give detailed instructions on how to remove the drive from your particular system. Look closely for caddy releases or retaining screws. Close inspection and a little logic will usually make it clear how to remove the drive. Make notes of how the drive comes out; you'll have to reinstall it later.

Step 7 With the hard drive out of the system and on a static-free surface, ground yourself, pick up the drive, and examine it carefully.

Note its dimensions; it should measure about 6" × 3.5" × 1", the same as a PATA drive. Here, too, the bottom of the drive boasts the hard drive controller, and the top of the drive is normally labeled with the drive's specifications.

Write down all the information on the label. Be sure to include the manufacturer and the model number for future reference.

_____

_____

_____

Step 8 To demonstrate one of the benefits of SATA—hot-swapping—you will now reinstall all the drives you removed and, if necessary, install an additional SATA drive to be hot-swapped. With the PC still powered down, insert all of the original drives back into your system, and at least one additional SATA drive with no critical data. Secure the drives with the proper screws, connect all the data cables, and connect the SATA power connectors using Molex-to-SATA adapters if required.

Leave the system case off to verify that everything is working properly and to facilitate the last steps.

✔ **Hint**

If you are performing this lab using a PCIe or PCI SATA controller card, you'll have to install the expansion card and load the drivers for the card. If you haven't loaded drivers for the SATA controller, you should do so now. Otherwise, this is going to be a very frustrating lab for you!

Power up the PC and boot into Windows. Windows should pick up the drive(s) with no problems at all. Check My Computer/Computer to verify that the drive is installed and functional. If the drive has no partition, then of course it won't show up in My Computer/Computer; if this is the case, you can use the Computer Management console to verify that the drive works.

Step 9   With Windows still running, disconnect the SATA data cable from the additional drive. What happened?

_____

Step 10   Plug the data cable back in. Does Windows see the drive?

_____

Step 11   Try the same hot-swap test with the SATA power cable—unplug it, then plug it back in. Does this produce the same effect as the hot-swap with the data cable?

✔ **Cross-Reference**

Windows won't redetect the SATA drive if AHCI mode is not enabled in CMOS. For more information, reference the "AHCI" section in Chapter 11 of *Mike Meyers' CompTIA A+ Guide to Managing and Troubleshooting PCs*.

 30 MINUTES

Lab Exercise 11.03: Configuring CMOS Settings

After installing either PATA or SATA devices, the second step you'll want to perform is the configuration of the BIOS to support these devices. On most motherboards, the BIOS automatically detects devices, so you will primarily be confirming the detection of all the devices and configuring advanced features such as RAID, S.M.A.R.T., and boot options. Autodetection does not render CMOS irrelevant, though; you can do or undo all kinds of problems relating to hard drives using CMOS setup. This lab walks you through the important configuration options.

Learning Objectives

At the end of this lab, you'll be able to

- Configure the CMOS settings for the hard drive
- Confirm that the hard drive is indeed installed properly

Lab Materials and Setup

The materials you need for this lab are

- A fully functioning PC with PATA and/or SATA devices installed
- Optional: A second drive with no important data

Getting Down to Business

There are many possible CMOS settings for the hard drive, depending on the BIOS installed on the motherboard. For example, every motherboard gives you the option to disable the built-in hard drive controllers. Why is this relevant? You can install a drive into a perfectly good system, but it won't work if the controllers are disabled!

Step 1 Turn on your system, and enter the CMOS setup program by pressing the appropriate key(s) while your system is booting.

Select the Integrated Peripherals option from the main menu, or the Drive Configuration option from the Advanced menu (you may have to hunt around for where you enable the PATA/SATA devices in your CMOS setup program), and look for the various controllers. You can enable or disable the controllers here.

✔ **Hint**

This option may look somewhat different depending on the version of CMOS you are using. Look for a menu option such as one of these:

- Onboard Primary PCI IDE
- Onboard Secondary PCI IDE
- PCI Primary and Secondary IDE
- Onboard IDE

- Use Automatic Mode

- SATA Port 0

When the controllers are disabled in CMOS, no device attached to them can be used—not even optical drives. This is why some systems will not let you disable the controllers at all.

If you are performing the labs in sequence, and have arrived at this lab directly from Lab Exercise 11.01 or Lab Exercise 11.02, here's where you find out whether or not you installed and jumpered the drive correctly.

Make sure all controllers are enabled, and then look for the Autodetection option in the CMOS settings. Older systems have a separate category in CMOS, appropriately named Autodetect or something similar; newer systems have it integrated into the main settings screen. Run this utility now. If your hard drive shows up in Autodetect as the drive you thought it would be—primary master, secondary master, SATA Port 0, or what have you—then you installed and (if necessary) jumpered it properly (see Figure 11-9).

Step 2 Save your settings, exit CMOS, and reboot your PC. You should boot into Windows normally. Check My Computer/Computer to verify that you can see and access all drives.

Step 3 Reboot your PC and go into CMOS. Access the settings to enable or disable the various controllers, and disable them all. (This won't affect your data; it will just prevent drive access for the next couple of steps in this lab.)

Step 4 Save your settings, then exit CMOS to reboot the system. Watch the monitor display for messages.

```
                  Phoenix - Award BIOS CMOS Setup Utility
                         Standard CMOS Features

    Date (mm:dd:yy)          Wed, Jun 7 2006    ▲        Item Help
    Time (hh:mm:ss)          13 : 19 : 35
                                                    Menu Level    ▶
  ▶ IDE Channel 1 Master     WDC WD1200JB-75CRA0
  ▶ IDE Channel 1 Slave      None                     Change the day, month,
  ▶ IDE Channel 2 Master     SONY    CD-CW   CRX17     year and century
  ▶ IDE Channel 2 Slave      TOSHIBA CD/DUDW SDR5
  ▶ IDE Channel 3 Master     None
  ▶ IDE Channel 4 Master     None
  ▶ IDE Channel 5 Master     WDC WD2000JS-00MHB0
  ▶ IDE Channel 6 Master     None

    Drive A                  1.44, 3.5 in.
    Drive B                  None
    Floppy 3 Mode Support    Disabled
    Halt On                  All , But Keyboard

    Base Memory                  640K
    Extended Memory          1047552K            ▼

 ▲▼▶◀:Move  Enter:Select   +/-/PU/PD:Value  F10:Save   ESC:Exit  F1:General He
          F5:Previous Values     F6:Fail-Safe Defaults   F7:Optimized Defaults
```

FIGURE 11-9 Various drives and their roles as listed in CMOS setup

What message is displayed last? _____

With most systems, the PC searches its various storage devices for a way to boot. It looks for a bootable drive (connected to an EIDE, SATA, or SCSI controller), a bootable optical disc, a USB drive, a floppy disk, or a network connection—not necessarily in that order—and then stops if it cannot find the operating system. It then displays a message indicating "no bootable device" and waits for your instructions to continue.

✖ Warning

If your system is connected to a network and uses the network boot option, disconnect the network cable for this exercise to get the desired results. Be sure to plug the network cable back in when finished.

When the system is not able to find a disk (because you disabled the controller), it will probably hang for a long period of time and then return a Primary Hard Drive Failure code or error message. Some systems try to recognize that you have a hard drive regardless of the disabling of features, but this is rare.

Okay, so the system can't find your hard drive. You obviously know why—you turned off the controller!

Step 5 Reboot your system and enter the CMOS setup program by pressing the appropriate keystroke combination while your system boots. Navigate to the menu where you disabled all of the controllers and reenable them.

Step 6 Now that the controllers are enabled, go back to the autodetection utility and look for any drives connected.

If autodetection still does not see a hard drive, save your settings, reboot your system, and reenter the CMOS setup program. Then try it again.

Do you now see all of the storage devices that are installed in the system?

Step 7 While you're still in CMOS, navigate to the menu where all of the storage devices can be configured. Use this screen (sometimes there are multiple screens) to examine the device settings and answer the following questions:

Are there any devices listed as ATA/IDE devices (Primary Master, Primary Slave, Secondary Master, or Secondary Slave)? _____

Are there any SATA controllers present? If yes, are there any SATA devices installed on the system (SATA Port 0, SATA Port 1, and so on)? _____

Is the motherboard capable of implementing RAID? If yes, how is it currently configured?

Exit CMOS without saving changes and let the PC reboot.

Step 8 At this point, if you did everything as described and if you started with a known good hard drive containing a working operating system, the system will boot back into the operating system. Otherwise, you'll have to wait until you partition and format the drive to see if everything is working as it should (for example, if your instructor gave you, to use, a demo hard drive with nothing on it).

✔ **Cross-Reference**

For details about partitioning and formatting drives, refer to Chapter 12 in *Mike Meyers' CompTIA A+ Guide to Managing and Troubleshooting PCs.*

 30 MINUTES

Lab Exercise 11.04: Comparing Solid-State Drives and Magnetic Hard Drives

PATA and SATA hard disk drives store data magnetically and have moving parts, but solid-state drives (SSDs) store data on dynamic RAM (DRAM) or flash memory boards and have no moving parts. In other words, SSDs use *nonvolatile* memory—memory that retains data even when it's not powered on—to store data and emulate a hard drive. Most common uses of SSDs have been in what are called flash drives or thumb drives, but now PC users are installing SSDs as their primary storage in desktops and laptops. SSDs have no moving parts, which makes them tougher, quieter, and oftentimes faster than hard disks.

Learning Objectives

This lab explores the differences between solid-state drives and magnetic hard drives and is designed to help you recommend drives to clients as the need arises.

At the end of this lab, you'll be able to

- Explain solid-state drives
- Explain magnetic hard drives
- Discern which one will be best for your clients

Lab Materials and Setup

The materials you need for this lab are

- Access to a PC system and the Internet

- A solid-state drive and a magnetic hard drive

Getting Down to Business

It's so cool to see how technology has changed over the years and migrated to smaller, less noisy equipment. Heck, I remember when we used to have to park the heads to move a hard drive, and now we just pull them out and put them in our pocket—what will they think of next?

In this scenario, your boss is not convinced that SSDs are all that great, so your job is to explain to him why you think SSDs are better than magnetic hard drives.

Step 1 Search the Internet for "solid-state drives." Use manufacturer and retailer Web sites to find the information listed in the following table. Record your findings.

Maker	Cost	Capacity	Pros	Cons	Unique Features

Step 2 Now do the same thing for "hard drives" and note whether it's a PATA or SATA drive.

Maker	Cost	Capacity	Pros	Cons	Unique Features	PATA or SATA

Step 3   Now that you've compiled some hard facts about SSDs and magnetic hard drives, prepare (electronically) a proposal to your boss explaining why you think SSDs are superior to magnetic hard drives. Be prepared to share your proposal with the class.

 60 MINUTES

Lab Exercise 11.05: Exploring SCSI and RAID

As you inventory the machines that were just donated to your nonprofit organization, you discover two additional machines with small computer system interface (SCSI) controllers. You want to use them in a RAID array, but don't know much about either technology.

Learning Objectives

This lab touches on important tech skills, helping you research hardware so you can provide good information to clients. With the introduction of the SATA interface, the need for SCSI implementation on desktop machines is quickly fading. However, SCSI—which is well over 20 years old—is still used in large-capacity, data server environments.

At the end of this lab, you'll be able to

- Explain key features of SCSI
- Define the levels of RAID

Lab Materials and Setup

The materials you need for this lab are

- Access to a PC system and the Internet
- A trip to the local computer store for research
- A notepad and pen to take notes at the store

Getting Down to Business

Limber up your surfing fingers, as you'll start your search on the Internet. Then you might want to make a visit to the local computer store to explore further how the technologies of SCSI and RAID are being used in today's computing environments.

Step 1   Access the Internet and search for information on parallel SCSI devices, primarily hard drives. Use keywords such as *Ultra320, Ultra640, white paper, controllers,* and *storage solutions.* Then answer the following questions:

a.   What speed of data transfer can be achieved with parallel SCSI?

_____

b.   How many drives can be attached to a single controller?

_____

c.   What is the price range of parallel SCSI drives?

_____

d.   What is a SCSI chain?

_____

✔ **Cross-Reference**

For more information on SCSI, refer to the "SCSI: Still Around" section in Chapter 11 of *Mike Meyers' CompTIA A+ Guide to Managing and Troubleshooting PCs.*

Step 2   As you surfed around to the different sites on SCSI, you probably noticed that many of these drives are implemented in different RAID configurations. With the overall cost of hard drives dropping, many desktop motherboard manufacturers (ASUS, Gigabyte, Intel, and so on) are incorporating RAID controllers into their motherboards. Visit a few of the motherboard manufacturers' Web sites and research their implementation of RAID. Use the following questions to refine your focus.

✔ **Cross-Reference**

For more information on RAID, refer to the "Protecting Data with RAID," "RAID," and "Implementing RAID" sections in Chapter 11 of *Mike Meyers' CompTIA A+ Guide to Managing and Troubleshooting PCs.*

a.   What are the most popular implementations of RAID used on desktop machines?

_____

b.   How many drives are required to support the various RAID levels?

_____

    c.   Can you configure desktop RAID using both PATA and SATA drives?

        _____

    d.   What are the two goals when implementing a RAID solution?

        _____

        _____

Step 3   Gather the information you've found in your Internet research and head to your local computer store. Explore the current trends, based on the systems and components your local supplier is promoting. Write (on a separate sheet of paper) a brief summary of your findings and share it with your instructor and classmates.

 45 MINUTES

Lab Exercise 11.06: Troubleshooting Hard Drive Installations

The newest tech in your office has had trouble installing hard drives properly. In fact, he's tried it on four different machines with eight different drives and succeeded only once! You've been asked to troubleshoot his failed installations and patiently explain the proper installation process to him. What fun!

Learning Objectives

This lab walks you through the errors new techs typically make on hard drive installation, particularly with PATA drives. The lab also addresses the main problems with SATA drives—usually faulty hardware—and how to address this in the field.

At the end of this lab, you'll be able to

- Troubleshoot hard drive installation problems effectively
- Explain the proper installation techniques for PATA and SATA drives

Lab Materials and Setup

The materials you need for this lab are

- Access to a PC system with PATA and SATA interfaces
- At least one PATA or SATA hard drive (preferably two or more)

Getting Down to Business

It might seem odd to mess up a hard drive installation deliberately, but you can't hurt anything, so give it a whirl. Seeing how the PC responds to mistakes when you know specifically what's wrong can help you when you run into similar situations later in the field.

Step 1 You must have a properly functioning PC for this lab to be effective, so verify first that you have a system up and running with one or more hard drives installed.

Step 2 Power down the system. Disconnect the data cable for the hard drive used to boot the system, then power up the system. What happens? Will the PC autodetect the drive?

It is difficult to imagine not connecting the data cables to hard drives, but many times to add RAM or new devices, we have to disconnect the cables to gain access to the component. It is easy to miss reconnecting one of the cables after installing the new device.

Disconnecting the cable also simulates a broken IDE or SATA cable. These cables are somewhat delicate, and can fail after a sharp crease or a crimp from the system case. If you're having unexplained problems with your drive, check the cables prior to replacing the drive.

Step 3 Power down the PC and put the cable back on properly.

Step 4 On a PATA drive, change the jumper for the primary master hard drive to slave, and then power on the PC. What happens? Will the PC autodetect the drive? How should the jumper be installed?

Step 5 Power down the PC and put the jumper back on properly.

Step 6 Install a second PATA drive onto the primary controller, and set the jumpers on both drives incorrectly. Try variations: both as master; both as standalone; both as slave; both as cable select. Power on the PC and test each variation. What happens? Will the PC autodetect the drives? How should the jumpers be set for two PATA drives to work properly on the same controller?

 30 MINUTES

Lab Exercise 11.07: Installing Multiple Hard Drives in Preparation for RAID

Remember those two extra machines you discovered—the ones with the dual CPUs and the SCSI controllers? Well, each of them has eight 150-GB SCSI hard drives ready to be installed. You haven't had the opportunity to configure a RAID system before, so you ask a colleague for advice. She recommends that you install some additional drives in one of the workstations and then practice configuring RAID.

Learning Objectives

In this lab, you will install additional hard drives—PATA, SATA, or both—in an existing system. You will access CMOS to verify that all of the drives have been recognized by the system. You will then use your motherboard's RAID controller to configure a RAID array (or set the system aside to be used in Lab Exercise 12.05, "Implementing Software RAID 0 with Disk Management," in Chapter 12).

At the end of this lab, you'll be able to

- Install multiple hard drives in computer systems

- Verify multiple drives in CMOS

- Configure a hardware RAID array

Lab Materials and Setup

The materials you need for this lab are

- A working PC with PATA or SATA interfaces and Windows XP Professional, Windows Vista, or Windows 7 installed

- At least two additional (preferably three), system-compatible hard drives—PATA or SATA as appropriate

Getting Down to Business

Even though you haven't been reminded during the past few exercises, you know that you should always take the proper anti-static precautions when opening the system case and working with the delicate components inside. Take those precautions now, and get ready to install a few extra hard drives into your system. In this exercise, you'll make sure these drives are recognized by the system; in the next chapter's labs, you'll configure them.

✔ **Hint**

For many of the exercises in the next chapter, it is very important that you have a working system with either Windows XP Professional, Windows Vista, or Windows 7 installed. Obviously, you will need to keep the system partition and boot partition intact (usually these are the same partition, and are the first partition on the first hard drive of the system) with the operating system running. Even if you have available space on the first hard drive, it is much cleaner if you can install at least two additional hard drives. That way, you can partition, format, and convert to dynamic disks to your heart's content, without the worry of losing data (or the operating system).

Follow these steps to install an additional PATA drive.

Step 1 Determine on which controller, and in which order, you will be installing the drives.

Step 2 Set the jumpers properly for both the master and slave drives. (Usually, the boot device is the master drive on the primary controller, whereas the optical drive is the master drive on the secondary controller, so the new drive is likely to be a slave to one of those drives.)

Step 3 Physically install the second drive, connecting the power and data cables properly.

Follow these steps to install additional SATA drives.

Step 1 Determine which controller you will use for the first additional drive and connect the SATA data cable to the controller on the motherboard.

Step 2 Physically install the first additional drive and connect the SATA power and data cables to the new drive.

Step 3 Determine which controller you will use for the second additional drive and connect the SATA data cable to the controller on the motherboard.

Step 4 Physically install the second additional drive and connect the SATA power and data cables to the new drive.

Follow these steps to verify the drives in CMOS.

Step 1 After installing all of the hard drives, plug the power back in and boot the machine.

Step 2 Press the appropriate key(s) to enter CMOS setup, and navigate to the configuration screen for installed devices.

Step 3 Perform autodetection if required, and confirm that all of the installed devices are present. If any of the devices are missing (and you remembered to reboot the machine if your system requires it), power the machine down, disconnect the power, and double-check all of the cables and drive settings.

→ **Note**

Your motherboard must support RAID in order to complete the following section of this lab. Check your motherboard manual to ensure the motherboard can do RAID! If not, you'll still configure a software RAID setup in the next chapter.

Follow these steps to implement RAID.

Step 1   Enter the CMOS setup program and find where you can enable the RAID controller on your motherboard. Usually this is in the same place where you disable your PATA and SATA controllers. Save your configuration and exit.

Step 2   Watch the boot screens. A new screen should appear now that you have enabled RAID in CMOS. If the screens go by too fast, press the PAUSE/BREAK key to pause the screen during boot-up. To enter the RAID setup utility, press the key combination required by your motherboard, similar to the key you press to enter CMOS. Which button must you press to enter your RAID setup utility?

_____

Step 3   Once you are in the RAID setup utility, set up different styles of RAID that your motherboard supports. Every configuration screen is different. As in the CMOS setup program, each setting should have an explanation to help you figure out what to do. Because you are using hard drives with no important data (right?), feel free to experiment. Remove drives once you have set up a particular RAID, such as RAID 0, 1, or 5. What are the results?

_____

_____

_____

Step 4   Once you have completed the RAID configurations, return to the CMOS setup program and reset it to the original settings.

Lab Analysis Test

1.   Matthew has decided to use the RAID integrated into the SATA controller on his new system. He uses the system for high-end video editing, and would like to improve the performance of the system for this task. What implementation of RAID would you recommend to improve performance?

2.   In what situation(s) might it be appropriate to disable the motherboard's hard drive controllers?

3.   Brock, a new tech in your firm, informs you that the PC he's working on can't autodetect a hard drive he installed. He thinks the motherboard is broken. What's the more likely problem here?

4.   The second SATA hard drive on your company's server has just died. You have a replacement drive, but it's critical that the server remain up and functioning. What, if anything, can you do to resolve this problem and get the second drive replaced?

5. Sean would like to install four additional hard drives in his system. His motherboard has two IDE controllers and two SATA controllers. There is one SATA drive installed, and the optical drive is an IDE device. How would you configure Sean's system?

Key Term Quiz

Use the following terms to complete the following sentences. Not all terms will be used.

autodetect

cable select

master

PATA

platters

RAID

SATA

sectors

slave

SSD

1. A(n) _____ uses memory chips to store data and has none of the moving parts of traditional hard drives.

2. The data in a traditional hard disk drive is actually stored magnetically on disks called _____.

3. One type of IDE drive transfers data in a parallel fashion. The other type of IDE drive transfers data in a serial fashion. These two types are known as _____ and _____, respectively.

4. To secure data in servers and high-end PCs, use a(n) _____ controller.

5. A great way to determine whether a new drive is installed and configured correctly is to run _____.

Chapter **12**

Implementing Hard Drives

Lab Exercises

Once you've installed a new drive on a PC and it has been recognized by the system, you have two more steps to complete before you can start storing data: partitioning and formatting.

✔ Hint

The tasks of partitioning and formatting have really become automated into the installation of the operating system (and the tools included in the operating system). Many of the steps are now completed in sequence, blurring the line between partitioning and formatting. Make sure you're clear on the distinction between partitioning and formatting, because you must do them in the proper order. Partitioning the disk simply means defining physical sections that are used to store data. Formatting the disk means *configuring the partition* with a file system.

In the early days of DOS, Windows 3.x, and Windows 9x, your hard drive had to be partitioned and formatted before you could run the installation setup routine. Windows now incorporates these disk-preparation steps into the installation routine itself. However, it's still important for you to be able to perform these tasks from scratch as part of your basic PC tech repertoire.

You have a number of tools at your disposal for performing partitioning and formatting tasks. If you are working with a fresh hard drive, you need to get to these tools without necessarily having an operating system installed (this may be the first disk in the system, and you are preparing it for the OS installation). The first of these tools is the Windows installation media. A number of third-party utilities are available for partitioning and formatting, such as Avanquest's Partition Commander, EaseUS Partition Master, and the open source Linux tool Gnome Partition Editor, affectionately known as GParted. These specific tools are beyond the scope of the CompTIA A+ exams; however, a good tech should develop skills in the use of these tools. The second tool you'll explore in this chapter is a live CD of GParted.

Once you have an operating system up and running, you should have some type of partitioning and formatting tool that you can run from the GUI. Windows uses a tool known as the Disk Management utility. Disk Management enables you to create, modify, and format partitions. You can also format partitions from within My Computer/Computer on the Windows desktop.

After looking at how to create and format partitions using the Windows installation media and the live CD of GParted, you'll start up Windows to look at how to accomplish these tasks using the built-in tools. Next, you'll use the Disk Management utility to convert basic disks to dynamic disks and implement a RAID 0 stripe set. Then you'll look at the procedures for performing regular hard drive maintenance and troubleshooting tasks.

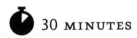 30 MINUTES

Lab Exercise 12.01: Creating and Formatting Partitions with the Windows XP and Vista/7 Installation Media

As you'll recall from the labs in Chapter 11, you have just worked with a number of donated machines, physically installing and configuring multiple hard drive technologies, primarily PATA and SATA hard drives. Once these drives have been recognized in CMOS, you are only halfway to your goal of using the drives for data storage. You must now partition each drive into usable space (even if only one partition uses all of the available drive space) and then format each partition with a file system.

In this lab, you will use the Windows installation media to partition and format hard drives in your system. You will be left with blank partitions, one of which needs an operating system. In the labs for Chapter 14 you will complete the process of installing the operating system.

✔ **Cross-Reference**

For details about partitioning and formatting drives with the Windows installation disc, refer to the "Partitioning During Windows XP Installation" and "Partitioning During Windows Vista/7 Installation" sections in Chapter 12 of *Mike Meyers' CompTIA A+ Guide to Managing and Troubleshooting PCs*.

Learning Objectives

In this exercise, you'll use the Windows installation media to partition a hard drive and format the partition for use.

At the end of this lab, you'll be able to

- Set up a primary partition on a hard drive

- Format the partition with the NTFS file system

Lab Materials and Setup

The materials you need for this lab are

- The PC from Lab Exercise 11.07 with a primary hard drive that holds your Windows OS, and the two blank hard drives that you can partition and format to your heart's content

- Optional: A system with one hard drive that you can safely erase

- The Windows XP or Vista/7 installation media

✖ Warning

Partitioning and formatting a hard drive destroys any data on it! Practice this lab using only drives that don't store any data you need.

Getting Down to Business

In this exercise, you'll start the system by booting from the Windows installation media (you will have to configure your system CMOS to boot from the optical drive or, if available, a USB device). You'll partition a portion of one of the hard drives and format it with the NTFS file system, as if you're preparing to install the operating system.

The instructions for Windows XP are first, followed immediately by the instructions for Windows Vista/7.

Step 1   Enter the CMOS setup program and configure the boot order, selecting the optical drive as the first boot device. Also make sure that the setting called "Boot Other Device" (or something similar) is enabled; otherwise, your system may not recognize the optical drive as a bootable drive.

Step 2   Place the Windows installation CD in the optical drive tray and boot the machine. Windows Setup copies a number of files and then presents you with the screen shown in Figure 12-1. Press ENTER to set up Windows now.

Step 3   Press F8 to accept the license agreement and enter the main partitioning screen.

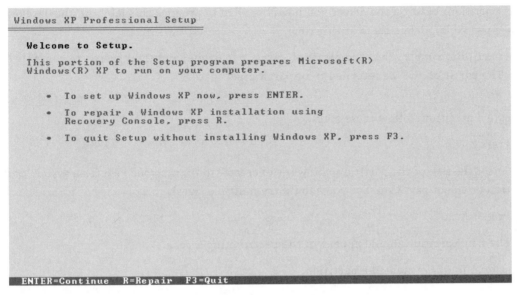

FIGURE 12-1 The first Windows XP Setup screen

✔ **Hint**

If you are using the machine configured in Lab Exercise 11.07, Windows XP has been installed on one of the drives in the system. Setup asks if you would like to repair this installation, and advises you to press ESC if you want to install a fresh copy. Press ESC to progress to the next step—partitioning the drive.

The screen displays the installed drives and any partitions and/or file systems that have been configured on the drives prior to this session (see Figure 12-2).

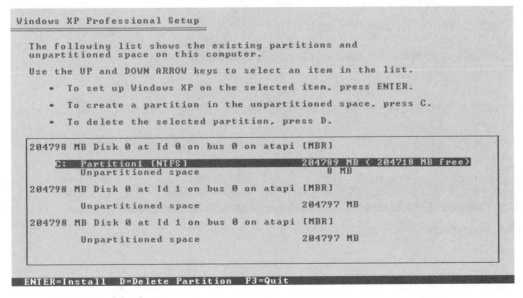

FIGURE 12-2 Partitioning screen

Step 4 If any partitions exist on the drives you have installed to practice this lab (and the data on these drives is expendable), delete them at this time.

To delete a partition, simply select the partition, press D to delete, and then press L to commit the delete process. The partition will be returned to unpartitioned space.

Step 5 To create a partition, follow these steps:

    a.   Press C.

    b.   Select the size of the partition you want to create (10 GB is a good size for a system partition or a boot partition, but you should try multiple sizes).

    c.   Press ENTER.

    d.   The new partition should appear in the partitioning screen.

Congratulations! You have created a partition.

Step 6 Press ENTER to see a list of file system options, as shown in Figure 12-3. Choose a file system (NTFS is the default) and indicate whether you will perform an exhaustive formatting process or the "Quick" formatting process.

Press ENTER. Windows formats the partition and proceeds with the operating system installation. You can shut down the PC once this step is completed.

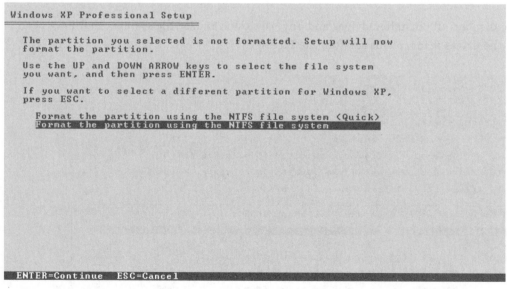

FIGURE 12-3 Format screen

Step 7   Reboot the machine and allow Windows to boot. Then use the Disk Management tool to verify the partition(s) you have created with the installation CD. Alternatively, you can verify the partitions you created and the file systems you configured when you use the GParted tool in the next lab.

Step 8   Practice deleting, creating, and formatting different combinations of partitions and file systems to become comfortable with the tools used in this exercise. Have fun!

Here are the same instructions, but for Windows Vista/7.

Step 1   Enter the CMOS setup program and configure the boot order, selecting the optical drive (or, if necessary, a USB device) as the first boot device. Also make sure that the setting called "Boot Other Device" (or something similar) is enabled; otherwise, your system may not recognize the optical drive as a bootable drive.

Step 2   Place the Windows installation media in the optical drive tray and boot the machine. Set your language and regional preferences on the first screen, and then click Next.

Step 3   Click the large Install Now button on the next page. Setup will then ask for a product key, but you do not need to enter one right now. Click Next to move on.

Step 4   Pick the edition of Vista/7 you wish to install. Your product key will only activate the edition that you purchased. Click Next to continue, and then agree to the license agreement on the next page.

Step 5   Click the Custom install button on the following screen. The screen displays the installed drives and any partitions and/or file systems that have been configured on the drives prior to this session (see Figure 12-4).

Step 6   If any partitions exist on the drives you have installed to practice this lab (and the data on these drives is expendable), delete them at this time.

To delete a partition, simply select the partition, click on *Drive options (advanced)*, and then click Delete. The partition will be returned to unpartitioned space.

Step 7   To create a partition, follow these steps:

    a.   Click the Drive options (advanced) button.

    b.   Click New.

    c.   In the Size field, type **50000** and click Apply to end up with a ~50-GB partition.

Step 8   Click the Format button. The installer will automatically set up an NTFS file system for the partition and proceed with the operating system installation.

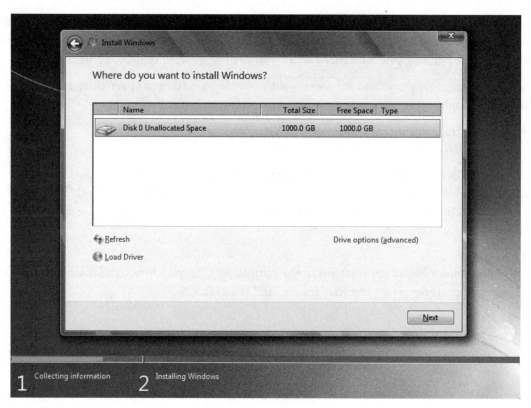

FIGURE 12-4 Where do you want to install Windows?

Step 9 Reboot the machine and allow Windows to boot. Then use the Disk Management tool to verify the partition(s) you have created with the installation disc. Alternatively, you can verify the partitions you created and the file systems you configured when you use the GParted tool in the next lab.

Step 10 Practice deleting, creating, and formatting different combinations of partitions and file systems to become comfortable with the tools used in this exercise. Enjoy!

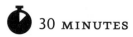 30 MINUTES

Lab Exercise 12.02: Creating and Formatting Partitions with Gnome Partition Editor (GParted)

As a competent tech, you want to keep up with the newest methods for accomplishing old tasks. Using the donated computers as an example, you might want to partition and format all of the machines before installing an operating system and deploying the machines to users. To accomplish this task, it might be easier to use a standalone partitioning/formatting tool such as the open source Gnome Partition Editor (GParted). Gnome is one of the many versions of the Linux operating system. GParted uses a basic, bootable version of Gnome with disk management tools built in. This method is somewhat beyond the scope of the CompTIA A+ exams, but the skills and techniques you will practice in this lab are valuable to a real-world tech, and can help you gain a deeper understanding of partitioning and formatting hard drives.

✔ **Tech Tip**

Many techs, and specifically techs employed by the IT departments of small to large businesses, often use one of the popular drive-imaging tools such as Symantec's Norton Ghost. Drive imaging is used to roll out the operating system and applications on multiple machines expediently. This method creates the partition, and copies the OS, applications, and user profiles onto the file system that was used to make the image, all in one step.

In this exercise, you will use the live CD of GParted to partition and format the two additional hard drives installed in your lab system. If you are working in a classroom setting, the instructor should be able to provide copies of the GParted live CD to you for this exercise. Alternatively, you could jump ahead to Lab Exercise 13.05, where you will create a live CD by burning a CD with an ISO image.

✔ **Cross-Reference**

For additional details about the GParted live CD, refer to the "Third-Party Partition Tools" section in Chapter 12 of *Mike Meyers' CompTIA A+ Guide to Managing and Troubleshooting PCs.*

Learning Objectives

In this exercise, you'll use the GParted live CD to partition a hard drive and format the partition for use.

At the end of this lab, you'll be able to

- Set up primary and extended partitions on hard drives
- Format the partitions with various file systems

Lab Materials and Setup

The materials you need for this lab are

- The PC from Lab Exercise 11.07 with a primary hard drive that holds your Windows OS, and the two blank hard drives that you can partition and format to your heart's content
- Optional: A system with one hard drive that you can safely erase
- A GParted live CD

✖ **Warning**

Partitioning and formatting a hard drive destroys any data on the drive! Practice this lab only on drives that don't store any data you need.

Getting Down to Business

In this exercise, you'll start the system by booting from the GParted live CD. (You will have to configure your system CMOS to boot from the CD.) You'll then partition a portion of one of the hard drives and format it with the file system of your choice.

Step 1   Enter the CMOS setup program and configure the boot order, selecting the optical drive as the first boot device. Also make sure that the setting called "Boot Other Device" (or something similar) is enabled; otherwise, your system may not recognize the optical drive as a bootable drive.

Step 2   Place the GParted live CD in the optical drive tray and boot the machine. GParted displays an introduction screen, as shown in Figure 12-5. Press ENTER to boot; Gnome Linux should begin to load. As the system loads, you will be queried a number of times for settings related to boot options, language,

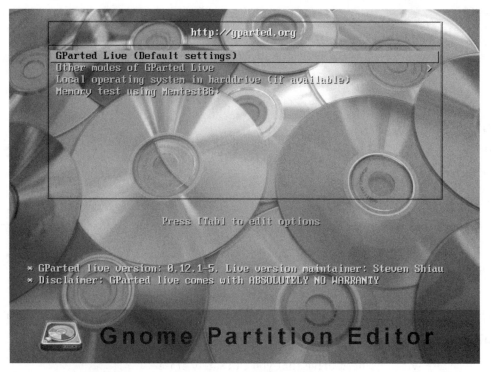

FIGURE 12-5 The Gnome Partition Editor initial screen

keyboard, and screen depth and resolution. Unless told to do otherwise by your instructor, select the defaults for these settings by highlighting OK and pressing ENTER.

GParted should finish booting and arrive at a screen displaying various menu items, icons, and the current drive focus with strange Linux names such as /dev/hda1, /dev/hda3, and so forth. Notice the item at the far right of the menu bar; here, you can click the drop-down arrow to select which physical drive the GParted screen is focused on (see Figure 12-6).

Step 3 Now change the focus to the second or third drive installed on your system. This will probably be labeled /dev/hdb or /dev/hdc in the drop-down list of hard drives.

✔ **Hint**

If you are using the machine that you configured in Lab Exercise 11.07, Windows has been installed on one of the drives in the system (most likely the first drive). When GParted first launches, the screen focus will be on this drive and the label will probably read /dev/hda1. Make sure that you select one of the drives that has been set up to be partitioned and formatted, or you'll find yourself reinstalling Windows.

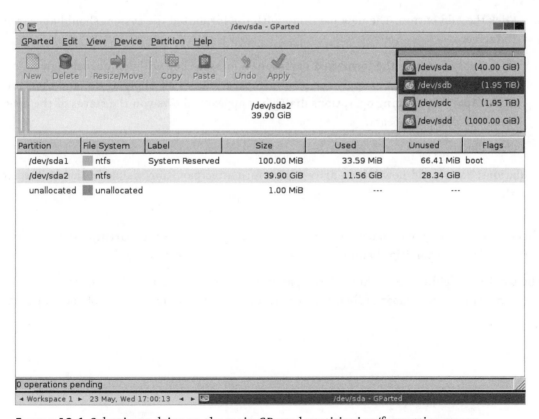

FIGURE 12-6 Selecting a drive on the main GParted partitioning/formatting screen

The screen now focuses on the drive you've selected and shows any partitions and/or file systems that have been configured on that drive prior to this session. If any partitions are displayed, highlight the partition, right-click, and select Delete.

Step 4   GParted requires that you commit any changes that you make to the partitions on the disk, so after deleting the partition, you must click the Apply button to apply the settings and actually delete the partition.

When you click Apply, GParted applies the pending operations. You should now have a drive visible with all of the available space denoted as unallocated space.

Step 5   Select the unallocated space, right-click, and select New. Then follow these steps:

    a.   Enter the size of the partition in megabytes; either type a number or use the up and down arrows to select a size. For the purposes of practice, 4000 MB (4 GB) to 10,000 MB (10 GB) is a good size for the partition.

    b.   Select Primary Partition or Extended Partition; primary is a good choice for the initial partition on the drive.

    c.   Select the NTFS file system.

    d.   Click the Add button. The new partition with the formatted file system should appear on the screen.

    e.   Click Apply to create the formatted partition. A message box will pop up, asking you to confirm that you want to apply the pending operations. Click Apply again, and then watch as the Applying pending operations dialog box appears, shows you the status of the operation, and then disappears.

    f.   Click Close.

Congratulations! You should now have a drive with a formatted partition visible in the main screen (see Figure 12-7).

Step 6   There is one last step, which depends on whether you plan to use this partition to boot the machine with an OS (active partition) and which file system you have selected.

With the partition highlighted, right-click the partition and select Manage Flags. A small window appears in which you'll see a number of flags that you can set (see Figure 12-8). Many of these apply to

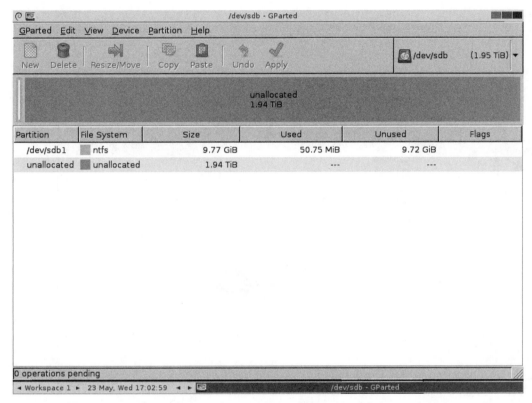

FIGURE 12-7 The GParted screen with a newly partitioned and formatted drive

operating systems other than Windows, but one of them must be set if you are to use the partition in Windows: boot. This flag must be set if the partition is to be the active partition in the system (this is usually the first partition on the first hard drive in the system).

Set the appropriate flags for your partition and file system and close the Manage flags window. Notice that you will not have to apply changes, as the settings take effect immediately.

Step 7   Reboot the machine and allow Windows to boot. You can then use Disk Management to verify the partition(s) you have created with GParted.

Step 8   Practice deleting, creating, and formatting different combinations of partitions and file systems to become comfortable with the GParted program.

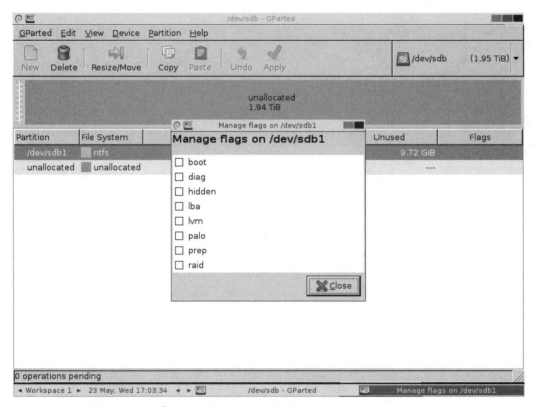

FIGURE 12-8 The Manage flags window in GParted

 30 MINUTES

Lab Exercise 12.03: Using Windows Tools to Create and Format Partitions

Once you have all of the donated machines' drives configured, partitioned, and formatted, and you've installed Windows, working with hard drive storage becomes much more intuitive. Windows includes tools that let you create, modify, and format partitions "on the fly" from within Windows. One of these utilities is called Disk Management.

✔ **Cross-Reference**

For details about creating and formatting partitions using Disk Management, refer to the "Disk Management" section in Chapter 12 of *Mike Meyers' CompTIA A+ Guide to Managing and Troubleshooting PCs.*

This lab exercise assumes that you want to create a partition on the second or third hard drive installed on the Windows lab system and then format that partition with a file system. Disk Management will enable you to format the partition right away; however, you can also use another Windows utility that you should be intimately familiar with by now: My Computer/Computer. Follow the steps in this lab exercise to create and format a new partition.

✔ Hint

Each version of Windows can read from and write to the FAT16, FAT32, and NTFS file systems. However, only Windows XP can be installed to a FAT16 or FAT32 partition—Windows Vista/7 must be installed on an NTFS partition.

Learning Objectives

In this exercise, you'll use the Disk Management program to partition a hard drive and format the partition with a file system.

At the end of this lab, you'll be able to

- Set up a primary, active partition on a hard drive

- Set up an extended partition and logical drives in that partition

- Format partitions with various file systems

Lab Materials and Setup

The materials you need for this lab are

- The PC from Lab Exercise 11.07, with a primary hard drive that holds your Windows installation and the two blank hard drives that you can partition and format

---

✖ Warning

Partitioning a hard drive destroys any data on it! Practice this lab only on drives that don't contain any data you need.

Getting Down to Business

The steps for partitioning drives and formatting partitions in each version of Windows are very similar.

Step 1   Right-click the My Computer/Computer icon and select Manage to open a Computer Management window. Under the Storage node, click Disk Management.

Step 2   As in prior lab exercises, if there are any existing partitions on the second or third drive, highlight the partitions and either right-click and delete the partitions or simply press DELETE.

Step 3   Start the process of creating a partition by right-clicking an unpartitioned section of drive space and, in Windows XP, selecting New Partition (see Figure 12-9). In Vista/7, select New Simple Volume. This will start the New Partition Wizard or the New Simple Volume Wizard, depending on the OS.

Step 4   Click Next, and, in Windows XP, select Primary Partition (in Windows Vista/7, you will not have to select Primary Partition). At the next screen, enter the size of your new partition in megabytes.

Step 5   You can now assign a drive letter or mount the partition to an empty folder. For now, go with the default drive letter assignment and click Next again.

Step 6   The next screen offers you the option to format the new partition with a file system. Select a file system: FAT, FAT32, or NTFS. (Note that Windows will not allow Disk Management to create a FAT16 partition larger than 4 GB or a FAT32 partition larger than 32 GB.) Then enter a volume label if you want and click OK. Figure 12-10 shows this selection screen in the Disk Management utility.

Step 7   The utility warns you that formatting will erase all data on the drive. Click OK to begin formatting.

Step 8   You can also format partitions in My Computer/Computer, but generally speaking you'll use this method only to format removable media, such as USB thumb drives.

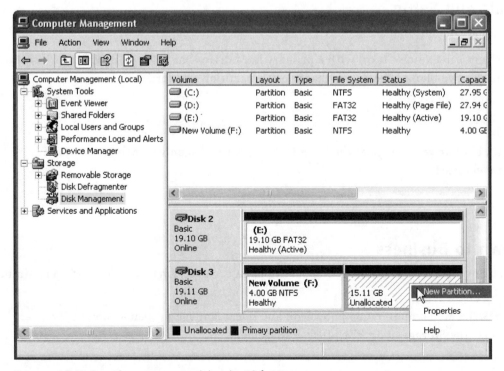

FIGURE 12-9   Creating a new partition in Disk Management

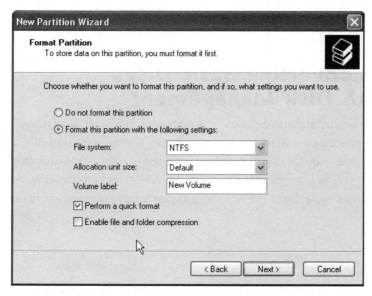

FIGURE 12-10 Formatting a partition in Disk Management

Right-click a drive icon in My Computer/Computer and select Format to open the Format dialog box (see Figure 12-11). Now proceed as in Step 6.

Step 9 Practice deleting, creating, and formatting different combinations of partitions and file systems to become comfortable with the Disk Management utility.

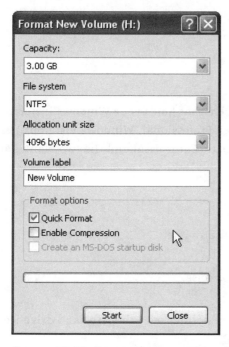

FIGURE 12-11 Formatting a partition in My Computer

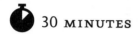 30 MINUTES

Lab Exercise 12.04: Converting Basic Disks to Dynamic Disks with Disk Management

In Lab Exercise 11.07, you configured two additional hard drives in a system to facilitate a software implementation of RAID. Windows XP Professional, Windows Vista Business/Ultimate/Enterprise, and Windows 7 Professional/Ultimate/Enterprise require that a disk be converted to a dynamic disk to allow the implementation of RAID. In this lab, you will prepare the two additional drives to be used in the next lab exercise by using Disk Management to perform the simple, nondestructive conversion from basic disks to dynamic disks.

✔ Cross-Reference

To learn more about dynamic disks, refer to the "Dynamic Disks" section in Chapter 12 of *Mike Meyers' CompTIA A+ Guide to Managing and Troubleshooting PCs*.

Learning Objectives

In this exercise, you'll use the Disk Management utility to convert basic disks to dynamic disks.

At the end of this lab, you'll be able to

- Convert basic disks to dynamic disks

Lab Materials and Setup

The materials you need for this lab are

- The PC from Lab Exercise 11.07 with a primary hard drive that holds your Windows installation (converting to dynamic disks requires Windows XP Professional, Windows Vista Business/ Ultimate/Enterprise, or Windows 7 Professional/Ultimate/Enterprise) and the two blank hard drives that you will convert to dynamic disks

Getting Down to Business

The steps to convert a basic disk to a dynamic disk are really quite simple.

Step 1 Open the Disk Management utility as in the previous exercise.

Step 2 Select the first drive to be converted. Position the mouse pointer over the left-hand drive icon, right-click, and select Convert to Dynamic Disk (see Figure 12-12).

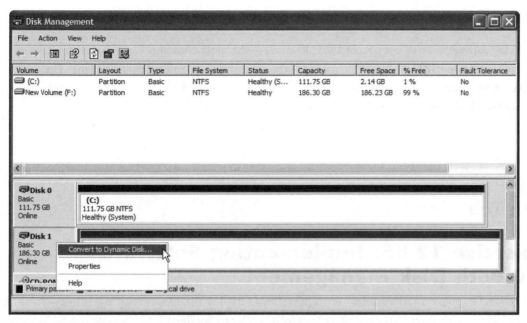

FIGURE 12-12 Selecting Convert to Dynamic Disk in the Disk Management utility

Step 3 Follow the wizard's instructions to complete the dynamic disk conversion. Reboot the PC (if necessary) and then open Disk Management again. The disk should now be labeled as a dynamic disk instead of a basic disk (see Figure 12-13).

Step 4 Repeat Steps 2 and 3 on the third drive in the system (you will need two dynamic disks to implement a RAID 0 stripe set), and then proceed to Lab Exercise 12.05.

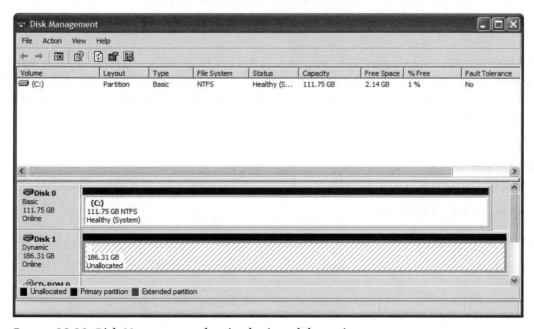

FIGURE 12-13 Disk Management showing basic and dynamic storage

> **→ Note**
>
> You can also convert master boot record (MBR) disks—the most common basic disk format—to GUID partition table (GPT) disks. GPT supports larger hard drives and more partitions. The instructions are identical to converting a basic disk to a dynamic disk, except that you select Convert to GPT Disk from the hard drive's context menu instead.

 30 MINUTES

Lab Exercise 12.05: Implementing Software RAID 0 with Disk Management

It's finally time to flex your RAID muscles in preparation to deploy the two server machines—remember, these are the systems with dual CPUs and SCSI controllers. (Many modern RAID setups use SATA instead of SCSI, but you'll probably find both in the field.) Windows XP Professional, Windows Vista Business/Ultimate/Enterprise, and Windows 7 Professional/Ultimate/Enterprise allow you to configure software RAID implementations using Disk Management and multiple hard drives. At the end of this lab, you will have configured a stripe set using two disks.

> **✔ Cross-Reference**
>
> Additional information on RAID 0, 1, and 5 may be found in the "Dynamic Disks" section in Chapter 12 of *Mike Meyers' CompTIA A+ Guide to Managing and Troubleshooting PCs*.

This lab exercise guides you through the creation of a RAID 0 stripe set using free, unpartitioned space on the second and third hard drives installed on the Windows lab system. These are the same disks that you converted from basic disks to dynamic disks in the prior exercise. Disk Management allows you to configure simple volumes, spanned volumes, and striped volumes on dynamic disks.

Learning Objectives

In this exercise, you'll use the Disk Management program to configure a RAID 0 striped volume.

At the end of this lab, you'll be able to

- Create and configure a RAID 0 striped volume

Lab Materials and Setup

The materials you need for this lab are

- The PC from Lab Exercise 11.07 with a primary hard drive that holds your Windows installation (Windows XP Professional, Windows Vista Business/Ultimate/Enterprise, or Windows 7 Professional/Ultimate/Enterprise) and the two blank hard drives that have been converted to dynamic disks

✖ Warning

Partitioning a hard drive destroys any data on the drive! Practice this lab only on drives that don't contain any data you need.

Getting Down to Business

You're in the home stretch now! Once you've worked with the Disk Management tool and converted basic disks to dynamic disks, it's just a matter of using the Disk Management New Volume Wizard, choosing the size allocated to the striped volume, and formatting the striped volume.

Step 1 Launch the Disk Management utility and right-click the unallocated space on the first disk of the planned striped volume. Select New Volume and then select Striped (see Figure 12-14).

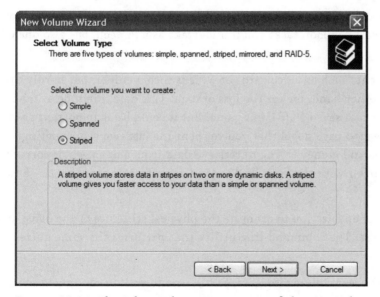

Figure 12-14 The Select Volume Type screen of the New Volume Wizard

Step 2 The wizard asks you to select at least one additional dynamic disk for the striped volume. You will then select the size of the volume you want to create and decide what file system to use to format the striped volume.

Are there any restrictions on the size of the volume? _____

Step 3 Disk Management now allocates the space on the drives and formats them with the file system you've selected. You should now have a healthy, formatted, striped volume.

Step 4 Practice deleting and creating various sizes of striped volumes using various file systems. Can you format a striped volume with FAT? Why or why not?

_____

_____

 60 MINUTES

Lab Exercise 12.06: Maintaining and Troubleshooting Hard Drives

Of all the devices installed in a PC, hard drives tend to need the most attention. Maintaining and troubleshooting hard drives is one of the most common tasks you'll undertake as a PC tech, but also one of the most important.

After all, the loss of other components such as video cards or NICs is inconvenient, but hardly disastrous. The loss of a hard drive, on the other hand, means the loss of data. This data might be as trivial as your favorite bookmarked Web pages or a saved Half-Life 2 game. But it could be as important as your business records, family photos, or the 1200-page novel that you've spent the last two years writing! Unless you want to spend valuable time and money trying to retrieve data from a damaged or corrupted hard drive, you should familiarize yourself with the built-in Windows drive maintenance tools. These tools include

- **Error-checking** This GUI tool enables you to examine the physical structure of the drive and retrieve data from bad clusters. The command-line utility that performs the same duties is called chkdsk.

- **Disk Defragmenter** This tool reorganizes disorganized file structures into contiguous clusters.

- **Disk Cleanup** This tool reclaims wasted space on the hard drive by deleting unneeded files and compressing files that are rarely accessed.

Learning Objectives

At the end of this lab, you'll be able to

- Use error-checking to scan for and fix physical errors on the hard drive
- Use the Disk Defragmenter utility to reorganize the hard drive's file structure
- Use the Disk Cleanup utility to reclaim wasted disk space

Lab Materials and Setup

The materials you need for this lab are

- A fully functioning Windows PC

Getting Down to Business

Performing regular maintenance on your hard drives can keep them running more smoothly and efficiently. If you're getting obvious disk-related errors (such as error messages indicating that your disk has bad clusters or cannot be read), or if files are missing or corrupt, a tune-up is in order. Another sign that your drive needs maintenance is excessive disk activity, or disk "thrashing." It's also a good idea to do some maintenance after a serious system crash or virus infection by scanning your drive for damage or fragmentation.

✔ **Tech Tip**

In a computer system, the hard drive wins the prize as the most critical storage device and for having the most moving parts of any of the components. For this reason, it is extremely important that you not only perform routine preventive maintenance (error-checking, defragmentation, and disk cleanup), but also regularly back up critical data.

Step 1 To scan a hard drive for physical problems, open My Computer/Computer and right-click the drive's icon. Select Properties, and then select the Tools tab, shown in Figure 12-15. Click Check Now to start the Error-checking utility.

In the Check Disk dialog box, you can opt to fix file system errors automatically, scan for and attempt to recover bad sectors, or both. When you've made your selections, click Start.

✔ **Hint**

The Error-checking utility must have *exclusive* access to the drive to finish scanning it. If you have services or applications running in the background, the utility will halt. In most cases, the utility will ask you if you want to check the hard disk for errors the next time you start your computer.

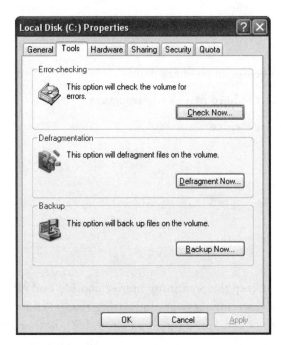

FIGURE 12-15 Disk Properties Tools tab

Step 2 To launch Disk Defragmenter, click Defragment Now on the Tools tab. The Windows XP version of Disk Defragmenter is shown in Figure 12-16.

Disk Defragmenter offers you a choice: You can click Analyze to examine the disk to see if a defragmenting operation is needed, or simply click Defragment to start the process without first analyzing the drive.

Step 3 Click the General tab, and then click Disk Cleanup. Disk Cleanup calculates the space you'll be able to free up, and then displays the Disk Cleanup dialog box, shown in Figure 12-17.

Near the top of the dialog box you can see how much disk space (maximum) you could free up using Disk Cleanup. But look carefully! Depending on which categories in the *Files to delete* list are checked, the actual amount of disk space you'll gain could be much smaller than the estimate at the top. As you select and deselect choices, watch this value change. Disk Cleanup can remove Recycle Bin files and temporary Internet files, and can also compress old files.

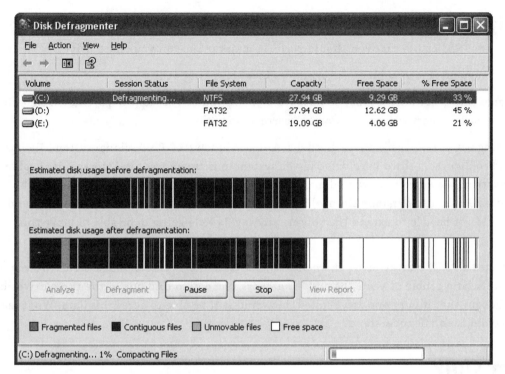

FIGURE 12-16 Disk Defragmenter

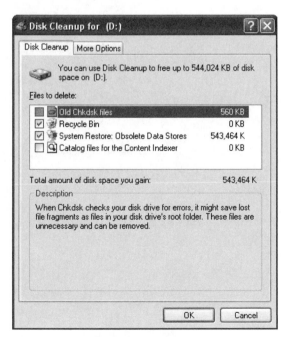

FIGURE 12-17 Disk Cleanup

Lab Analysis Test

1. Name at least two indicators that you should perform maintenance on your hard drive.

2. What is the command-line version of the Windows Error-checking utility?

3. Amanda argues that a hard drive must be formatted before you can set up the partitions. Samantha says the drive must be partitioned first. Who is correct, and why?

4. Kyle is running out of disk space on his hard drive on a Windows XP Professional system. He has installed and configured a third hard drive in the system to increase the total storage. He is planning on converting his current drive to dynamic storage and extending the storage space to the newly installed drive (also dynamic storage). Pablo argues that the conversion is destructive and that Kyle would not be able to extend the volume anyway. Is Kyle going to be able to make this work?

5. Sean has created a RAID 0 array using three drives on a Windows 7 Professional system. After running the system for a couple of years, he arrived at work one day to find one of the three drives had failed. He thought that if only one drive failed, he would still be able to access his data. What facts about RAID 0 did Sean misunderstand?

Key Term Quiz

Use the following terms to complete the following sentences. Not all terms will be used.

basic disk

chkdsk

defragmentation

Disk Cleanup

Disk Management

dynamic disk

Error-checking

format

GParted

partition

volumes

Windows installation media

1. To partition and format a hard drive when no operating system has been installed, you may use either _____ or _____ to boot the system and run disk setup utilities.

2. Use a(n) _____ tool to fix noncontiguous file clusters on a hard drive.

3. The _____ tool enables you to partition and format drives in Windows.

4. Microsoft supports two types of storage configurations now; the _____ uses partitions, whereas the _____ uses _____.

5. If your hard drive is running out of free space, you should use the _____ utility.

Chapter 13

Removable Media

Lab Exercises

Removable media storage is one of the fastest-changing components of the PC, and these days it's also very much in the public eye. With the advent of USB thumb drives, iPods, and digital cameras using CompactFlash and Secure Digital memory cards, all kinds of people—from children to great-grandmothers, from artists to zookeepers—are using removable storage. With the high resolution of today's audio and video files, photographs, and games, the need for portable large-capacity storage is greater than ever.

The lowly floppy drive has the distinction of being the only component of a "modern" PC to employ basically the same technology as the original IBM PC. It's hard to believe, but when the first PCs came out, the entire data storage system consisted of a single floppy drive and multiple floppy disks holding a little more than 300,000 bytes of data each! Floppy drives (and disks) have been around ever since, but with the recent advances in storage technology, the floppy has finally entered its twilight, due mostly to its tiny capacity.

Technicians were the last holdout in keeping floppy drives around. Although hard drives can contain trillions of bytes of data, they can also fail; until recently, techs could still depend on the floppy drive, and a disk that can hold less than 2 MB of data, to boot a failed system and provide troubleshooting utilities that might breathe life back into the PC. While techs still need these tools, they now come in the form of bootable CDs, DVDs, and USB thumb drives.

As a budding tech, you'll work with all types of removable media. The labs in this chapter will introduce you to the installation, configuration, and use of optical drives, burners, and media. You'll work with thumb drives and even learn to install the venerable floppy drive—this is important because the CompTIA A+ 220-801 exam thinks you should still know how to deal with floppy drives. The final lab in the chapter looks at some troubleshooting techniques for removable media.

 30 MINUTES

Lab Exercise 13.01: Installing Floppy Drives

Your boss recently approved the purchase of a number of new workstations, all without floppy drives. "Times are changing," he explained, "and floppies just hold too little data. Plus they're slow and cumbersome!" But the employees assigned to the new machines complained so much that the boss has decided to retrofit all the new workstations with 3.5-inch floppy drives. Some manufacturers offer external USB 3.5-inch floppy drives, but you found a supply house closeout on old, internal floppy drives. You've been assigned the task of installing them into each system.

✔ **Cross-Reference**

To review the details of floppy drive installation, refer to the "Installing Floppy Drives" section in Chapter 13 of *Mike Meyers' CompTIA A+ Guide to Managing and Troubleshooting PCs*.

Learning Objectives

In this lab, you'll practice removing and installing a floppy drive.

At the end of this lab, you'll be able to

- Remove a floppy drive safely and correctly

- Install a floppy drive safely and correctly

Lab Materials and Setup

The materials you need for this lab are

- A working computer system with a floppy drive installed

- A known good floppy disk with data

Getting Down to Business

Although this lab starts with a working floppy drive installed in a PC—a likely scenario in a classroom setting—you would obviously need to install one yourself when building a system.

Step 1 Begin with the PC turned on and the standard Windows desktop displayed. To verify that the floppy drive works, insert a known good floppy disk containing files into the drive, and then view the files on it by following these steps:

    a. Double-click the My Computer/Computer icon on the desktop.

    b. Double-click the 3½ Floppy Disk Drive (A:) icon in the window (see Figure 13-1).

    c. Observe the files and folders displayed.

        Do you see files displayed? _____

✔ **Hint**

If no files are displayed, try another floppy disk. Also, be sure to insert the disk properly. You should hear a ratcheting sound when you double-click the floppy drive icon. This is the sound of the read mechanism opening the metal cover so that it can read the data on the disk.

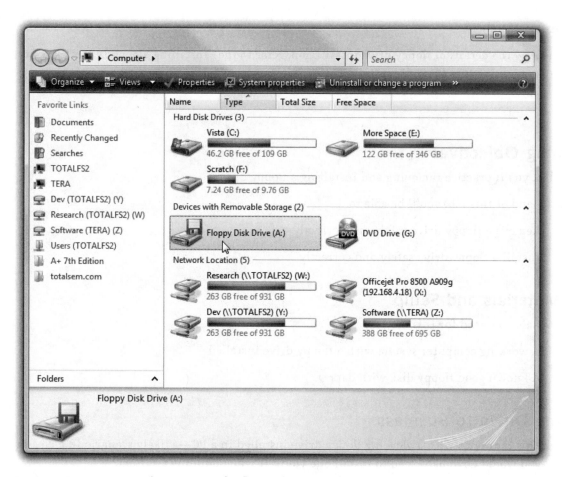

FIGURE 13-1 Accessing the contents of a floppy disk in Windows Vista

Step 2 Properly shut down the system, unplug the main power cable, and open the case following good ESD procedures.

Step 3 Carefully disconnect the two cables from the back of the floppy drive. One is the four-wire cable from the power supply (with its mini power connector), and the other is the flat ribbon cable that carries the data to and from the drive.

✖ Warning

Be sure to notice the seven-wire twist in the ribbon cable before you disconnect it. Is the twist closer to the drive or to the motherboard? If you put this cable back on incorrectly, the floppy drive will not work. The end with the twist (see Figure 13-2) always goes closest to the floppy drive.

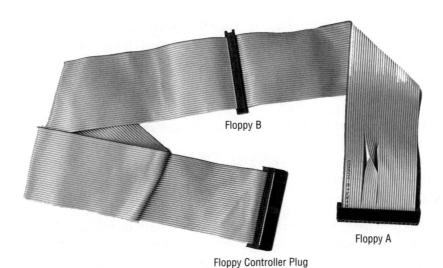

Floppy B

Floppy A

Floppy Controller Plug

FIGURE 13-2 The twist in one end of the floppy drive ribbon cable

---

✔ **Hint**

If your lab uses rounded data cables rather than the traditional flat ribbon cables, you can safely assume that one of the connectors will have a marking for the A: drive.

Now disconnect the other end of the ribbon cable from the motherboard. These cables can be quite firmly attached to the motherboard, so use caution! Grab the connector (or grab as close to the connector as you can) and pull straight up firmly but gently. Sometimes a connector will seem to stick on one side—make sure that you don't pull unevenly, or you may bend the pins on the motherboard.

a. How many wires make up the ribbon cable? (Go ahead, count 'em!)

_____

b. Is one of the wires a different color from the rest, and if so, what does that mean?

_____

c. Look at the motherboard where the cable was attached, and examine the pins. How many pins do you count?

_____

d. Look at the shape of the connection. Is it symmetrical, meaning you can plug the connector in either direction, or is one side of the connector keyed to prevent you from inserting it backward?

_____

Locate pin 1 (where the colored wire attaches) and pin 34. The thirty-fourth pin is the drive change signal/disk change signal. It indicates when a disk has been physically changed. If this wire is broken or not connected, the system will read the initial disk placed in the floppy drive after power is applied and remember the contents for that disk, no matter how many times you change disks during a session, until you reboot the system.

Compare your motherboard connection for the floppy drive with the one shown in Figure 13-3.

Step 4 Remove the floppy drive from the case. There are so many different ways that floppy drives are held into system cases that it would be impossible to list all of the various carriers, caddies, bays, and so on, that might be used to hold your floppy drive.

Almost all floppy drives are secured to these carriers, caddies, and bays with fine-threaded screws. The threads on these screws are narrower than those on the screws commonly used to secure expansion cards and the case cover. There should be two screws in each side of the floppy drive for support.

✔ **Hint**

Get in the habit of storing screws safely while you're changing out or inspecting hardware. You can use a small plastic bowl, a coffee cup, or an empty baby food jar or breath mint tin—but if you let those screws roll around loose, you may not have enough of them the next time you need to install a device!

Step 5 Now that you've removed the floppy drive, give it a thorough inspection. Look at the area where the cables connect (see Figure 13-4).

a. Is this ribbon cable area keyed or notched? _____

b. Find the indicator for the location of pin 1 on the floppy drive. What and where is it?

_____

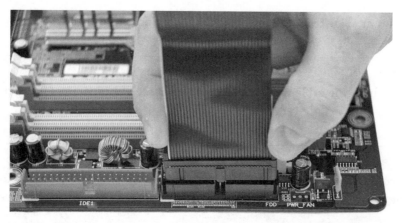

FIGURE 13-3 The orientation of the floppy drive connector on the motherboard

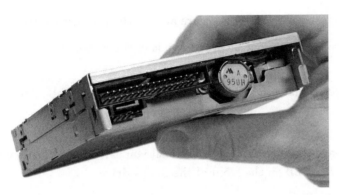

FIGURE 13-4 Examining the connections for the ribbon cable (top) and power cable
(bottom) on the back of a floppy drive

c. On which side of the connector does the red (or other colored) orientation stripe of the cable
    go—toward the center or toward the outside?

    _____

d. How many physical pins are on your floppy drive? _____

e. Look at the area where the power is attached. How many pins are there? _____

f. Take a moment to experiment to see if you can insert the power connector into the floppy
    drive incorrectly. Be gentle!

g. Can you connect it upside down? _____

h. Can you connect it without covering every pin? _____

i. On which side of the mini connector does the orientation stripe go: toward the center or
    toward the outside?

    _____

✖ **Warning**

It is possible to force the power connector on incorrectly, which will cause damage to the drive.
Practice how it feels to make this connection properly and improperly, so that when you do it
from an odd angle (for example, lying on your back under a desk), you know how it should feel.

Step 6 Reinstall the floppy drive by placing it back where you found it in the case. Be sure to use the
proper fine-threaded screws to secure the drive.

Now attach a mini connector to the floppy drive to provide power, and attach the 34-pin ribbon
cable securely to the drive.

Attach the ribbon cable to the motherboard. Make sure it is secure and all the pins are covered.

a.   Did you make sure that pin 1 was connected properly at both ends of the ribbon cable?

_____

b.   Are the connectors properly aligned so that pin 34 is connected on both ends of the cable?

_____

Step 7   Once everything is back in place, leave the system cover off so that you can make adjustments if needed. Start the system and watch the green LED on the front of the floppy drive.

If the green LED does not turn on at all during the boot process, then check your power connection.

If the green LED comes on and stays on all the time, then the ribbon cable is not connected properly (it is probably reversed either on the motherboard or on the floppy drive).

Is everything working properly? _____

After you confirm that everything is working, place the cover back onto your system. Start Windows and test your floppy drive as you did in Step 1 of this lab.

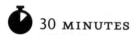 30 MINUTES

Lab Exercise 13.02: Installing Optical Drives

Your supervisor calls you in one day and announces that he wants to simplify the daily database backup procedures for your company. You will still use tape backups for archival backups, but he wants all the CD-R/RW drives on your company's servers replaced with DVD-R/RW drives. The increased storage capacity of this type of drive will enable you to back up onto a single disc most of the critical files that change during the day. To accomplish this task, you must physically uninstall all the existing CD-R/RW drives and replace them with DVD-R/RW equivalents.

You should be comfortable removing and installing optical drives. Many optical drives still use the PATA interface to connect to your system, making the installation process fairly simple. If you are lucky enough to be working with a newer system, you will probably uninstall and install SATA optical drives. The CompTIA A+ exams assume you know how to install both PATA and SATA optical drives!

Learning Objectives

In this lab, you'll remove and inspect an optical drive, and then reinstall the drive.

At the end of this lab, you'll be able to

- Remove and install an optical drive safely and properly

- Identify the physical features of an optical drive

Lab Materials and Setup

The materials you need for this lab are

- A working computer with Windows and an optical drive of some type installed (what type you use doesn't matter, but it's helpful if you have both a PATA and a SATA drive)

Getting Down to Business

Removing an optical drive is almost too easy. The only real secret here is to remember which cable you removed and how the cable ends were oriented—you've got to make sure you can put it back! Also, PATA optical drives use the standard master/slave jumpers—these also need to be inspected to make sure that the drive runs properly on the PATA connection. For a quick look at jumper settings check out the PDF file at www.wdc.com/en/library/eide/2579-001037.pdf.

Step 1 Properly shut down your system. As I've mentioned before, there are so many different ways that drives are held into system cases that it would be impossible to list all of the various carriers, caddies, bays, and so on, that might be used to hold your drive. Using whichever method is appropriate, remove the cover from the PC case so that you can access the screws on both sides of the drive. Using proper ESD procedures, perform the following steps to remove the drive from your system:

   a. Unplug the connections. First unplug the Molex or SATA power connection from the back of the drive, and then disconnect the PATA ribbon cable or SATA cable from the drive. Unplug the audio cable coming from the sound card (if present) that plugs into the back of the drive.

   b. Using a Philips-head screwdriver, remove the screws holding the drive in place. Notice that the screws are small-threaded screws—the same type you encountered when you removed and installed your floppy drive.

✔ **Hint**

Some optical drives are held in their bays by rails. Simply squeeze the rail toggles (sticking out of the front) and remove the drive by pulling it forward.

Step 2 Inspect the optical drive. Look at the front of the drive. Do you see a tiny hole near the edge of the tray door? Most drives have such a hole. You can take a straightened-out paper clip and push it into this hole to release the tray. This is handy in case you accidentally leave a disc in the drive when you remove it from the system. Go ahead and push a straightened-out paper clip into the hole to eject the tray.

Look at the back of the drive. You should see several areas for connections:

- The Molex or SATA power connection

- The connection for the PATA or SATA cable

- An audio connection for a cable to the sound card (there may be more than one connector because of different styles of cables, but only one cable should be connected)

- Jumper settings: master, slave, and cable select (PATA only)

✔ **Hint**

On PATA drives, look for the orientation of pin 1. It is usually closest to the power connection.

Step 3   Reinstall the optical drive into your system. It can be a master drive or a slave drive, depending on what other PATA devices are installed. Figure 13-5 shows a properly installed drive.

Now answer these questions:

a.   Did you fasten the drive using the correct screws? _____

b.   Is the master/slave jumper set correctly? _____

c.   Is the PATA/SATA cable connected properly? _____

d.   Is the power plug fully inserted? _____

e.   Is the audio cable connected to the drive? _____

Step 4   Leave the cover off the system and boot the PC to the Windows desktop.

Step 5   Select My Computer/Computer. Notice if the drive's icon is present. If so, all is well. If not, repeat Steps 2 and 3. The most common problem when installing hardware is a loose connection, so recheck your cable ends and try again. Replace the PC cover once the drive is recognized in Windows.

FIGURE 13-5 Viewing a properly installed optical drive

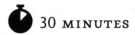 30 MINUTES

Lab Exercise 13.03: Working with USB Thumb Drives

Your company is finally being forced to provide larger-capacity removable storage for all of the sales organization staff. In the not-so-distant past, PowerPoint presentations were moved from machine to machine via floppy disks, and then via CD-Rs. With the ease of use and convenient size of USB thumb drives, all sales personnel will now be issued 4-GB thumb drives. Your mission (should you choose to accept it) is to teach the field sales personnel how to properly use their new thumb drives.

✔ **Cross-Reference**

For a primer on USB flash memory drives (often called thumb drives), see the "USB Thumb Drives" section in Chapter 13 of *Mike Meyers' CompTIA A+ Guide to Managing and Troubleshooting PCs*.

Learning Objectives

In this lab, you'll learn to insert, use, and safely remove USB thumb drives.

At the end of this lab, you'll be able to

- Insert and remove USB thumb drives

- Save and transfer data using USB thumb drives

Lab Materials and Setup

The materials you need for this lab are

- A Windows PC

- A USB thumb drive

Getting Down to Business

In Lab Exercise 13.01, you physically removed and reinstalled a floppy drive, but as you are aware, this technology is quickly being retired. This lab exercise uses the newest technology to replace the function and ease of the floppy disk, the USB flash drive (thumb drive). You will use a USB thumb drive to transfer a large file by inserting the drive into a Windows system, copying some data onto it, removing it, and reinserting it into a new system (or the same lab machine) and transferring the data to the new machine.

Step 1 USB thumb drives come in many shapes and colors, as well as many data capacities. An older thumb drive might be as small as 256 MB, while a newer thumb drive might be as large as 256 GB. They are typically a few inches long, and most provide protection for the USB connector using either a cover of some type or a retractable mechanism as shown in Figure 13-6.

    a.   Boot your lab system and allow it to finish displaying the Windows desktop. Insert the USB thumb drive and note any activity on the screen.

    b.   Did a window appear asking what you want Windows to do? _____

    c.   If yes, what were some of the options you could choose?

_____

_____

Close the options window.

Step 2 Open an application on your PC, such as Word or PowerPoint, and select and open a file. If you can find a file larger than 1.44 MB, you can experience firsthand the benefit of USB thumb drives over floppy drives.

Step 3 In the application window, select File | Save As. In Windows XP, click the drop-down arrow for the Save in field. You will see a number of folders and drives where you could choose to save the file. One of these should be the thumb drive, as shown in Figure 13-7. Select the thumb drive and save the file. In Windows Vista/7, click Browse Folders (if necessary). In the list that appears, click Folders. Then scroll until you see the thumb drive. Select it and save the file. Close all open windows.

Step 4 In the system tray, find and click the Safely Remove Hardware icon, which in Windows XP is a green arrow and a gray rectangle, and in Vista/7 is a white checkmark on a green circle in front of a tiny USB symbol. A tiny pop-up message appears adjacent to the icon, listing all removable devices;

FIGURE 13-6 A USB thumb drive with a retractable connector

click the name of the thumb drive. In XP, an information balloon with a *Safe to Remove Hardware* message should notify you that you can now remove the USB mass storage device. In Vista/7, an announcement will appear with the same message.

Remove the thumb drive from the USB port.

✔ **Hint**

If you forget to close one or more windows with a focus on the thumb drive, you will receive an error message: *The device "Generic Volume" cannot be stopped right now. Try stopping it later.* If you receive this message, just click OK, close all open files and folders on the thumb drive, and try again.

If you have some open files or folders on the thumb drive and you just pull it out of the machine, you may receive an error message such as *Fail Write Delay.* Most of the time the files and folders will remain intact, but this is not the recommended removal method.

Step 5   At this point, if you have a second machine where you can plug in the thumb drive, it will make the lab exercise more realistic. If you don't, you can just use the same system again for this step. Insert the thumb drive into a USB port and again note any activity on the screen. This time, double-click *Open folder to view files using Windows Explorer.*

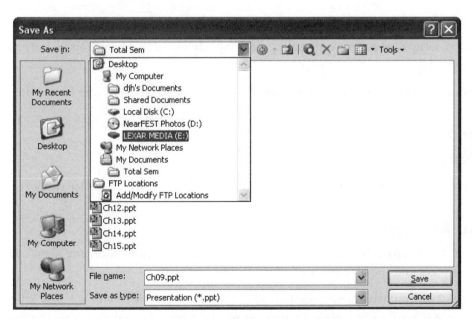

FIGURE 13-7 The Windows XP Save As dialog box showing a Lexar Media thumb drive

Step 6 Double-click the file you saved previously; if the file has an associated application, this should launch that application and open the file.

You have now successfully used a USB thumb drive—also referred to as a *jump drive*—to "jump" files from one machine to another.

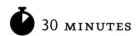 30 MINUTES

Lab Exercise 13.04: Configuring Removable Media Drives

A new client has very specific needs for the boot order and access to removable media in his computer center's seven computers. For the two servers, the floppy drive and USB ports will be installed, but the floppy drive will be disabled in CMOS. Three of the five workstations need the optical drive set as the first drive in the boot sequence, but the other two need the USB drive to be first in the boot sequence, with the optical drive second. It's your job to set up these PCs properly, so get to work!

Learning Objectives

In this lab, you'll use the CMOS setup program to configure the settings for the floppy drive, USB devices, optical drive, and boot order.

At the end of this lab, you'll be able to

- Locate the CMOS setup screens for configuring the floppy drives, USB devices, optical drives, and boot order

- Configure various scenarios for the floppy drive, USB devices, optical drive, and boot order

Lab Materials and Setup

The materials you need for this lab are

- A working computer system with a floppy drive, an optical drive, and USB device support

Getting Down to Business

This lab exercise involves the floppy drive controller, optical drive, and USB controller, and shows you how to configure these devices and the boot order of these devices in CMOS.

Depending on your BIOS manufacturer and version, you may or may not be able to perform all of the following steps. Explore the different screens to discover whether you can enable/disable the floppy drive controller (FDC) and the USB controller, and which devices you can put in the boot order (floppy drive, optical drive, hard drive, and USB devices).

Step 1 You will start by disabling the floppy drive. Enter the CMOS setup program by pressing the appropriate key or key combination (which you should remember from Lab Exercise 8.02) while your system is booting.

Having previously browsed through your version of CMOS, you should be able to locate the screen that contains settings for the FDC. If you can't remember which screen deals with the FDC, browse through the CMOS screens until you find it.

   a.   Do you have an option in CMOS to disable the FDC? _____

   b.   Under what title heading did you find this option?

   _____

   c.   How do you disable this setting?

   _____

   Now disable it.

✔ **Hint**

Disabling the FDC is a good way for a network administrator to prevent users from using floppy disks to either take information off the network or introduce viruses into the network.

Step 2 Restart your system and see if you can access the floppy drive. Did the LED on the front of the floppy drive turn on as the system booted up?

_____

Step 3 Re-enter the CMOS setup utility and turn the FDC back on. Reboot the system, and test the floppy drive. Does it function properly?

_____

Step 4 One of the most important aspects of removable media is that you can boot a nonfunctioning system from a device other than the hard drive with the diagnostic and troubleshooting tools included. The next CMOS setting to play with is the boot sequence.

When you boot up a PC, the system needs to know where to get the operating system software to load into memory. The three standard places to store this software are the hard drive, the optical drive, or a USB thumb drive. In some cases, you might boot from a server somewhere on your network.

Using the CMOS setup utility, you can designate the order in which your system will check the devices for the operating system software. Specifying the proper boot sequence—that is, the search order—saves time by telling the system where to look first. After all, if your operating system is on the hard drive, why should your system waste time looking on the optical or USB thumb drive every time you boot?

Enter the CMOS setup utility, and look for a screen that includes a boot sequence setting.

a.   How many different boot sequences can you configure in CMOS? _____

b.   How many different devices can be in the search sequence? _____

Set your system to boot from the optical drive first (see Figure 13-8).

Step 5   Restart your system. Typically, the boot screen will prompt you with the message *Press any key to boot from the CD*. If there is a bootable CD in the drive, the system will boot from that disc. Leave this boot order in place for the next lab exercise, in which you'll learn how to create bootable CDs.

Step 6   Re-enter the CMOS setup utility, and note whether your system will allow you to boot from a USB device, such as a USB thumb drive.

If your machine is capable, you can substitute a USB thumb drive for the optical drive in the next lab exercise and create a live USB of the GParted partition editor. For now, leave the optical drive as the first device in the boot order and shut down the machine.

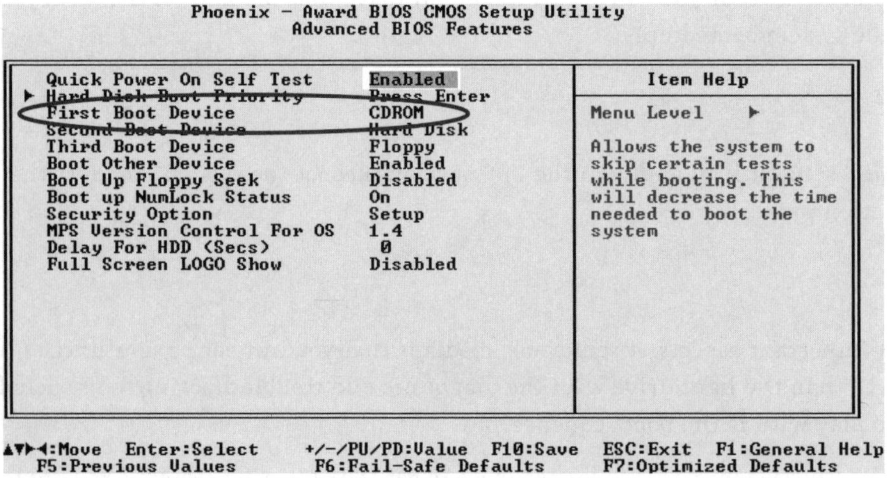

```
              Phoenix - Award BIOS CMOS Setup Utility
                      Advanced BIOS Features

  ┌─────────────────────────────────────────┬──────────────────────┐
  │ Quick Power On Self Test    Enabled      │     Item Help        │
  │▶ Hard Disk Boot Priority    Press Enter  │                      │
  │ First Boot Device           CDROM        │  Menu Level    ▶     │
  │ Second Boot Device          Hard Disk    │                      │
  │ Third Boot Device           Floppy       │  Allows the system to│
  │ Boot Other Device           Enabled      │  skip certain tests  │
  │ Boot Up Floppy Seek         Disabled     │  while booting. This │
  │ Boot up NumLock Status      On           │  will decrease the time│
  │ Security Option             Setup        │  needed to boot the  │
  │ MPS Version Control For OS  1.4          │  system              │
  │ Delay For HDD (Secs)        0            │                      │
  │ Full Screen LOGO Show       Disabled     │                      │
  │                                          │                      │
  │                                          │                      │
  │                                          │                      │
  └─────────────────────────────────────────┴──────────────────────┘
 ▲▼◄:Move   Enter:Select    +/-/PU/PD:Value  F10:Save   ESC:Exit  F1:General Help
    F5:Previous Values      F6:Fail-Safe Defaults       F7:Optimized Defaults
```

FIGURE 13-8   Boot sequence screen from CMOS with the optical drive as first boot device

 60 MINUTES

Lab Exercise 13.05: Burning Optical Discs

PCs today are used more than ever for storage of digital photographs, music, and video, in addition to more traditional types of data. Even a modest collection of MP3 files, family photos, and home video clips requires many gigabytes of space! Hard drives do have space limits, and at some point they tend to fail, so wise PC users turn to recordable CDs, DVDs, and Blu-ray drives. These discs provide an affordable large-capacity portable storage option; you can put your important data onto a disc, or make multiple copies of that disc to store in two or more secure locations.

This lab will introduce you to the process by which we record, or *burn*, optical discs. Rather than burning a disc full of your favorite tunes or photos, you'll be making the type of disc that a technician would have in his toolkit when troubleshooting a machine that won't boot.

→ Note

If your systems have Blu-ray drives, you will be burning your disc the same way. However, be aware that Blu-ray Discs are better armed than current DVDs. They come equipped with a secure encryption system—a unique ID that protects against video piracy and copyright infringement.

✔ Cross-Reference

For additional information on burning optical discs, refer to the "Applications" section in Chapter 13 of *Mike Meyers' CompTIA A+ Guide to Managing and Troubleshooting PCs*.

Learning Objectives

In this lab, you'll use a third-party burning program to create bootable ISO images on recordable optical discs.

At the end of this lab, you'll be able to

- Work with optical discs and burning tools
- Create a bootable optical disc

Lab Materials and Setup

The materials you need for this lab are

- A working computer system with a CD-RW or DVD-RW drive installed

- Internet access (preferably a high-speed connection) for downloading

- An optical disc burning application such as the included tool in Windows 7, ISO Recorder, Nero Burning ROM, or freeware CDBurnerXP

- Blank optical discs (more than one if possible)

Getting Down to Business

In Chapter 12, you were asked to prep a number of newly donated PCs by preparing their hard drives for the installation of an operating system; you already partitioned and formatted the drives. To do that, you used the open source utility called GParted. GParted is a Gnome Linux live CD with the Gnome Partition Editor application installed. Your instructor may have provided you with the bootable CD or DVD, or you may have jumped ahead to this lab to make it yourself. In this lab, you will burn the ISO image of the open source, bootable live CD of Gnome Linux and the utility GParted.

Step 1   Ensure that you have optical disc burning software that will enable you to burn ISO images. An ISO image is a complete copy of a disc, including all of the boot information in the boot record. Popular third-party products include the freeware ISO Recorder for Windows XP, Vista, or Windows 7 (http://isorecorder.alexfeinman.com/isorecorder.htm) and the commercial Nero Burning ROM (www.nero.com). Windows 7, helpfully, includes the ability to burn ISO images without the need for a third-party tool.

You can also try CDBurnerXP, an excellent freeware burning tool that supports the burning of ISO images; it's available at www.cdburnerxp.se. Just go to the CDBurnerXP Web site, follow the instructions, and run the installation. After you've successfully installed the program, you should have all the tools necessary to burn ISO images (see Figure 13-9).

Step 2   Now visit the GParted Web site at http://gparted.sourceforge.net. Click Downloads and follow the instructions. You can download the full ISO, or download the .zip file to improve transfer times (remember you will have to expand the .zip file after it's on your system).

Step 3   Once you have the ISO image, open the tray on your optical drive and insert a blank optical disc. Close the tray and launch your optical disc burning software. Navigate to the GParted ISO file and follow the instructions to burn the ISO image onto the optical media. Most programs will eject the tray with the disc once the writing process is complete.

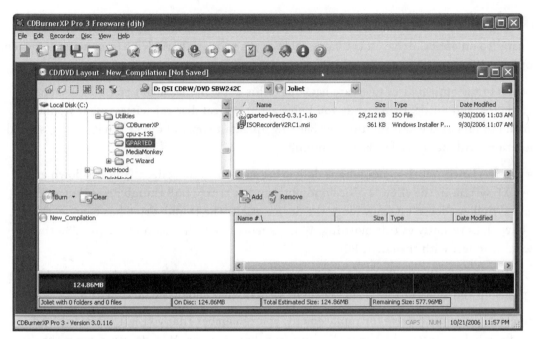

FIGURE 13-9 CDBurnerXP

Step 4 Place the newly created disc into the optical drive tray, close the tray, and reboot the computer. If all has gone well, GParted will boot, detect your hard drives, and give you the option to partition and format these drives.

✖ Warning

Remember, any time you format a hard disk, you delete the data currently on that disk. Do not run GParted on the disk containing your operating system unless you have been instructed to delete this system's OS.

→ Try This: Ultimate Boot CD

Now that you have an understanding of why you might want to boot a machine from removable media—to perform low-level diagnostics, troubleshoot, or just prep the disk before installing an operating system—take a cruise over to www.ultimatebootcd.com.

You can download the ISO image of Ultimate Boot CD (UBCD), which has over 100 different freeware tools, all placed on a live CD. Use the method you learned in this exercise to burn the ISO image to a CD, boot a machine with the UBCD, and explore some of the tools. You might find that using some of the drive manufacturer's low-level formatting tools will bring a dead drive back to life.

Lab Analysis Test

1. Jovan installed an optical drive on the same cable as his primary hard drive, and now the system will not boot. What could be causing this?

2. Mark wants to use optical discs to create backups of his data. He has about 20 GB of documents, movies, photos, and music. Using what you know about optical disc capacities, what would you recommend to him as the best solution for backing up data to optical discs? What, if any, special considerations will Mark need to keep in mind?

3. Cecelia is a freelance Web designer who is delivering some files to a client. She sits down at a Windows XP system in the client's office and plugs in her trusty USB thumb drive, but nothing happens—Windows doesn't acknowledge the device at all. The thumb drive has been working perfectly well, as recently as this morning. What is most likely the reason that the USB thumb drive won't connect with the client PC?

4. When Philip puts his CD-RW disc in the drive and copies files to and from it, he notices that the drive speeds up and slows down. Is this normal? If not, what should he do to fix it?

5. After removing an optical drive for replacement, you remember that you left a disc in the drive. You look for a hole to insert the paper clip into, but there is none. How do you remove the disc?

Key Term Quiz

Use the following terms to complete the following sentences. Not all terms will be used.

Blu-ray

CMOS

disc

DMA

label

optical drive

scratches

spiral

surface

USB 1.0

USB 2.0

USB 3.0

1. An optical drive must be identified in the _____ settings.

2. _____ Discs can hold and play back large quantities of high-definition video and audio, as well as photos, data, and other digital content.

3. Any drive that uses a laser of some sort to read data from a disc is called a(n) _____.

4. The _____ version of thumb drives supports a maximum throughput of 480 Mbps.

5. The reflective aluminum layer of an optical disc can be damaged by _____.

Chapter 14

Installing and Upgrading Windows

Lab Exercises

As a PC technician, you'll spend a lot of time installing and upgrading operating systems. For this reason, it's important that you become familiar with the tasks involved; otherwise, you might find yourself in a tight spot when Windows won't install on the laptop that your boss needs for a presentation this afternoon.

A number of different operating systems are in use today, including Apple Mac OS X, several different flavors of Linux, and of course the Microsoft Windows family. Because the CompTIA A+ certification focuses primarily on Microsoft products—and because Microsoft products represent the majority of the market—these lab exercises are dedicated to the installation of Windows.

Just about anyone can install software if everything goes right and no problems come up during the process; plenty of people with minimal software knowledge have upgraded Windows without the slightest incident. Even an experienced technician may have problems, though, if the system has incompatible expansion cards, broken devices, or bad drivers. As a PC technician, you'll need to handle both the simple installations—the ones with only new, compatible components—and the more complex installations on older and more problematic systems.

Installing and upgrading Windows requires more than just popping in the installation disc and running the install program. You need to plan the installation thoughtfully, check for component compatibility, and thoroughly understand the installation options and how to configure them. Good planning up front will give you the best chances for a successful installation or upgrade.

Be sure to have everything you need before you start, from the installation disc to the discs containing your device drivers. Remember the old adage, "Measure twice, cut once." Believe me, it's no fun to start over on an installation or upgrade if you mess it up! Do it right the first time—you'll be glad you did.

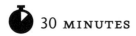 30 MINUTES

Lab Exercise 14.01: Installing/Upgrading Considerations

Your client has asked you to upgrade his system to Windows 7 Professional 64-bit. He's currently running Windows Vista Business 64-bit, and everything works fine. He has the documentation that came with his system, which states that it has an ASUS P5E Deluxe motherboard. He isn't sure how fast the processor is, but he does know that the system has 1 GB of memory. Where do you start the planning process?

✔ Cross-Reference

To review the details of pre-installation planning, refer to the "Preparing for Installation or Upgrade" section of Chapter 14 of *Mike Meyers' CompTIA A+ Guide to Managing and Troubleshooting PCs*.

Learning Objectives

In this lab exercise, you'll become more familiar with using the Internet to help answer pre-installation questions.

At the end of this lab, you'll be able to

- Access the Microsoft Support Web site

- Determine the minimal requirements for a system installation

- Determine whether to perform an upgrade installation or a clean installation

Lab Materials and Setup

The materials you need for this lab are

- A working PC

- Internet access

- A notepad and pencil

Getting Down to Business

The first step in a successful Windows installation or upgrade is to determine whether the hardware meets the requirements of the new operating system. Your first stop in this process is the Microsoft Support Web site, found at http://support.microsoft.com/findsolutions/.

Microsoft has invested massive amounts of energy and time in building its Support Web site. Digging through all of the articles on the huge number of Web pages can be overwhelming, but I'm a firm believer in this site's usefulness. When I have a question that directly concerns a Windows operating system (or any Microsoft product, for that matter), I check this site first, and I'm rarely disappointed. In fact, while searching for the answer to a problem or question, I usually learn two or three new, sometimes unrelated, things just by reading through the search results. Also, my search techniques improve with each visit. I consider the Microsoft Support Web site an invaluable tool and resource.

Step 1 You'll first need to make sure that your client's computer is capable of running Windows 7 Professional 64-bit. To do this, you will need to attain a copy of the Windows 7 Upgrade Advisor. Go to www.microsoft.com/download/en/details.aspx?id=20 and click the DOWNLOAD button, which will take you to the actual download page. Microsoft will suggest other applications to download with the Upgrade Advisor, but you can ignore these and click Next. Depending on your Web browser, you will either be asked to save the file to your hard drive or the download will begin automatically.

✔ Hint

Web sites change or disappear all the time—especially Microsoft Web sites. If the Microsoft Web site should change significantly from the time this book was printed to the time you're reading this, and you find that a link listed here is no longer valid, a quick search with Google for "Windows 7 Upgrade Advisor" should get you where you need to be.

When the file is downloaded, double-click it to start the installation process, and then follow the onscreen prompts to install the Upgrade Advisor. When it's finished installing, it should start up automatically, so just click the Start Check button and wait for it to complete.

Once the scan completes, it will show you detailed results of the scan (see Figure 14-1). This will tell you whether or not your system is Windows 7-capable. Further down the page, you can click on a set of links to view details about the system requirements, device compatibility, and program compatibility.

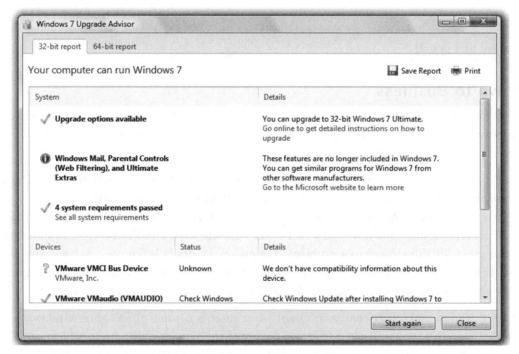

FIGURE 14-1 A Windows 7 Upgrade Advisor scan's results

Step 2   Once you've seen the scan's results, answer the following questions:

   a.   What version of Windows 7 does the Anytime Upgrade allow you to migrate to?

   _____

   b.   What's the minimum CPU speed requirement?

   _____

   c.   What's the minimum amount of RAM?

   _____

   d.   How much available hard drive space is required?

   _____

   e.   Does your graphics adapter support Aero?

   _____

   f.   List a few devices or programs that the Upgrade Advisor says are "Not Compatible":

   _____

   _____

→ Note

At the time of this writing, the Windows 8 Consumer Preview has been released to the public. The guys here at Total Seminars installed it on a computer that was previously running Windows 7 Professional 64-bit and it ran without a hitch. As I type this, there is no separate Windows 8 Upgrade Advisor. Microsoft plans to include it directly inside the Windows 8 installation process.

Step 3   Now you know whether or not your client's computer can run Windows 7 Professional 64-bit, and, if not, what you need to upgrade in order to get it to run. Next, you need to find out whether you can do an upgrade installation, where the new OS is installed on top of the old one, or a clean installation, where the drive is erased before installation of the new OS.

Doing an upgrade installation is based both on the version of Windows Vista you're upgrading from and the edition of Windows 7 that you're upgrading to, so it's a fairly complicated subject. In order to find out the possible upgrade paths, you'll need to do a bit of searching.

Go to www.microsoft.com/ and do a search for **Windows 7 Upgrade Paths**. The first search result should give you the information you need, but if not, search around a little. This sort of research will make up a substantial part of your life as a tech, so get used to it!

Step 4   When you've found information about Windows 7 upgrade paths, answer the following questions:

    a.   Can you do an upgrade installation from Windows Vista Business 64-bit to Windows 7 Professional 64-bit? _____

    b.   Can you do an upgrade installation from Windows XP to Windows 7 Professional? _____

    c.   Can you do an upgrade installation from Windows Vista Business 32-bit to Windows 7 Professional 64-bit? _____

    d.   Can you do an upgrade installation from Windows Vista Business 32-bit to Windows 7 Home Premium 32-bit? _____

✔ **Cross-Reference**

For a refresher on the considerations that come into play when you install or upgrade Windows, refer to the "Deciding What Type of Installation to Perform" section of Chapter 14 of *Mike Meyers' CompTIA A+ Guide to Managing and Troubleshooting PCs*.

 30 MINUTES

Lab Exercise 14.02: Using Windows Easy Transfer

You're about to upgrade a client's computer from Windows XP to Windows 7, but the client doesn't want to lose any of her important data. She doesn't have a lot of data to transfer, just a gigabyte or so, but that data is absolutely essential to the operation of her business. Fortunately, you're a savvy tech and you know that Windows Easy Transfer will enable you to back up her documents onto a flash drive and then transfer them to her new OS after it's installed.

Learning Objectives

You'll learn how to use Windows Easy Transfer effectively to back up files and transfer them to a new operating system.

At the end of this lab, you'll be able to

- Use Windows Easy Transfer to back up files onto a USB thumb drive

- Use Windows Easy Transfer to transfer files onto a new OS installation

Lab Materials and Setup

The materials you need for this lab are

- A PC running Windows XP or Windows Vista

- A PC running Windows 7

- Internet access

- A USB thumb drive (1 GB or more)

Getting Down to Business

Microsoft's Windows Easy Transfer has made moving data to a new computer as easy as it could be, but it's still a somewhat complicated program. In this lab, you'll learn all the necessary steps you need to take to move a customer's data from one computer to another. If you ever work as a tech in a retail store, this sort of information will be vital when trying to convince customers to upgrade their PCs.

Step 1   The first thing you need to do to use Windows Easy Transfer, of course, is to get a copy of Windows Easy Transfer for Windows XP. Microsoft offers Windows Easy Transfer as a free download, so go to www.microsoft.com/downloads and do a search for **Easy Transfer** to locate the specific version for the OS from which you are upgrading. Click the search result and then download the program to your hard drive. I'd give you the direct link to the download page here, but it's Microsoft's Web site, so it'll probably change in six months.

→ **Note**

You can also perform this exercise using Windows Vista, though some of the screens may differ.

After you've downloaded a copy of Windows Easy Transfer to your XP machine, run it and follow the onscreen prompts to install the program. Once it's installed, run it from the All Programs menu. (It should be listed as Windows Easy Transfer for Windows 7.) The first screen (see Figure 14-2) gives you information about the transfer process, so once you've read all of that, click the Next button.

Step 2   The next screen (see Figure 14-3) offers you several different options from which to choose how you want to transfer the files and settings to your new computer, whether by Easy Transfer Cable (a special USB cable sold by Microsoft), by a network connection (useful if you're transferring between two computers on a local area network), or by an external hard disk or USB flash drive. Since you're using a USB flash drive, a type of removable media, select the third option.

Once you've selected the removable media option, the wizard asks you which computer you are using now (see Figure 14-4). The only option you have is *This is my old computer*. Makes sense, right? You can't use Easy Transfer to migrate *to* Windows XP, only *from* Windows XP. Click on *This is my old computer*.

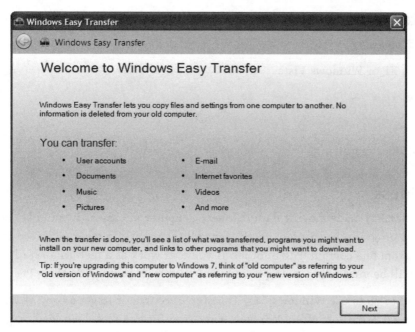

FIGURE 14-2 Running Windows Easy Transfer

On the next screen, you can pick which account's files and settings you want to move to the new Windows 7 computer (see Figure 14-5). After it finishes scanning, choose all of them by selecting the checkboxes and then click Next.

The next page enables you to enter a password to encrypt your data for added security (see Figure 14-6). After adding a password that you can remember, click Save.

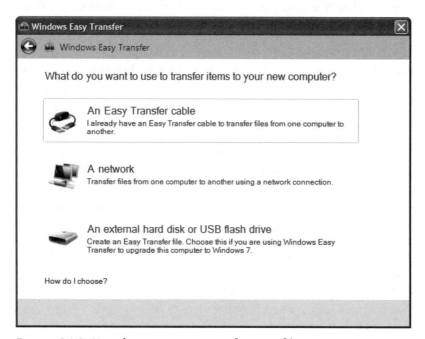

FIGURE 14-3 How do you want to transfer your files?

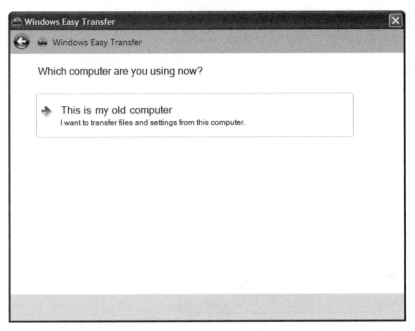

Figure 14-4 Which computer are you using now?

Save your Easy Transfer file to your flash drive. Depending on the size of the files belonging to each user account, this can take some time. Once all the files have been saved, Windows Easy Transfer will prompt you. Click Next, and then click Close. It's time to go to the new Windows 7 computer!

Step 3 Once you've transferred all your files onto your USB thumb drive, you can remove the drive and move it to your PC running Windows 7. If you don't have a PC with Windows 7 already installed,

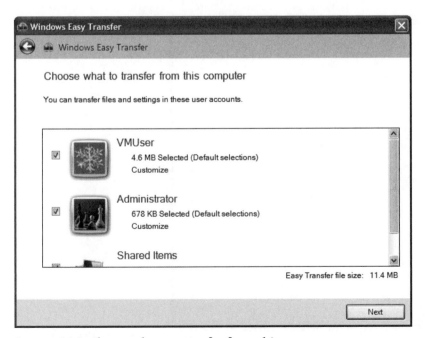

Figure 14-5 Choose what to transfer from this computer

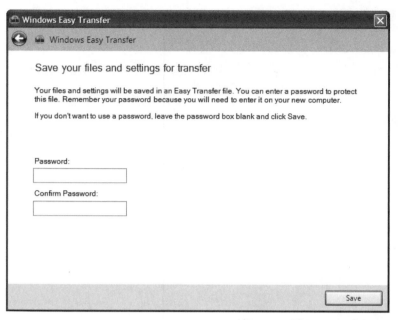

FIGURE 14-6 Password protection

skip to Lab Exercise 14.04 and then come back when you're finished with it. Once you are on your Windows 7 PC, open Windows Easy Transfer by going to Start | All Programs | Accessories | System Tools | Windows Easy Transfer.

When the wizard starts, you can once more click Next past the welcome screen. The next screen will present you with the same options as before. Your choices are an Easy Transfer Cable, a network, an

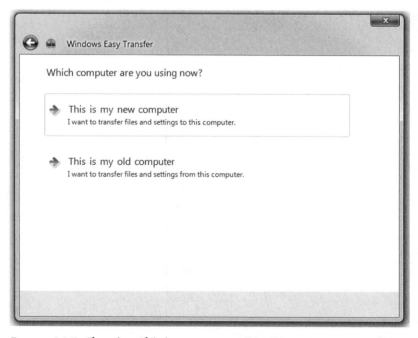

FIGURE 14-7 Choosing This is my new computer

external device, or a USB flash drive. Since you've backed up the files from the old computer onto a flash drive, select *An external hard disk or USB flash drive*.

The next screen asks which computer you are using right now. Since you are now on the Windows 7 computer, choose *This is my new computer* (see Figure 14-7).

Next, the wizard will ask you if Easy Transfer already saved the files from your old computer to an external hard disk or USB drive. Yes it did! Choose the correct path to the file saved on your flash drive and open it.

You will then need to enter the password you created back on the Windows XP computer to access your content. Then click Next.

Windows Easy Transfer will then take a moment to scan the file. Eventually, it will display a screen for you to select which account's files and settings you want to transfer to the new PC. Select all of them if they aren't already selected (see Figure 14-8).

Finally, click the Transfer button, and all of your information from the Windows XP computer will be transferred to the Windows 7 computer.

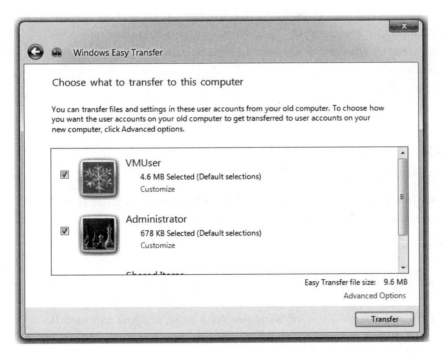

FIGURE 14-8 Choose what to transfer to this computer

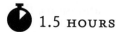 1.5 HOURS

Lab Exercise 14.03: Upgrading a Windows Operating System

A client running Windows Vista Home Premium, decides to modernize by moving to a more recent OS. He asks you to upgrade his system to Windows 7 Home Premium. You agree to upgrade the system for him.

Learning Objectives

You need to perform at least one complete upgrade, both for practice and to prepare for questions asked on the CompTIA A+ exams.

At the end of this lab, you'll be able to

• Upgrade an operating system

✔ Cross-Reference

To refresh your memory about the ins and outs of performing a Windows upgrade, read the "Installing or Upgrading to Windows XP Professional," "Installing or Upgrading to Windows Vista," and "Installing or Upgrading to Windows 7" sections in Chapter 14 of *Mike Meyers' CompTIA A+ Guide to Managing and Troubleshooting PCs*.

Lab Materials and Setup

The materials you need for this lab are

• A working Windows Vista Home Premium PC with a hard drive that you can write to without negative consequences (make sure it can also run Windows 7)

• A Windows 7 installation disc

✔ Hint

A Windows Vista installation disc has every edition of Windows Vista on it, and you can install any edition you want on your computer for a 30-day trial without a product key. Each edition of Windows 7, however, has its very own installation disc.

Getting Down to Business

You'll need quite a bit of time to complete this lab; most of that time will be spent waiting for Windows to install files. The exercise will walk you through upgrading a Windows Vista Home Premium system to Windows 7 Home Premium. Depending on the systems and software licenses you have available, you may not be able to do this lab exactly as it's laid out here. The important thing is that you actually perform a Windows upgrade, to see the questions that are asked during the installation, and to become familiar with the process so that you're prepared for the CompTIA A+ certification exams.

Step 1 You've completed the compatibility exercise in the earlier labs, and you know whether or not your system can handle Windows 7. Since you won't actually be *using* Windows 7, just installing it, the main consideration for performing this installation is hard drive space. Make sure you have at least 40 GB of hard drive space available on the computer you're upgrading.

The first step to doing an upgrade installation to Windows 7 is to make sure your computer is booted into Windows Vista. Because an upgrade installation is meant to be installed on a computer with a pre-existing OS, Windows 7 will not allow you to do an upgrade installation unless you start the installation while booted into another Windows OS. So, with your computer booted up, insert the Windows 7 installation disc, wait until the Setup program starts, and click *Install now*.

Step 2 When asked whether or not you want to download the latest updates for installation, choose the second option, *Do not get the latest updates for installation*. Ordinarily, you would agree to do this, but it can take a long time to complete this download, and you'll be updating this computer in Lab Exercise 14.05, so you don't need to bother right now.

Step 3 The next screen is the End User License Agreement (EULA), shown in Figure 14-9. This document enumerates the deal made between you and Microsoft that you agree to by installing their software. EULAs typically contain a great deal of legalese, and are generally quite lengthy, and the Windows 7 EULA is no exception. You are certainly free to read through it if you like, but you don't have to. When you're done, check the box that says *I accept the license terms* and click Next.

Step 4 The next screen enables you to choose either an upgrade installation or a custom installation. For this lab, you're doing an upgrade installation, so select Upgrade. This option may or may not be available to you based on the version of Windows Vista that you're starting with and the edition of Windows 7 you're installing to, as you saw in the first lab in this chapter. The Windows 7 installer may give you an error at this point, and if it does, follow any instructions it gives you and start the installation process again. If there are no errors, click Next.

Step 5 Wait around for a while as Windows installs itself.

Step 6 Wait some more.

Step 7 Twiddle your thumbs. Did you know that Windows 7 can be installed from a thumb drive? Use another computer to go online and search for **Windows 7 USB tool**. This tool will take the contents of your Windows 7 disc and place it on your thumb drive. That might speed up this process (for the next time you install Windows 7, at least).

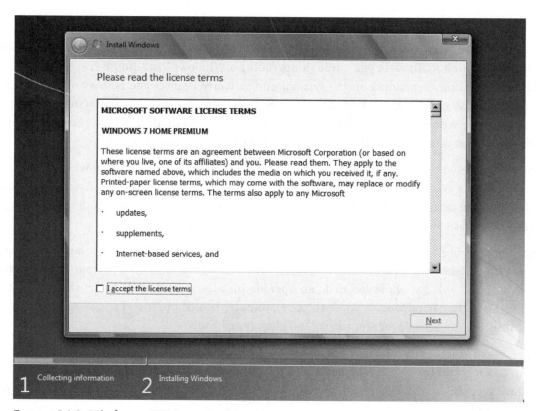

FIGURE 14-9 Windows 7 EULA agreement screen

Step 8   Why does it have to copy files and then "gather" them? What does that even mean?

Step 9   Oh, hey! It finished! Once the installer's done copying files, it will need to reboot the computer to continue setting up Windows 7.

Step 10   If you have a legitimate Windows 7 product key, enter it on the next screen (see Figure 14-10). If not, just click Next and then answer No to the dialog box that pops up asking you if you want to enter your product key.

Step 11   On this next screen you will decide how you want the operating system to interact with Windows Update. I suggest clicking on *Use recommended settings* in order to keep your computer fully patched from vulnerabilities.

Step 12   Now you're asked to set your time zone, the time, and the date. Make sure all the settings are correct and click Next.

Step 13   If your computer has network access, the installer will ask you whether you are on a home, work, or public network. Answer appropriately.

Step 14   You're done! Type in your credentials to log on. Click Start and enjoy the Windows 7 experience. After installing Windows 7, you will have 30 days to run the Windows Activation Client to activate Windows, or else the OS will stop functioning, so keep that in mind, especially if you didn't enter a product key.

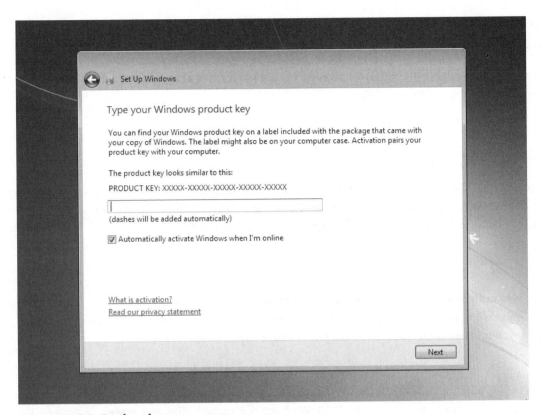

FIGURE 14-10   Product key screen

 60 MINUTES

Lab Exercise 14.04: Performing a Clean Installation of Windows 7

Your boss has traditionally ordered new workstations already assembled and loaded with the desired Windows OS. She recently decided that with her great in-house techs, she should be buying PC parts from a wholesaler instead and having you and your team build the systems. You've enjoyed choosing the various hardware components and building these custom machines, but now it's time to bring your creations to life! You need to load Windows 7 Professional onto these new machines that have never seen the light of day.

Learning Objectives

You should complete at least one clean Windows installation, both for the experience and to prepare for questions asked on the CompTIA A+ exams.

At the end of this lab, you'll be able to

- Install a Windows operating system on a blank hard drive

Lab Materials and Setup

The materials you need for this lab are

- A working PC with a blank hard drive, or with a hard drive that you can write to without negative consequences

- A Windows 7 installation disc

Getting Down to Business

In this exercise, you'll be putting an operating system onto a hard drive that doesn't currently have one. Even if the hard drive has an operating system on it, doing a clean installation will format that drive and erase all its data, so be sure you've backed up any important files!

→ **Note**

This lab was designed for installing Windows 7, but you can very easily perform this lab exercise using Windows Vista. The order of some of the screens will change, such as when you put in the license key, but other than that, it should be a similar experience.

Step 1 Insert the Windows 7 installation DVD into the optical drive, close the tray, and reboot your PC. If prompted, press any key to boot from the DVD. Wait for the Install Windows screen to appear. Windows 7 will first ask you to select your preferred language (see Figure 14-11). After you do so, click Next. Then, click *Install now*.

✔ **Hint**

If you notice that it takes what feels like forever during the wait for the Install Windows screen to appear, go into your CMOS setting and disable the floppy drive. It will dramatically improve the speed for a Windows Vista or Windows 7 installation.

Step 2 This process is almost identical to the upgrade installation, with a few key differences, so if you start to feel a sense of déjà-vu, just stick with it. Here are the steps for performing a clean installation of Windows 7:

a. The next screen is your old friend, the End User License Agreement (EULA). When you're done reading it, check the box that says *I accept the license terms* and click Next.

b. The next screen, shown in Figure 14-12, is the fork in the Windows 7 installer's road. You've already tried the Upgrade, so go ahead and click Custom (advanced) to do a clean installation.

c. The next screen is the disk partitioning page, where you can select which drive to install Windows 7 on to, as well as how to partition that drive. You should already be familiar with partitioning drives using this screen, but that's not important for now. Simply select the drive you wish to install to and click Next.

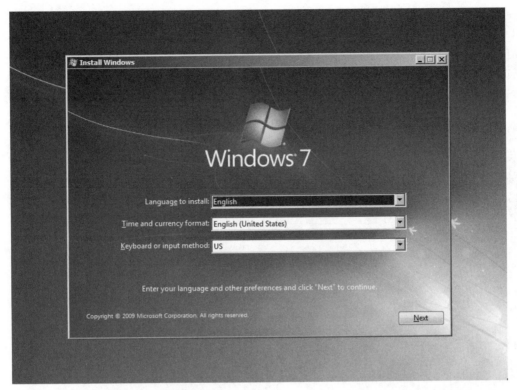

Figure 14-11 Language selection screen

d.   Wait, once again, for Windows 7 to install itself.

e.   Once the installer is done copying files, it will need to restart the computer.

f.   Once the computer finishes restarting, type in your name. This will be the user name for the computer. Next, type in a computer name. If you want to, you can choose to keep it set as the default, but you also have the option of changing how your computer appears on the network. When you are finished, click Next.

g.   Type in a password for your user account that you can remember, and give yourself a hint. Click Next. You have the option of skipping this step and going without a password. Doing so can be a huge security risk.

h.   If you have a legitimate Windows 7 product key, enter it in the appropriate box. If not, just click Next and then answer No to the dialog box that pops up asking you if you want to enter your product key.

i.   Now you're back in familiar territory, at the screen asking how you want to set up Windows Update. Generally, there's no reason not to select the first option, *Use recommended settings*, so click that now.

j.   Now you're asked to set your time zone, the time, and the date. Make sure all the settings are correct and click Next.

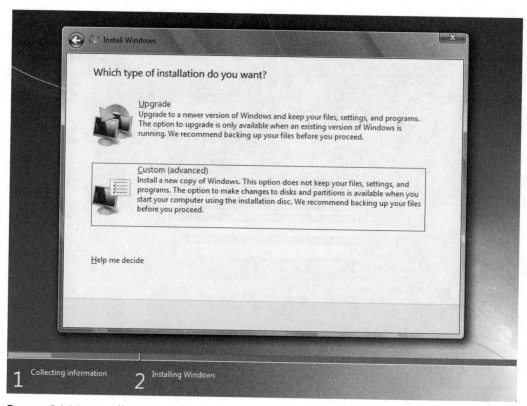

FIGURE 14-12 Installation selection

k. If your computer has network access, the installer will ask you whether you are on a home, work, or public network. Answer appropriately. If you select home, you will be prompted with the option of setting up a homegroup. For now, skip this step.

l. You're done! Click Start and enjoy the Windows 7 experience.

 60 MINUTES

Lab Exercise 14.05: Performing a Clean Installation of Windows XP

You work for a school and you have just received some old computer equipment from a few local businesses. These computers don't meet the minimum requirements for Windows Vista or Windows 7, so you have no option but to load the longest running operating system that Microsoft ever released, good ol' Windows XP.

Learning Objectives

You should complete at least one clean Windows installation, both for the experience and to prepare for questions asked on the CompTIA A+ exams.

At the end of this lab, you'll be able to

- Install a Windows operating system on a blank hard drive

Lab Materials and Setup

The materials you need for this lab are

- A working PC with a blank hard drive, or with a hard drive that you can write to without negative consequences

- A Windows XP Professional Edition CD-ROM with a valid product key

Getting Down to Business

In this exercise, you'll be putting an operating system onto a drive that doesn't currently have one. If the hard drive that you plan to use currently has data on it (even data that no one needs), then you must wipe that drive clean before you begin the exercise. Once you have a clean hard drive, you can proceed as directed.

Step 1 Turn on the computer and insert the Windows XP CD-ROM into the optical drive, close the tray, and boot from the optical drive. Ensure that your boot order is correct in CMOS.

Step 2 The Windows setup will begin in text mode, which means you won't have any mouse support and everything feels like the old days of the command-line interface. It is at this point you will notice a bunch of text cycling through at the bottom of your screen. These are drivers being loaded. During this process, you will have the option to press F6 to load third-party drivers. This is essential if you are installing Windows XP on an SCSI drive or on a RAID setup. If you are installing Windows XP onto a SATA hard drive with an installation disc that has a pre–Service Pack 1 version of Windows XP, you will need to press F6 to load SATA drivers.

Step 3 You will then see the Welcome to Setup screen. Press ENTER to set up Windows. Read the EULA (End User License Agreement) and agree to it to proceed by pressing F8.

Step 4 When the Setup program prompts you to partition your drive, set up a single NTFS partition that uses all the available drive space. Then you'll simply need to wait and watch while the Setup program does its magic and reboots the computer.

Step 5 When the computer has rebooted, work through the graphical portion of the installation process by carefully reading each screen and filling in the appropriate information. Be sure to enter the product key correctly, as you won't get past that screen with an invalid key.

Step 6 When you come to the Networking Settings screen, ask your instructor (if you're in a classroom setting) whether to choose Typical settings or Custom settings, and what specific information to use. If you're not in a classroom setting, select Typical.

Step 7 Click Next. Your computer will reboot one more time. You'll need to adjust your display settings by following the prompts.

Step 8 The Welcome to Microsoft Windows screen appears. Press Next to continue.

Step 9 Click the option to protect your computer by having it pull down updates from Microsoft's Web site.

Step 10 Next, you have the option to register your copy of Windows XP. Keep in mind that registration is completely optional.

Step 11 Who will use this computer? Type in the names that identify as many users as you would like (up to five users during the setup of Windows XP).

Step 12 Click Finish. Welcome to Windows XP!

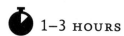 1–3 HOURS

Lab Exercise 14.06: Post-Installation Tasks: Drivers and Updates

As a tech, you will run into countless well-meaning, industrious, but ultimately hopeless customers who have taken their OS installation into their own hands, only to find that some critical piece of hardware doesn't work properly post-installation. Because of this, you absolutely must become well versed in the art of finding and installing hardware drivers and Windows updates.

Imagine, then, that you have a friend who has been happily using Windows XP Professional on his custom-built PC for a few years. The PC recently grew unstable, so your friend decided to do his own migration to Windows 7, which seemed to go pretty well. Now, however, his wireless networking card doesn't work. And his graphics card seems to be acting kind of funny. And he can't hear any sound. And ... you get the picture. Because you're an excellent tech, you instantly recognize the problem, and you graciously let him know that the problem is a result of his not properly following up his Windows installation with the appropriate driver installations. Then, of course, you offer to help him out.

✔ **Cross-Reference**

To review the process of installing drivers and updates, refer to the "Post-Installation Tasks" section in Chapter 14 of *Mike Meyers' CompTIA A+ Guide to Managing and Troubleshooting PCs*.

Learning Objectives

In this exercise, you'll learn how to finish up an installation by installing hardware drivers and operating system updates.

At the end of this lab, you'll be able to

- Find and install the correct hardware drivers for your operating system

- Install updates to the operating system

Lab Materials and Setup

The materials you need for this lab are

- A working Windows 7 PC

- Internet access

- A notepad and pencil

- Possibly a second PC and a thumb drive or other removable media

Getting Down to Business

The first thing you should do post-installation is to update your operating system, so you'll learn how to do that before you move on to finding and installing drivers.

Step 1   When you install Windows 7, it installs basic drivers for a wide range of products, so it's highly likely that Windows 7 will immediately have Internet access. If that isn't the case, you will have to use another computer to find network drivers for your Windows 7 PC, and then use a thumb drive or other removable media to transfer them over. For more information on how to do that, see the next step of this lab.

Once you have Internet access, click Start | All Programs | Windows Update. Over the years, Microsoft has made this a fairly painless process, so all you have to do is click the *Check for updates* button and wait.

When Windows Update has finished finding updates for your OS, click the *Install updates* button to begin the installation process. If you're curious about the updates being installed, you can click the *View available updates* button for more information.

After clicking the *Install updates* button, you may be asked to agree to further license agreements, which you should agree to. Then, Windows 7 will download and install any updates it found. Note that for a just-installed OS, this can take a long time, so you may have to be patient for this step.

Once the updates have all been downloaded and installed, you will be asked to restart your computer. Do so, and you're done. Sometimes, it's a good idea to run Windows Update again after updating, just to make sure it got everything, but that's really up to you.

Step 2 Once you've got your operating system updated (or if you need drivers to access the Internet), it's time to install hardware drivers. On a custom-built PC, this step can be pretty intimidating, since you can't just go to, say, Dell's Web site and download all the drivers in bulk. Instead, you have to track down drivers for each and every component in your system. This can be a time-consuming process, but there are a few tools that all good geeks should know about that can drastically reduce the frustration of this process.

The first thing to do when looking for drivers is to check Device Manager to get an idea about what drivers you should be looking for. To get to Device Manager in Windows XP, right-click My Computer, go to Properties, select the Hardware tab, and click Device Manager (in Vista/7, just open the Start menu, type **Device Manager** into the Search bar, and then click the Device Manager icon).

If you see "Video controller (VGA compatible)" listed in Device Manager with a yellow question mark next to it, you know you need to look for graphics drivers. If you see "Ethernet controller" listed, you know you need to look for drivers for your network interface card, and so on. Most of the missing-driver descriptions should give you a hint as to what they are for.

To find the drivers, you'll need to know the model name or number of your devices. Shut down your computer, open the case, and look at the motherboard, graphics card, and any other expansion cards the PC may have, like sound cards, TV tuners, and so forth. Often, these parts will have a manufacturer and model number on them somewhere, such as Gigabyte GA-MA790GPT-UD3H written on your motherboard, or NVIDIA GeForce GTX 560 on your graphics card. Write those things down and then do a Google search for them. If you can find the manufacturer, just go to its Web site, look up your product, and follow the link to download drivers.

Sometimes, you're not lucky enough to get a manufacturer or model number, but just about every device out there should have a sticker with some sort of part number or serial number on it. Usually, doing a quick Google search for that number and the word "driver" will get you the results you need. Finding drivers can be pretty frustrating, but keep searching and you're almost guaranteed to find what you're after.

In today's computing world, if you can find your motherboard's chipset drivers, most of the unknown driver icons in Device Manager will go away, so concentrate on finding your motherboard drivers first, and the expansion cards second.

Lab Analysis Test

1. Phyllis wants to do an upgrade installation from Windows Vista Business to Windows 7 Professional, and the Windows 7 Upgrade Advisor says her computer is eligible for an upgrade installation. When she boots her computer from the Windows 7 installation disc, however, the Upgrade option is grayed out. Why is that?

2. What's the recommended CPU speed and amount of RAM needed to install Windows 7 Professional 32-bit? How about 64-bit?

3. Dwight wants to upgrade his old Windows XP system to Windows Vista, but he isn't sure whether his hardware is sufficient to support Vista. Since the Windows Vista Upgrade Advisor is no longer available, what would you recommend that he use to check his system?

4. Michael is about to replace his aging Windows XP Home machine with a hotrod PC running Windows 7 Ultimate, but he wants to transfer all his documents to the new computer. What tool can you recommend that he use to do that?

5. What happens if you don't run the Windows Activation Client for Windows 7 within 30 days of installation?

Key Term Quiz

Use the following terms to complete the following sentences. Not all terms will be used.

1 GHz

2 GHz

BD-ROM

CD-ROM

clean installation

DVD-ROM

Easy Transfer

network drive

Upgrade Advisor

upgrade installation

Windows 7

Windows Vista

Windows XP

1. If you plan to install Windows Vista onto a system, it must have a(n) _____.

2. You can start with a blank hard drive to perform a(n) _____ of Windows 7.

3. You can use the _____ to see if your computer is capable of running Windows 7.

4. If you want to migrate your data from a Windows XP or Vista computer to a Windows 7 computer, you can use the _____ tool.

5. _____ can be upgraded to Windows 7.

Chapter 15
Windows Under the Hood

Lab Exercises

While Windows is arguably one of the most accessible operating systems available, Microsoft doesn't plaster your desktop with every single feature and option. In fact, certain options are well hidden so that less technically inclined users don't break anything. As a PC tech, of course, you'll be the one digging up these options and understanding how they work. The Registry rests at the heart of Windows, storing everything there is to know about your computer. The Windows boot files are special files used to load the OS. The Task Manager utility enables you to control programs, processes, services, and more. While all of these tools hide under the hood, they are key to controlling how Windows functions.

 30 MINUTES

Lab Exercise 15.01: The Windows Registry

The Registry stores everything about your PC, including information on all the hardware in the PC, network information, user preferences, file types, and virtually anything else you might run into with Windows. The hardware, software, and program configuration settings in the Registry are particular to each PC. Two identical PCs with the same operating system and hardware can still be remarkably different because of user settings and preferences. Almost any form of configuration done to a Windows system results in changes to the Registry.

> ✖ **Warning**
>
> When changing the Registry, proceed with great care—making changes in the Registry can cause unpredictable and possibly harmful results. To paraphrase the old carpenter's adage: consider twice, change once!

Learning Objectives

Most of the common tools used to modify the Registry are contained in the Control Panel. When you use the Display applet to change a background, for example, the resultant changes are added to the Registry. The Control Panel applets are what you should normally use to configure the Registry. However, there are times—a virus attack, perhaps, or complete removal of a stubborn application—when direct manipulation of the Registry is needed. In this lab, you'll familiarize yourself with the Windows Registry and the direct manipulation of the Registry using the regedit command.

At the end of this lab, you'll be able to

- Access the Registry using regedit

- Export, import, and modify Registry data subkeys and values

- Define the function of the five top-level Registry keys

Lab Materials and Setup

The materials you need for this lab are

- A working computer running Windows XP, Windows Vista, or Windows 7

Getting Down to Business

A technician needs to know how to access the Registry and modify the configuration based on solid support from Microsoft or other trusted sources. As mentioned in the Learning Objectives, your main interface to the Registry is the Control Panel. Changes made through the applets in the Control Panel result in modifications to the Registry settings. To see what's going on behind the scenes, though, you'll explore the Registry directly in this exercise using the regedit command.

✔ Cross-Reference

For more details on the Windows Registry and working with regedit, refer to the "Registry" section in Chapter 15 of *Mike Meyers' CompTIA A+ Guide to Managing and Troubleshooting PCs*.

Step 1 You almost never need to access the Registry directly. It's meant to work in the background, quietly storing all the necessary data for the system, updated only through a few menus and installation programs. When you want to access the Registry directly, you must use the Registry Editor (regedit or regedt32).

✔ Hint

This lab exercise was written using a system running Windows XP Professional and works in Vista/7. Windows XP and all later versions have combined the two versions of the Registry Editor—regedit and regedt32—into simply regedit (although you can still use either command to open the editor).

To edit the Registry directly, follow these steps:

a. Select Start | Run, type **regedit**, and then click OK (see Figure 15-1) to start the Registry Editor.

b. Note the five main subgroups or root keys in the Registry (see Figure 15-2). Some of these root key folders may be expanded. Click the minus sign by any expanded folders. Do a quick mental review—do you know the function of each Registry key? You should!

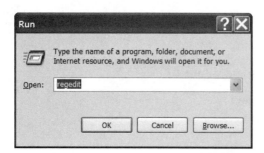

FIGURE 15-1 Starting the Registry Editor

c. Now test your knowledge of the Registry. Referring to the textbook as necessary, match the listed keys with their definitions by writing the definition letter next to the corresponding key:

HKEY_CLASSES_ROOT	
HKEY_CURRENT_USER	
HKEY_LOCAL_MACHINE	
HKEY_USERS	
HKEY_CURRENT_CONFIG	

A. Contains the data for non-user-specific configurations, and includes every device in your PC and those you've removed

B. Contains the personalization information for all users on a PC

C. Contains additional hardware information when there are values in HKEY_LOCAL_MACHINE such as two different monitors

D. Defines the standard class objects used by Windows; information stored here is used to open the correct application when a file is opened

E. Contains the current user settings, such as fonts, icons, and colors on systems that are set up to support multiple users

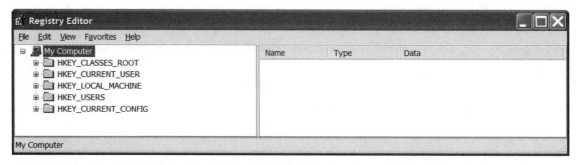

FIGURE 15-2 Viewing the five main subgroups of the Windows XP Registry

Step 2 One of the reasons you might want to edit the Registry directly would be to implement or expand a component of Windows that is not accessible through the Control Panel interface. A favorite of many techs is to enable the Rename function for the Recycle Bin. Expand the HKEY_CLASSES_ROOT key by clicking the plus sign. Notice that there are more subkeys underneath it, some of which have sub-keys of their own, and so on. Search down to the CLSID subkey and expand the key by clicking the plus sign. You will see hundreds of long identification codes. Now use the Find utility (CTRL-F) and enter the following string into the text box: **645FF040-5081-101B-9F08-00AA002F954E**. Make sure you enter the numbers correctly. Expand the subkey and click the ShellFolder icon. You should see the information shown in Figure 15-3.

Before you start changing the Registry, it's a good idea to learn how to "back up" the keys by exporting and importing them. This will enable you to reset the subkey to its original state if you make a mistake in your entries.

   a. Highlight the ShellFolder subkey, and then select File | Export to open the Export Registry File dialog box. Save the key in a folder where you can find it again, and give it a useful name that you won't forget.

   b. Highlight the key again, and double-click the Attributes REG_BINARY file. Replace the hexa-decimal number 40 01 00 20 with **50 01 00 20** and click OK.

   c. Double-click the CallForAttributes REG_DWORD file. Replace the 40 with **00** and click OK.

   d. Minimize the Registry Editor and find the Recycle Bin on your desktop.

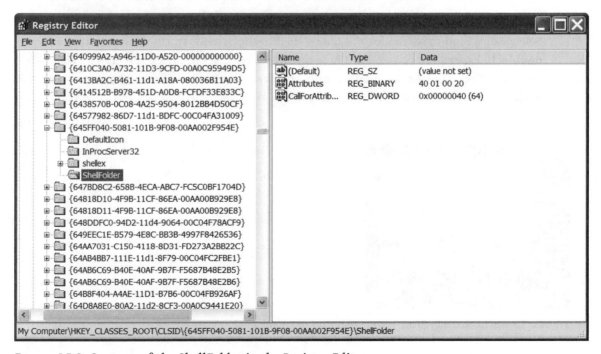

FIGURE 15-3 Contents of the ShellFolder in the Registry Editor

e.   Right-click the Recycle Bin icon. In the drop-down menu there is now a Rename option (see Figure 15-4). Click Rename and change the name of the Recycle Bin. Fun, eh?

f.   To return the Recycle Bin to its natural state, first rename it back to Recycle Bin. Now navigate to your exported Registry file and double-click the file. You will be asked if you are sure you want to add this information to the Registry. Click Yes. You should see a message that the information was successfully added to the Registry.

g.   To confirm that your backup Registry information has taken effect, right-click the Recycle Bin. Can you still rename it? _____

Step 3   Imagine you're in the Control Panel adjusting your mouse settings, and you adjust the mouse double-click speed to the maximum (fastest) and close the window without testing it. When you try to use the system, you can't double-click the mouse fast enough even to get back into the Control Panel to fix it. (This is a bit of a stretch, as you could always use the keyboard to access the Mouse applet, but go with me here to see the Registry in action.) So, what do you do? Follow these steps to view your current Mouse applet double-click speed setting and then use regedit to change it:

a.   Access the Control Panel and open the Mouse applet.

b.   On the Buttons tab, adjust the slider for the double-click speed to the middle position, and test to be sure it works.

c.   Click Apply and then OK. Close the Mouse applet and the Control Panel.

d.   Open the Registry Editor, and make sure that My Computer is highlighted at the top of the left pane.

e.   Select Edit | Find to search for the mouse double-click speed. In the Find What field, type **doubleclickspeed** (be sure to spell it as one word, no spaces). Check the Match Whole String Only box. Click Find Next. You want only the first occurrence it finds. There are other things with that name that you don't want to change.

FIGURE 15-4 The Recycle Bin's newly added Rename option

f. When regedit finds the file, right-click the word DoubleClickSpeed in the right pane and select Modify.

g. Change the value to something between 100 and 900 (milliseconds); 100 is very fast. Click OK and then close the Registry Editor.

h. Reopen the Mouse applet in the Control Panel. Did the slider move from where it was?

    _____

i. For more practice, set your double-click speed to the fastest setting in the Control Panel and go to the Registry to slow it down.

✔ **Hint**

The Web site www.pctools.com/guides/registry is full of working Registry fixes.

 30 MINUTES

Lab Exercise 15.02: Windows XP Boot Files

In Windows XP, there are important system files that are required for the operating system to load properly. These files are vital to the boot process of any Windows XP–based operating system. Becoming more familiar with their purpose and where they reside on a Windows system can help you when you get in a situation that calls for you to replace corrupted system files.

Learning Objectives

At the end of this lab, you'll be able to

- Locate and understand the different boot files associated with Windows XP

- Make changes to the boot.ini file

Lab Materials and Setup

The materials you need for this lab are

- A working computer running Windows XP

Getting Down to Business

A technician needs to understand the location of important system boot files on a Windows XP system so that he or she can troubleshoot any corrupted files quickly and efficiently.

→ **Note**

This exercise was done on a computer with a clean installation of Windows XP Professional. Although the edition of your Windows XP operating system will not affect this lab, having multiple operating systems installed could alter the results you see in your lab environment.

Step 1   By default, Microsoft hides important system files. This is a good thing, because normal users don't need access to these files. However, we aren't normal users!

    a.   To see all the files that Microsoft hides, click on Start | My Computer. Click Tools | Folder Options.

    b.   Click on the View tab. In the Advanced settings area, select the *Show hidden files and folders* radio button.

    c.   Uncheck *Hide protected operating system files (Recommended)*.

    d.   Finally, uncheck *Hide extensions for known file types* so that you can see the files in all of their glory. Click OK. Windows will ask if you are sure you want to reveal everything. Click OK again to confirm.

Step 2   You should now see many new files in your C: drive, as shown in Figure 15-5.

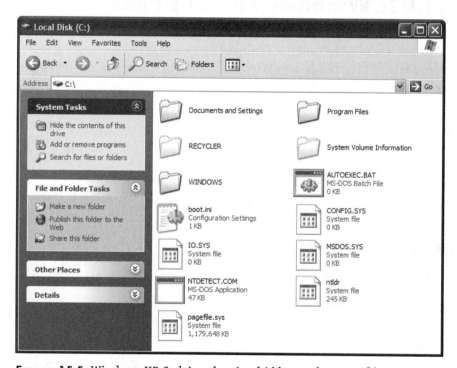

FIGURE 15-5   Windows XP C: drive showing hidden and system files

a. There should be about eight freshly revealed system files on your screen. Pick five of these files (not folders) and give a short description of each.

_____

_____

_____

_____

_____

b. All of these files are important for the booting of Windows XP. Some are extremely relevant and some are meant for backward compatibility with legacy operating systems.

c. List the four files that are kept around for legacy operating systems.

_____

_____

_____

_____

d. Double-click on the boot.ini file. Given your first impression of the boot.ini file, describe its function and purpose. Notice that the boot.ini file is just a text file. Close the file when you are finished.

_____

Step 3 Next, let's find another way to view the boot.ini and how your system boots up.

a. Open the System Properties applet by pressing WINDOWS LOGO KEY-PAUSE/BREAK. Click on the Advanced tab. Under Startup and Recovery, click Settings. This will open the Startup and Recovery dialog box. The first section is all about system startup.

b. Click Edit. Now that should look familiar! Pretty cool, eh? Close out of the boot.ini file to return to the Startup and Recovery dialog box.

c. Change the *Time to display list of operating systems* setting to 15 seconds. Click OK.

d. Return to the Startup and Recovery dialog box by clicking Settings again. Click Edit to view the boot.ini file again. Your new timer of 15 seconds should be listed. Your boot.ini file should look something like the one shown in Figure 15-6.

e. Now, let's really go to town on the boot.ini file. First, we need to save a backup on the C: drive. Use File | Save as and name it **bootini.bak**. Close Notepad.

f. Click on Edit to open the original boot.ini file again.

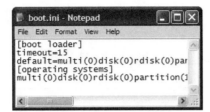

Figure 15-6 Boot.ini showing a 15-second timeout

✔ **Cross Reference**

If you want more clarity on the syntax used in the boot.ini file, refer to the "The Windows XP Boot Process" section in Chapter 15 of *Mike Meyers' CompTIA A+ Guide to Managing and Troubleshooting PCs.*

---

    g.   This is an example of what your boot.ini file should look like:

```
[boot loader]
timeout=30
default=multi(0)disk(0)rdisk(0)partition(1)\WINDOWS
[operating systems]
multi(0)disk(0)rdisk(0)partition(1)\WINDOWS="Microsoft Windows XP Professional" /
fastdetect /NoExecute=OptOut
```

    h.   Change your boot.ini file to say this:

```
[boot loader]
timeout=20
default=multi(0)disk(0)rdisk(0)partition(2)\WINDOWS
[operating systems]
multi(0)disk(0)rdisk(0)partition(1)\WINDOWS="Microsoft Windows XP Professional"
multi(0)disk(0)rdisk(0)partition(2)\WINDOWS="I Love Lamp"
```

    i.   Save your settings. Close out of boot.ini. Reboot the computer.

    j.   Give a detailed description of what happens.

_____

_____

_____

_____

Step 4 Reboot the computer and this time choose to enter Microsoft Windows XP Professional instead of I Love Lamp.

Log on to the computer and delete the boot.ini file that you altered during the lab exercise. Restore the original that you created by renaming it from bootini.bak to **boot.ini**.

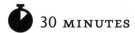 30 MINUTES

Lab Exercise 15.03: Windows Vista/7 Boot Files

Just like in Windows XP, there are important system files that are required to let the operating system load when a computer is turned on for Windows Vista/7. These files are essential to the Windows Vista and Windows 7 boot process. Becoming more familiar with their purpose and where they reside on the system can help you when you need to replace corrupted system files.

Learning Objectives

In this lab, you will practice locating the Windows Vista/7 boot files and using the bcdedit program.

At the end of this lab, you'll be able to

- Locate and understand the different boot files associated with Windows Vista/7

- Use bcdedit.exe

Lab Materials and Setup

The materials you need for this lab are

- A working computer running Windows Vista/7

Getting Down to Business

Just like in Windows XP, the boot files in Windows Vista/7 are hidden to protect them from users. A technician, though, needs to know where to find them and how to fix them if there are any problems. Unfortunately, just because Windows Vista and Windows 7 use the same files to manage the boot process doesn't mean that they store them in the same location.

Step 1 Where are my boot files? Well, the answer isn't easy. It really depends on your operating system and the motherboard you are using. To figure it all out, let's do a series of "If-Then" statements—if this, then that. Follow along and it will all make sense.

    a. If your computer is a Windows Vista computer, then all of your important system boot files will be stored in the following path:

       C:\Boot\

    b. If your computer is a Windows 7 computer using a motherboard with a traditional BIOS, then your computer will have a special 100-MB system partition. You can view the contents of this partition by going to Disk Management and mounting the 100-MB partition with any drive letter you want. The path will be the same as above, except you need to replace "C:" with the drive letter you chose to assign to the tiny system partition.

➜ **Note**

In order to see any of these files, you need to go to the Folder Options dialog box and select the *Show hidden files, folders, and drives* radio button and uncheck the *Hide protected operating system files (Recommended)* checkbox. You can reach these options from any Windows Explorer view in Windows Vista/7. Click **Organize | Folder and search options**, and then click on the **View** tab.

c.   If your computer is a Windows 7 computer using a motherboard with an EFI/UEFI BIOS, your computer will still have that same 100-MB system partition. For security reasons, however, you will not be able to access the contents of the system partition through the Windows GUI. If you really want to—I don't recommend it—you can mount the drive letter by opening a command prompt with elevated privileges and typing **mountvol /s**. This command mounts the EFI/UEFI system partition to a drive letter of your choosing. Unfortunately, you still can't access this drive letter from the Windows GUI. With a little more command-line interface knowledge, you might stand a chance to navigate your way around the EFI/UEFI system partition. Good luck!

➜ **Note**

To determine if you have an EFI/UEFI motherboard, go to Disk Management. If the system partition is labeled "EFI," you have an EFI/UEFI motherboard. You can also check if your motherboard supports EFI/UEFI by looking at the box it came in or the manual.

Step 2   In order to see some of the important system files in action for a Windows Vista/7 system, we are going to have to venture into the realm of the command-line interface.

a.   Open the Start menu and type **cmd** in the Search bar. Don't press ENTER. Right-click on cmd.exe and select *Run as administrator*. You will then be presented with a confirmation from UAC. Click Yes.

b.   At the command prompt, type **bcdedit**. It will take a few moments to load completely.

c.   What would happen if you ran the command bcdedit without choosing *Run as administrator* in Step 2a?

_____

d.   You use the bcdedit utility to edit the BCD. Describe, in your own words, the BCD.

_____

_____

e.   The bcdedit screen can be overwhelming. Fill in the following values based off the Windows Boot Manager section of bcdedit. If the values don't exist on your PC, then skip them.

Identifier   _____

Devices   _____

Path   _____

Description   _____

Timeout   _____

f.   You should also have a section in bcdedit called Windows Boot Loader. You may have one or more sections depending on how your system is configured. Pick one of the listings and fill in the following values.

Identifier   _____

Devices   _____

Path   _____

Description   _____

Osdevice   _____

g.   Make a backup copy of the BCD by exporting it. To export the BCD, type in the following command:

bcdedit /export "C:\backup\bcdbackup"

h.   This command will export the BCD into the path of your choice. In this case, we chose C:\backup\bcdbackup. Browse to your C:\backup folder that you just created to ensure that it created the backup file. List the size of the file in the space provided.

_____

i.   Close all open windows and command prompts to return to your desktop.

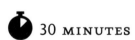 30 MINUTES

Lab Exercise 15.04: The Task Manager

All Microsoft operating systems include a utility that enables you to view all of the tasks running on your system. Since the days of Windows NT, Windows has used the Task Manager to accomplish this. The Task Manager is arguably one of the most important troubleshooting utilities included in Windows. The Task Manager enables you to start, view, and end tasks. You can also see the resources being used by each running task. This lab exercise will show you how to best use the Task Manager, as well as introduce you to a third-party tool that makes the Task Manager look like a child's toy by comparison.

Learning Objectives

In this lab, you'll learn how to use the Task Manager and Process Explorer to work with running applications and processes.

At the end of this lab, you'll be able to

- Locate and use the Task Manager
- Download and run Process Explorer

Lab Materials and Setup

The materials you need for this lab are

- A working computer running Windows XP, Windows Vista, or Windows 7

Getting Down to Business

Your friend Max just bought a new computer. He's loaded it up with new games and applications, but after he finished installing everything, he noticed his computer slowing down. He has no idea what could be causing this and needs help! Assist Max by using the Task Manager and a third-party tool called Process Explorer.

Step 1   Opening the Task Manager can be done in a variety of ways on a Windows computer. Try each of the following:

- CTRL-ALT-DEL

→ **Note**

If you are on a PC with the Welcome screen disabled, you will need to click on Select Task Manager (Windows XP) or Start Task Manager (Windows Vista/7).

- CTRL-SHIFT-ESC
- Right-click on the taskbar and select Task Manager (Windows XP) or Start Task Manager (Windows Vista/7)

Step 2   The first screen you will see is the Applications tab. This shows you the currently running programs on your system. This list should comprise any open applications on your taskbar.

a.   With the Task Manager still open, open Notepad.

b.   Notepad should now be listed as a task in the Task Manager. The Status column should list it as Running. This is good—we like it when applications (or tasks) are running. If you ever see an application listed as Not Responding, the application is having issues.

    c.   With Notepad selected in the Task Manager, click End Task. Describe the results.

_____

Step 3   Open Windows Media Player. Then open the Task Manager (if you closed it). You should now see Windows Media Player listed in the tasks under the Applications tab.

    a.   Sometimes, using the End Task button doesn't end the task. The application might feel stuck and won't close. When this happens, we need to turn to the Processes tab. Right-click on the Windows Media Player task in the Applications tab and select Go To Process. This opens the Processes tab with the appropriate process selected.

    b.   Record the process that is associated with Windows Media Player as well as how much memory is allocated to it.

        •   Process name: _____

        •   Mem Usage: _____

    c.   Right-click on the process name and click End Process. Describe what happens.

_____

➜ **Note**

If you ended the process and Windows Media Player didn't go away, then you ended the wrong process. Whoops!

    d.   You may have also noticed the End Process Tree option next to the End Process option. We'll use this feature later in this exercise.

Step 4   With the Task Manager open, click on the Performance tab. This is another great area for troubleshooting and diagnosing a Windows PC. You'll notice that you can monitor the CPU and RAM usage from this tab.

    a.   Record the following based on your operating system. For Windows XP users, record the Commit Charge. For Windows Vista/7 users, record the Physical Memory percentage. Both of these values are located in the bottom-right corner of the window.

_____

    b.   Open 15 instances of Microsoft WordPad. Record the new Physical Memory percentage or Commit Charge.

_____

    c.   Close all 15 instances of Microsoft WordPad.

Step 5   Switch back to the Processes tab. Scroll down until you find winlogon.exe. This process is a bit odd because, even on Windows Vista/7, there is no description listed.

a.   Try to end the process winlogon.exe. Record the results.

_____

b.   You might think this process is some type of malware that has infected your system, but before you do anything else, you need to be sure.

c.   Open a Web browser and search for **Process Explorer**. Clicking the first search result should take you to the Windows Sysinternals Web site (see Figure 15-7).

d.   Download the latest version of Process Explorer. Once downloaded, extract the contents of the zipped archive to a folder on your desktop or another location of your choosing.

e.   Open the folder with the extracted files and run the program **procexp.exe**. It should look familiar. Think of Process Explorer as a super-advanced Task Manager.

FIGURE 15-7   The Windows Sysinternals Web site

f.   Look around the Process Explorer application. Notice that certain processes branch off of other processes. This is where that End Process Tree option from earlier can come in handy. You can end all the connected processes at once.

g.   Scroll down and find winlogon.exe. You'll notice that pretty much every process shows how much RAM is allocated to it, along with descriptions of the process—except for winlogon.exe again! Right-click on winlogon.exe and select Search Online. Give a detailed description of winlogon.exe.

_____

_____

Step 6   It's a good thing we were unable to end that process—looks like Windows needs that one. Take some time to become more familiar with Process Explorer. You'll see that it's more powerful than the Task Manager. You can even use Process Explorer to replace the traditional Task Manager when you press CTRL-ALT-DEL.

a.   Click Options | Replace Task Manager.

b.   If you want to undo the replacement of the Task Manager, just repeat the previous step.

c.   Close out of all the open windows and programs to finish the exercise.

Lab Analysis Test

1.   Sally says that her computer runs slowly and that it doesn't respond like it used to. How could you use the Task Manager to check out the problem?

2.   Jim receives an error message on startup that says "NTLDR is Missing." What can you tell Jim about ntldr that will help him understand why it is so important to a Windows computer?

3.   Why would a user ever want to edit their boot.ini file?

4.   Describe the function of the Registry and explain why someone would edit it.

5.   John wants to access the Task Manager so he can end some processes. What are the three ways he could open it?

Key Term Quiz

Use the following terms to complete the following sentences. Not all terms will be used.

bcdedit

boot.ini

bootmgr

HKEY_CLASSES_ROOT

HKEY_CURRENT_CONFIG

HKEY_CURRENT_USER

HKEY_LOCAL_MACHINE

HKEY_USERS

ntdetect.com

ntldr

Process Explorer

regedit

Registry

Task Manager

winload.exe

1. The Registry contains all the configuration data and can be accessed directly using _____.

2. The _____ file is used to manage the boot process of Windows Vista/7.

3. The _____ is a built-in Windows tool used to start and end processes.

4. _____ is the Registry key that stores the plug-and-play information about your computer.

5. Windows Vista/7 use the _____ tool to view and edit the boot configuration.

Chapter 16

NTFS, Users, and Groups

Lab Exercises

Not every computer is a part of some vast corporate network. Not everyone logs on to a domain and manipulates multiple file servers to carry out their business. Sometimes, a system stands alone. And lest you take pity on this lonely PC—or worse, ignore it entirely—you must still think about its security. Even without a network, a single computer contains plenty of vital data, and it is these very systems that will be accessed by multiple users (because, well, it's the only one). Without taking the necessary security precautions, your data could easily be stolen or destroyed by anyone else who uses that computer. This is why user accounts, permissions, and encryption in Windows are so important.

As a PC tech, you may be called upon to set up a new user account. But simply adding a new user is just the beginning. You will need to keep in mind what sort of powers or permissions you want each user to have—do they need to be able to install new software, or is just being able to open and edit files enough?

But sometimes, the general set of abilities granted by each type of user account isn't specific enough—maybe certain files or folders should be accessed only by certain users, or groups of users. Then there are the files that should only be seen or touched by you, with access granted by your password alone. Or the opposite—maybe you need to share some folders so that everyone on that PC can get to them. This chapter will show you how to implement these security features in Windows so that a single system can have multiple users working with and sharing files securely.

 15 MINUTES

Lab Exercise 16.01: Managing Users in Windows

Any time you access a PC, you do so through a local user account, whether Windows makes it obvious or not. A lot of home PCs have only one user, without a password, so this process becomes transparent. But that would not be the ideal setup for the workplace, unless you want everyone to be able to go through everyone else's bank records, e-mail messages, personal photos, and so on. Having local user accounts provides a means of authentication—making sure that Steve *is* Steve—and authorization—allowing Steve to delete this, but not install that.

Learning Objectives

In this lab, you'll practice creating and managing new users.

At the end of this lab, you'll be able to

- Create and manage a new local user account
- Work with user groups

Lab Materials and Setup

The materials you need for this lab are

- A PC running Windows

Getting Down to Business

Your client is a small business with four employees and one computer. They each need their own user account so that they can keep their personal data private and so that they stop accidentally deleting everything while logged on as an administrator. Adam is the only one with enough knowledge of computers to have a more powerful account. Betsy, Carol, and Dale each need more limited accounts, because they aren't tech savvy and could easily break something.

This exercise works with any version of Windows, but for the sake of instruction, the steps will be repeated for Windows XP, Windows Vista, and Windows 7.

✔ **Cross-Reference**

For more information on users and groups, refer to the "Managing Users in Windows XP," "Managing Users in Windows Vista," and "Managing Users in Windows 7" sections in Chapter 16 of *Mike Meyers' CompTIA A+ Guide to Managing and Troubleshooting PCs.*

Step 1   Follow these steps to create a new user account for Betsy in Windows XP:

a.   Make sure to sign in as an administrator, so that you can create the user account. Then click Start | Control Panel.

b.   If Classic view is not enabled in the Control Panel, enable it now by clicking Switch to Classic View.

c.   Double-click User Accounts. Then click *Change the way users log on or off*. Deselect the *Use the Welcome screen* option (see Figure 16-1). This also disables Fast User Switching. Now each user will have to type in their user name and password at the login screen. Click Apply Options.

d.   Click *Create a new account*. Enter a user name, and then click Next.

e.   For the account type, choose Limited. Then click Create Account (see Figure 16-2).

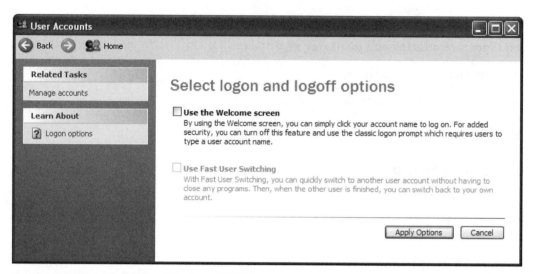

FIGURE 16-1 Disabling the Windows XP Welcome screen

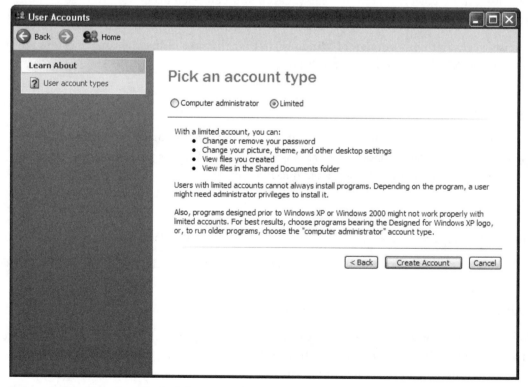

FIGURE 16-2 Choosing Limited for account type

f.   Windows XP creates user accounts without passwords by default, so you need to add the password manually. Select the user you just created by clicking her icon. Then click *Create a password*. Type in a memorable password and confirm it. Then create a hint phrase to remind you of the password if you forget it. *Do not* use the password as the hint phrase, since this makes having a password pointless. Click *Create password*.

Step 3   Follow these steps to create a new user account for Carol in Windows Vista:

a.   Make sure to sign in as an administrator, so that you can create the user account. Then click Start | Control Panel. Click Switch to Classic View, and then double-click User Accounts.

b.   Select *Manage another account* (see Figure 16-3). Then click *Create a new account*.

c.   Type in a new account name. Standard user should already be selected. Click Create Account.

d.   Select Carol's user account from the Manage Accounts screen. Click *Create a password*. Type in a memorable password, confirm it, and then create a password hint to remind yourself in case you forget. Click *Create password*.

Step 4   Follow these steps to create a new user account for Dale in Windows 7:

a.   Make sure to sign in as an administrator, so that you can create the user account. Then click Start | Control Panel. Under the link to User Accounts and Family Safety, click on the link *Add or remove user accounts*.

b.   Click on *Create a new account*.

c.   Type in a new account name. Standard user should already be selected. Click Create Account.

Figure 16-3 Selecting the Manage another account link

    d.   Select Dale's user account from the Manage Accounts screen. Click *Create a password*. Type in a memorable password, confirm it, and then create a password hint to remind yourself in case you forget. Click *Create password*.

Step 5   Now that you have standard users created, your client decides that he really needs another administrator besides Adam. Based on the operating system you are doing this exercise on, choose an account to upgrade to Administrator.

    a.   As usual, make sure your account is set to Administrator. Click Start, right-click My Computer/ Computer, and select Manage.

    b.   On the left side of the screen, select Local Users and Groups. On the right side, double-click Groups, and then double-click Administrators.

    c.   In the Administrators Properties window, click Add. Type the user name in the *Enter the object names to select* box, and then click Check Names. Click OK.

    d.   Click OK in the Administrators Properties dialog box. Find the name of the group that the user had been in previously, most likely Users. Double-click it to open the Properties dialog box.

    e.   Find the user name in the list, click it, and then click Remove. Click OK. Now the user is an administrator!

 15 MINUTES

Lab Exercise 16.02: Defining NTFS Permissions

Now that you've learned how to set up authentication, it's time to talk about authorization—what a user can do with files, folders, or any other resource. Granting NTFS permissions is a powerful and complex tool that allows you to define precisely who can do what on a system. Depending on your needs, this can quickly become a complicated and sticky web of overlapping settings that you don't want to deal with. But it's important to know how to define these permissions so that each user has the specific powers and limitations he requires. It's best to start thinking about it one folder at a time: who can open it, and who can edit it?

Learning Objectives

In this lab, you'll use NTFS permissions to define which users can access specific files and folders.

At the end of this lab, you'll be able to

- Set up NTFS permissions for files and folders

Lab Materials and Setup

The materials you need for this lab are

- A PC running Windows XP Professional, Windows Vista Business/Ultimate/Enterprise, or Windows 7 Professional/Ultimate/Enterprise on an NTFS partition

Getting Down to Business

Now that your client has a set of user accounts for his employees, he wants to set up a folder on the C: drive for everyone to use. But there's one text file he doesn't want Dale to touch—he doesn't even want Dale to be able to open it, let alone make any changes. He's asked you to set up the file with the right permissions so that Dale can't access the file.

Setting up permissions for files and setting up permissions for folders are very similar procedures. In this exercise, you'll work with setting up permissions for a text file, but the same procedure will also work with folders.

Step 1   The rest of the steps in this lab will be more straightforward if you first deactivate simple file sharing (in Windows XP only). To do so, open any folder in Windows Explorer, such as My Documents. Select Tools | Folder Options. Switch to the View tab. At the bottom of the list of Advanced settings is the *Use simple file sharing (Recommended)* option. Deselect the box. Click OK.

Step 2   If you haven't done so already, create an account for Dale on your computer using Lab Exercise 16.01. Make sure Dale *isn't* an administrator and *you* are. Then navigate to My Computer/Computer and double-click the C: drive. Right-click an empty area in the right pane of the window and select New | Folder. Rename it **Work**.

Step 3   Open the Work folder you just created. Right-click an empty area again and select New | Text Document.

Step 4   Right-click the text document and select Properties. Then open the Security tab. Click Edit. This opens a more detailed version of the tab you were just looking at. Listed should be several users and groups, but Dale might not be listed. To add him, click Add. Type **Dale** in the *Enter the object names to select* box (see Figure 16-4) and click Check Names. Click OK.

Step 5   Now that Dale is on the list, you can set his permissions. Select Dale from the list of Group or user names. The bottom half of the window shows a list of permissions for Dale. Everything should be set to Allow. Scroll until you see Read. Check the Deny box next to Read. Click Apply. A dialog box will pop up explaining how this will change the permission of this file and how it could affect other files. Choose Yes.

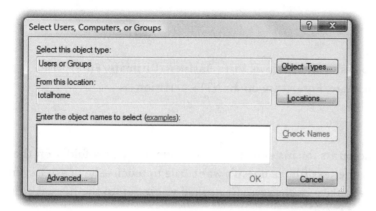

Figure 16-4 The Select Users, Computer, or Groups applet

Step 6 Log off of the administrator account and log in as Dale. Go back into My Computer/Computer, double-click the C: drive, and open the Work folder you created. Double-click the new text file.

What happens?

_____

If all goes well, Notepad should open, but Windows should deny you (Dale) access to the text file. Congratulations! You just set a permission!

 10 MINUTES

Lab Exercise 16.03: Sharing Files and Folders

There are plenty of times when delving into specific NTFS permissions is overkill. Sometimes, you just want to share a folder, one that everyone can freely add to, edit, and so on. Windows makes it incredibly easy to share a folder with multiple local user accounts. Most versions even come with a folder set up for this purpose, like Public Documents in Windows Vista/7. But one shared folder isn't always enough.

Learning Objectives

In this lab, you'll use sharing in Windows to set up a folder that can be accessed by all users.

At the end of this lab, you'll be able to

- Set up a shared folder

Lab Materials and Setup

The materials you need for this lab are

- A PC running Windows XP Professional, Windows Vista Business/Ultimate/Enterprise, or Windows 7 Professional/Ultimate/Enterprise

Getting Down to Business

In the previous lab, you created the Work folder on the C: drive of your computer. But the only account that has complete control of that folder is the one used to create it. Your client wants to make sure that every user on that system has full access to the contents of that folder. The easiest way to accomplish that is to use the share feature of Windows.

This is pretty easy, but to make it clear, the exercise will be divided between Windows XP and Windows Vista/7. You'll need the professional editions of these operating systems (Windows XP Professional, Windows Vista Business/Ultimate/Enterprise, or Windows 7 Professional/Ultimate/Enterprise) because the Home editions of Windows can only use simple file sharing.

✔ **Hint**

Just because you know how to set up sharing in one operating system doesn't mean you shouldn't practice in another. Remember that the CompTIA A+ certification exams aren't just testing you on the OS you already know. Take time to check out all the differences between the Windows versions.

Step 1 Windows makes the basic process of sharing files and folders over a network pretty easy. File sharing in Windows, however, is an incredibly deep and complex topic, and you're only going to scratch the surface in this lab. Entire books have been written about share permissions and proper sharing security. With that said, here are the basic steps for sharing a file over a network with Windows XP:

a. In Windows XP, navigate to the C: drive in My Computer. If you haven't already done so, create a Work folder in the root folder of the C: drive. Then right-click the folder and click Properties.

b. Open the Sharing tab. Select Share This Folder. Then click Permissions. From the choices given, select Everyone. On the bottom half of the window, under Permissions for Everyone, check the Allow box next to Full Control. Click OK. Now you are sharing the Work folder with everyone!

Step 2 The process for sharing folders in Windows Vista/7 has changed significantly. Here are the steps for accomplishing in Vista/7 what you did in XP in Step 1:

a. In Windows Vista/7, navigate to the C: drive in Computer. If you haven't already done so, create a Work folder in the root folder of the C: drive. Then right-click the folder and select Share or Share With, depending on the operating system.

b. Select *Specific people*. From the drop-down menu, select Everyone. Click Add. Then, in the list of Names and Permission Levels below, click Everyone. Open the drop-down menu for the Permission Level and select Read/Write or Co-owner, depending on the operating system. Then click Share. Done!

 10 MINUTES

Lab Exercise 16.04: Encrypting Important Data

So far, you've gone through several methods of securing data on a machine accessed by multiple users. But these features don't secure the data itself as much as put a wall around it to keep people out. The data inside is (as of yet) defenseless. If a system has two administrator accounts, and one administrator sets up file permissions to keep the other out, the second administrator has the power to undo those permissions and access the data—unless you activate encryption.

When you encrypt a file, it becomes absolutely secure from everyone else but you or, more specifically, your password. If you were to lose your password, or an administrator were to change it for you, that data would be lost forever, because that password is *the only way* to get it back. So be careful!

Learning Objectives

In this lab, you'll use encryption to protect sensitive data.

At the end of this lab, you'll be able to

*   Use the Encrypting File System in Windows

Lab Materials and Setup

The materials you need for this lab are

*   A PC running Windows XP Professional, Windows Vista Business/Ultimate/Enterprise, or Windows 7 Professional/Ultimate/Enterprise

Getting Down to Business

Your client has several personal documents that she keeps copies of on her computer at work. But she isn't the only administrator on that system, so to fully secure the data, she wants it to be encrypted.

Thanks to the Encrypting File System (EFS) introduced with NTFS, encrypting files in Windows is simple. Be warned, however, that if you lose access to the user account that you used to encrypt the files, you will lose those files forever!

✔ **Hint**

The Home editions of Windows, such as Windows XP Home, Windows Vista Home Premium, and Windows 7 Home Premium, do not include a utility to encrypt data. If you are using one of these operating systems and still want to or need to use encryption, check out TrueCrypt. Open source (and free), TrueCrypt provides advanced encryption features across multiple platforms. Check it out at www.truecrypt.org.

Step 1 Navigate to the files or folder in question (for the purposes of the lab, use the Work folder you already created). Right-click the Work folder and select Properties. Next to the Attributes checkboxes, click the Advanced button. At the bottom of the Advanced Attributes dialog box, check the box for *Encrypt contents to secure data* (see Figure 16-5). Click OK.

Step 2 Now switch to another user, even another administrator. Navigate back to the folder that you just encrypted. Try opening it.

What happens?

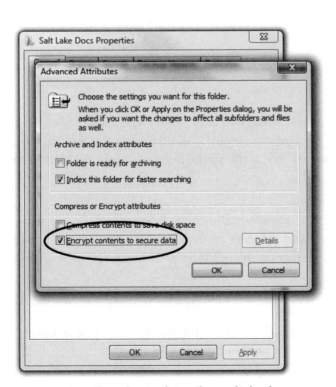

FIGURE 16-5 The Advanced Attributes dialog box

 10 MINUTES

Lab Exercise 16.05: Configuring User Account Control

Starting with Windows Vista, Microsoft introduced users to a new feature called User Account Control (UAC). User Account Control was designed to put controls in place to stop malicious code from spreading on a computer. UAC ensures that important changes cannot be made to a Windows Vista/7 computer without the permission of an administrator. When it debuted with Windows Vista, users were less than enthusiastic about this new feature. Many, myself included, turned the feature off almost immediately because of how invasive it was. With Windows Vista, UAC could either be on or off—there was no middle ground. Microsoft fixed this in Windows 7 and has enabled users to choose four distinct levels of how UAC presents itself. Note that this feature is not available in Windows XP Home or Professional.

Learning Objectives

In this lab, you'll learn the effects of the different UAC settings.

At the end of this lab, you'll be able to

- Understand the effects of User Account Control

Lab Materials and Setup

The materials you need for this lab are

- A PC running Windows 7

Getting Down to Business

You have set up a client, Taylor, with a new computer using Windows 7 Home Premium. Taylor has just downloaded and installed a copy of Ventrilo, a popular Voice over IP (VoIP) application used in the world of online gaming. When she clicks on the icon to start Ventrilo, her screen goes dark and a small prompt appears. She is scared and calls you for help!

Step 1   Open your favorite Web browser and visit www.ventrilo.com/. From that page, visit the Download section and download the appropriate client software package for your version of Windows 7 (see Figure 16-6). After you have downloaded the program, install it on your computer.

→ **Note**

We won't actually be using Ventrilo for anything other than testing out the functions of UAC. So after we are finished with this exercise, feel free to uninstall the application.

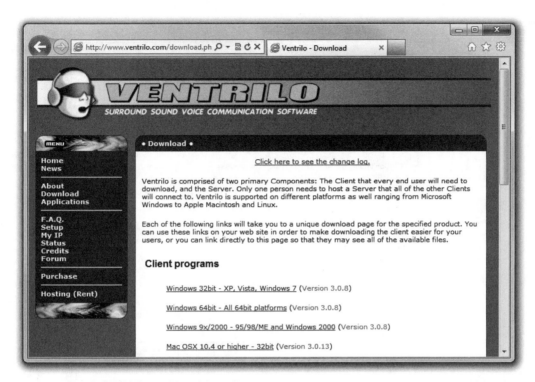

Figure 16-6 Downloading Ventrilo

Step 2 Now, before we get crazy checking out how UAC reacts to Ventrilo, let's see what User Account Control looks like and the different settings it offers in Windows 7.

  a. Click Start | Control Panel | System and Security. Under the Action Center section, click on the *Change User Account Control settings* link.

→ Note

  Alternatively, you can click Start, type **UAC** into the Search bar, and click on the *Change User Account Control settings* link at the top of the search results. However, even when searching, CompTIA still wants you to know the path of how to find the different utilities in Windows.

  b. You should now be in the User Account Control Settings window. If the default settings aren't being used on this machine, go ahead and switch to the default settings (see Figure 16-7). Give a short description of what the default settings are.

_____

_____

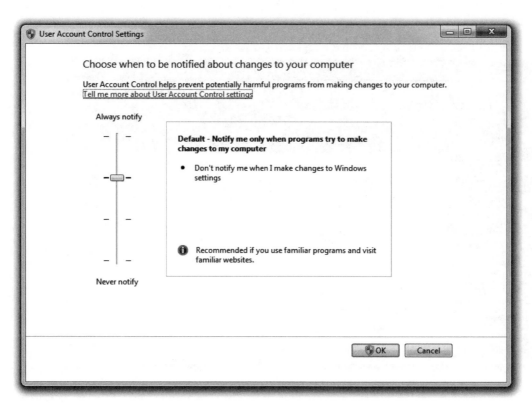

FIGURE 16-7 User Account Control Settings window

c. Click OK to confirm your settings changes, or minimize the UAC window if you made no changes, and open Ventrilo. Describe what happens.

_____

_____

d. Go ahead and click No on the prompt. Return to the User Account Control Settings window as described in Step 2a.

e. Move the slider down one notch, just above Never notify. Click OK to confirm your settings.

f. Open Ventrilo again. Describe what happens this time.

_____

_____

g. Go ahead and click No on the prompt.

Step 3

a.   Click Start | Control Panel | System and Security.

b.   Notice the links to items such as Allow remote access, Device Manager, and Create and format hard disk partitions. What is a similarity between those links and the Ventrilo icon in your Start menu?

_____

c.   Open any of those utilities and record what happens.

_____

d.   This similarity between these items ties directly into how UAC interacts with programs and utilities that are either third-party applications or built directly into the Windows operating system. Return to the User Account Control Settings window as described in Step 2a.

e.   Move the slider bar to the very top for Always notify. Click OK to save the changes. Instantly, you should see the UAC dialog box prompt appear. Click Yes to proceed.

f.   Click on Start | Control Panel | System and Security. Try to click on *Allow remote access, Device Manager,* or *Create and format hard disk partitions.* Also, try to open Ventrilo again. Record the results.

_____

_____

Step 4

a.   This exercise was designed to help you become more familiar with UAC. Why do you think this feature is useful in modern computing?

_____

_____

b.   Which level of User Account Control best fits your needs as a user and why?

_____

_____

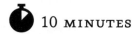 10 MINUTES

Lab Exercise 16.06: Using BitLocker To Go with Windows 7

Starting with Windows Vista, Microsoft introduced users to a new feature called BitLocker. BitLocker is drive-level encryption, meaning it enables you to encrypt your entire hard drive so that no one else can access it. BitLocker requires two volumes (partitions) on your disk. This can take a lot of partition resizing and hassle in Windows Vista, but Windows 7 creates a 100-MB system partition during the installation that fills this requirement. You also need a Trusted Platform Module (TPM) chip to store the encryption key. If you do not have a TPM chip, you have the option of using a USB flash drive to store the key.

Windows 7 added a new feature called BitLocker To Go, which enables you to encrypt flash drives and other similar devices, instead of just entire hard disk drives. While Windows Vista Enterprise/Ultimate and Windows 7 Enterprise/Ultimate all support BitLocker, only Windows 7 Enterprise/Ultimate supports BitLocker To Go. Because you can use BitLocker To Go without all of the hassle of multiple partitions, you'll use it here to learn more about drive encryption.

Learning Objectives

In this lab, you'll learn how to use BitLocker To Go.

At the end of this lab, you'll be able to

- Use BitLocker To Go to encrypt a flash drive

Lab Materials and Setup

The materials you need for this lab are

- A PC running Windows 7 Enterprise or Ultimate
- A PC running Windows Vista or Windows XP
- A USB flash drive

Getting Down to Business

Nikki works for a company that has highly sensitive data stored on its servers. The network administrator is concerned about possible data theft when users like Nikki take work home on a flash drive. He wants to train Nikki and users like her to use BitLocker To Go so that lost flash drives won't be readable by any stranger who picks them up.

Step 1 First, you'll use BitLocker To Go to encrypt the flash drive.

   a. Go to Start | Control Panel | System and Security. Select BitLocker Drive Encryption (see Figure 16-8).

   b. From here you have the ability to turn on BitLocker for your entire hard drive, but we're here for the BitLocker To Go feature. Attach your USB flash drive.

   c. You should see the flash drive appear in the BitLocker Drive Encryption window.

   d. Click Turn On BitLocker. This will begin the BitLocker To Go wizard (see Figure 16-9).

   e. Enter a password that will later unlock the drive. BitLocker To Go also has another way of unlocking the drive besides a password. What is the other method of unlocking the drive?

   _____

   f. Click Next. This screen asks you where you want to store the recovery key in case you forget the password. What options are available for storing the recovery key?

   _____

   g. Choose either option available.

   h. The last screen begins the encryption process. This can take a while, depending on the size of the flash drive.

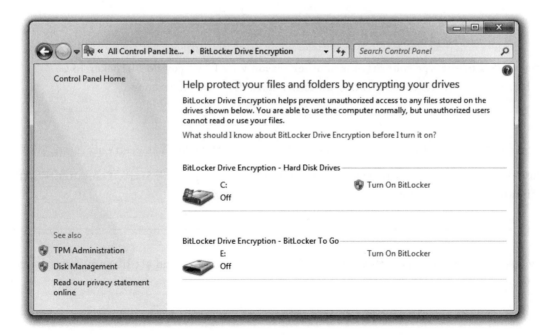

FIGURE 16-8 BitLocker Drive Encryption applet

FIGURE 16-9 BitLocker To Go wizard

→ **Note**

The time it takes to encrypt your drive is another reason why I had you do BitLocker To Go rather than regular BitLocker. Encrypting an entire hard drive can take hours!

i.   Upon completion, you will receive a message stating that the drive has been encrypted. Click OK.

j.   Close out of all the open windows and return to your desktop. Click Start | Computer. What is different about the icon of your flash drive?

_____

k.   Try opening and working with your flash drive. It should work and act like any other flash drive.

Step 2   To test what happens when you connect to your PC a flash drive encrypted using BitLocker To Go, you'll need to disconnect it from your PC, then reconnect it.

a.   Remove your flash drive from the computer.

b.   Wait a minute and then reinsert your flash drive into the computer.

c.   Immediately you should be prompted with a BitLocker Drive Encryption window to supply your password. Click *I forgot my password* and supply it with the recovery key from Step 1. You can also automatically unlock the drive on this computer from now on. When might you check the option?

_____

d.   Click Unlock.

e.   Once you click Unlock, you will be able to read and write to the drive without any problems.

f.   BitLocker To Go also gives you the ability to manage your device by right-clicking on the drive and selecting Manage BitLocker.

g.   List the five options you can choose from while managing BitLocker.

_____

_____

_____

_____

h.   Close the Manage BitLocker dialog box.

→ Note

You will only be able to do Step 3 if you have an available Windows XP or Windows Vista computer.

Step 3 What about other versions of Windows? You know that only Windows 7 Enterprise and Ultimate can configure BitLocker To Go thumb drives. You'll now see what happens when you try to read the encrypted thumb drive on a Windows XP or Windows Vista PC.

a. Take your BitLocker encrypted flash drive and insert it into your Windows XP or Windows Vista computer.

b. Click Start | My Computer/Computer. Double-click to open your flash drive. You should notice two files listed. Open the BitLockerToGo file.

c. Supply BitLocker To Go with your password and click Unlock.

d. You can now drag and drop the files that are located on your flash drive onto the local computer to view them using BitLocker To Go Reader, which enables Windows XP and Windows Vista machines to read your BitLocker-encrypted files.

e. Take a file that is on your Windows XP computer and attempt to drag and drop it onto the flash drive. What happens?

→ **Note**

With BitLocker To Go Reader, you can only read files from an encrypted drive. You can't write to it.

Lab Analysis Test

1. Jonas has an administrator account and sets up the permissions for a folder on the C: drive to deny anyone else from accessing it but himself. If another administrator account was created, would the folder still be secure? Why or why not?

2. Reginald needs to set up a folder that can be seen by the administrator and two standard users, but can be edited only by the administrator. How would he make this work?

3. Arnold wants to implement BitLocker on his hard drive at home because he heard a technician from his IT department at work tell him how much it has helped them at the office. Unfortunately, Arnold has no idea what BitLocker is. Explain to him what BitLocker does and what he will need in order to implement it.

4. Nina created several user accounts in Windows Vista for her family, but forgot to give each of them passwords. List the steps to take to add a password to a user account in Windows Vista.

5. What makes EFS a great security feature in Windows?

Key Term Quiz

Use the following terms to complete the following sentences. Not all terms will be used.

administrator

authentication

authorization

BitLocker

BitLocker To Go

BitLocker To Go Reader

group

limited user

NTFS permissions

simple file sharing

standard user

Trusted Platform Module

User Account Control (UAC)

Users group

Welcome screen

1. A(n) _____ cannot install software or delete system files.

2. Typing your user name and password is a means of _____.

3. Windows Vista introduced a new feature called _____. Windows 7 improved on it by adding _____.

4. _____ are used to define specific rules for which users and groups can and cannot access files and folders.

5. _____ prevents a program from running unless a user authorizes it to.

Chapter 17
Maintaining and Optimizing Windows

Lab Exercises

Imagine that your company has just acquired a small architectural firm. One of the principals of the firm informs you that they haven't really had any IT support to speak of in a few years. You visit the new office and determine that the computers are about five years old. They were good machines when they were purchased, and as long as the hardware is not failing, they should be more than adequate for a year or two more. The architects do complain that their machines are running slowly and that it's affecting productivity. You would like to avoid a complete rollout of new PCs, since you're looking at a replacement expense of thousands of dollars. Consequently, you decide it would be worthwhile to spend a day trying to figure out if anything can be done to make the machines run faster.

After checking out a few of the systems, you determine that they could definitely benefit from additional memory, but that's not the only issue—none of the systems have been updated in over three years! Even though most versions of Windows are optimized when they're installed, time and use can alter that fact significantly. It's important, therefore, to be able to take what you know about navigating and manipulating the Windows environment and put it to work figuring out what needs to be fixed, updated, or improved. Sometimes a simple tweak is all it takes to make a sluggish system run like it's fresh out of the box.

One of the first tasks is to make sure that all of the systems have the latest service packs and Windows updates. Before you do that, however, it's recommended that you back up all of the data on the systems, as this can be a pretty major upgrade. Another item that needs to be checked is whether the device drivers are all up to date. Neglected PCs will definitely require updated device drivers.

First, you will learn how to back up and restore your system as preparation for updating and optimizing Windows. You'll then explore the various troubleshooting tools included with Windows. It's time to drop a few sticks of memory into the pilot machines, back them up, run them through the service packs and updates, and get this office back on its feet!

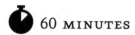 60 MINUTES

Lab Exercise 17.01: Performing a Backup and Restoration

Windows offers simple backup/restoration utilities that you can use to back up system data and program data and files, and an advanced recovery feature, in case the system becomes so unstable that it won't even boot.

Windows XP introduced the Automated System Recovery (ASR) routine, and Windows Vista/7 uses the Backup and Restore Center (though Windows 7 drops the "Center" part). The ASR creates nonbootable disks with tools to restore a system (along with a backup of the system and boot partitions), whereas Vista/7's Backup and Restore Center will make a full (or partial) backup of your entire system that is restored using the System Recovery Options. It is important to understand—and the CompTIA A+ certification exams expect you to know this—that none of these options are bootable.

This lab introduces you to the ASR process in Windows XP Professional and the Backup and Restore Center in Windows Vista/7.

Learning Objectives

Performing backups of any kind is a critical responsibility of a PC technician. The Windows XP Professional Automated System Recovery and the Vista/7 Backup and Restore Center are excellent representations of the steps required to back up and restore an OS.

At the end of this lab, you'll be able to

- Prepare a backup

- Perform a restoration

Lab Materials and Setup

The materials you need for this lab are

- A working PC with Windows XP Professional, Windows Vista, or Windows 7 installed

- Some form of backup media/device (CD/DVD drive, tape drive, network drive, separate partition)

- A blank, formatted floppy disk (XP only)

- The Windows XP Professional or Windows Vista/7 installation media

Getting Down to Business

The time to prepare a backup is while the system and data are in a state of complete integrity. It's when they crash or get corrupted that you'll need the backup! The following steps create an ASR set and then use that ASR set to restore a Windows XP system to working condition. The steps for the Windows Vista/7 Backup and Recovery Center will follow.

AUTOMATED SYSTEM RECOVERY PREPARATION

Step 1   Launch the Windows Backup or Restore Wizard by clicking Start | Run and typing **ntbackup.exe** in the dialog box. Alternatively, you can click Start | All Programs | Accessories | System Tools | Backup. Click the Advanced Mode text link to bring up the screen shown in Figure 17-1.

Step 2   Launch the Automated System Recovery Wizard and perform the following steps:

  a.   Click Next, and in the *Backup media or file name* dialog box, type or browse for the location in which you want the backup to be placed. This backup includes your entire system and boot volumes, which, in most cases, is your C: drive. Your backup media (second hard drive or optical disc) will need to be big enough to hold the contents of that drive.

  b.   Name the backup file, being careful to preserve the .BKF file extension. If you are using a second hard drive, for example, you might enter D:\MyASRBK.BKF to create the file on the D: drive.

  c.   Click Next and then click Finish to start the backup of your system files.

  d.   When the backup completes, the ASR Preparation Wizard instructs you to insert a formatted 1.44-MB floppy disk. Click OK. ASR copies the required files onto the floppy disk.

  e.   When instructed, remove and label the floppy disk and then click OK. You have completed the preparation for an Automated System Recovery.

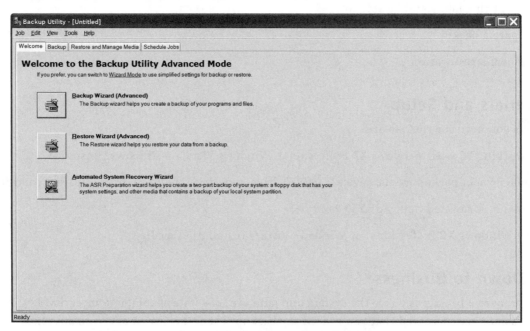

FIGURE 17-1 Windows XP Backup Utility's Advanced Mode screen

→ **Caution**

When you run the ASR restoration, you will format the C: drive. Make sure you've backed up everything you want to keep!

AUTOMATED SYSTEM RECOVERY RESTORE

Step 1 Boot the system using the Windows XP Professional installation CD-ROM.

Step 2 When prompted with *Press F2 to run Automated System Recovery (ASR)*, press the F2 key.

Step 3 Insert the ASR floppy disk and press any key when ready.

Step 4 The Windows XP Installer will copy files to a temporary folder, format the partition where XP will be installed, and prompt you to remove the installation CD-ROM and reboot.

Step 5 After rebooting, the Windows XP installation continues.

    a. During the installation, you'll be prompted for the location of the ASR backup file.

    b. Enter the file location or use the Browse button to enter the location and name of the ASR backup file.

    c. Click OK.

    d. The installation now completes. All of the Windows XP configuration settings and preferences should be as they were on the original system.

BACKUP AND RESTORE CENTER

Step 1 Open Control Panel. Switch to Classic View (if you haven't already) and double-click Backup and Restore Center (Vista) or Backup and Restore (Windows 7).

Step 2 To set up the backup, decide first whether to back up certain files or the whole computer. (In Windows 7, use the *Create a system image* option to create a complete backup of your system.) The Back Up Files wizard will open. Select where to save the backup and click Next. If you chose only a partial backup, select the file types you wish to back up from the list provided. Click Next. For partial backups, Windows also asks how often you want the backup to be updated. Click *Save settings and start backup*.

Step 3   To restore files, choose whether to restore only certain files or to restore a Windows Complete Backup and Restore image (referred to as a System Image in Windows 7). If you are performing a partial restoration, click *Restore files*. Select whether to restore the latest backup or an older one. Click Next. Then select where to restore the backup files to and click Start Restore. If you are overwriting any files, a window will pop up asking how to resolve the conflict.

→ **Note**

> To do a complete restoration, you must reboot your system and open the System Recovery Options from the installation media.

 30 MINUTES

Lab Exercise 17.02: Upgrading to Windows Vista SP2 and Configuring Automatic Updates

These systems have been around for some time, so there are probably a number of outdated patches and drivers. Windows Vista went through a major upgrade with Service Pack 2, so this is where you'll start. If you are working with a new installation of Windows Vista, Service Pack 2 should already be incorporated into the cabinet files, but these are old machines, so they will need some attention. Upgrading to Service Pack 2 is imperative to keeping the system up and running, secure, and compatible with new technology. To bring the OS up to date, you will first manually download and install Service Pack 2, and then configure Automatic Updates so Windows will take care of future updates on its own.

Learning Objectives

A competent technician should understand the importance of upgrading an OS with the latest service pack.

At the end of this lab, you'll be able to

- Upgrade Windows Vista to Service Pack 2
- Configure Windows Automatic Updates to update drivers, security patches, and utilities

Lab Materials and Setup

The materials you need for this lab are

- A working PC with Windows Vista (prior to Service Pack 2) installed
- An Internet connection

> ➔ **Note**
>
> The procedures for updating Windows and setting up Automatic Updates are very similar between Windows XP, Windows Vista, and Windows 7. Although this lab describes a Windows Vista upgrade, the concept remains the same for Windows XP and Windows 7.

Getting Down to Business

You will begin by downloading and installing Service Pack 2 for Windows Vista. Then you will learn how to configure Automatic Updates.

Step 1 You will need to procure Windows Vista Service Pack 2. Go to Microsoft's Web site and search for "Vista Service Pack 2," or go straight to http://technet.microsoft.com/en-us/windows/dd262148.aspx. The search should return a page with the title Service Pack 2 for Windows Server 2008 and Windows Vista; follow the directions on this page to download Service Pack 2. (You'll look at getting updates through Automatic Updates next.)

Step 2 Once the download finishes, log on to the system that you want to update. Open the folder where you have placed the files and complete the following steps:

    a.   Double-click the setup file you downloaded.

    b.   The Windows Vista Service Pack 2 setup wizard welcome screen appears (see Figure 17-2). Click Next to continue.

    c.   The End User License Agreement screen displays next. Accept the agreement and click Next to continue.

    d.   The setup wizard now inspects your machine, installs files, and upgrades your system. When the upgrade is complete, the wizard informs you that "Windows Vista Service Pack 2 is now installed on your computer" (see Figure 17-3).

    e.   Click Finish and let the system reboot.

    f.   After the machine reboots for the first time with Service Pack 2 installed, Windows gives you the opportunity to turn on Automatic Updates before it presents the logon screen. Decline this option for now; you will manually configure this in the next step.

Step 3 You will now configure the system to perform automatic updates. Log on to Windows and complete the following steps:

    a.   In Windows XP, click Start | All Programs | Accessories | System Tools | Security Center. In Windows Vista, type **Security Center** in the Start Search bar. This opens the Windows Security Center window, where you'll find the configuration utility for Windows' Automatic Updates feature. Click Automatic Updates. In Windows 7, go to Control Panel | Windows Update.

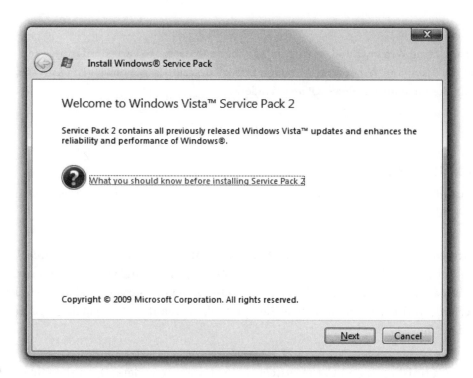

FIGURE 17-2 Welcome to the Windows Vista Service Pack 2 setup wizard

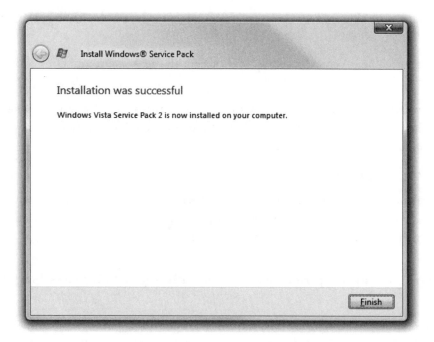

FIGURE 17-3 Completing the Windows Vista Service Pack 2 setup wizard

FIGURE 17-4 Automatic Updates configuration screen

✔ **Cross-Reference**

You will have the opportunity to work with antivirus software in Chapter 29.

b.   This brings up the Automatic Updates configuration screen (see Figure 17-4) in Windows XP. Select the Automatic (recommended) option button and then click Apply. In Windows Vista/7, click *Change settings*, and then choose *Install updates automatically* from the drop-down menu.

 30 MINUTES

Lab Exercise 17.03: Installing Device Drivers in Windows

Installing new devices under Windows is easier than it has ever been. Assuming, of course, that you start with compatible hardware, Windows will detect the new device and install the correct driver with little prompting. If that doesn't work, it is often just a matter of updating the driver or using Roll Back Driver. It's best to check the Internet for new drivers whenever you install a new device.

Even after a device has been installed, you should check for newer drivers periodically, even for devices that have been working fine. Manufacturers occasionally release new drivers aimed at optimizing the device or enabling it to work with some new technology. Keep in mind, however, that a new driver may cause unexpected problems with your operating system. Because of this, Windows XP introduced a feature that enables you to roll back to the previous (working) driver if something should go wrong with a driver update.

One of two wizards will assist you when you need to load a driver: the Found New Hardware Wizard or the Add New Hardware Wizard. Windows starts the Found New Hardware Wizard when it discovers some new hardware device while booting. If Windows has a driver in its database, it proceeds on its own. If not, the Found New Hardware Wizard will prompt you for one. The Add New Hardware Wizard enables you to add or update hardware manually at any time. There's a lot of overlap in how the two wizards work, so you'll look at just the Add New Hardware Wizard, which you can activate at any time.

Learning Objectives

Loading and removing device drivers is one of the basic skills that any good PC tech should have. The following lab exercise walks you through the process.

At the end of this lab, you'll be able to

- Load a device driver in Windows

- Roll back to a previously working driver

Lab Materials and Setup

The materials you need for this lab are

- A working PC with Windows XP, Windows Vista, or Windows 7 installed

- An Internet connection

Getting Down to Business

This lab covers the steps for installing and updating device drivers. You'll also look at the steps to roll back (uninstall) device drivers that turn out to be incompatible.

→ **Note**

Adding hardware in Windows 7 has become so automated that you can't pretend to install a piece of hardware like you could in Windows XP and Windows Vista (as this lab exercise is about to instruct you to do). In the case of Windows 7, make sure your device is plugged in properly, and the OS will take care of the rest (though you might still need to supply drivers).

Step 1   The first step before you begin installing any new device is to make sure it's compatible with your current Windows OS. Microsoft has removed the Windows XP and Windows Vista Web sites that detail device compatibility with those OSs, but you can find the Windows 7 Compatibility Center at www.microsoft.com/windows/compatibility/windows-7/en-us/default.aspx.

Step 2   Now you'll walk through the process of adding a device using the Add Hardware Wizard:

    a.   From the Window XP/Vista Control Panel, double-click Add Hardware. In Windows 7, open the Devices and Printers applet and click *Add a device*.

    b.   On the Add Hardware Wizard's welcome screen, click Next. (Windows 7's Add a device wizard skips this step.)

✔ **Hint**

If the Add Hardware Wizard doesn't find any new hardware, it asks, "Have you already connected this hardware to your computer?" Select Yes or No, and follow the directions.

---

    c.   Select the device you want to install or update by either selecting from the given list or choosing the Add a New Hardware Device item in the list box. In Windows 7, select the device from the list. If it's not on the list, chances are the device is not properly plugged in. (Windows 7 users should stop here.) For Windows XP/Vista users, select the last item in the list—*Add a new hardware device*—and then click Next.

    d.   Click the *Install the hardware that I manually select from a list (Advanced)* option button, and then click Next.

    e.   Select the type of hardware you're trying to install or update from the list. If your device doesn't fit the descriptions, select the Show All Devices item. When you've made your selection, click Next.

    f.   If you chose the Show All Devices item, the wizard displays the *Select the device driver you want to install for this hardware* screen. If you chose a specific type of hardware, you'll be led off into a series of options for that type of hardware.

    g.   Choose the Windows driver for your device, or click Have Disk and point to the location of the new driver you want to install. This driver generally is located either on the installation CD-ROM that came with the device, if you have it, or on your hard drive if you downloaded it from the manufacturer's Web site.

    h.   Click Next. Windows is ready to install the driver.

    i.   Click Next again, and click Finish when the installation is complete.

You should now have a driver that runs your newly loaded device. If the device isn't working properly and you're sure the driver loaded correctly, you can check online and see if there's a newer driver that you can download from the manufacturer's Web site.

Step 3 What if you have a device already installed and you want to update the driver to address a problem, improve performance, or just add a new feature? This step will take you through updating new drivers.

a. Begin by locating the updated driver. In most cases, the best way to obtain the updated driver is to search the Internet for the manufacturer's Web site. Search its site for your specific model, and download the most recent driver.

b. Go to Device Manager and expand the appropriate device category. Locate the device you want to update.

c. Double-click the device.

d. Select the Driver tab and click the Update Driver button (see Figure 17-5). This launches a wizard similar to the Add New Hardware Wizard.

✔ **Hint**

In all modern Windows operating systems, you can right-click on the device in Device Manager and update the driver without accessing its properties.

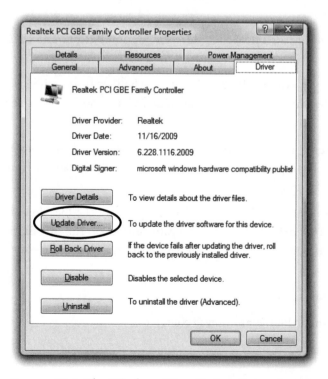

FIGURE 17-5 The Windows Vista Update Driver button

For Windows XP, select *Install from a list or specific location (Advanced)* and click Next. Select *Include this location in the search,* and browse to where you have saved the new driver.

For Windows Vista/7, click *Browse my computer for driver software.* Then choose *Let me pick from a list of device drivers on my computer.* Click the Have Disk button and then click Browse. You can locate the file from there.

You may be wondering, "What if I load a new driver, and my system doesn't work correctly anymore?" Well, you're in luck! Read the next step, and your question will be answered.

Step 4   If a driver is corrupt or if the wrong driver is installed, Windows has a bad habit of stopping dead in its tracks, rendering your PC useless. Windows XP and Vista/7 have a feature that keeps track of the drivers you install on a system and allows you to roll back to a previous one when a new one isn't working as it should.

a.   Go to Device Manager and locate the device you want to roll back.

b.   Double-click the device.

c.   Select the Driver tab. You can revert to the previous driver by clicking Roll Back Driver (see Figure 17-6).

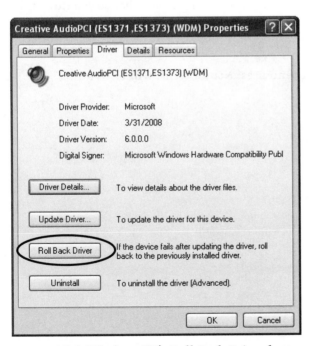

Figure 17-6 Windows XP's Roll Back Driver button

Lab Analysis Test

1. Tommy wants to install a service pack for his Windows operating system but is unsure because he doesn't know what a service pack actually is or how to get one. Explain to Tommy what a service pack is and how to install one.

2. Jackie has a Windows 7 Professional computer with thousands of pictures and music files. Needless to say, she is very concerned about losing her data. She heard from a technician at her work that she should create an image of her computer every week and have it saved to her network storage device. Can Jackie's computer do this? If so, how would she make this happen?

3. Tammy has Windows 7 Ultimate 64-bit installed on her PC and is attempting to install drivers for a USB scanner that she was previously using on a Windows Vista Ultimate 32-bit PC. She has not been successful thus far and continues to get errors. She knows the scanner is fully functional. List some plausible reasons for the failure of the scanner installation.

4. Laurie has been given six computers in various stages of disrepair. None of the systems will boot. They are all Windows XP systems. A friend gives her some floppy disks labeled "ASR" and recommends that she boot the machines using these floppies. When she tries it, the machines display the message *Non-System disk or disk error, replace and press any key when ready.* Why?

5. William has been running his Windows XP system for a few days and notices a small yellow shield icon in the system tray/notification area. He calls you to ask what it might be. What do you think it is?

Key Term Quiz

Use the following terms to complete the following sentences. Not all terms will be used.

Add Hardware Wizard

ASR

Automatic Updates

Backup

Backup and Restore Center

Roll Back Driver

ntbackup

System Recovery options

service packs

Windows 7 Compatibility Center

1. To assist in the recovery of a system crash, Windows XP uses the _____ process, which requires a floppy disk to store critical system files.

2. If you update a driver on your computer for a video card that you have been using for a year and it ends up not working, you could use _____ to restore the original driver.

3. As operating systems age, many of the system files, drivers, and utilities are updated. It is recommended that Windows always has the latest _____ installed.

4. Use the _____ to ensure that your devices will work with Windows 7.

5. In Windows XP, you can use _____ from the command line to make and restore backups.

Chapter 18

Working with the Command-Line Interface

Lab Exercises

The CompTIA A+ certification exams' objectives stipulate that PC technicians should know some of the basic commands and functions available at the command-line interface in all versions of Windows. Why? Because they still work, and good techs use the command line often. You'll need a solid understanding of several basic command-line commands and a few advanced tasks. Commands such as cd, copy, and attrib, as well as the tasks of starting and stopping services, editing files, and converting file systems, should be part of your PC tech arsenal.

If you have a system crash and are able to gain access to the machine using Windows XP's Recovery Console or Windows Vista's or Windows 7's System Recovery Options menu, you'll really need to know the proper commands for navigating around your drives, folders, and files, and launching utilities that will get your OS up and running again. Also, when you start working with networks, the command-line interface on all Windows systems is invaluable.

✔ **Cross-Reference**

You will further explore the use of the Recovery Console and System Recovery Options in the lab exercises for Chapter 19. You will also have the opportunity to work with additional networking command-line utilities in the lab exercises for Chapter 22.

The command line can often provide a quicker way to accomplish a task than the graphical alternative. In cases where a virus, hard drive failure, or OS problem prevents you from booting to Windows, you need to know how to get around with the command line. The following labs are designed to give you the chance to practice your basic command-line skills so that when the need arises, the command line will be your friend.

✔ **Hint**

As you have worked through the labs in this manual, I have recommended often that you explore features, options, and components not specifically covered in the lab exercises. You have embarked on the journey to become a CompTIA A+ certified technician! Natural curiosity, enthusiasm, and determination will go a long way toward developing the understanding and experience you need to become a competent technician and pass the exams. These qualities are especially important when it comes to working with the command-line interface. As you navigate through the following labs, it is easy to take a left when you should have taken a right and get lost in subdirectories, mistype a command, or delete a file you didn't want to. Don't let it discourage you.

Making mistakes while learning is good, and learning from those mistakes is great! If you get lost, explore ways to get back to where you need to be—you're unlikely to hurt anything. If you really get lost, work with your instructor or a more experienced classmate to determine where you went astray, then work through it again.

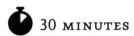 30 MINUTES

Lab Exercise 18.01: Configuring the Command-Line Window

Before you can use the command line, you need to know the basics: ways to access it, manipulate and customize the look of it within the GUI, and close it down properly. This lab covers those basics.

Learning Objectives

In this lab, you'll practice opening, resizing, customizing, and closing a command-line window.

At the end of this lab, you'll be able to

- Open a command-line window from within the Windows operating system

- Resize the command-line window

- Customize the look of the command-line window

- Exit the command-line window

Lab Materials and Setup

The materials you need for this lab are

- A PC with Windows installed

Getting Down to Business

The first thing you'll need to do, obviously, is get to a command line. Spend the next several minutes becoming familiar with accessing the command-line window.

✔ Cross-Reference

For details on how to access the command-line interface, refer to the "Accessing the Command Line" section in Chapter 18 of *Mike Meyers' CompTIA A+ Guide to Managing and Troubleshooting PCs*.

Step 1   Turn on your system, and wait for the Windows desktop to appear. Then follow these steps:

    a.   In Windows XP, select Start | Run, then type **cmd** (see Figure 18-1). In Windows Vista/7, select Start, then type **cmd** into the Search bar.

    b.   In XP, click OK to open a command-line window. In Vista/7, press ENTER.

Step 2   There are three ways to change the size of the command-line window for better viewing:

- Use the resize arrows along the edges of the windows (this will not work when the window is maximized).

- Use the minimize/maximize button in the upper-right corner of the window.

- Press ALT-ENTER to toggle between the full screen mode and a window.

Step 3   Windows XP's default prompt displays C:\Documents and Settings\username>, while the Windows Vista/7 prompt displays C:\Users\username>.

To the right of the prompt, you'll see a flashing cursor indicating that it's waiting for your input. There's also a scroll bar along the right side of the window. Sometimes your command causes more information to be displayed than the window can hold, and it's really useful to be able to scroll back up and see what messages were displayed.

You'll now execute a few commands, for the purpose of exploring the scrolling issue. The change directory command (cd) lets you change the focus of the working directory displayed in the command-line window. The directory command (dir) lists the filename, extension, file size (in bytes), and creation date/time of the files in the current folder.

You are going to change from the current working directory to a subdirectory with hundreds of files. Type **cd C:\Windows\System32** (C:\ is the root directory, Windows is the system folder, and System32 is where many of the system configuration and driver files are stored). You may have to use a different drive letter or system folder name to arrive at the System32 directory.

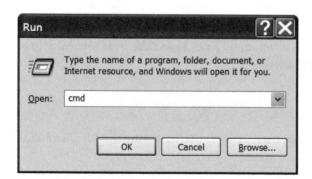

FIGURE 18-1 Opening the Windows XP command-line window

Now type **dir** and press ENTER. The System32 folder contains over 15,000 files, so the command-line window will not be able to display all of the information at once. If there's more than one screen's worth of information, it will keep scrolling out of sight until everything has been displayed. You can use the scroll bar to go back a few screens' worth—give it a try.

If you were actually trying to work with a few of the files in the folder, you'd probably be out of luck, because you can't scroll back more than a few screens. To address this problem, there's a command you can use that forces the information to be displayed one screenful at a time. Type **dir /p** and then press ENTER. Adding the /p switch to the command tells it to pause after each screenful of text. Press the SPACEBAR to display the next screenful. You can't go back if you're too quick with the SPACEBAR, so take a good look at each screen! If you tire of paging through the screens, you can end the command by pressing CTRL-C.

Step 4 Just as with most applications in the Windows environment, if you right-click the title bar and select Properties, you can configure some of the features of the command-line window. The following tabs appear in the Command Prompt Properties dialog box:

- **Options** Configure the cursor size, command history, display options, and edit options

- **Font** Select from a limited set of command-line fonts and sizes

- **Layout** Set the screen buffer size and window size, and position the window on the monitor screen

- **Colors** Configure the color of screen text, screen background, pop-up text, and pop-up background

→ **Note**

Some features differ depending on which operating system you are using. For example, Windows Vista does not offer the Display Options panel in the Command Prompt Properties dialog box.

Explore some of the settings you can change, and feel free to set up the command-line window to your personal taste. I grew up on early IBM machines, in the days when owning a color monitor meant that you had an electric green or bright orange character on a black monochrome screen. See if you can re-create this wonderful look!

Step 5 There are two common ways to close a command-line window:

- Click the × in the upper-right corner of the window. This method isn't recommended if the window is actively running a program. You should wait until you see the prompt before clicking the ×.

- Type **exit** at the command line, and press ENTER. I prefer this method, because I can be sure the window is inactive when I quit.

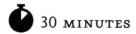 30 MINUTES

Lab Exercise 18.02: Navigating Basic Commands

Before you can really use the command line, you must know the basic commands needed to navigate around a drive to locate and modify files. In this lab exercise, you'll learn more basic command-line commands that you would need to know when troubleshooting your or your client's PC.

✔ **Hint**

For the most part, mistakes such as spelling a command or filename incorrectly won't be disastrous for you. But it is possible to misspell just incorrectly enough to delete the wrong file, or something similar, especially if you're using wildcards (I'll get to those in a bit). Typically, though, if you misspell a command or filename, the command line won't know what you're asking it to do and therefore won't do anything, or won't know what file you're asking to work with, and will return an error message.

Learning Objectives

In this lab, you'll learn or review commands for directory and file management while using the command line.

At the end of this lab, you'll be able to

- Use commands to view, navigate, create, and delete directories using the command line
- Use commands to copy, move, rename, and delete files using the command line

Lab Materials and Setup

The materials you need for this lab are

- At least one working computer running Windows

✔ **Hint**

Any version of Windows will work just fine for this exercise, as long as you understand that the results may appear differently on your screen.

Getting Down to Business

Hundreds of commands and switches are available to you from the command-line interface. Although it is beyond the scope of these exercises to explore every possible command and its associated switches, you should spend the time in this lab exercise working with the specific ones that form the cornerstone of command-line navigation. These are the basic commands you'll use most often when working with the command line.

Step 1   Follow these steps:

    a.   Launch the command-line interface in Windows XP by typing **cmd** in the Run dialog box and either clicking OK or pressing ENTER. In Windows Vista/7, access the command-line interface through the Start menu Search bar with the same command.

    b.   When you first open the command-line window, your prompt might not be focused on the root directory. Because you want to focus on the root directory at this time, you must change directories before continuing.

The cd (change directory) command changes the directory the system is focused on. When you use the cd command, you must type the command followed by a space and then the name of the directory you want to view. This is true of all command-line commands. First, type the command followed by a space and then any options. Because you want to focus on the root of C: and the name of the root is the backslash (\), you'd type in the following and press ENTER (assuming that you're in the C: drive to begin with):

```
C:\Documents and Settings\username>cd \
```

Notice that the prompt has changed its focus to C:\> (see Figure 18-2).

Step 2   Probably the most frequently typed command is the request to display the contents of a directory (dir). Because the command-line interface doesn't continually display everything the way a GUI does, you have to ask it to display specific information. The way you display the contents a directory is to focus on the particular directory or subdirectory, and enter the command **dir**.

Let's take a look at the contents of your root (C:\) directory. You should already be focused there from the previous step in this exercise. Type **dir** at the command prompt and press ENTER.

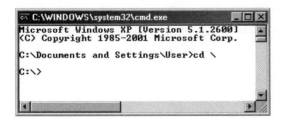

FIGURE 18-2 Changing the command-line focus

✔ **Hint**

From now on, when you see an instruction to type a command, assume that you should press ENTER afterward to complete the request (command). Otherwise, the command line will sit there, waiting patiently until the sun grows cold.

Now here's where it gets a little gray. Because I don't know what's in your root directory, there's no way to predict exactly what your C:\ contents will look like—but it's a good bet that *something* will be different from what I show you here! In theory at least, your display should be similar to Figure 18-3. Windows XP, Vista, and 7 will have the same basic look.

Notice that using the dir command in any Windows operating system gives you the following information:

- Filename
- File extension
- Date and time of creation
- Size in bytes
- Designation as either a directory (<DIR>) or a file
- The number of files in the directory
- The amount of free space on the drive

Look at your particular results and note the mixture of files, which display a size in bytes, and directories, which have the annotation <DIR> after their name. In the preceding examples, AVG7QT.DAT is a file of 12,288,463 bytes, and Windows, Program Files, and Documents and Settings are all names of directories.

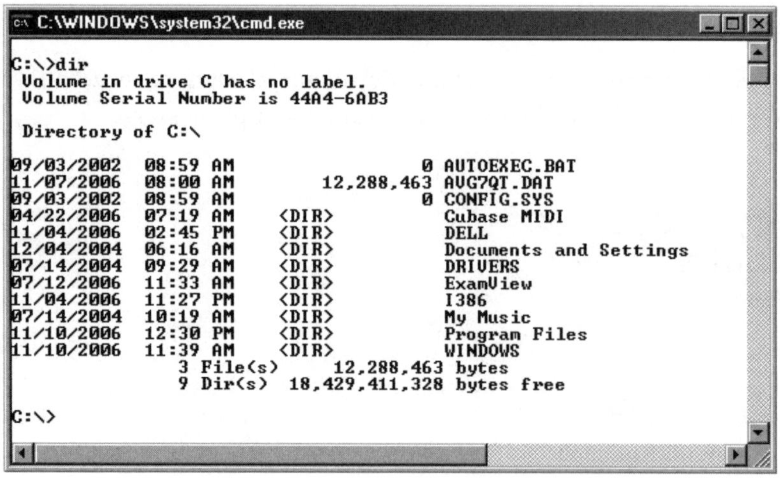

FIGURE 18-3 Viewing a sample Windows XP root directory

Note whether you see the following files or folders in your root (C:\) directory (you won't see them all):

	Yes	No
autoexec.bat		
config.sys		
WinNT		
Windows		
Documents and Settings		
Program Files		

List the names of all the directories you see displayed in your root directory:

_____   _____

_____   _____

_____   _____

_____   _____

_____   _____

Step 3   The biggest challenge when working with the command prompt is remembering what exactly to type to achieve your goal. Learning the commands is one thing, but each command can have switches and options that modify it somewhat. Also, you may have noticed that the screen fills up and scrolls from top to bottom, making it difficult to view all the information you might need. Let's look at a command to clear the screen and another to provide assistance with how to use the commands.

    a.   Type the command **cls**. What happened? _____

    b.   Type the command **dir /?**. What happened? _____

The question mark (/?) is a standard help switch for most commands. Even though I've used these commands for decades, I still use the /? switch occasionally to remember what options are available for a specific command.

✔ **Hint**

Be careful not to confuse the backslash (\) and the forward slash (/). In a command-line world, the path uses the backslash and command switches use the forward slash.

At this point, a huge amount of help information is displayed (see Figure 18-4), so you may feel like you're in command overload! Take comfort in the fact that dir is the most complex command. Other

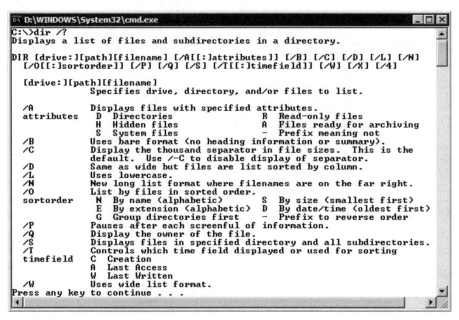

```
D:\WINDOWS\System32\cmd.exe                                    _□×

C:\>dir /?
Displays a list of files and subdirectories in a directory.

DIR [drive:][path][filename] [/A[[:]attributes]] [/B] [/C] [/D] [/L] [/N]
  [/O[[:]sortorder]] [/P] [/Q] [/S] [/T[[:]timefield]] [/W] [/X] [/4]

  [drive:][path][filename]
              Specifies drive, directory, and/or files to list.

  /A          Displays files with specified attributes.
  attributes    D  Directories            R  Read-only files
                H  Hidden files           A  Files ready for archiving
                S  System files           -  Prefix meaning not
  /B          Uses bare format (no heading information or summary).
  /C          Display the thousand separator in file sizes.  This is the
              default.  Use /-C to disable display of separator.
  /D          Same as wide but files are list sorted by column.
  /L          Uses lowercase.
  /N          New long list format where filenames are on the far right.
  /O          List by files in sorted order.
  sortorder     N  By name (alphabetic)    S  By size (smallest first)
                E  By extension (alphabetic) D  By date/time (oldest first)
                G  Group directories first  -  Prefix to reverse order
  /P          Pauses after each screenful of information.
  /Q          Display the owner of the file.
  /S          Displays files in specified directory and all subdirectories.
  /T          Controls which time field displayed or used for sorting
  timefield     C  Creation
                A  Last Access
                W  Last Written
  /W          Uses wide list format.
Press any key to continue . . .
```

FIGURE 18-4 Viewing the syntax of the dir command

commands are more straightforward with their help. You don't need to know what all the switches are—just know how to use the help switch (/?) to find them! The main thing to learn is the syntax of the commands.

Everything in brackets ([ ]) is optional for the command. Notice that dir is the only mandatory part in that command even though there are several optional switches and parameters. This is the same for all the commands. The system will use defaults if you don't specify a switch or optional parameter. It's the defaults that can cause problems if you're not careful when using these commands. Now follow these steps:

c. Put a known good disc with files in your optical drive and let it spin up and come to rest. Cancel any windows that automatically open and proceed to the next substep.

d. Type **dir**, and examine the resulting list of files and folders. Did they change from the previous step? _____

    Do you think it read the disc? Probably not, because your prompt is still focused on the root directory of the hard drive.

e. Type **dir d:** (replace d: with the appropriate drive letter for your optical drive, if necessary) and examine the resulting list of files and folders. Did they change this time? Aha! The option of [drive:] was needed to change the focus of the dir command to the optical drive.

The [drive:] option will work for any of the drive letters. Optical discs and USB thumb drives are all fair game as well. When you use this option, you can look at those other drives without switching from the directory you're in.

Step 4 Type **dir /?** to look at two more optional switches: /p and /w. The /p switch is used when all the information will not fit on one screen, and /w is used to see a condensed listing of the directory.

Let's focus on a different directory. Remember, the cd command will let you change the directory you want to focus on:

a. Type **cd \Windows**.

b. Type **cls**.

c. Type **dir** at the command prompt. This shows way too much data for the screen to display all at once.

d. Type **dir /p** at the command prompt. This very useful switch causes the display to stop scrolling (pause) after each screen, waiting until you press the SPACEBAR to show you more. In directories with lots of files, this is a lifesaver!

✔ **Hint**

If you want to stop a process that seems to be running forever, you can press CTRL-C. The process will end, and you'll get the prompt back.

---

e. Type **dir /w** at the command prompt. This switch is convenient when you're simply looking to see if a particular file resides in a particular directory, because it shows a "wide" list with filenames but no details.

f. Now practice moving around in the command window. Right now you're focused on the Windows directory. Go back to the root directory by typing **cd **. To change the focus to another directory, use the **cd** command as you've learned. Use the **dir** command to see what directories you have available in your current folder.

g. Try going to a subdirectory in another subdirectory and listing the contents. Look back at the list of directories you made previously and select one. Issue the **cd** command followed by a backslash (\) and the name of the target directory. For example, to switch to the Documents and Settings directory in the previous listing, type this:

```
C:\Windows>cd \Documents and Settings
```
Do this using several of the directory names you wrote down previously, and then type **dir** to see what's there. Are there any subdirectories in this directory? Make a note of them.

_____   _____

_____   _____

_____   _____

✔ **Hint**

After you've changed the prompt focus many times, you may become confused about exactly where you are. You can always get to the root directory from any focus by typing **cd **.

Step 5 A Windows installation creates a Drivers directory, within a directory called System32, under the Windows directory in the root of the C: drive. To go to the Drivers directory, you don't have to do the cd command three times unless you really want to. If you know the path, you can go directly to the subdirectory with one cd command.

Go to the Drivers subdirectory by typing this at the command prompt:

```
C:\>cd \Windows\System32\Drivers
```

Your prompt should now look like Figure 18-5.

Type **dir** to see what's there.

One final navigation hint—you can change directories going back up toward the top level without returning directly to the root. If you want to go up a single directory level, you can type **cd** followed immediately by two periods (sometimes referred to as *cd dot dot*). For example, typing this takes you up one level to the System32 directory:

```
C:\>\Windows\System32\Drivers>cd..
C:\>\Windows\System32>
```

Do it again to go to the Windows directory:

```
C:\>\Windows\System32>cd..
C:\>\Windows>
```

Type the command once more to arrive at the root directory:

```
C:\>\Windows>cd..
C:\>
```

Take a minute and practice using the cd command. Go down a few levels on the directory tree, and then jump up a few, jump back to the root directory, and then jump down another path. Practice is the only way to get comfortable moving around in a command-prompt environment, and a good PC technician needs to be comfortable doing this.

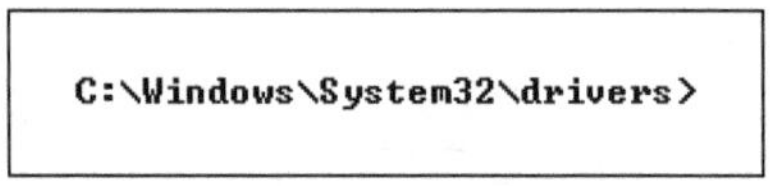

```
C:\Windows\System32\drivers>
```

FIGURE 18-5 Focusing on the Drivers subdirectory

Step 6   Sometimes a technician needs to make a directory to store files on the system. This could be a temporary directory for testing purposes, or maybe a place to store something more permanently (diagnostic reports, for example). In any case, it's important that you know how to create and remove a directory. The CompTIA A+ exams will test you on this. Follow these steps:

a.   Be sure you're in the root directory. If you aren't there, type **cd ** to return to the root directory, where you'll add a new top-level directory. Actually, you can make a directory anywhere in the file structure, but you don't want to lose track of where it is, so make your new directory in the root. Do this using the md (make directory) command.

b.   Type **md /?** to see how the command is structured and view the available options (see Figure 18-6).

c.   At the command prompt, type the following:

`C:\>md Corvette`

d.   When the command line just presents a fresh prompt, it means that everything worked correctly. But to verify that the directory was actually made, type **dir** to see your new directory in the list. It's as simple as that!

✖ Warning

Be careful—the new directory will always be created wherever the prompt is focused when you issue the command, whether that's where you meant to put it or not.

---

e.   Be sure you're in the root directory (type **cd**), and prepare to remove your new Corvette directory.

Removing a directory requires the RD (remove directory) command and two conditions: First, the directory must be empty, and second, your system must not currently be focused on the directory about to be deleted.

f.   Type this command:

`C:\>rd Corvette`
The directory has been deleted.

g.   Type **dir** to confirm that Corvette has been removed.

```
C:\>md /?
Creates a directory.

MKDIR [drive:]path
MD [drive:]path
```

FIGURE 18-6 Using the md command

✔ **Hint**

Be *very* careful when you remove directories or delete files in the command line. It isn't as forgiving as Windows, which allows you to change your mind and "undelete" things. When you delete a file or directory using the command line, it's gone. If you make a mistake, there's nothing left to do but pout. So think carefully before you delete, and be sure you know *what* you're deleting before you do it—you'll save yourself a great deal of agony. Also pay attention to the directory you're currently focused on, to ensure that you're in the correct one.

Step 7   Sometimes you know the name of the file you want to use, but you don't know in which directory it's located. In this case, working with files and directories can become quite tedious. To help you locate files more easily, here are some switches and wildcards you can use with the dir command:

a. Look again at the results of the **dir /?** command, and find the /s switch. The /s switch will look for a file(s) in the specified (focus) directory and all subdirectories under that directory.

b. Windows has a file named xcopy.exe somewhere on the drive. Locate the path to the xcopy.exe file using the **/s** switch.

c. Start with your command prompt at the root directory (**cd **).

d. Type this command:

```
C:\>dir xcopy.exe
```
If the file isn't in the root directory, nothing will be displayed.

e. Now try the new switch you just learned about to search all subdirectories. Type this command:

```
C:\>dir /s xcopy.exe
```

f. On my system, the file shows up in two places: in the C:\Windows\System32 directory and in the C:\Windows\System32\dllcache directory (see Figure 18-7).

Another way to look for a file is to use a *wildcard*. The most common wildcard is the asterisk character (*), which you can use in place of all or part of a filename to make a command act on more than one file at a time. Wildcards work with all commands that use filenames.

The * wildcard replaces any number of letters before or after the dot in the filename. A good way to think of the * wildcard is "I don't care." Replace the part of the filename that you don't care about with *.

For example, if you want to locate all the readme files on a hard drive and you don't care what the extension is, type the following:

```
C:\>dir /s/p readme.*
```

The result is a list of all the readme files on the hard drive. Notice that I used the /s switch to look in all the directories and used the /p switch so that I can view one screenful of results at a time (see Figure 18-8).

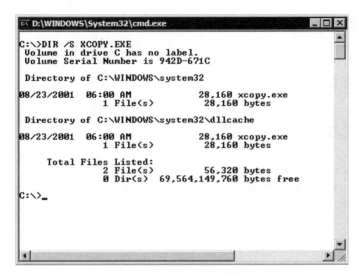

FIGURE 18-7 Locating the xcopy.exe file

You can use the * wildcard for any number of characters. For example, not all companies use readme.txt as the help filename. Some use read.me, and others may use read.

Because read is common to all those variations, let's find all the files with "read" in the filename. You should be prepared to see a long list of every file with "read" in the name, not just the readme files.

Type the following:

```
C:\>dir /s/p *read*.*
```

Figure 18-9 shows the first screenful of results from my system. I found 104 files with "read" somewhere in the filename. How many files and directories did you find with "read" as part of the name?

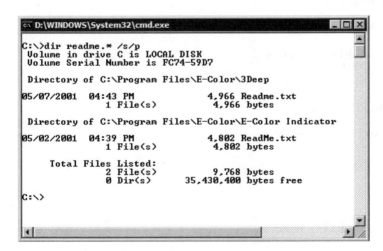

FIGURE 18-8 Using a wildcard to locate files

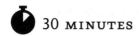

FIGURE 18-9 Using a wildcard to locate *read*.* files

30 MINUTES

Lab Exercise 18.03: Using Command-Line Tools

Commands such as type, copy, move, rename, and delete are used for manipulating files, such as you would be doing while troubleshooting a client's PC. These are more of the commands that every working tech should know by heart.

Learning Objectives

In this lab, you'll use commands for file management.

At the end of this lab, you'll be able to

- View text (.txt) documents from the command-line interface
- Rename files using the command-line interface
- Copy files using the command-line interface
- Move files using the command-line interface
- Delete files using the command-line interface

Lab Materials and Setup

The materials you need for this lab are

- At least one working computer running Windows

Getting Down to Business

You might refer to these as the "second-tier" commands. Once you've used commands such as dir, md, and cd to navigate and create folders, you can use the following commands to manipulate individual files.

→ **Note**

This lab exercise is written assuming you are using Windows XP. However, you can perform the entire exercise in Windows Vista/7 by using C:\Users\%USERNAME%\Documents instead of C:\Documents and Settings\%USERNAME%\My Documents.

Step 1   Open Notepad by clicking Start | All Programs | Accessories | Notepad. Type the following sentence and save the file in the My Documents or Documents folder as **command line test.txt**:

This is a small sentence of text created in Notepad.

Close Notepad.

Step 2   You will now navigate to your My Documents/Documents folder using the command-line interface and verify that the file is there and contains readable text:

a.   If you don't already have the command-line window open, get to a command prompt.

b.   Enter the following commands:

```
C:\>cd \Documents and Settings\%USERNAME%\My Documents
C:\Documents and Settings\%USERNAME%\My Documents\>dir /p
```

✔ **Hint**

The variable %USERNAME% (including the preceding and trailing percent signs) in the command-line syntax represents the user name you're currently using. Microsoft has assembled many variables that can be used in this manner, such as %SYSTEMROOT% to represent the system folder (usually named Windows). You may actually use the variable in the command-line syntax to have the system insert your user name (the folder where all of your personal settings and saved documents are) in the path. I have included a generic example of the use of this variable in Figure 18-10.

Do you see the file you created? (It should be called command line test.txt.) _____

FIGURE 18-10 Using an environment variable to insert the user name

Now you will use another command to verify that the file is a text file containing readable text. There are many ways to do this; you'll use one of the simplest methods. The type command displays the contents of a text file, but doesn't allow you to edit or manipulate the text in any way.

c. Enter the following (carefully enter the line in the exact syntax as shown, including the quotation marks):

    C:\Documents and Settings\%USERNAME%\My Documents\>**type "command line test.txt"**

You should see the text that you entered earlier. All of the text should be displayed, although you may have to resize your command-line window to see all of it, and even then it won't be pretty.

The other thing you may have noticed is that to access the text file, you had to add quotation marks to the beginning and the end of the filename. This is because the command line only understands spaces as breaks between commands and operators or switches. Leave the quote marks out of the command line and run the **type** command again. What happened?

You should see something similar to the output in Figure 18-11.

You're going to use this file in the next few steps, and it will be easier to work with if its format conforms to the 8.3 rule. In the early days of MS-DOS, filenames could only be eight characters long, with a three-character extension after the period. The three-character extension has remained throughout all versions of Microsoft operating systems (though there are common exceptions to that rule, such as .docx for Microsoft Word files), but you can now use up to 255 characters (with spaces) as the filename. To make

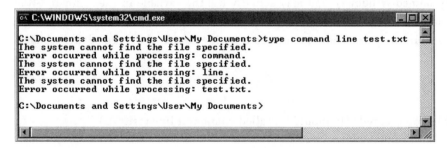

FIGURE 18-11 Results of running type without using quotation marks

this file easier to work with in the command line, you'll use the ren (rename) command to change the filename.

    d.   Type the following command:

        `C:\Documents and Settings\%USERNAME%\My Documents\>`**`ren "command line test.txt"`**

    e.   Now confirm that this has worked by typing the following command:

        `C:\Documents and Settings\%USERNAME%\My Documents\>`**`type cmdlntst.txt`**

        Great! Now you will be able to type the filename more quickly as you complete the rest of the exercise.

Step 3   At the command prompt, type **cd ** to change your focus to the root directory.

You'll now create a new directory called Study in the root so that you can do some copying and moving. The only difference between copying and moving is that copy leaves the original file in the same place (as a backup) with a duplicate made elsewhere, whereas the move command relocates the original file to a new location with no backup available. They're otherwise similar, so once you've learned the copy command, you've pretty much learned the move command too! Follow these steps:

    a.   Make a directory named Study by typing the following:

        `C:\>`**`md Study`**

    b.   Verify that the directory is there by using the **dir** command.

        Now follow these steps for copying your file named cmdlntst.txt to the new Study directory:

    c.   Change the focus of the command prompt to the Study directory:

        `C:\>`**`cd Study`**

    d.   Copy the cmdlntst.txt file to the Study directory:

        `C:\Study>`**`copy "C:\Documents and Settings\%USERNAME%\My Documents\cmdlntst.txt"`**
        `C:\Study\cmdlntst.txt`

        Here, copy is the command, "C:\Documents and Settings\%USERNAME%\My Documents\ cmdlntst.txt" is the current location and name of the file (notice the use of the quotation marks and the %USERNAME% variable once again), and C:\Study\cmdlntst.txt is the target location and name of the file.

        The entire command and response will look similar to Figure 18-12.

FIGURE 18-12 The copy command and response

e.   Run the **dir** command to see if you copied the file. If the file isn't there, carefully repeat the previous steps or ask your instructor for help.

f.   Change your directory focus back to the My Documents folder (**cd \Documents and Settings\%USERNAME%\My Documents**) and run the **dir** command to see if the original cmdlntst.txt file is still there.

✔ Hint

If you're already in the target directory, you don't need to include the target path in the command. My idea of copying or moving files is to start in the directory to which you want to copy the files. Then you can bring the files to where you are. Each time you copy or move a file, you can run the dir command to see if it's actually there. The other way of sending a file to a directory can be troublesome if you're moving files, because you may accidentally send them to a wrong directory and waste time looking for them.

Another good use of the copy command is to make a backup copy of a file and rename it at the same time, so that the two files can reside in the same directory.

g.   To make a backup of the cmdlntst.txt text file, type the following command:

```
C:\Study\>copy cmdlntst.txt cmdlntst.bak
```

You now have three copies of the same file; you will clean these up in the last step.

Step 4   The last two commands you will work with in this step are the move and del (delete) commands. First, you will delete the copy of cmdlntst.txt that you copied into the Study folder in the last step. You will then move the file permanently from the My Documents folder to the Study folder. Follow these steps:

a.   Change the focus of the command prompt to the Study directory:

```
C:\>cd Study
```

b.   Delete the cmdlntst.txt file from the Study directory:

```
C:\Study\>del cmdlntst.txt
```

c.   Run the **dir** command to see if you deleted the file. If the file isn't there, you deleted it.

Now you will follow the steps to move the file from My Documents to the Study folder. You will then verify that the file is in the Study folder and no longer in the My Documents folder.

d.   Make sure the focus of the command prompt is still the Study directory.

e.   Move the cmdlntst.txt file to the Study directory:

```
C:\Study>move "C:\Documents and Settings\%USERNAME%\My Documents\cmdlntst.txt"
C:\Study\cmdlntst.txt
```

In this case, move is the command, "C:\Documents and Settings\%USERNAME%\My Documents\cmdlntst.txt" is the current location and name of the file (notice the use of the quotation marks and the %USERNAME% variable once again), and C:\Study\cmdlntst.txt is the target location and name of the file.

f.   Run the **dir** command to see if you moved the file. If the file isn't there, repeat the previous steps or ask your instructor for help.

g.   Change your directory focus back to the My Documents folder (**cd \Documents and Settings\%USERNAME%\My Documents**) and run the **dir** command to see if the original cmdlntst.txt file is still there.

Do you see it? _____

Why or why not? _____

You should now have two copies of the file in the Study directory, cmdlntst.txt and cmdlntst.bak. The file should have been moved from the My Documents directory.

 60 MINUTES

Lab Exercise 18.04: Advanced Command-Line Utilities

In Windows, you can perform many tasks either from the GUI or from the command-line window. The CompTIA A+ exams want you to be comfortable with both methods to accomplish these tasks. To practice your skills with the command-line versions of these tasks, work through the following scenarios and steps to explore the attributes, the Print Spooler service, and the NTFS file system, all with the view from the command prompt.

Learning Objectives

In this lab, you'll work through three scenarios.

At the end of this lab, you'll be able to

- Work with the attrib and edit utilities

- Start and stop services with the net command

- Convert file systems

Lab Materials and Setup

The materials you need for this lab are

- At least one working computer running Windows

- A hard drive with at least 1 GB of unallocated space, or a 1-GB or greater partition formatted with the FAT32 file system

---

✔ Hint

If the machines configured with multiple hard drives are still available from Lab Exercise 12.05, "Implementing Software RAID 0 with Disk Management," you can convert these back to basic disks and format them with FAT32 to use in Step 3 of this exercise.

Getting Down to Business

Working through commands as you have in the prior exercises is an excellent method to explore the commands and their usage, but it can seem a little sterile since the commands are isolated and out of context. The next few steps are built around scenarios common in the workplace, requiring you to perform tasks that incorporate both commands you have learned in prior exercises and new commands that will be introduced as needed.

Step 1   In the steps that follow, you will use the attrib command to alter the attributes of a text file.

    a.   Create a new folder in the root directory. Name it **Folder**. Inside that folder, create a new text document and name it **text.txt**.

    b.   Using your favorite method, launch the command prompt and change your focus to the new folder you created.

    c.   To list the files and all of their attributes, use the attrib command:

```
C:\Folder>attrib
```

Because the folder contains one file, the only file that should be listed is your new text document. Notice the *A* to the left of where text.txt is listed. This means that the Archive attribute has been applied. To make this blank text file more secure, we'll add two more attributes: r (read-only) and h (hidden). For more options, type **attrib /?**.

    d.   To change the attributes for text.txt, type the following command:

```
C:\Folder>attrib +r +h text.txt
```

This will add the read-only and hidden attributes to the text file. Verify this by using My Computer/Computer to navigate to the folder and checking its contents. Do any files show up in the folder? _____

e. Now change the attributes for text.txt again so that it's not read-only or hidden anymore. Type the following command:

```
C:\Folder>attrib -r -h text.txt
```

Return again to the folder in My Computer/Computer and verify that the text file has reappeared.

Step 2 One recurring problem you will run into in the field is that one of the services in Windows will stall—in particular the Print Spooler. The Print Spooler is a holding area for print jobs, and it's especially important for network printers. If the print device runs out of paper while printing a document, you may have to stop and start the Print Spooler to allow the print device to receive jobs again. Typically you just open the Computer Management console, select Services, and restart the service. However, there may be times when it is more convenient or just plain necessary to accomplish this task from the command-line interface.

The following steps walk you through stopping and starting the Print Spooler from the command-line interface:

a. Launch the Services console by opening the Control Panel, launching the Administrative Tools applet, and double-clicking Services.

b. Scroll down and highlight the Print Spooler, then select Action | Properties. You should see that the Print Spooler is started and running (see Figure 18-13).

FIGURE 18-13 The Print Spooler Properties dialog box

c.   Launch the command-line interface and change the focus to the root directory.

d.   Type the following command at the prompt:

C:**net stop spooler**

The command line should inform you that the Print Spooler service is stopping, and then that the Print Spooler service was stopped successfully (see Figure 18-14).

✔ **Cross-Reference**

You will explore the net command-line utility in the lab exercises for Chapter 22. If you would like to explore the net command while working on this lab, type **net /?.**

---

e.   Using ALT-TAB, change your focus to the Print Spooler Properties dialog box you opened earlier. You should be able to confirm that the Print Spooler service has been stopped (see Figure 18-15).

f.   Change the focus back to the command-line window, and type the following command at the prompt:

C:**net start spooler**

The command line should inform you that the Print Spooler service is starting, and then that the Print Spooler service was started successfully (see Figure 18-16).

In the real-world scenario, your Print Spooler service would be restarted, and you should have a healthy, functioning print server once again. Now you just have to figure out where you stored the extra toner!

Step 3   Many of the legacy systems in the field started out as Windows 2000 machines. Often, these systems' hard drives were partitioned and formatted with the FAT32 file system. As you upgrade these systems, you may want to leave the FAT32 file system intact until you verify that the upgrade has been successful. After successful completion of the upgrade, it is recommended that you convert the file system to NTFS. This is a nondestructive, one-way conversion! Once you switch to NTFS, you will have to delete the data and reformat the partition if you want to revert to FAT32.

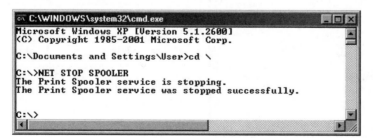

FIGURE 18-14 Stopping the Print Spooler service from the command-line interface

FIGURE 18-15 The Print Spooler Properties dialog box after stopping the service

In this step, you will create a FAT32 partition (unless you already have one from earlier labs) and then use the command-line utility called convert to convert the partition to NTFS.

a. Boot a computer system with at least 1 GB of unallocated hard drive space. If you have access to the system you used to explore RAID 0 (striping), you can use the extra hard drives installed in the system.

b. Launch the Disk Management console. Right-click My Computer/Computer and select Manage.

c. Click Disk Management.

d. Right-click an area of unallocated space and select New Volume from the drop-down menu.

e. Follow the wizard instructions to create a FAT32 partition of at least 1 GB.

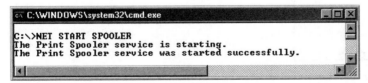

FIGURE 18-16 Starting the Print Spooler service from the command-line interface

✔ **Cross-Reference**

To refresh your Disk Management skills, refer to Chapter 12, Lab Exercise 12.03, "Using Windows Tools to Create and Format Partitions."

f. Close the Disk Management console and double-click My Computer/Computer. Create and save a text file to the new drive to verify that the drive is accessible. Right-click the drive and select Properties; notice the tabs and file system (see Figure 18-17).

Now that you have a FAT32 partition, you can launch the command-line window and convert the file system from FAT32 to NTFS. You will then verify that the conversion was indeed non-destructive by opening the text file you created earlier.

g. Launch the command-line window and change the focus to the root directory using the **cd ** command.

h. Type the following command at the prompt (substitute the drive letter for your FAT32 partition):

```
C:\convert e: /fs:ntfs
```

Your results should look similar to Figure 18-18.

i. Exit the command-line window and double-click My Computer/Computer.

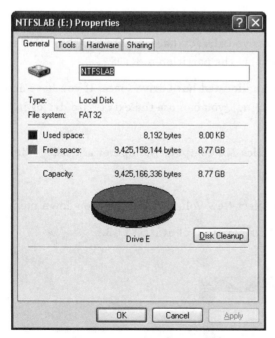

FIGURE 18-17 FAT32 partition properties

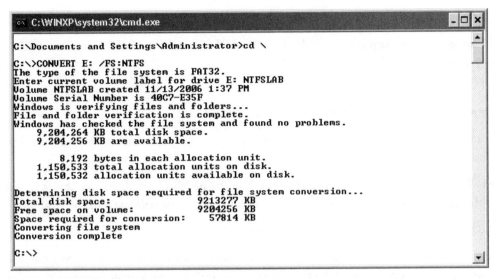

FIGURE 18-18 Converting a partition from FAT32 to NTFS

j.   Right-click the drive that you just converted and select Properties. Your drive should now be formatted with the NTFS file system. Notice the additional tabs for Security and Quota (see Figure 18-19).

k.   Close the Properties dialog box and double-click the drive. The text document you created earlier during the setup should still be there and accessible.

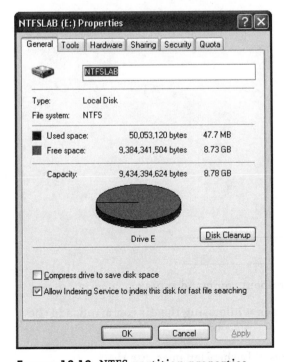

FIGURE 18-19 NTFS partition properties

Lab Analysis Test

1. Nate would like to make backup copies of all of his Word documents in the root directory. He types the following at the command prompt:

    ```
    C:\>copy c:\*.docx
    ```

    Will this command work? Why or why not? What will it do?

2. Which command(s) would you use to make a full copy of a file in the same directory under a different name?

3. The xcopy.exe file is in the System32 directory, which is in the Windows directory that's in the root directory of the primary hard drive. What's the complete command-line path to the file?

4. Explain the 8.3 rule. What does the 8 mean? How about the 3?

5. Thomas was messing around one day and deleted a file named critical.dll from the System32 directory. His friend gave him a copy on a USB thumb drive. What's the exact command he'd use to copy it back to the correct place (assuming the E: drive is his USB thumb drive)?

Key Term Quiz

Use the following terms to complete the following sentences. Not all terms will be used.

/?

/p

/w

cd

copy

del

dir

md

rd

ren

1. The command used to create a new directory is _____.

2. The command used to create a duplicate file is _____.

3. The _____ switch is used to get help about command syntax.

4. When there are too many files to show on the screen while using the dir command, add the _____ switch.

5. For a listing of a directory's contents that displays only the filenames, use the _____ command with the _____ switch.

Chapter 19
Troubleshooting Windows

Lab Exercises

Recall from Chapter 17 that your company has just acquired a small architectural firm. You have patched and updated all of the firm's machines, but users are still managing to find ways to render their PCs unusable. As a technician, you need to use Event Viewer to log what they do to their computers. A few of the computers have contracted malware, corrupting the valuable master boot record (MBR), making the computers nonbootable. You'll need to be more than competent in navigating the Recovery Console to get these systems up and running. Let's take some time in this chapter to discover and use some of the available Windows troubleshooting tools.

 30 MINUTES

Lab Exercise 19.01: Examining and Configuring Log Files in Event Viewer

Windows Event Viewer is a valuable tool to anyone who maintains or troubleshoots systems. It's mostly run as a standalone program, but it can also be added as a snap-in to the MMC (as described in Chapter 4).

Event Viewer monitors various log files and reveals things about the health of the operating system. This utility reports real-time statistics, but normally, this data is only used with servers. Desktop computer users are less proactive and usually depend on the after-the-fact log files to help determine the cause of a problem.

Event Viewer displays important events from multiple log files. The log files you see depend on your system. The three most important log files include Application, Security, and System. (More log files are available in the server versions of Windows.) Figure 19-1 shows the contents of the System event log in Event Viewer.

Notice in Figure 19-1 that there are three kinds of log entries: Information, Warning, and Error. The Security event log also shows two other types of entries: Success Audit and Failure Audit. These types of events are logged only when auditing is turned on; again, this is normally done only on servers.

Learning Objectives

You'll become familiar with using Event Viewer to analyze the different logs kept by the system.

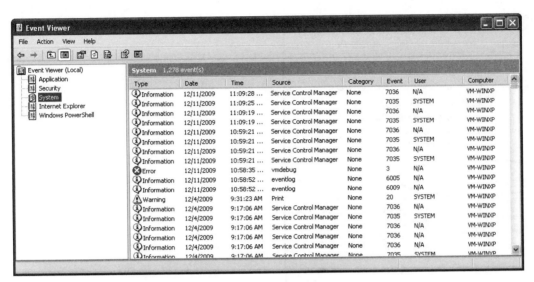

FIGURE 19-1 Viewing the System log in Event Viewer

At the end of this lab, you'll be able to

- Run the Event Viewer program

- Examine an event log entry

- Save the event log

Lab Materials and Setup

The materials you need for this lab are

- A working PC with Windows installed

Getting Down to Business

In Windows XP, you can start Event Viewer from the Control Panel by double-clicking the Administrative Tools applet and then double-clicking Event Viewer. In Windows Vista/7, go to the Start menu Search bar and type **Event Viewer**. Click the program that appears in the search results.

Step 1 Follow these steps to change the size of a log file:

a. In Event Viewer's left panel, right-click System and select Properties. (In Windows Vista/7, you'll first need to expand the Windows Logs subfolder.)

b. Change the number in the *Maximum log size* box to **40960** KB (512 is the default in Windows XP, 20480 is the default in Windows Vista/7) and, if it isn't selected already, select *Overwrite events as needed* (see Figure 19-2).

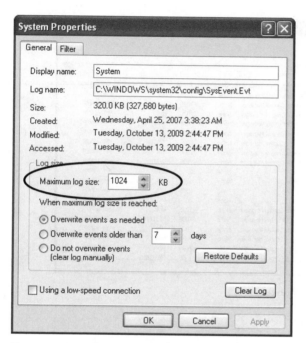

FIGURE 19-2 Changing the size of a log file

c. Do this for the Application, Security, and System logs.

d. Sometimes the log can be completely full before you get a chance to look at the entries. Scrolling through all the events can be a little boring and time-consuming, but you can fix that with filter settings. In Windows XP, click on the Filter tab of the log's Properties dialog box (see Figure 19-3). In Windows Vista/7, select the log from the main Event Viewer screen and click on Filter Current Log in the Actions list. The Windows XP and Windows Vista/7 versions differ in appearance, but they accomplish the same task.

You can filter events based on type/level, source, category, ID, user, computer, and more. This only controls what Event Viewer displays; all the events information will still be logged to the file, so you can change your mind about filter settings. Click OK to close the Properties dialog box.

Step 2 To clear, archive, and open a log file, follow these steps:

a. Clear the System log by right-clicking System and selecting *Clear all Events* in Windows XP (see Figure 19-4) or *Clear Log* in Windows Vista/7.

b. When you're prompted to save the System log, click Yes in Windows XP or Save and Clear in Windows Vista/7.

c. You can archive log files using different filenames each time (recommended) and select a location other than the default. Give your file a name you can remember and save it.

d. To open a saved file, click the Action menu and select Open Log File in Windows XP or Open Saved Log in Windows Vista/7. Select the file and click Open.

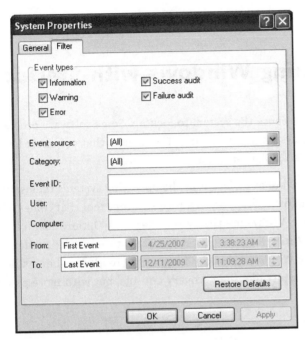

Figure 19-3 Viewing Event Viewer's settings

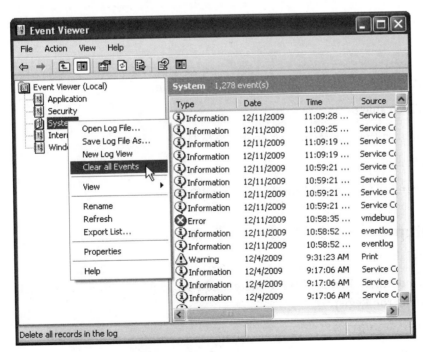

Figure 19-4 Clearing the System log

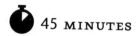 45 MINUTES

Lab Exercise 19.02: Repairing Windows with Startup Options and Tools

An errant upgrade or a poorly written driver can cause the system to lock up. Some software problems, such as corrupt Registry files, will even prevent the system from booting. This means that you must be ready to use alternative methods to boot the system to make repairs or replace files.

Windows has several ways to boot, and these ways are as different as the operating systems themselves. A Safe Mode boot is available in every version of Windows. There's also a nice recovery tool that comes with Windows XP known as the Recovery Console. Windows Vista/7 use the System Recovery Options menu (also known as the Windows Recovery Environment, or WinRE) on the bootable installation media; available tools include Startup Repair, System Restore, and the Windows Memory Diagnostic (Tool). Another available option is access to the Command Prompt, which works just like the Recovery Console, but with more power.

→ **Note**

From the System Recovery Options menu, you can also use the System Image Recovery (Windows 7) or Windows Complete PC Restore (Windows Vista) option to restore a previously created backup. Return to Chapter 17 to refresh your memory on backing up files.

Learning Objectives

You'll become familiar with alternative methods of booting a faulty system.

At the end of this lab, you'll be able to

- Boot to Windows Advanced Options Menu and enable Safe Mode
- Install the Recovery Console
- Repair the Registry using the Recovery Console/Command Prompt

Lab Materials and Setup

The materials you need for this lab are

- A working PC with Windows XP installed (preferably a non-production system, as you will be corrupting and repairing the Registry)
- A working PC with Windows Vista/7
- The Windows XP installation media

Getting Down to Business

If your system won't boot normally because of some system problem, you need a way to gain access to the hard drive and your files to troubleshoot the problem. There are, happily enough, troubleshooting tools that give you access to these files if the normal boot process won't work. You'll begin this exercise with the first line of defense, the Advanced Options Menu, and boot to Safe Mode. Then, Windows XP users will install and explore the Recovery Console, eventually repairing the Registry manually. Windows Vista/7 users should follow along until they are instructed to skip ahead.

Step 1 Power up a machine with any version of Windows installed. After the POST messages, but before the Windows logo screen appears, press F8. Depending on your system, you will see a number of different boot options. Record the various modes and provide a short description for each:

_____

_____

_____

_____

✔ **Cross-Reference**

For definitions of each of the boot modes, refer to the "Advanced Startup Options" section in Chapter 19 of *Mike Meyers' CompTIA A+ Guide to Managing and Troubleshooting PCs*.

Step 2 Select Safe Mode and press ENTER. The system will proceed to boot into the operating system, but it will inform you many times that it is running in Safe Mode (see Figure 19-5).

Safe Mode is often used when video settings have been changed and the new settings render the display unusable. In Safe Mode, a standard VGA driver is installed, and the minimal settings (16 colors, 640 × 480 resolution) are set. This enables you to revert to previous drivers, and/or correct the settings for the current display or monitor you are using. Complete the following steps to explore the display properties:

    a.   Right-click somewhere in the empty space of the desktop and select Properties from the drop-down menu. This brings up the Display Properties dialog box.

    b.   Click the Settings tab and note the display, color, and screen resolution settings. Record your settings here: _____

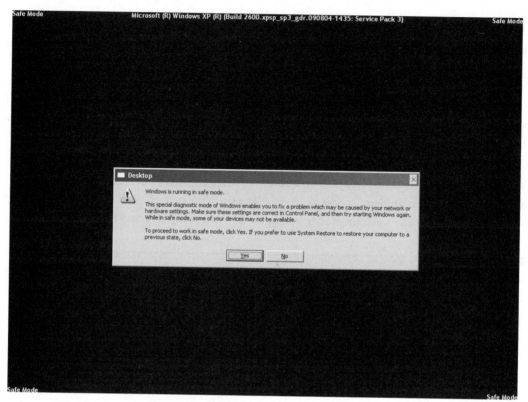

FIGURE 19-5 Windows running in Safe Mode

    c.   Click Cancel to close the Display Properties dialog box.

    d.   Click Start | Shut down.

Step 3   Windows XP users will now use the Repair menu item from the Windows installation media to launch the Recovery Console. If you're using Windows Vista or Windows 7, skip ahead to Step 5.

    a.   Insert the Windows installation disc and then reboot the system, making sure your CMOS is set to boot from your optical drive. The installation program loads a number of files and then displays a screen with the following information:

```
Welcome to Setup
This portion of the Setup program prepares Microsoft
Windows XP™ to run on your computer
        To set up Windows XP now, Press ENTER.
        To repair a Windows XP installation, press R.
        To quit Setup without installing Windows XP, press F3.
```

b. Press R to select the Repair function.

You'll now see a command-line interface asking which installation you want to access. If you have a dual-boot system, you'll have to choose an operating system; type its number from the list and press ENTER. Then type the administrator's password. This is the password for the first account created when you initially installed the operating system. You now have a command-line prompt from which to work.

✖ Warning

Be sure you know what you're doing here. You have access to files that you can add, change, rename, or delete. The old DOS command set is only partially available.

c. To see a list of commands, type **help** and note the results.

d. Type a command followed by **/?** to get an explanation of that command. You'll explore some of these commands later when you install the Windows XP Recovery Console.

→ Note

The Recovery Console operates very similarly to the Windows Command Line that you learned about in Chapter 18.

e. Type **exit** to quit the Recovery Console; the system will reboot.

Step 4 Although you can run the Recovery Console by booting directly to it from the Windows XP installation disc, it's much more convenient to set it up as a startup option on your boot menu (see Figure 19-6). In this step, you'll install the Windows XP Recovery Console as a boot option. (Windows Vista's and Window 7's System Recovery Options menu is located on the installation media or in the Advanced Boot Options menu on boot.)

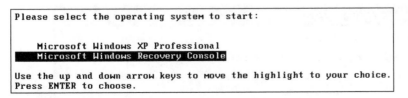

FIGURE 19-6 Recovery Console option in Windows XP startup

✔ **Hint**

To install the Recovery Console, you must have administrative rights on the computer.

---

   a.   Put your Windows XP installation CD-ROM into the optical drive; if it autostarts, select Exit. You can also press and hold SHIFT until the disc stops loading.

   b.   Select Start | Run.

   c.   In the Open box, type **D:\I386\Winn32.exe /cmdcons** (where D is the drive letter for your optical drive).

   d.   A Windows Setup dialog box appears, which describes the Recovery Console option. The system prompts you to confirm installation. Click Yes to start the installation procedure.

   e.   When the installation is complete (see Figure 19-7), restart the computer. You will see a Microsoft Windows Recovery Console entry on the boot menu.

→ **Note**

When you're installing the Recovery Console, you must use a Windows installation disc with the same version of Windows that was used for the system's main OS installation. For example, if you used a Windows XP Service Pack 3 installation disc to install Windows on this system, you should not use a pre–Service Pack 3 disc for this procedure. You can, but it may have adverse effects on the system.

It's wise to install the Recovery Console on important servers and on critical workstations.

Step 5   For Windows XP machines, reboot your system, and at the boot menu screen, select the Recovery Console. For Windows Vista/7 users, access the System Recovery options menu either by booting from the installation media and choosing Repair or by opening the Advanced Boot Options menu and choosing Repair Your Computer. Then open the Command Prompt.

FIGURE 19-7 Completing the Recovery Console installation in Windows XP

To see a list of the commands, type **help** at the command prompt. Type a command followed by **/?** to get an explanation of the command's use.

Several commands are worth reviewing; for the CompTIA A+ exams, you should know what the following commands do:

- **chkdsk** Checks the clusters and sectors of a disk (fixed or removable) and, if possible, repairs bad clusters or sectors

- **diskpart** A partitioning tool

- **exit** Closes the Recovery Console and restarts your computer

- **expand** Extracts copies of single files from the CAB files

- **fixboot** Writes a new partition table

- **fixmbr** Fixes the master boot record

- **help** Displays a Help screen

✔ **Hint**

Many techs resort to the Recovery Console when a system fails to boot in the normal fashion (from the hard drive). Three of the commands, fixboot, fixmbr, and chkdsk, are particularly important when it seems that the hard disk, the master boot record, or the system partition is missing, corrupt, or damaged. If you come across a system exhibiting these symptoms (and you will), follow good troubleshooting procedures, but remember that you have these tools available to you.

→ **Note**

Windows Vista/7 replaced fixmbr and fixboot with the bootrec command. The old commands still exist, but are hidden inside bootrec. To access them, you must use bootrec /fixmbr and bootrec /fixboot. Other available options include /scanos, which scans for Windows installations not in the boot configuration store, and /rebuildbcd, which does the same but allows you to add the installation to the boot configuration store.

The files that make up the Windows XP Recovery Console reside on the system partition, making the Recovery Console useless for a system partition crash. In such a situation, you would use the optical drive to access the Windows XP Recovery Console or Windows Vista/7 Command Prompt. The Recovery Console/Command Prompt shines in the business of manually restoring Registry files, stopping problem services, rebuilding partitions (other than the system partition), or using the expand program to extract copies of corrupted files from removable media.

Step 6 As mentioned in the previous step, the Recovery Console/Command Prompt is excellent when you need to restore Registry files. In the following steps, you will crash a system by deleting the System folder, and then repair the folder and recover the system.

✖ Warning

As mentioned in the "Lab Materials and Setup" section for this lab exercise, you are going to purposefully delete/corrupt the System folder of a working Windows system. For this reason, the system you use must be a noncritical, non-production system. Don't risk your family's financial records or your 40-GB photo archive—find another system to use for this exercise!

✔ Cross-Reference

The following steps use many components of Windows and the Recovery Console/Command Prompt. To understand better the files, folders, and Registry components involved, be sure to read the "Registry" section in Chapter 15 of *Mike Meyers' CompTIA A+ Guide to Managing and Troubleshooting PCs*. Microsoft has also gathered invaluable information in their Knowledge Base articles (a component of TechNet). The following lab steps incorporate valuable information from Knowledge Base articles 307545 and 309531. As previously mentioned, Web sites change over time, so if you don't find these exact articles, use your favorite search engine and locate similar articles related to the Recovery Console/Command Prompt and repairing the Registry.

---

a. Some preparation may be required to complete the steps to corrupt and restore your Registry folders. In Windows XP, open My Computer, then select Tools | Folder Options. In Windows Vista/7, select Start, then type **Folder Options** in the Search bar and press ENTER. Click the View tab. Turn on *Show hidden files and folders* (or *Show hidden files, folders, and drives*), turn off *Hide extensions for known file types*, and turn off *Hide protected operating system files (Recommended)*. Click OK.

b. Boot to the Recovery Console/Command Prompt, and after logging on as administrator (if needed), type the following commands at the prompt:

```
md C:\%SYSTEMROOT%\Tmp
copy C:\%SYSTEMROOT%\System32\Config\System C:\%SYSTEMROOT%\Tmp\system.b
delete C:\%SYSTEMROOT%\System32\Config\System
exit
```

c. At this point, the Recovery Console/Command Prompt closes. Restart Windows. Allow Windows to boot normally. Did anything inhibit the normal loading and startup of Windows?

    d.   Boot to the Recovery Console/Command Prompt once again, log on as administrator (if needed), and type the following commands at the prompt:

```
copy C:\%SYSTEMROOT%\Repair\System c:\%SYSTEMROOT%\System32\Config\System
exit
```

    e.   The Recovery Console/Command Prompt again closes. Reboot Windows. Allow Windows to boot normally. Did Windows boot properly this time?

→ **Note**

Windows Vista/7's System Recovery Options menu also includes a handy tool called Startup Repair. It scans your computer for any problems and automatically repairs them. The next time you think you need to delve into Windows Vista/7's Command Prompt to fix any startup-related troubles, try Startup Repair first—it might just save you from having to type all of those backslashes!

 30 MINUTES

Lab Exercise 19.03: Troubleshooting Startup Problems

When it comes to troubleshooting tools, the latest versions of Windows inherited the best of both the Windows NT and 9x OS families. They have vintage tools such as the Last Known Good Configuration startup option for startup failures and the Task Manager for forcing errant programs to close. There is also the Recovery Console/Command Prompt, and Windows Help.

I'll leave the finer details of these tools for you to explore through Windows Help, the main textbook, and other labs. In this lab, you'll explore a simple tool known as the System Configuration utility. The System Configuration utility has been around for some time, having been introduced in Windows 98. It was never incorporated into Windows NT or 2000, but it is included in Windows XP and Windows Vista/7.

Learning Objectives

You'll be reintroduced to some troubleshooting tips using a vintage tool with Windows XP/Vista/7.

At the end of this lab, you'll be able to

- Use the System Configuration utility to perform diagnostic startups

Lab Materials and Setup

The materials you need for this lab are

- A working Windows system

Getting Down to Business

Many systems have way too many startup options enabled. This isn't only a source of boot problems; it can also slow down the boot process and hog RAM from programs that need it. When Windows experiences failures during startup, consider using the System Configuration utility to discover and fix the problem.

Step 1 In Windows XP, select Start | Run, type **msconfig**, and then press ENTER. In Windows Vista/7, select Start, type **msconfig** into the Search bar, and then press ENTER.

The System Configuration utility opens (see Figure 19-8).

Notice that on the General tab, you can select Diagnostic startup. This is useful if you have just added new hardware that's causing intermittent problems, because it enables you to boot with only basic devices.

The Selective startup feature is also nice; it lets you bypass some configuration files to see which one contains the errors that are causing problems.

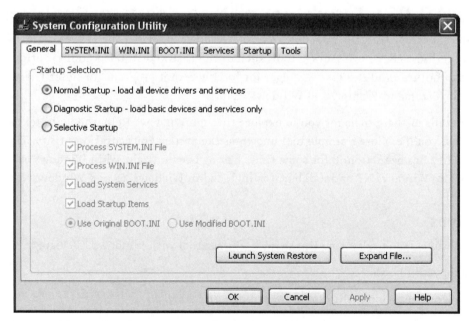

FIGURE 19-8 Using the System Configuration utility

Notice the SYSTEM.INI and WIN.INI tabs, which provide settings that enable you to change the load sequence of your drivers and edit the entries when you find an error.

→ **Note**

The SYSTEM.INI and WIN.INI tabs are not present in Windows Vista/7. Those files still exist, but only for backward compatibility with 16-bit applications.

Step 2   The BOOT.INI tab (labeled Boot in Windows Vista/7) is powerful (see Figure 19-9) and goes well beyond the CompTIA A+ exam requirements, but there are a couple of options you should know about.

One important option for troubleshooting is to create a log of what transpired during the boot process. On the BOOT.INI/Boot tab, you can enable a bootlog to be created each time the system boots.

If you're troubleshooting a problem and you need to start in Safe Mode every time, instead of pressing F8, you can enable the Safe boot (/SAFEBOOT in Windows XP) option.

Step 3   One item that I find useful is under the Services tab. Microsoft has many services that you can disable during bootup if you believe they're causing problems. The Hide All Microsoft Services option, when enabled, only displays those services you've installed—like my VMware Tools Service driver in Figure 19-10.

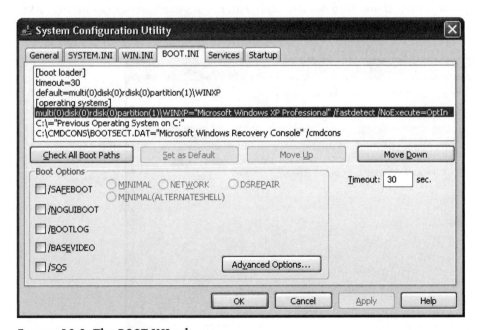

FIGURE 19-9 The BOOT.INI tab

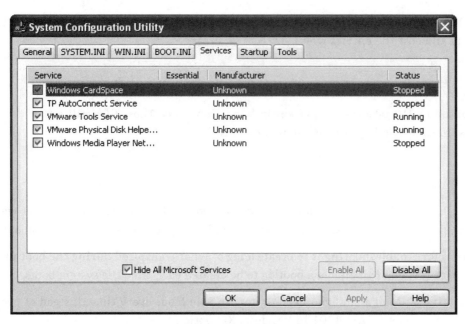

FIGURE 19-10 Using the Services tab with Microsoft Services hidden

Step 4 The Startup tab is perhaps the most useful. You can enable or disable any of the terminate and stay resident (TSR) programs that are installed. This is a good place to look if some unexplained program is trying to load every time you boot, even though you thought you'd uninstalled it.

Notice in Figure 19-11 that one program on the list doesn't have a name. I'm kind of suspicious about what this program might be doing! If you find questionable entries in your Startup tab listing, you should fire up a browser and do some research to see whether or not they're harmful.

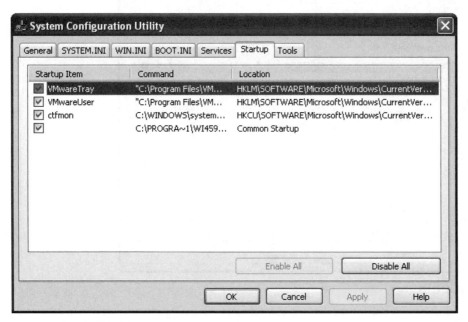

FIGURE 19-11 Checking your startup programs

✔ **Hint**

You can also run the System Configuration utility in Safe Mode. If you're having problems, you can boot to Safe Mode and then use this utility to identify the source of the problem.

Lab Analysis Test

1. John has just been infected with malware on his Windows XP computer and his computer now says "NTLDR is Missing" upon bootup. Give John a detailed description of the steps he needs to take to fix the computer.

2. You've installed a new network card and sound card. Every time you boot, the system locks up, and you must boot into Safe Mode to get to a GUI. What tool can you use to locate the source of the problem?

3. Tim is a Windows XP user who feels he's really a programmer at heart—he always seems to be opening the Registry with regedit and changing settings directly in the Registry. Today, it doesn't go so well, and he ends up with the Blue Screen of Death (BSOD). What can Tim use to make his system work again?

4. Laurie suspects that someone is trying to log on to her computer and is failing over and over again. She wants to know when this intrusion attempt is happening, so she has set up auditing for login events on her Windows 7 computer. Where will she go to see the intrusion attempts?

5. William has a computer that has been on the fritz, so he decided to enter Safe Mode. What are the features of Safe Mode that make it so good for troubleshooting?

Key Term Quiz

Use the following terms to complete the following sentences. Not all terms will be used.

Advanced Startup Options menu

Application logs

bootrec

diskpart

Event Viewer

F8

fixboot

fixmbr

msconfig

Recovery Console

Safe Mode

security logs

system logs

System Recovery Options menu

1. You can repair the master boot record on a Windows Vista computer using the _____ command.

2. The _____ can be added as a boot menu option.

3. The _____ in Windows 7 includes Startup Repair, System Restore, Windows Memory Diagnostic, and Command Prompt.

4. The _____ utility is used to troubleshoot startup issues when you can't get into the GUI of Windows.

5. _____ provides three log files to assist with the troubleshooting of a Windows operating system.

Chapter 20

Input Devices

Lab Exercises

The world of input and output is one full of peripherals. These range from the more obvious (keyboards and mice) to the more specialized (digital cameras, bar code readers, and KVM switches) devices. It is these components that allow you to interact with the computer. Without a keyboard or mouse, you would be sitting in front of a computer all day *waiting* for something to happen spontaneously. While you are most likely familiar with the use of input devices such as keyboards and mice, you may not be as intimately acquainted with their connection method or maintenance.

Most peripherals use a USB connector of one kind or another. While USB is a plug-and-play technology, the device itself still requires a driver, and you need to know where to find that driver and how to install it. Maintaining peripherals is also important. Keyboards, in the wrong hands, can be quite breakable, but even well-kept keyboards can't last forever. Of course, there is more to life than just plain text. With the rise of digital photography and online image-sharing services, more people than ever want to keep their photos on their computers. Two peripherals can help them do just that—scanners and digital cameras. But these devices are not all built the same. Cost and quality can vary dramatically, and even a single device is capable of producing images of different qualities, depending on its settings and how it is used.

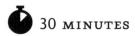 30 MINUTES

Lab Exercise 20.01: Using USB Drivers

USB's incredible ease of use makes it the most popular type of general-purpose connection used on PCs. USB is so popular that every type of peripheral (other than monitors) has someone making a USB version. The downside to this ease of use is that it can be a challenge to deal with USB when it doesn't work as specified.

Learning Objectives

At the end of this lab, you'll be able to

- Diagnose and repair common USB driver failures
- Recognize the limitations of built-in Windows USB device drivers

Lab Materials and Setup

The materials you need for this lab are

- A Windows system using USB

- At least one "human interface" USB device, such as a mouse or keyboard

- At least one mass storage USB device, such as a USB thumb drive

- At least one USB device that is neither a human interface device nor a mass storage device (for example, a wired NIC, Bluetooth hub, or wireless NIC)

- A notepad and pencil

Getting Down to Business

The biggest problems you'll see with USB are the result of improper drivers. If you know how to recognize these problems from error messages or by using third-party tools, you shouldn't have too much trouble fixing them.

Windows comes with very good built-in support for what it calls human interface devices (HIDs), such as keyboards and mice. It also does a good job supporting most USB mass storage devices such as USB thumb drives. Once you move outside these two classes of devices, however, Windows won't work properly (if at all) without the drivers supplied by the manufacturer.

✔ Cross-Reference

For more information on setting up USB devices, refer to the "USB Configuration" section in Chapter 20 of *Mike Meyers' CompTIA A+ Guide to Managing and Troubleshooting PCs*.

Step 1   Connect any HID or mass storage USB device to the Windows system *without* first installing the supplied driver. Does the device work as expected? Is it missing any features? Does the device even come with drivers? Write down your conclusions and unplug the device.

_____

_____

_____

Step 2   Check the Web site of the manufacturer of the USB device you just installed to see if a driver exists. If there is a driver, download it and install it into your system. Now connect the device again. Does the device work the same as it did before?

_____

_____

Step 3   Select another USB device—specifically, one that is neither an HID nor a mass storage device—and connect it to the same system *without* first installing the supplied driver. Does the device work as expected? Is it missing any features? Does the device even come with drivers? Write down your conclusions and unplug the device.

_____

_____

_____

Step 4   Check the Web site of the manufacturer of the USB device you just installed to see if a driver exists. If there is a driver, download it and install it into your system. Did the installation work? In many cases installation will fail because Windows may have loaded an improper driver when you first installed the device. Does the device work the same as before? You'll probably find that it doesn't, for the same reason.

_____

Step 5   Go to the manufacturer's Web site and see how to remove the device driver properly. Delete the driver and then remove the device.

✔ Hint

Installing a USB device without first installing the proper driver on a non-HID or mass storage device will almost always require you to uninstall the USB device completely from Device Manager. Even so, you should still check the manufacturer's Web site first!

Step 6   With the previous drivers properly removed, again install the drivers you downloaded earlier. Then insert the USB device. Does the device work as expected? Are there features now that did not appear earlier? What does this tell you about the importance of installing USB device drivers before you install the actual USB device?

_____

_____

_____

_____

Step 7   As time and available hardware allow, practice installing other USB devices and document how they work, both with and without proper drivers.

 30 MINUTES

Lab Exercise 20.02: Paging Dr. Keyboard!

Keyboards are plentiful and common, and a new basic keyboard is very inexpensive. Even with cheap keyboards, users tend to get attached to these devices over time—and in the case of an expensive keyboard with lots of extra buttons and features, the user may have both a financial *and* an emotional attachment! For these reasons, it's important that you learn to play "Dr. Keyboard," fixing these devices when they break.

Learning Objectives

At the end of this lab, you'll be able to

- Repair stuck keyboard keys

- Dismantle and clean a keyboard

Lab Materials and Setup

The materials you need for this lab are

- A Windows system

- As many "throw-away" keyboards as possible (functional keyboards that you won't mind throwing away at the end of this lab; connection type is unimportant as long as they're usable by a Windows system)

- A medium-sized flathead screwdriver

- Compressed air

- A lint-free cloth

✔ Hint

Try to avoid using older (pre-2004) laptop keyboards, as many older laptop keyboards used a delicate type of scissors key connector that would shatter if pried off.

Getting Down to Business

In this exercise, you'll dismantle one or more keyboards, cleaning up the keyboard components in the process, and then reassemble the device(s) and test for functionality.

Step 1   Disconnect the keyboard from the Windows system. Try prying off two or three keys using the flathead screwdriver (see Figure 20-1). Include more difficult keys such as the SPACEBAR, ENTER/RETURN, and a key from the center of the keyboard such as the letter G. Inspect the bottom of the key and the key post that it sits on—how much dirt is there? Reinsert the keys, making sure they are snapped all the way down.

Step 2   Test the keyboard by installing it into a Windows system. If any of the keys you removed aren't working, double-check that they're properly snapped in. Shut down the system and remove the keyboard. Repeat this process until all keys are working.

> ➜ **Note**
>
> What should you do if you break a key? Well, nobody sells replacement parts for keyboards—they're just too darn cheap to bother! You might be lucky enough to have a nonworking keyboard that's the exact same model, which you can cannibalize; otherwise, just consign the affected keyboard to the scrap heap after you've used it for this lab.

Step 3   Insert the nozzle of the compressed air under a key and start blasting away. If the keyboard is really old or looks dirty, you may want to do this outside! Did you see any dust or crumbs come out?

Step 4   Completely dismantle the keyboard. Most keyboards have a number of screws underneath that you must first remove to begin this process. Inspect the screws—are they different sizes? Keep track of which screw goes into which hole.

FIGURE 20-1   Removing the CTRL key with a screwdriver

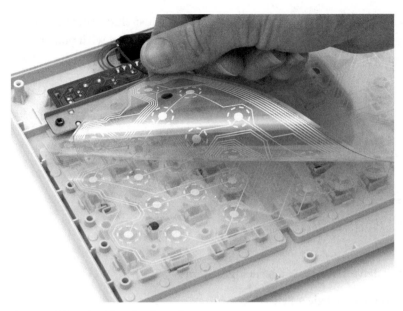

FIGURE 20-2 Inside a keyboard

Step 5 The inside of the keyboard will have a number of plastic contact templates (see Figure 20-2). Remove these, keeping track of their relation to each other so you can reassemble them. Wipe down each template with the lint-free cloth dampened with water. If you run into serious dirt, add a bit of mild detergent and repeat until the keyboard is clean.

✔ **Hint**

All keyboards have small circuit boards inside as well. Don't get them wet!

Step 6 After allowing everything to dry, reassemble the keyboard and test it on a Windows system. If the keyboard is not working properly, dismantle it and try again.

 30 MINUTES

Lab Exercise 20.03: Exploring Scanners

With the near ubiquity of digital cameras, most people keep the majority of their photographs in digital form, whether on their hard drive or uploaded to a photo-sharing Web site like Flickr.com. But what do you do with all of those photographs from the old days of film cameras? Sadly, you can't just shove them into your hard drive and have them magically appear on your computer. Instead, flatbed scanners are a popular choice for those people who wish to preserve their photographs or just share them online with friends and family. There are several image-editing applications that will interface with your scanner. You can often scan, import, edit, and upload from a single application!

Learning Objectives

At the end of this lab, you'll be able to

- Use and configure a scanner

Lab Materials and Setup

The materials you need for this lab are

- A Windows system

- A scanner with the proper drivers for your operating system

- An image-editing utility, such as Google's Picasa

- A photograph or document to scan

Getting Down to Business

In this exercise, you'll scan various images at different resolutions to see how various settings impact the speed of the scanner and the quality of the images. Make sure that your scanner is hooked up to your system and properly set up with the correct drivers. Also, make sure you have software capable of interfacing with your scanner. This exercise is written for use with Google's Picasa, but you should be able to follow along with any image-editing utility.

Step 1   If you haven't already, download Google's Picasa from http://picasa.google.com, install it, and open it. (Now would be a good time to check and make sure your scanner is turned on!) Meanwhile, find something (preferably flat) that you can scan. The best things to use include old photographs and paper printouts. Newspapers and magazines are good, too, but depending on the resolution used to print them, you may have mixed results. Place the item facing down on the scanner bed.

Step 2   With Picasa open, select File | Import From. At the very top of the screen is a drop-down box. Use it to select your input device (your scanner).

Step 3   When you select your scanner from the list, the configuration utility for your particular scanner should appear. This will be different for every scanner, but it should have some common features. The most important setting is quality, or resolution. The resolution your scanner uses is the number of dots per inch (dpi) used to create the digital image on your computer. You might have settings called Draft, Good, or Best quality, or they may be more specific, such as 150 dpi, 600 dpi, or 2400 dpi. You might even be able to type in any number you want, up to the maximum resolution of the scanner. There are probably other settings available, but you can play with these later. For now, choose the lowest quality setting available, such as Draft, 150 dpi, or what have you.

Step 4   Click the Preview button. This will scan the entire bed of the scanner at a low resolution so you can accurately select where you want to scan the final image. When the preview is complete, use the tool that is (hopefully) provided to select or highlight the photo, document, or whatever you're scanning. Click the Scan button.

Step 5   Your scanner will now begin to hum and buzz and maybe even shake a little—do not be alarmed. This is the part of the process when whatever you put on the scanner bed is actually *scanned*. When finished, you may be able (or asked) to scan another image, but for now, close the scanner utility.

Step 6   Back in Picasa, your image should appear in the Import window. At the bottom of the screen, select Import All. You'll be asked to name the folder that the image is saved to as well as designate where that folder goes. Click Finish, and you'll be returned to Picasa's main gallery.

Step 7   Find and double-click the image you just scanned. Zoom in and out and pan around. At 150 dpi or Draft settings, the picture will be very small, and any attempt to enlarge it will cause severe pixilation and loss of quality.

Step 8   Now that you know how to scan an image, repeat the process, but this time, select Best quality, or the highest resolution available. Preview and scan the image.

Step 9   Notice anything about the humming and buzzing this time around? Unless you have a magic make-believe scanner, it probably took a lot longer to finish scanning the image this time. That's because the scanner needed to create more digital dots per inch, which takes more time. Import the image into Picasa and open it. Zoom in and out and pan around. Compare this second scan to the first one.

Which scanned image is better? Why?

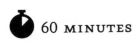 60 MINUTES

Lab Exercise 20.04: Testing Digital Cameras

As much as we would all like to always be working with the latest and greatest equipment and most advanced technology around, there is one limiting factor that always seems to get in the way: cost. Some people firmly believe in the mantra, "You get what you pay for." And they may be right. But with all of the different features and specifications of digital cameras, some of which are nice and some of which are needless, it is very possible to spend way too much on a bad camera. Personally, I like to focus (an unfortunate pun) on the quality of the pictures taken, and *then* look at the available features, because a camera with more features doesn't necessarily take better pictures. It's possible to buy a cheaper camera with fewer features that takes better pictures—the trick is to know how to find it.

Learning Objectives

At the end of this lab, you'll be able to

- Use a digital camera

- Compare digital cameras

- Upload photos to a computer

- Research digital cameras

Lab Materials and Setup

The materials you need for this lab are

- At least two digital cameras, preferably more if possible

- Cables to connect the digital camera to a computer

- A Windows system with access to the Internet

- An image-editing utility, such as Google's Picasa

- Something to photograph

Getting Down to Business

In this lab exercise, you will compare the quality of images taken by multiple digital cameras in order to determine which camera is the best. To facilitate this, try to use as many different digital cameras as possible. If students have access and permission, they could use their own. The school may also have digital cameras available for student use.

Step 1　To ensure proper testing, you'll need to set up a test shot—something that can be photographed by each digital camera but won't move or change. This can be either a single object or an arrangement of several objects. You may even want to put people in the picture, but make sure they don't move! The object or scene should have color, depth (objects in the foreground and background), and contrast. It should also be adequately lit.

Step 2　Using each digital camera, take a picture of the object or scene. For best results, you may wish to mount the digital cameras on a tripod so that the picture is taken from the same spot each time and the images don't turn out blurry.

Step 3　With all of the pictures taken, plug in each digital camera to your computer using the cable that came with the camera. The image-editing utility will often open automatically when the computer detects a camera has been plugged in, but if not, open your image-editing utility. Find the Import feature for your particular program. In Picasa, you'll find it under File | Import From. Select the digital camera and import your images. Make sure to label the images in a way that lets you know which camera was used; the image itself will store this data, but depending on your software, this information could be difficult to find. Repeat this step for each digital camera used.

Step 4 With all of the images imported into your image-editing utility, open each of them and take a good look. Zoom in and out and pan around. Look at colors (are they accurate?), detail (is this image clear or grainy?), and any obvious flaws (artifacting, pixilation, and so forth). Then, using the following chart, rank each camera in each category to determine which is the best.

Camera	Quality/Clarity	Color Accuracy	Absence of Flaws	Overall

Step 5 Now it's time to do some research. Using Google or a digital camera review Web site (Steve's Digicams, CNET.com, and Digital Camera Resource Page are all good sources of information), find the cameras you used, read about them, and fill in the following chart. Try to use the same Web site for each review score to keep it consistent. Then answer the questions following the chart.

Camera	Average Cost	Review Score

Compare the cost of each camera with its review score and your own findings. Is there a connection between the cost of the digital camera and the quality of its output? If so, what is the connection? Do you think this is true of all digital cameras? Why or why not?

_____

_____

_____

_____

Lab Analysis Test

1. Beth's brand-new USB keyboard has a piece of the packaging stuck under the keyboard in such a way that she simply can't pull it out, even with a pair of needle-nose pliers. What should she do to fix this problem?

2. Mario recently purchased a used digital camera capable of taking pictures with a resolution of up to 2 megapixels. He wants to eventually make printouts of these images at 8 × 10 inches or larger. Why or why not is this a good idea?

3. Edward is on a trip with his family and has been taking pictures using a traditional film camera. He has had several rolls of film developed and wants to share some pictures online. Fortunately, he has packed his laptop and a portable scanner for the trip. But when he goes to scan the pictures, the scanner doesn't work. He tries again, with the lid of the scanner opened this time, and notices the light of the scanner is on, but won't move. What's wrong?

4. Whitney sits down at her Windows Vista computer one day to do some work, but notices that something is different about her mouse clicks. She finds it difficult to double-click fast enough for anything to open. Describe how to fix this in Windows Vista.

5. Rita has been using two different computers at her desk at work. She has two cases, two monitors, two keyboards, and two mice. What device could she use to simplify this setup, and how would she set it up?

Key Term Quiz

Use the following terms to complete the following sentences. Not all terms will be used.

bar code reader

biometric device

device driver

digital camera

keyboard

KVM switch

optical resolution

scanner

touch screen

USB

webcam

1. An example of a(n) _____ would be a fingerprint scanner.

2. A(n) _____ usually has two types of zoom: optical and digital.

3. The color depth of a(n) _____ is commonly measured in bits, such as 24-bit, 36-bit, and 48-bit.

4. When installing any USB device, make sure you have the appropriate _____.

5. The main interface for most smartphones is a(n) _____.

Chapter 21

Video

Lab Exercises

Few components affect the PC user like the video system, the primary output for the PC. As you know from the textbook, the video system has two main hardware components—monitor and display adapter—that work together to produce the image on your screen. Both components must be installed and configured properly in Windows, or your viewing pleasure will be seriously compromised. Good techs know how to do video right!

In this set of labs, you'll install a display adapter, hook up a monitor, load video drivers, and configure Windows for optimal viewing. You'll then work with the growing practice of using multiple monitors (for example, a projector and a laptop screen) to expand your desktop viewing area. The last lab exercise will run you though some of the typical troubleshooting issues that techs face when dealing with video.

✖ Warning

It is critical to understand that only *trained* monitor technicians should remove the cover of a video monitor (or a television set, for that matter). The inside of a traditional monitor might look similar to the interior of a PC, with printed circuit boards and related components, but there's a big difference: No PC has voltages up to 50,000 volts or more inside, but most CRT monitors *do*. So be sure to get one thing clear—casually opening a monitor and snooping around has the potential to become harmful to you and the monitor—and in cases of extreme carelessness, it can even be deadly! Even when the power is disconnected, certain components (capacitors) still retain substantial levels of voltage for an extended period of time. Capacitors work like batteries. Yes, they can maintain 50,000 volts! If you inadvertently short one of the capacitors, a large discharge will occur into the monitor circuits, destroying them. If you're touching the metal frame, you could fry yourself—to death. Given this risk, certain aspects of monitor repair fall outside the necessary skill set for a standard PC support person, and definitely outside the CompTIA A+ exam domains. Make sure you understand the problems you can fix safely and the ones you need to hand over to a qualified electronics repair shop.

 30 MINUTES

Lab Exercise 21.01: Installing Video

Your office staff's computers need a serious video upgrade. Some of the PCs have tiny 17-inch LCD monitors that simply have to go, while others have decent 19-inch and 20-inch LCDs that have a year or two of life left in them. Your boss has bought new PCIe video cards and some 24-inch-widescreen LCD monitors. You're tasked with installing the cards, loading drivers, and setting up everything in Windows.

✔ Cross-Reference

For the details of CRT versus LCD monitors, refer to the "CRT Monitors" and "LCD Monitors" sections in Chapter 21 of *Mike Meyers' CompTIA A+ Guide to Managing and Troubleshooting PCs*.

Learning Objectives

At the end of this lab, you'll be able to

- Identify the make and model of a video card

- Install a video display adapter card

- Check BIOS for proper video settings

- Adjust the monitor for the proper display

- Optimize the video settings in Windows

Lab Materials and Setup

The materials you need for this lab are

- A working PC with Windows installed

- A working monitor (access to both a CRT and an LCD monitor is recommended)

- A working computer system with access to the Internet

✔ Hint

Classrooms that have a variety of different monitor types and video display adapter cards are a plus.

Getting Down to Business

To begin this lab, you'll become familiar with the video components in your system. You'll then step through the proper installation and configuration of a video adapter.

✖ Warning

Some versions of Microsoft Windows operating systems have problems when you make changes to the video display adapters, even when you're simply removing and reinstalling the same card into a different slot. If you perform this lab on a test machine, you should have no real problem if things go wrong. If you're using your primary PC to do the lab, however, make certain you have current drivers available for your video card, or a source to get drivers if necessary.

Step 1   Shut down your system properly and unplug the power cable from the system unit and the wall. Remove the cover from the PC to expose the expansion buses.

   a.   Find your video display adapter card (the one to which the monitor is attached). What type of video display adapter is installed: PCIe, AGP, or PCI? _____

✔ **Hint**

Many laptop computers and some low- to mid-level desktop systems include display adapters integrated right into the electronics of the motherboard. On desktop systems with this configuration, the connector will appear in line with the PS/2 and USB ports. If your system uses this type of display adapter, the overall performance of the system may suffer because the display typically "steals" system RAM to serve as video RAM. Laptops are usually designed around this limitation, but if your desktop system is of this type, you can increase the performance (and usually the video quality) by installing a display adapter card and disabling the onboard video in the BIOS.

---

   b.   Detach the monitor's cable from the video card. Using good ESD avoidance procedures, remove the screw that holds the card in place, put it in a secure location, and then remove your video display adapter card (see Figure 21-1). Examine it closely to answer the following questions. Be careful not to touch the expansion slot contacts on the card!

   c.   Look for a name or model number on the adapter's circuit board or chipset.

   Who is the manufacturer, or what is the model number? Write it down. (Note that for this lab's scenario, you'd actually be looking up the information for the new video cards, not the ones already installed—*those* will most likely be donated to charity!)

FIGURE 21-1 This video card has a large cooling fan for the graphics processing unit (GPU) and its onboard RAM chips

Be sure to write down as much information as you can collect from the display adapter for a later assignment.

   d.   Reinsert the video card into the same slot, and make sure it is properly seated. Reattach the monitor cable and test your system with the case still open to see if it works. This could save you the frustration that results when you close the case, fire up the system, and get a video error. (Not that I've ever done that!)

✔ **Hint**

AGP and PCIe cards can be a little tricky. They must be seated perfectly or they will not work. Many of these types of cards use slots with locking levers—if you were observant when you removed the card initially, you'll know what you have to do now for proper physical installation.

   e.   Boot your system and open your favorite browser to search the Web.

Conduct your search using the information you've gathered about the manufacturer and model number of your card.

Can you find the specifications for your display adapter? _____

What is the highest resolution you can achieve with your video adapter according to these specifications? _____

How much memory is available? _____

What type of memory is used? _____

Does the adapter support SLI or CrossFire? _____

Does the adapter have any other features, such as an HDMI connector?

_____

_____

Step 2   Reboot your system and press the proper key sequence to enter the system setup utility. Depending on the BIOS manufacturer and version, there can be as many as five or more video-related settings. My lab system has 10 settings directly related to video or the PCIe slot. Complete each of these questions based on your specific BIOS. Some of the names of the sections will undoubtedly differ from the ones presented here. Search around a bit and you'll find video options in your CMOS.

On the Standard CMOS Setup or similar screen, how many choices are there for video, and how is your video set? _____

On the Chipset Features Setup or similar screen, what is the value for your Video RAM Cacheable setting? _____

Are there any PCIe-specific settings? _____

Are there any settings for the amount of RAM the onboard adapter will use? _____
_____

On the Power Management Setup or similar screen, do you have settings to control how the monitor and video adapter will react when not in use for a period of time? What are your settings?

_____

On the Integrated Peripherals or similar screen, do you have an Init Display First setting? What are the choices?

_____

What does your setting say?

_____

Know that when this setting is wrong, the display might not work.

Step 3 You'll now examine a monitor and see what external controls it has. If you're not in a computer lab, you can go to your local computer store and examine a wide variety of monitors.

Figures 21-2 and 21-3 show the control buttons for adjusting the display attributes for an LCD and a CRT monitor, respectively. Both of these have the controls on the front of the monitor, but some have the controls behind a door under the front of the monitor screen, and others may have them on the back.

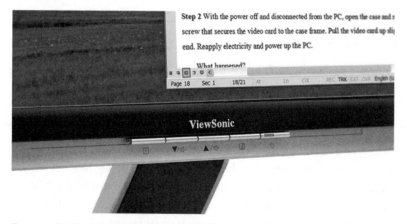

FIGURE 21-2 An LCD monitor with front-panel buttons for adjustments

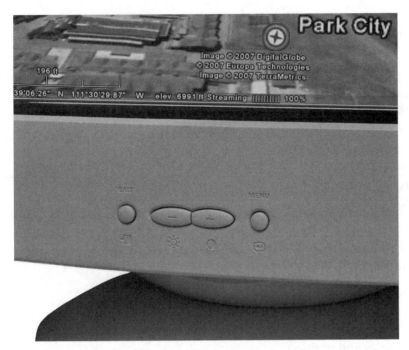

FIGURE 21-3 Front controls on a CRT monitor

A monitor can have quite a few adjustable features. How many of the following can you adjust on your LCD monitor?

Brightness	
Contrast	
Clock	
H-position	
V-position	
Color temperature	
Auto balance	
Sharpness	
Gamma	
Signal select (for LCDs with both VGA and DVI inputs)	
Full screen	
Language	

How many of these can you adjust on your CRT monitor?

Brightness	
Contrast	
Color saturation	

Vertical size	
Vertical position	
Horizontal size	
Horizontal position	
Pincushioning (for adjusting displays that are narrow in the middle but flare out at the top and bottom)	
Keystoning (for adjusting displays that are narrow at the top but flare out at the bottom)	
Degauss (for adjusting displays that have become fuzzy due to electromagnetic interference)	

Play with the controls of your monitor or a test monitor. If the current settings use percentages, write down the settings before doing any adjustments. Then follow these steps:

a.   Change the settings such as color and sizing. Don't be shy!

b.   Put the settings back as close as possible to their original positions.

c.   Optimize the screen for clarity and position.

Step 4   The hardware is set up properly and the BIOS settings should be correct, so now you need to configure and optimize the Windows settings that determine your video display characteristics. To do this, you need to use the Display applet (or Display Settings applet in Windows Vista).

✔   **Hint**

This lab simulates a working PC that you upgrade with new hardware and drivers. All the steps can work just as well for installing a video card into a new system, although the pace of that installation would differ. In a new system, you would physically install the video card, let Windows use generic VGA drivers until you make sure you can boot properly, and only then install the drivers for the video card. Finally, you'd go to the Display/Display Settings applet and optimize the video card settings. Windows is fairly good at finding a suitable driver the first time around, but you should still understand how to locate and update drivers for your video card.

In Windows XP, navigate to the Display applet and click the Settings tab. In Windows Vista, go to Control Panel | Personalization | Display Settings. In Windows 7, go to the Display Control Panel applet and click on *Change display settings*. This displays the monitor settings, such as those shown in Figure 21-4.

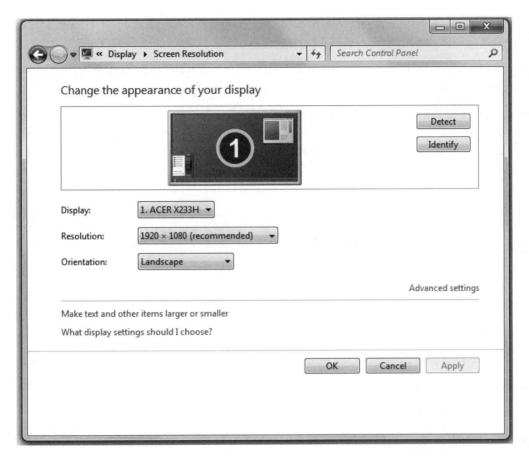

Figure 21-4 The Screen Resolution dialog box in the Display applet of Windows 7

✖ **Warning**

You're going to make changes to the look and feel of Windows. Making some of these changes can result in frustrating and time-consuming problems. Use a test machine if you have one available. If you must use your own machine, write down all your display settings before you make any changes.

Each video display adapter manufacturer has different options for its cards. By clicking the Advanced button (Advanced settings in Windows 7), you can access more information about the display adapter. You may see a choice for setting the refresh rate, as well as other features. Look through the settings on the Advanced tab or Properties dialog box, and see what your display adapter manufacturer provides. Remember that the video adapter "pushes" the monitor. If you set the refresh too high, it can cause problems, and in the case of older CRTs may even damage your monitor.

Write down your display's current resolution, color depth, and refresh rate. In Windows 7, you may need to look around to find these. Go ahead and explore!

Close the Advanced/Properties dialog box (if you selected it), but leave the Display Properties/Screen Resolution dialog box open.

Make some changes to the background and colors on your screen. In Windows XP, you'll find these options on the Desktop and Appearance tabs, respectively. In Windows Vista/7, you'll find these options in the Personalization applet. Be sure to note the original settings so you can change things back when you're done.

✔ **Hint**

The setting changes suggested in this step are perfectly safe and easy to undo.

Change the desktop background to something you might like better. Then try the following:

- Experiment with color combinations.

- Make some changes to the displayed fonts and menu bars.

- Experiment with changing the colors and resolution of your display.

    Can your machine run in 16-bit color? _____

    How about 24-bit color? _____

    Can you run 800 × 600 resolution? _____

    Can you run 1024 × 768 resolution? _____

    Can you run 1280 × 960 resolution? _____

    Do you have any other options? _____

In Windows XP, click the Advanced button again. In Windows Vista, click Advanced. In Windows 7, click on the Advanced settings link. Open the Monitor tab. Experiment with changing the refresh rate (see Figure 21-5).

✔ **Hint**

Because of the way that LCD monitors work, the refresh rate setting doesn't really apply to them. As a general rule, LCD monitors display a stable, flicker-free image at 60 hertz (Hz). There are no visible differences between 85 Hz and 60 Hz.

FIGURE 21-5 A typical refresh setting on the Monitor tab

Can you make specific numeric changes? _____

Are the Optimal and Adapter Default settings the only choices you have? _____

✔ Hint

The refresh rate is not an option on all video adapters. This setting may be in a different location, or not on your system at all.

Make sure you return all the settings to their original values, and then close the dialog box.

Check the drivers for your video card and monitor. Are they "standard" drivers, or are they specific to your hardware? Follow these steps:

a. Go to Device Manager, locate your display adapter, right-click, and select Properties.

b. Locate your driver information.

c. Can you identify the version number(s) of your video drivers? Write them down.

_____

d. Go online and find the manufacturer's Web site.

e. Check to see if newer drivers are available. If so, download and install them. (Do this on a test machine first. Get comfortable with the whole process before you do this on your personal computer.)

How did this affect your machine?

_____

✔ **Hint**

New drivers will sometimes fail to work properly, thereby crippling your PC. Windows XP and higher have the Roll Back Driver feature that enables you to go back to a driver that worked correctly in case this should happen. Refer to Chapter 17 for a refresher on how to do this.

Step 5 One more place to look for video settings is the Power Options Control Panel applet. Take a look at any power management settings you may have.

Go to the Control Panel and double-click the Power Options applet.

Read through the list of available power management schemes.

Which one do you have running? _____

How long is the period of inactivity before your monitor shuts off? _____

Close the applet and the Control Panel.

 30 MINUTES

Lab Exercise 21.02: Configuring Multiple Displays

Your consulting firm has just been awarded a contract to perform complete upgrades on the 12 digital audio workstations at a local recording studio. Among the various considerations for this type of application—large data storage, backups, fast processors, and loads of memory—the application also requires high-performance display adapters with multiple monitors for each station. It is not unusual for a recording engineer to have three or four critical windows open simultaneously during a session, so the studio design has included three widescreen monitors for each station.

You jump on the project and immediately stage one of the systems in the shop to run it through its paces. You decide to use one of the new ASUS motherboards with three PCIe slots and three high-performance NVIDIA display adapters. You finish the video configuration and attach three 30-inch widescreen monitors—this system looks impressive!

✔ **Cross-Reference**

For additional information on configuring your multiple displays, refer to the "Installing and Configuring Video" section in Chapter 21 of *Mike Meyers' CompTIA A+ Guide to Managing and Troubleshooting PCs*.

Learning Objectives

At the end of this lab, you'll be able to

- Install an additional video display adapter card

- Configure a system to use multiple displays

- Expand the desktop across two or more displays

Lab Materials and Setup

The materials you need for this lab are

- A working PC with Windows installed

- At least one additional display adapter or a display adapter that supports multiple monitors

- At least one additional working monitor (CRT or LCD)

✔ **Hint**

This lab exercise does not require any of the high-end equipment discussed in the scenario. You should be able to complete the steps to configure multiple monitors using a few video cards and the monitors in your classroom lab. You can even use the integrated display adapter on many motherboards and install one additional video card to complete the lab steps. If time permits, hop on a system with Internet access and explore some of the components discussed in the scenario. Manufacturers such as ASUS, NVIDIA, and NEC are always adding new technology to their product lines.

Getting Down to Business

To explore the system configuration presented in the opening scenario, you will install at least one additional display adapter and monitor on a working system. You will then use the Display applet in Windows to configure the multiple monitors for use as an expanded desktop.

Step 1 Shut down your system properly and unplug the power cable from the system unit and the wall. Remove the cover from the PC to expose the expansion bus slots.

a. Verify the type (PCI, AGP, or PCIe) and location of the current video display adapter. Using proper ESD avoidance procedures and one of the available expansion slots (depending on the additional video card available to you), install a second video display adapter in your system. Remember that AGP and PCIe cards can be a little finicky during installation, so make sure they are inserted securely.

→ **Note**

You may have a display adapter that already supports multiple monitors and has two display ports on a single card. If this is the case, you don't need to add a second adapter to set up multiple monitors, but it's good to practice, either way.

b. Attach the second monitor cable to the new display adapter, and test your system with the case still open to see if it works.

To verify that the second display adapter and monitor have been installed correctly, are recognized by the system, and have drivers available, open Device Manager and expand the display adapter's icon. View the properties of the newly installed card and select the Drivers tab. Does everything appear to be in order?

c. If the new display adapter is not working properly, you may need to install specific drivers or updated drivers. Access the Internet to download and install the appropriate drivers for your display adapter.

Step 2 Now that the hardware is set up and functioning properly, you will configure Windows to expand your desktop across two or more displays. To do this, you will again open the Display applet.

In Windows XP, navigate to the Display Properties dialog box's Settings tab. In Windows Vista, go to Control Panel | Personalization | Display Settings. In Windows 7, go to the Display applet and click on *Change display settings*. This shows the monitor settings and should now display two monitor icons, as shown in Figure 21-6.

Now complete the following steps to expand your desktop across the displays you have installed.

a. Click the drop-down arrow next to the Display field. Are both of your display adapters available?

_____

b. Select the second monitor icon. In Windows XP, check the *Extend my Windows desktop onto this monitor* box, and click the Apply button. In Windows Vista/7, click on the Multiple displays drop-down box and select *Extend these displays*. Your monitor icons should now look something like Figure 21-7, and the display on your monitors should change accordingly.

c. Click and drag the dialog box or another open window from one monitor to the other. Notice that the standard setup has the second display as the display to the right, so the expansion should allow you to use the second monitor as the rightmost portion of the desktop. Open a few windows and place them in different locations on the two monitors (see Figure 21-8).

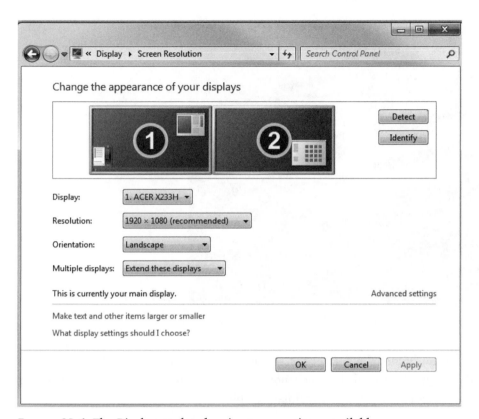

Figure 21-6 The Display applet showing two monitors available

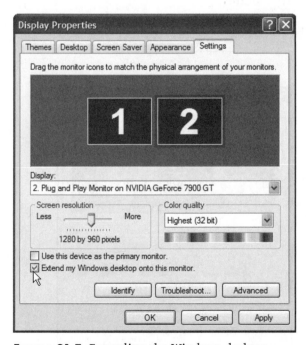

Figure 21-7 Extending the Windows desktop

FIGURE 21-8 Dual monitors displaying multiple open windows

d.   Experiment with the "virtual" placement of the monitors by clicking one of the numbered monitors and dragging it around the other monitor(s). Also click and highlight one of the numbered monitors and select it as the primary display.

Can you place the monitors on top of each other (see Figure 21-9)? _____

Can you set the second display as the primary monitor? _____

Right-click one of the displays in the Display Properties dialog box and select Identify. What are the results? _____

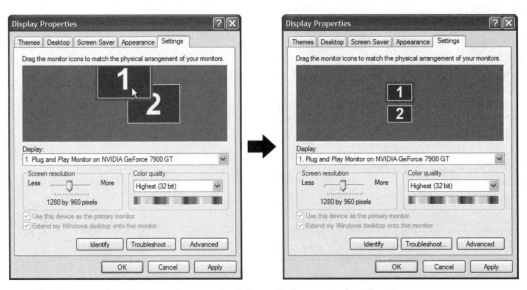

FIGURE 21-9 Configuring monitors to be "virtually" on top of each other

 30 MINUTES

Lab Exercise 21.03: Troubleshooting Video

Video troubleshooting really boils down to two distinct questions. First, are the physical video components installed and configured properly, as discussed in Lab Exercise 21.01? Second, do the current video display adapter and CPU support the software technologies you're trying to use? (Or have you loaded that killer game and completely overwhelmed your video subsystem?) In this lab exercise, you'll create connectivity problems to simulate real-world installation problems, and use the DirectX Diagnostic Tool to analyze your system.

Learning Objectives

At the end of this lab, you'll be able to

- Recognize and fix typical video installation and connectivity problems

- Use the Microsoft DirectX Diagnostic Tool to analyze and test the graphic display attributes of a PC system

Lab Materials and Setup

The materials you need for this lab are

- A working PC with Windows installed

- Any version of the Microsoft DirectX Diagnostic Tool installed

Getting Down to Business

If you went through Lab Exercise 21.01 and had typical results—video card not seated properly, forgetting to plug things in all the way, and so on—you can probably skip Steps 1 and 2 of this lab. If you had a perfect reinstall, on the other hand, then definitely do all of the steps!

Step 1   Loosen the screws that hold the monitor data cable securely to the video card. With the system fully powered up and in Windows—and being gentle with your hardware—partially disconnect the monitor cable.

What happened to the screen? _____

With many monitors, a loose cable results in a seriously degraded display. Colors fade out or a single color disappears, or the display may appear grainy or snowy, for example. If you run into these symptoms in the field, check your connectivity!

Connect the monitor cable and tighten the restraining screws to resume normal operation.

Step 2   With the power off and disconnected from the PC, open the case and remove the screw that secures the video card to the case frame. Pull the video card up slightly on one end. Reapply electricity and power up the PC.

What happened? _____

You might have to run through this a couple of times to get the desired effect, which is a seemingly dead PC and some beeping from the system speaker. That long-short-short beep code is pretty universally recognizable as the PC's cry for help: "Hey! My video card isn't seated properly!"

With the power off and disconnected, reseat your video card, reinstall the restraining screw, and power up your PC to resume normal operation.

Step 3   Access the Microsoft DirectX Diagnostic Tool. In Windows XP, select Start | All Programs | Accessories | System Tools | System Information. Select Tools | DirectX Diagnostic Tool. In Windows Vista/7, type **dxdiag** into the Start menu Search bar and press ENTER (see Figure 21-10).

✔ **Hint**

There is a faster way to get to the DirectX Diagnostic Tool in Windows XP too! Just go to Start | Run, type dxdiag, and click OK.

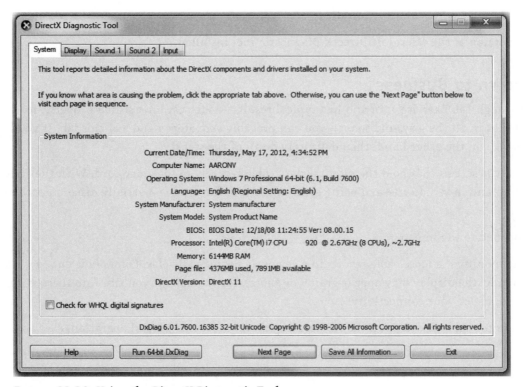

FIGURE 21-10 Using the DirectX Diagnostic Tool

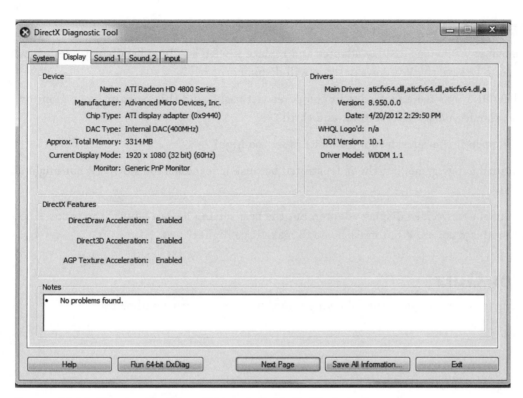

FIGURE 21-11 Viewing the DirectX Diagnostic Tool's Display tab

Step 4 Select the Display tab (see Figure 21-11).

What is the name of your display adapter? _____

How much total memory is on the adapter? _____

What is the current display mode? _____

What is the driver name and version? _____

Does it display a driver version date? _____

Should you look for a more current driver? _____

Step 5 Check out the Notes box at the bottom of the Display tab, and read the information provided. This is where you can find out about any conflicts or problem areas.

Do you see any information about conflicts or problems? If so, what's the conflict or problem?

_____

Lab Analysis Test

1. If you remove an AGP video display adapter and replace it with a PCIe video display adapter, what must you do to be sure the Windows desktop will display properly?

2. Your nephew Brian visited and used your computer last night, and this morning your monitor is dead. What should you do first, second, and third?

3. What can happen if the refresh rate for a CRT is set too high?

4. Teresa installed a new game, but she is frustrated because it responds too slowly. What might she check?

5. Taylor installed a new video display adapter, but the best setting he can adjust it to is 800 × 600 resolution with 256 colors. What must he do to make it go higher?

Key Term Quiz

Use the following terms to complete the following sentences. Not all terms will be used.

color depth

Direct3D

DirectX Diagnostic Tool

Display applet

Display Settings

Init Display First

refresh rate

resolution

1. Once software is installed, test your video using Microsoft's _____.

2. Erin's monitor was set to 640 × 480, a very low _____.

3. John complained constantly about getting headaches every day. When you looked at his PC, you noted that the screen flickered. John's monitor had the _____ set too low!

4. The _____ is the one-stop shop in Windows XP and Windows 7 for changing your video settings. In Windows Vista, many of these same settings can be found in _____.

5. You can adjust the number of colors displayed by the monitor by using the _____ option.

Chapter 22
Local Area Networking

Lab Exercises

In Chapter 5, you were introduced to basic networking concepts. You explored network topologies, devices, and settings. Now that you have that introductory knowledge, it's time to move on to tougher topics and more advanced exercises. This chapter is all about building and using a local area network.

In this chapter, you'll first learn how to construct an Ethernet patch cable. While you can easily find patch cables at any electronics store, a tech should be able to make his or her own. Next, you'll verify TCP/IP settings such as your IP address and default gateway using both the Control Panel and the command prompt. The third lab exercise in this chapter explains how you can share resources on your computer with the entire network. Finally, you'll return to the command prompt and work with several commands that enable you to test and troubleshoot your network connection.

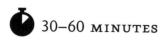 30–60 MINUTES

Lab Exercise 22.01: Building an Ethernet Patch Cable

CAT 5e and CAT 6 UTP cabling are now the dominant cabling media for wired networks. This is due to the fact that Ethernet has become the dominant networking technology, and Ethernet uses UTP cabling to electrically transmit the data frames. To ensure that these data frames are transmitted and received correctly requires that these UTP cables are wired to exacting specifications. The Telecommunications Industry Association/Electronics Industries Alliance (TIA/EIA) defines the industry standards for wiring Ethernet UTP cables.

Typical IT departments will have several lengths of premade patch cables on hand to be used as needed. Nonetheless, a well-versed tech should have a good command of assembling and testing UTP patch cables. Some folks refer to the building of UTP patch cables, which requires stripping the insulation, arranging the wires to meet the TIA/EIA standards, and crimping the RJ-45 connectors onto the ends of the wire, as an "art." You will now practice the art of building UTP patch cables.

Learning Objectives

In this lab, you'll assemble a TIA/EIA 568B patch cable.

At the end of this lab, you will be able to

- Identify proper orientation of RJ-45 connectors
- Identify the wire pairs of a UTP patch cable according to the specifications of the TIA/EIA 568A and 568B standards

- Successfully crimp an RJ-45 connector to the end of a UTP cable

- Verify proper wiring of a completed patch cable using a commercial cable tester

Lab Materials and Setup

The materials you need for this lab are

- A working computer with Internet access

- A length of CAT 5, CAT 5e, or CAT 6 UTP cable

- RJ-45 connectors

- Wire strippers

- Wire snips

- A crimping tool

- TIA/EIA 568B color codes

- A cable tester

→ **Note**

Though CAT 6 UTP cable is the current choice for high performance, it can prove much more difficult to use when making cables. CAT 6 cable has a plastic spine that must be trimmed before inserting it into the RJ-45 connectors. There are many variations on the RJ-45 connectors for CAT 6 cable, and special crimping tools may be required.

Getting Down to Business

The TIA/EIA 568A and 568B standards define the arrangement of four-pair UTP cabling into RJ-45 connectors. When purchasing commercial, premade cables, the emerging default standard to follow is TIA/EIA 568B. For the purposes of this lab, you will adhere to the default industry standard of TIA/EIA 568B.

You'll find that once you develop some technique, you will enjoy making patch cables. As mentioned earlier, in the eyes of some, this is an "art." I want to caution you against spending too much time making cables, however, or spending too much time completing this lab exercise. The skill you develop will not be tested on the CompTIA A+ exams, and even in the field, making cables will not be the prime example of your skills as a tech.

That said, you will want to spend enough time to know the basics so that you will not look like a novice when it comes to whipping up a few patch cables.

Step 1   You'll begin with a cut length of UTP cable. Your instructor may define the lengths based on actual implementation. Shorter, 2- to 5-foot cables may be made to patch in a new switch or router, and medium lengths of 15 to 25 feet may be used to connect computers and printers to wall jacks. What lengths of cable will you be using?

_____

Step 2   Using the Internet, conduct a search for TIA/EIA 568A and 568B wiring diagrams. There are many sites that offer color-coded diagrams of the standards for wiring both straight-through and crossover patch cables. I found a nice diagram on the Web site of the Internet Centre, an Alberta, Canada Internet provider, at www.incentre.net/content/view/75/2/. I have also included the wiring diagram from the *Mike Meyers' CompTIA Network+ Guide to Managing and Troubleshooting Networks* textbook (see Figure 22-1).

Using either the diagram shown in Figure 22-1 or a diagram you've found on the Web, record the proper color wire for each of the pins of the RJ-45 modular connector when assembled using the TIA/EIA 568B standard:

Pin 1: _____

Pin 2: _____

Pin 3: _____

Pin 4: _____

Pin 5: _____

Pin 6: _____

Pin 7: _____

Pin 8: _____

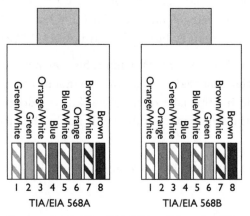

FIGURE 22-1 The TIA/EIA 568A and 568B standards

Step 3   Using wire strippers (often the crimping tool has wire strippers and snips built in), carefully remove approximately 0.5 inch of the outer insulating jacket of each end of the UTP cable.

→ **Note**

After removing the outer insulating sheathing, look for any damaged or cut wires. This is a very delicate procedure, so finesse is required. If any of the eight wires have been damaged, use the wire snips to cut off the entire end (all eight wires and insulation) and repeat Step 3.

Step 4   Separate each pair of wires and align them in the correct sequence according to the TIA/EIA 568B standards defined in Step 2. The next step, where you insert the wires into the RJ-45 connector, will go more smoothly if you take your time during this procedure. Once the sequence is correct, grasp the wires firmly between your thumb and forefinger, and carefully snip the edges of the wires to make them even, as shown in Figure 22-2.

Step 5   With the pins of the RJ-45 connector facing up and away from you, slide the wires all the way into the connector. The outer insulating sheath should be just past the first crimping point in the connector, and you should be able to see the copper of all eight wires if you look at the head of the RJ-45 connector, as shown in Figure 22-3.

Step 6   Place the RJ-45 connector into the crimping tool. Firmly squeeze the handle of the tool until the wires are crimped into place. The crimp should bind each of the wires tightly, and the connector

FIGURE 22-2 Aligning the wires and evening the ends

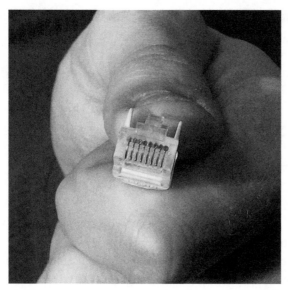

FIGURE 22-3 Head of an RJ-45 connector showing all eight wires firmly inserted

should bind the outer jacket. If any of the wires can be pulled from the connector with a gentle tug, the connection is incorrect. Snip the RJ-45 connector off and return to Step 3.

Step 7   To complete the assembly of the patch cable, repeat Steps 3–6 to add a connector to the other end of the cable.

 30 MINUTES

Lab Exercise 22.02: Verifying TCP/IP Settings

As you are probably aware, TCP/IP has emerged as the standard transport protocol for network communication. Microsoft operating systems normally use the Dynamic Host Configuration Protocol (DHCP), which automatically retrieves and assigns client TCP/IP settings from a DHCP server. This makes it easy to set up a small home or business network of PCs. All systems in the network will communicate with each other using these settings. The problem is that most businesses have their own set of TCP/IP settings (either automatically configured through DHCP or manually configured) that must be used for all new or repaired systems introduced into the network. Your responsibility as a PC technician is to verify the TCP/IP settings.

✔ **Cross-Reference**

To review additional details of TCP/IP, re-read the "Configuring TCP/IP" section in Chapter 22 of *Mike Meyers' CompTIA A+ Guide to Managing and Troubleshooting PCs.*

Learning Objectives

In this exercise, you'll access and verify the TCP/IP settings for a given PC system.

At the end of this lab, you'll be able to

- Define Automatic Private IP Addressing (APIPA)

- Use the ipconfig command-line utility

- Manually configure the TCP/IP settings on a PC

Lab Materials and Setup

The materials you need for this lab are

- A PC system that's properly configured for LAN access using Windows

- A list of TCP/IP settings provided by the instructor

Getting Down to Business

Typically, in corporate environments, the network protocol configuration scheme has been defined by the senior systems administrators. Unless you've had some experience with the configuration, you would not automatically know all of the TCP/IP settings for a network. For instance, even when you're setting up a small network (one that connects to the Internet), you'll need to contact your Internet service provider (ISP) to set up your router's TCP/IP settings. So don't worry if you have no idea what settings to use. The trick is to learn how to get them.

TCP/IP requires each system to have two basic settings for accessing a LAN and two additional settings for accessing other LANs or the Internet. You can configure your system to automatically obtain the following settings when you log on (Microsoft's default settings), or you can specify them, depending on the requirements of your network:

- IP address (unique to the PC)

- Subnet mask (identifies network information)

- Default gateway (address of the router to the external realm)

- Domain name service (DNS)

Step 1   First, you'll locate and verify your current TCP/IP settings.

   a.   You can accomplish this by going to the Control Panel. If you have a Windows Vista/7 system, open the Network and Sharing Center applet. In Windows Vista, click on *Manage network connections*, and in Windows 7, click *Change adapter settings*. Go to the Properties dialog box of the appropriate adapter. If you are on Windows XP, open the Network Connections applet, then open the Properties dialog box of the appropriate adapter. Highlight the Internet Protocol (TCP/IP) entry and click the Properties button. When the Internet Protocol (TCP/IP) Properties dialog box appears, one of the setting options shown in Figure 22-4 will be selected.

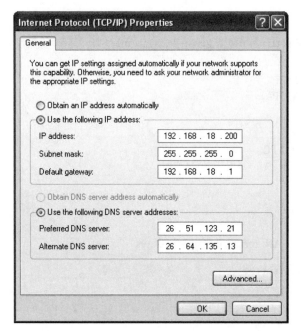

FIGURE 22-4 Viewing manually configured TCP/IP Properties in a Windows XP system

b. If the settings are manually configured, you will be able to verify them in the TCP/IP
    Properties dialog box. Write the settings down and verify them with the settings given to
    you by the instructor.

    IP address _____

    Subnet mask _____

    Default gateway _____

    Preferred DNS server _____

c. If the system is configured to use the Microsoft Automatic Private IP Addressing (APIPA) settings
    or if the network has a DHCP server (ask the instructor), the *Obtain an IP address automatically* and
    Obtain DNS server address automatically radio buttons will be selected. You will not be able to verify
    the values of the TCP/IP settings from this window. Close this window by clicking OK. To verify
    the settings, launch a Command Prompt window and, at the prompt, type the following
    command:

    `C:\Documents and Settings\%USERNAME%\>`**`ipconfig /all`**

This produces a listing similar to the one shown in Figure 22-5. Use these values to fill in the following settings and then verify them with your instructor.

IP Address _____

Subnet Mask _____

Default Gateway _____

DNS Servers _____

Step 2 You should be familiar with one final configuration: Automatic Private IP Addressing, or APIPA. If Windows is configured to obtain an IP address automatically and no DHCP server is available, Microsoft will automatically configure an address in the 169.254.0.0 network. Follow these steps to explore APIPA:

a. In a classroom lab environment, have the instructor disable the DHCP server if applicable. Alternatively, you can disconnect the DHCP server's UTP cable from the hub or switch.

b. Verify that your TCP/IP Properties settings are set to *Obtain an IP address automatically* and *Obtain DNS server address automatically*. Close all windows and reboot the system.

c. Launch a Command Prompt window and, at the prompt, type the following command:

```
C:\Documents and Settings\%USERNAME%\>ipconfig /all
```

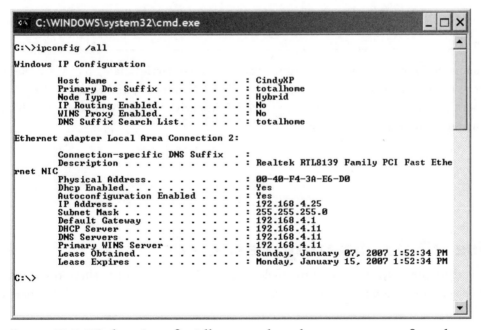

FIGURE 22-5 Windows ipconfig /all command results on a system configured to use DHCP

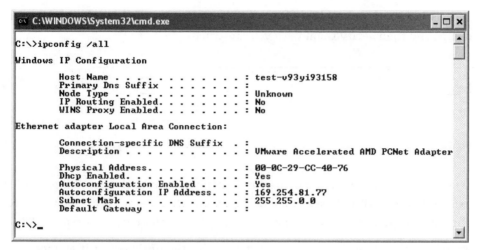

FIGURE 22-6 Windows ipconfig /all command results on a system using APIPA

This produces a listing similar to the one shown in Figure 22-6. Use these values to fill in the following settings and then verify them with your instructor.

IP Address _____

Subnet Mask _____

Default Gateway _____

DNS Server _____

d.   Exit the Command Prompt window and launch the TCP/IP Properties dialog box again. Return all settings to the normal classroom configuration. Click OK to finish, and close all the windows. Reboot the system, and verify that it's working properly and that you have reestablished network communication to its prior state.

 30 MINUTES

Lab Exercise 22.03: Sharing Resources

With the network all set up properly, the next thing to do is decide how you want to share resources. You can share any folder or other resource. Optical drives, hard drives, and printers can all be shared.

Learning Objectives

In this lab, you'll set up file sharing for others to access information from their system.

At the end of this lab, you'll be able to

- Enable and configure shared directories and other resources

Lab Materials and Setup

The materials you need for this lab are

- A PC system that's properly configured for LAN access using Windows

Getting Down to Business

Whew! That last exercise was interesting, but the job is only half done. Now you'll find where to set up sharing for a particular resource.

Step 1 Open My Computer/Computer, double-click the C: drive, and create a new folder on the C: drive. Name it **Shared**. Right-click the Shared folder icon to see the folder options, and select Properties. This will open the folder's Properties dialog box. Select the Sharing tab (see Figure 22-7).

✔ **Hint**

If the Sharing tab isn't there, you probably forgot to enable the File and Printer Sharing option in the Networking applet. Go back and do that.

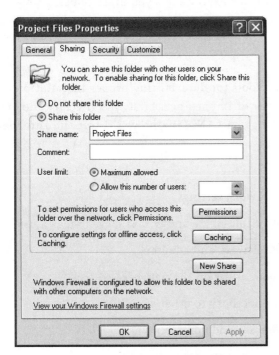

FIGURE 22-7 A folder's Properties dialog box with the Sharing tab selected in Windows XP

> ✔ **Hint**
>
> If you're running Windows XP Home Edition or Windows XP Professional Edition in a workgroup environment, the Sharing tab is much simpler. It contains *Do not share this folder* and *Share this folder* buttons and a space to provide a share name.

Step 2 Try sharing and unsharing the folder. Note that the share name and permissions are grayed out when you select *Do not share this folder*. Share the folder again, change the share name, and look at the various levels of permissions: Full Control, Change, and Read.

Step 3 When you're done, click OK to close the dialog box.

 30 MINUTES

Lab Exercise 22.04: Testing Your LAN Connections

Various tools are available that will help you test and troubleshoot your new network. The textbook covers using these tools in detail. Some of these tools will be beneficial to you as a CompTIA A+ certified technician and are covered on the CompTIA A+ exams. This lab exercise lets you practice using several key network troubleshooting tools.

Learning Objectives

In this exercise, you'll be introduced to troubleshooting tools for determining proper installation of the network components. These tools are covered in order of importance. First, you'll verify the local settings. Next, you'll try to access other systems on the same LAN. Finally, you'll test the Internet connectivity.

At the end of this lab, you'll be able to

- Use the ipconfig command to determine local network settings
- Use the net config command to check the local system name and who is logged on as a user
- Use the ping command to test the local TCP/IP software and adapter
- Use the net view command to check for other computers on the network
- Use the ping command with switches to test connectivity to other computers
- Use the nslookup command to translate IP addresses and domain names
- Use the tracert command to check the path to other computers

Lab Materials and Setup

The materials you need for this lab are

- A PC system that's properly configured for network access using Windows

- Access to the Internet

✔ **Hint**

The commands vary slightly, depending on the operating system you use. You should practice with each operating system if possible. Test the LAN first by accessing another computer on the network using My Network Places/Network.

Getting Down to Business

As a PC technician, you should be familiar with several networking tools, both for your own good and because they're covered on the CompTIA A+ exams. You'll begin by looking at ipconfig.

✔ **Hint**

Since you have already used the ipconfig /all command, run through the steps again, either on your own system or on a different lab machine. Ask the instructor if any different networks or system configurations are available to explore.

Step 1 You have already examined ipconfig in Lab Exercise 22.02. You'll now use the ipconfig command again to determine local network settings. As you have already learned, checking the automatic TCP/IP settings given to you by a DHCP server and verifying your manual settings is easy: just open a Command Prompt window, type **ipconfig /all**, and press ENTER. The details of your local network connection appear on the screen.

Does the display contain the settings that were automatically assigned by the DHCP server or the ones you entered manually?

_____

Record your settings here:

IP Address _____

Subnet Mask _____

Default Gateway _____

DNS Servers _____

Leave the Command Prompt window open; you'll use it throughout the rest of this exercise.

Step 2   You'll now use the net config command to check the local system name and to see who is logged on as a user. To confirm the computer name and discover who is currently logged on, you'll again use the command line.

Type **net config workstation** at the command prompt and press ENTER. You'll see how the identification is set up for your local PC. There's a lot of information listed, but you're only interested in a couple of items (see Figure 22-8).

How are these listed?

Computer name _____

User name _____

Workstation domain (workgroup) _____

Software version _____

Step 3   You'll now use the ping command to test the local TCP/IP software and adapter.

At the command prompt, type **ping 127.0.0.1** (including the periods) and press ENTER. This is known as the IPv4 loopback or localhost address and will test the TCP/IP software and the internal part of the local network card. Look at Figure 22-9 to see a successful test. If you don't see the test results, there are serious problems with the software. Reinstall your network drivers, and reconfigure the TCP/IP settings.

→ **Note**

Want to see some IPv6 action? At the command prompt, type **ping ::1**. The IPv6 loopback address is ::1. When you ping it, it's just like running ping using 127.0.0.1, but it uses IPv6 instead.

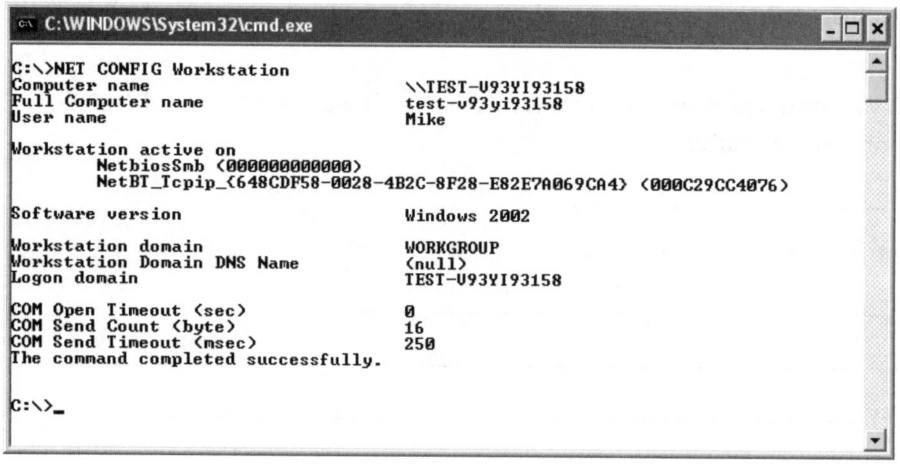

```
C:\WINDOWS\System32\cmd.exe                              - □ ×

C:\>NET CONFIG Workstation
Computer name                        \\TEST-U93YI93158
Full Computer name                   test-v93yi93158
User name                            Mike

Workstation active on
        NetbiosSmb (000000000000)
        NetBT_Tcpip_{648CDF58-0028-4B2C-8F28-E82E7A069CA4} (000C29CC4076)

Software version                     Windows 2002

Workstation domain                   WORKGROUP
Workstation Domain DNS Name          <null>
Logon domain                         TEST-U93YI93158

COM Open Timeout (sec)               0
COM Send Count (byte)                16
COM Send Timeout (msec)              250
The command completed successfully.


C:\>_
```

FIGURE 22-8 Using the net config workstation command in Windows XP

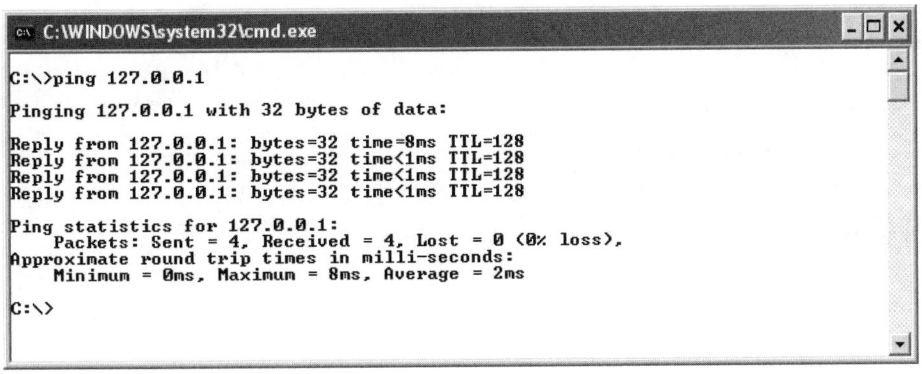

FIGURE 22-9 A successful ping test

Step 4 You'll now use the net view command to check for other computers on the network.

You want to establish that other computers are available on the network so that you can test that your network card can transmit and receive data in Step 5.

At the command prompt, type **net view** and press ENTER. You'll see which other computers are on the network by a listing of their computer names (see Figure 22-10).

Step 5 Now you'll use the ping command to test your ability to connect to other computers on the network.

In Step 4 you obtained the names of other systems on the LAN, so now you want to check whether you can actually communicate with them.

At the command prompt, type **ping** *computer name*, where *computer name* is another PC's host name on the network you found in Step 4, and press ENTER. The results will look the same as when you used ping to see your own computer, but with the other computer's IP address (see Figure 22-11). Be sure to put a space between the ping command and the computer name. If you get errors, use the net view command again to be certain of the computer name's spelling. If the DNS is down, you can adjust by pinging the other computer's IP address instead of its name.

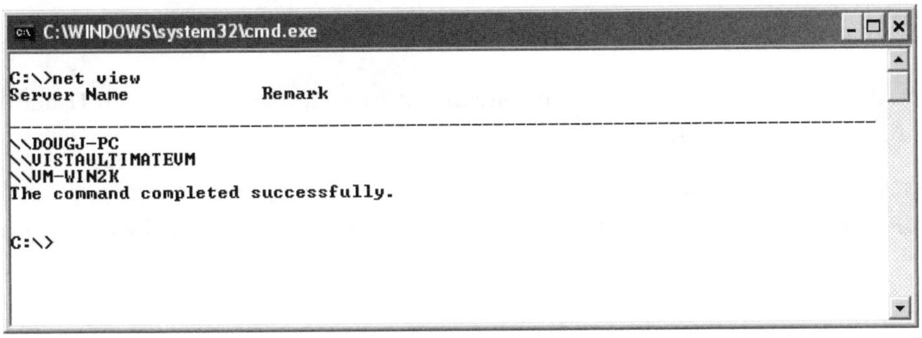

FIGURE 22-10 Using the net view command

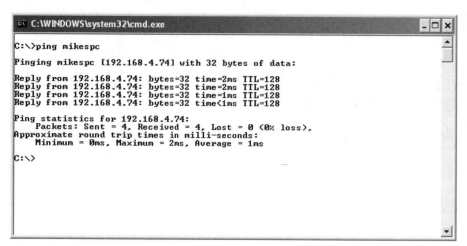

FIGURE 22-11 Pinging a computer by its name

→ Try This: Ping Switches

The humble ping command is one of the most frequently used troubleshooting tools for TCP/IP. As you saw in Step 5, you can actually use ping to test whether DNS is working. If you do not receive a response from the computer using its host name, but you do receive a response when using the IP address, this points to a problem with DNS.

Ping also has a number of switches that add to the functionality of the command. If you need to explore the switches, type the following at the command prompt:

```
C:\>ping /?
```

This will list all of the available switches and their functions. The following combination is typically used for a connection that seems to drop packets intermittently. You would run the command indefinitely and increase the packet size to overload the connection. Type the following command:

```
C:\>ping -t -l 65000 computername
```

To stop the continuous ping, press CTRL-c to break the program.

Step 6   You'll now use the nslookup command to translate an Internet domain name to an IP address or an IP address to an Internet domain name.

This is a good command for finding out the IP addresses of Web sites. Why do I want this, you ask? Well, when you use a URL in your browser, it has to be translated somewhere to an IP address. This slows down your access time. If you know the IP address and type that into the address of your Internet browser, the site will pop up faster. Follow these steps:

  a. Type **nslookup microsoft.com**, and then press ENTER.

      What's the IP address(es) of http://www.microsoft.com? _____

      Try **nslookup totalsem.com.**

      What's the IP address(es) of http://www.totalsem.com? _____

  b. Now enter the IP address you got when you did a lookup for http://www.microsoft.com. If you get a different result, it could be that a Web site is being hosted by someone other than the original domain you looked up.

Step 7   You'll now use the tracert command to check the path to other computers or Web sites on the Internet.

This command will show you where the bottlenecks are in the Internet. The tracert command will list the time it takes to get from your PC to the Web site or other system you're accessing. Follow these steps:

  a. Type **tracert google.com**, and then press ENTER.

      Was it successful? _____

      How many hops did it take? _____

      What's the IP address of the first hop? _____

  b. Use the nslookup command with the IP address of the first hop to see where your first server is located.

Go ahead—have fun with this! Part of the learning process with PCs is to dive in and tackle a subject that you're not completely familiar with. As long as you remember to write down any information you want to change before you change it, you can enjoy exploring the amazing world of computers and still have a recovery point.

Lab Analysis Test

1. A user complains that after you installed the new NIC in her system, she can see everyone on the network but can't access the Internet. What did you forget to do? Are there any other configuration problems that could cause this to happen?

2. What command would you use to test the NIC's internal TCP/IP capabilities? What would the "human readable" address be?

3. Jerry is attempting to make a crossover cable for a customer. Jerry has forgotten the wire pattern to create the cable. Remind Jerry of what the TIA/EIA standards are along with the color arrangement of the wires from left to right.

4. How do you access the Local Area Connection Properties dialog box in Windows 7?

5. Tanner has replaced his old 100BaseT NIC with a new 1000BaseT NIC. The office network is set up and works fine for everyone else. Now he can't see anyone on the network or access the Internet. Where should he start checking and in what order?

Key Term Quiz

Use the following terms to complete the following sentences. Not all terms will be used.

568A

568B

APIPA

crimpers

crossover cable

default gateway

DHCP

DNS

dynamic

IP address

ipconfig

net view

Network and Sharing Center

Network Connections

nslookup

ping

RJ-45

snips

static

straight-through cable

subnet mask

tracert

1. The _____ and _____ are the minimum addressing requirements for setting up a network card using the TCP/IP protocol.

2. A(n) _____ address is an address that is self-assigned by the computer to make local communication in the event that a DHCP server can't be reached.

3. A user should go to the _____ in Windows 7 to view and manage all of their network settings.

4. A(n) _____ is used to connect two similar devices together for communication, such as connecting two switches together.

5. The _____ command is used to query the state of DNS servers.

Chapter 23
Wireless Networking

Lab Exercises

Wireless networks are so common today that most people don't take the time to understand the differences between a hard wired network and a wireless one. With mobile computing on the rise, it's important for CompTIA A+ certified technicians to know as much about wireless networks as possible so that they are prepared to provide quality service in any situation to the users they support. New technicians may be asked questions like, "When should you set up a network with a server," and, "How do you set up a wireless network?" You need to know not only how to set up a wireless network, but also how to configure and secure that network. In the lab exercises in this chapter, you'll set up, configure, and secure a couple of wireless networks so that you are prepared to do the same in a real-world setting.

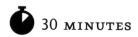 30 MINUTES

Lab Exercise 23.01: Setting Up a Wireless Network

Your neighbor is interested in starting a home business and has asked you to help him set up a wireless network. The only equipment he currently has is a desktop computer, a laptop computer, a mobile phone, and a USB printer, all of which he is considering using with his business. He wants to be able to communicate with his clients wirelessly from any room in his house. He's asked you to help him decide what additional equipment he needs to purchase.

Learning Objectives

This lab tests basic wireless network setup skills and helps you to think about scenarios you might encounter.

At the end of this lab, you'll be able to

- Recommend proper wireless equipment (for example, wireless cards and routers)
- Identify solutions for proper placement of equipment
- Set up and configure a wireless router

Lab Materials and Setup

The materials you need for this lab are

- A working desktop computer running Windows, with some form of broadband Internet connection

- A laptop with wireless connectivity

- Two Ethernet cables

- A wireless router

Getting Down to Business

First, you will need to tell your friend that he needs to buy a wireless router. He'll also need a Wi-Fi adapter (if he doesn't have one already). Once he's purchased the necessary equipment, he needs to connect it. It may seem strange, but you have to plug in several cables ("wires") when you set up a wireless network.

Step 1 Figure out how your neighbor's computer is physically connected to the Internet. If you are at his home, chances are that he has either a DSL or cable modem that connects to his computer via an Ethernet cable. In order to set up the wireless network, disconnect the Ethernet cable from your computer.

Step 2 Plug the Ethernet cable running from the wall jack or modem into the back of the wireless router. There is often a specific jack labeled "Internet" for you to use. Plug in the router and turn it on, if it doesn't turn on automatically. The router is ready when all the lights remain on and steady. There may be one or two blinking lights—it's okay.

Step 3 Now plug one end of the second Ethernet cable into the wireless router and the other end into the desktop computer's RJ-45 Ethernet port. You may be thinking that this wireless network isn't looking very wireless so far, but think of it this way: how often do you pick up your entire desktop setup and move it into another room? Not very often, I'd wager.

Step 4 Now that all the cables are in place, go to the laptop and see if you can find the wireless network. Windows alerts you with a pop-up once it locates a new wireless network (see Figure 23-1). Clicking on the message bubble will then present you with a list of all the found networks.

When you have finished the exercise, have your instructor initial here: _____

FIGURE 23-1 Windows has detected wireless networks

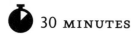 30 MINUTES

Lab Exercise 23.02: Configuring and Securing a Wireless Network

Now that you've installed a wireless router, you must configure it properly so that it is secure from pesky invaders. Be sure to follow these step-by-step instructions so you can reduce the chances of your data being exposed, stolen, or attacked by hackers.

Learning Objectives

This lab enables you to configure and secure your network.

At the end of this lab, you'll be able to

- Properly configure a wireless router

- Set up security options to keep intruders out

Lab Materials and Setup

The materials you need for this lab are

- A working desktop computer running Windows with some form of Internet connection

- A laptop with wireless connectivity

- A wireless router

Getting Down to Business

Failing to configure and secure a wireless network is like leaving your debit card on the sidewalk outside your house with the PIN written on it—chances are that someone will take advantage of the situation and do something unscrupulous. Configuring and securing your wireless network is a fairly easy task. Just be sure to do it. Many people will simply hook up a wireless router, turn it on, and go about their business, not realizing what they've opened themselves up to. For the sake of your private data, follow the steps in this lab exercise.

Keep in mind that configuring a wireless network depends heavily on the router/wireless access point being used. The following steps lead you through the basics, but for more details, check the manual that came with your device.

Step 1   To secure your wireless network, you will use the configuration tool included with your router/ wireless access point. To access it, open a Web browser and type **192.168.1.1** (or sometimes **192.168.0.1**) into the address bar. This is the most common address used for the setup utility. You may get a pop-up dialog box or other screen asking for a user name and password. Again, the defaults for these are often **admin** and **password**. This is true across multiple brands, which is all the more reason to change them as soon as possible!

Step 2   You should now be in the setup utility. Different devices use different names, but look for the Wireless Settings page (see Figure 23-2). If it's not called that, look for a screen with options for network name, security options, or MAC address options. Once you've found it, find the box used to enter a network name, or SSID. Delete the one that is there already and create a new one that is unique but memorable. When you try to connect to your wireless router, you'll want to know which one is yours, and changing the SSID will help your router stand out.

Step 3   Usually on the same page as the network name are wireless network security options. These include choices such as WEP, WPA, WPA2, and None. (You'll also see terms like Personal or PSK and RADIUS.) If it's available, select WPA2-PSK; otherwise, select WPA-PSK. WEP is an older encryption technology that is far less secure. There should also be an empty box labeled "password" or "passphrase" or "pre-shared key." Enter a unique and memorable password to be used whenever you want to connect to the wireless network. Save these settings.

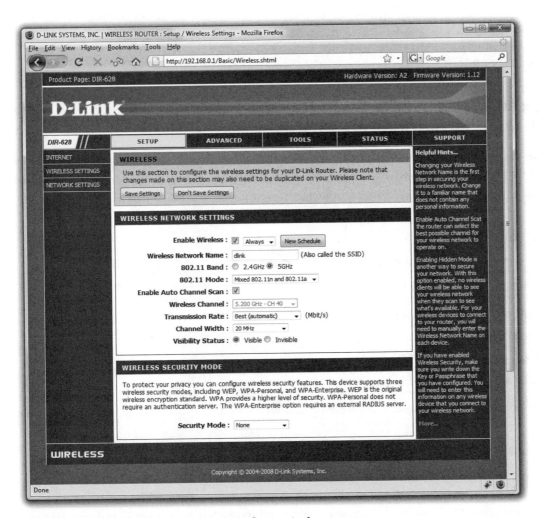

FIGURE 23-2 The Wireless Settings page for a wireless router

Step 4   Finally, now that you've secured the wireless connection by enabling WPA2 or another encryption option, you need to secure the router itself. Remember that 99 percent of routers use "admin" and "password" as the user name and password to access the router's setup utility. Failing to change these is an invitation to intruders. Find the setup utility's administration options, or something similar, and change the user name and password to something unique and memorable.

When you have finished the exercise, have your instructor initial here: _____

→ Note

> You may hear that turning off the SSID broadcast will help secure your wireless Internet. This is actually a bit of a mixed bag. Users will still need to learn the SSID of your network to join it, but modern versions of Windows display available wireless networks even if the SSID isn't broadcast. Disabling the SSID broadcast makes it more difficult to join a wireless network, but it doesn't entirely hide your network.

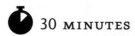 30 MINUTES

Lab Exercise 23.03: Setting Up an Ad Hoc Wireless Network

Okay, so you've set up a traditional wireless network and learned how to secure it. But what if all you really want to do is play a game with someone, share some files, or search the Internet without a bunch of wires and a router? In CompTIA A+ terminology, we would call this an ad hoc peer-to-peer network.

Learning Objectives

This lab gives you another option for setting up a network.

At the end of this lab, you'll be able to

- Connect two or more computers together wirelessly

Lab Materials and Setup

The materials you need for this lab are

- Two computers with wireless connectivity and Windows XP, Windows Vista, or Windows 7 installed

Getting Down to Business

The process for setting up an ad hoc wireless network is even simpler than the process for setting up a normal wireless network. However, due in part to their temporary nature, ad hoc wireless networks are not nearly as common. Still, the next time you've got two laptops but no network, and you desperately need to share some files, you'll be glad you know how to set up an ad hoc wireless network.

Step 1 (Windows XP) In Windows XP, open the Control Panel and double-click Network Connections. Right-click Wireless Network Connection and click Properties. In the Wireless Network Connection Properties dialog box, select the Wireless Networks tab. Verify that the *Use Windows to configure my wireless network settings* box is selected. If it is not, select it. Click Add.

Step 2 (Windows XP) The Wireless network properties dialog box opens (see Figure 23-3). In the Network name (SSID) text box, enter the name of the network you want to add. I suggest calling it something simple, like "temp." Create a password and confirm it. Uncheck the *The key is provided for me automatically* checkbox and check the *This is a computer-to-computer (ad hoc) network; wireless access points are not used* checkbox. Click OK. You are returned to the Wireless Networks tab, and the new network name appears in the Preferred networks list.

Step 1 (Windows Vista/7) In Windows Vista/7, go to the Control Panel and open the Network and Sharing Center. Select *Manage wireless networks* and click Add.

→ **Note**

The *Manage wireless networks* option appears only if you have a wireless network card.

Step 2 (Windows Vista/7) In the *Manually connect to a wireless network* dialog box, choose *Create an ad hoc network*. Click Next, and then create a simple network name. Select a security type from the menu

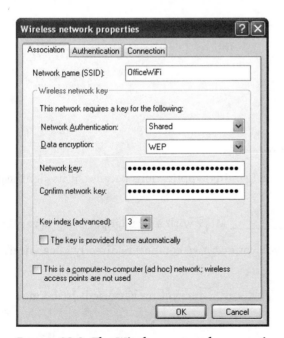

FIGURE 23-3 The Wireless network properties dialog box

provided (WPA2 is preferred) and enter a password. Check the *Save this network* checkbox and click Next. You've now set up the ad hoc wireless network.

When you have finished the exercise, have your instructor initial here: _____

Lab Analysis Test

1.   What are the primary differences between WEP, WPA, and WPA2?

2.   What are two common IP addresses for wireless routers?

3.   In what situations would you recommend an ad hoc network to a user?

4.   What is the path used to get to TCP/IP properties for a network adapter in Windows XP?

5.   How does a wireless router communicate signals?

Key Term Quiz

Use the following terms to complete the following sentences. Not all terms will be used.

49

54

802.11n

ad hoc

cell phone

WAP

WEP

WPA

WPA2

wireless router

1.   Network adapters wirelessly connect your computer to your _____.

2.   A(n) _____ router is ideal for multimedia (gaming) applications because of its significant range and speed.

3.   An 802.11g router can communicate up to _____ Mbps with a throughput of up to 22 Mbps.

4.   You create a(n) _____ network when you connect two computers directly via a wireless connection.

5.   When securing your wireless network, use _____ encryption because it is the most secure.

Chapter 24

The Internet

Lab Exercises

The Internet is a complex system of communication that enables computers, in-business networks, mobile computers, and home PCs to share information worldwide. Today we even have smartphones, tablets, and other personal devices that we can use to connect to the Internet and access e-mail, download MP3s, and do other tasks.

Because nearly everyone wants access to the Internet, implementing and troubleshooting Internet connectivity is a PC technician's bread and butter. The CompTIA A+ certification exams recognize this and test you on the details of installing and configuring a connection to the Internet. It may be a legacy dial-up analog modem used to connect to an ISP through a phone line, or a broadband cable modem using the local cable company as the provider. This heightened usage brings with it a new task for the PC technician: Internet security!

Since most computers are now communicating with the world through the Internet, the exposure to malicious intruders and programs has greatly increased. Two components that go hand-in-hand with the Internet are firewalls and wireless network security. You just finished setting up and configuring the hardware portion of a wireless network in the last chapter, so now you'll look at the software side of network security. This chapter's lab exercises first guide you through the properties of the current wide area network (WAN) connection technologies and then take you through the steps needed to perform the installation and configuration of these technologies. You'll also explore the configuration of Windows Firewall and Windows Internet Connection Sharing and learn how to upgrade to the latest version of the Internet Explorer browser.

✔ Cross-Reference

Computer security is such an important component of a PC technician's training that the topic receives its own chapter in both the textbook and the lab manual. Refer to Chapter 29 in *Mike Meyers' CompTIA A+ Guide to Managing and Troubleshooting PCs*. Chapter 29 of this lab manual also includes additional lab exercises to build your security awareness.

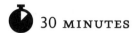 30 MINUTES

Lab Exercise 24.01: Identifying Internet Connectivity Properties

A new client has signed up with your firm, requesting that you evaluate their current Internet connectivity and recommend the best upgrade path for their 12-person office (six desktop PCs and two laptops). Your first job is to assess what method they are currently using to connect to the Internet and what methods are available in their location, and to make a recommendation for upgrades if necessary.

Learning Objectives

This lab exercise tests basic assessment skills. Every technician should be able to go into a situation and quickly understand the state of the technology in question—in this case, an Internet connection. You should also feel comfortable telling your clients about any concerns with aging technology and feel confident recommending upgrade paths to higher-performance technology.

At the end of this lab, you'll be able to

- Verify the Internet connectivity method

- Check the properties of the connection

- Perform an Internet search to learn about the performance of various connectivity methods

Lab Materials and Setup

The materials you need for this lab are

- A working computer running Windows with some form of Internet connection

- Internet connectivity to perform your research

Getting Down to Business

First, you will visually inspect your computer and its surroundings for the method used to connect to the Internet. Then you will run an Internet utility to determine the speed of your connection and appropriate upgrade paths.

Step 1 Look at the back of your computer:

- Is there a phone cable (RJ-11) plugged in? This could indicate that this computer is using an analog modem for the Internet connection.

- Are there any USB or network (RJ-45) cables plugged into the system? Trace the wires. Do they connect to a cable modem or DSL modem? This could be your connectivity method.

- Is there a network patch cable plugged into the NIC? You may be connecting to the Internet through the corporate LAN.

- Are you on a laptop with wireless connectivity? You could have access to the Internet through a wireless access point (WAP) connected to a cable or DSL modem.

These are the possibilities a technician is faced with today, so the more you can explore the various methods of connectivity, the more knowledgeable you will be. Figure 24-1 depicts a typical PC using a wired LAN patch cable to connect to a broadband cable modem.

Examine the physical components that constitute the method your system uses to connect to the Internet, and then record the details of the hardware/connectivity type here.

_____

_____

Step 2 Once you have determined the connectivity method, boot your system and launch your Internet browser (popular browsers include Microsoft Internet Explorer, Mozilla Firefox, and Google Chrome). In the address bar, type **http://reviews.cnet.com/internet-speed-test/** and press ENTER. This will take you to CNET's Bandwidth Meter Online Speed Test. Follow the onscreen instructions to test the speed of your connection.

What is the speed of your connection? _____

Step 3 Using the Bandwidth Meter Online Speed Test results (where possible), fill in the approximate data transfer speeds of the various Internet connection types:

Dial-up 56 Kbps modem _____

DSL _____

Cable _____

T1 _____

T3 _____

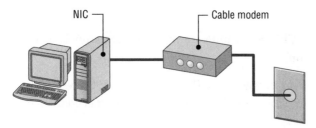

FIGURE 24-1 A PC and cable modem Internet connection

Step 4   Based on the results of the analysis of your client's Internet connection method and performance, are there any recommendations you would make to improve the performance of the connection?

_____

_____

_____

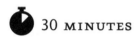 30 MINUTES

Lab Exercise 24.02: Installing and Configuring an Internet Connection

You determine that the client is currently using dial-up networking through analog modems to access the Internet. Though this is probably acceptable for occasionally connecting to the Internet, these folks have a business to run! You decide to recommend either high-speed DSL or cable. You explain to the client that unlike the analog modem they're currently using, the other methods use a standard network interface card (NIC) and an external device to interface between the DSL or cable lines. Ironically, this device is usually referred to as a DSL or cable _modem_. You will evaluate the current PCs and select one that will act as the interface to the Internet. If required, you'll add a PCI or PCIe NIC, connect the DSL or cable interface, and then configure the interface in Windows.

Learning Objectives

Installing DSL or cable high-speed Internet access requires four steps. First, you should verify whether your system is already equipped with an NIC, either integrated into the motherboard or as a PCI/PCIe card, and if not, physically install such a device. Second, verify that this device is operating properly and has the latest drivers installed. Third, connect the DSL transceiver or the cable modem, and finally, configure the proper settings required by the ISP.

At the end of this lab, you'll be able to

- Install a network interface card (if not already present)
- Verify proper operation, and install or update the drivers
- Install the DSL transceiver or cable modem
- Configure the connection in Windows

✔ **Cross-Reference**

Refer to the "DSL" and "Cable" sections in Chapter 24 and the "Installing Expansion Cards" section in Chapter 9 of *Mike Meyers' CompTIA A+ Guide to Managing and Troubleshooting PCs* for help installing and configuring NICs. It's a good idea to have the textbook handy while you progress through this lab.

Lab Materials and Setup

The materials you need for this lab are

- A PC system with or without an NIC
- A PCI or PCIe NIC
- Access to the proper driver software (either built-in Windows drivers or a separate disc)
- A copy of the Windows installation media (may be needed, depending on the system)
- A Phillips-head screwdriver
- An anti-static wrist strap

Getting Down to Business

Break out your trusty screwdriver and anti-static wrist strap. It's time to install an NIC! The process for physically installing an NIC is functionally identical to the process you've used to install expansion cards in the past, but the software side of things has a few differences that you should pay attention to.

✔ **Hint**

You can skip Steps 1–3 if the system is already equipped with a network interface card, as most systems are today. The steps are included here for completeness. You will be asked to install a second NIC in Lab Exercise 24.04, "Configuring Windows Internet Connection Sharing," so if you have that second NIC handy, go ahead and install it now.

Step 1   Make sure the PC is off and unplugged. While following proper ESD avoidance procedures, remove the cover of the PC. Choose any free PCI or PCIe slot to install the NIC. Remove the back plate if one exists.

Step 2   Plug the NIC into the PCI or PCIe slot (see Figure 24-2). Physically inserting the NIC into the PC is the easiest part of the task. Take care to avoid touching the pins or any of the chips on the NIC. Once the card is inserted, secure it by putting the proper screw through the metal tab of the card and screwing it to the case. Put the cover back on and restart your computer.

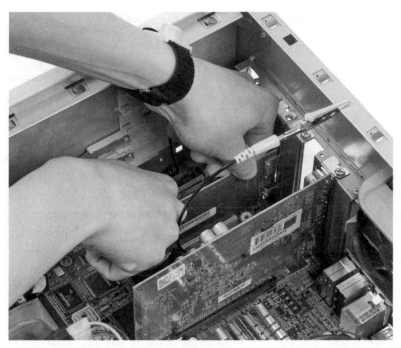

FIGURE 24-2 Inserting a PCI NIC

Step 3 Now that you have physically installed the NIC, turn on your PC. Windows should automatically detect the NIC. The operating system reports success installing the new device with a small balloon from the system tray.

✔ **Hint**

Every Windows operating system has a good selection of network interface drivers built in at the time of release, but your driver may not be one of them. For example, if the NIC you're installing was manufactured after the release of software you're using, the drivers may not be part of the operating system and will need to be manually installed or updated.

Step 4 Now that the drivers are installed, you should confirm the NIC properties and verify what drivers are installed.

a. Open the Control Panel. In Windows XP, open Network Connections. In Windows Vista/7, open the Network and Sharing Center. In Windows Vista, click *Manage network connections*. In Windows 7, click *Change adapter settings*.

b. Right-click Local Area Connection (note: if this is the second network interface, choose Local Area Connection 2) and click Properties. In the Local Area Connection Properties dialog box, click the Configure button next to the network interface adapter.

c. In the network interface adapter Properties dialog box, click the Driver tab (see Figure 24-3). Record all the information provided about the driver you installed.

_____

_____

Step 5 Now examine the physical device that has been provided by your ISP to connect the computer to the Internet. If the device is a DSL transceiver, it will typically have an RJ-45 Ethernet connection to connect to the NIC of the computer, an RJ-11 connector to connect to the telephone wall jack, and some sort of power adapter. If the device is a cable modem, it will typically have an RJ-45 Ethernet connection to connect to the NIC of the computer, an F-connector to attach to the cable, and some sort of power adapter (refer to Figure 24-1). Both interfaces may provide a USB connection, but for the purposes of the lab exercise, this will not be used.

✔ Hint

If you are in a classroom lab environment, you may not have access to the actual DSL transceiver or cable modem. Follow the instructor's directions to connect the computer to the Internet. You should conduct an Internet search or make a trip to the local technology store to explore the specifications of common DSL and cable interfaces. For the most part, going through the full configuration of the actual connection is beyond the scope of this book, but you should at least know where to go to follow instructions from your ISP; that's the purpose of these last steps.

FIGURE 24-3 Network interface adapter driver properties

Connect the interface device by following the instructions provided with the device or by your ISP. The layout and configuration of the device may differ somewhat from device to device, but you should be able to confirm that the device is working properly by observing the various indicator lights on the device.

Step 6   To finish this installation and gain high-speed access to the Internet, you will most likely have to follow specific directions from your ISP to configure Windows to communicate through the DSL or cable device. A technician may need to come to your home or office to configure some settings. Windows also provides a generic wizard to configure this communication. The following list walks you through this generic configuration by operating system:

- **Windows XP**   Open Network Connections and select *Create a new connection*. Click Next. Choose the Connect to the Internet option and click Next. Select the option to set up your connection manually and click Next. Pick the appropriate option on the next screen, most likely *Connect using a broadband connection that is always on*. Click Next, then Finish.

- **Windows Vista/7**   Open Control Panel. Open the Network and Sharing Center and select *Set up a new connection or network*. Select Connect to the Internet and click Next. Choose Broadband as your connection. Type in the relevant information and click Connect. Windows will then attempt to set up your Internet connection. When it is finished, click Close.

If you have followed these steps (and actually have installed a DSL or cable interface), you should now have high-speed access to the Internet.

 30 MINUTES

Lab Exercise 24.03: Enabling Windows Firewall

Your client is very pleased with how the rollout of the office's Internet connection upgrade is progressing. They have been surfing around a little, and are impressed with the speed at which the Web sites are loading. You explain that you must now configure a firewall to protect them from outside intrusion through the high-speed connection. Windows offers a very competent built-in firewall. In this lab you will enable Windows Firewall and explore some of the services (ports) that you can allow or block.

Learning Objectives

Completing the following steps, you will explore Windows Firewall and associated TCP and UDP service ports.

At the end of this lab, you'll be able to

- Enable Windows Firewall

- Identify various protocols and associated service ports

Lab Materials and Setup

The materials you need for this lab are

- A working computer running Windows XP, Windows Vista, or Windows 7

- Optional: A machine connected to the Internet

Getting Down to Business

Enabling the firewall is as simple as a few clicks of the mouse and verifying that you can communicate with the trusted sites that you prefer. Windows Firewall is practically self-configuring, but if you want to allow access to Web servers or e-mail servers in your organization, you will have to open some TCP ports. The CompTIA A+ certification exams will expect you to know some of these "well-known ports," so you'll explore them in Windows Firewall.

✔ **Hint**

If you are configuring a single machine for Internet access, you will want to implement Windows Firewall on that machine to protect it from malicious intrusion. However, if you are configuring machines as part of a LAN and using a proxy server or Internet Connection Sharing (as you will in the next lab exercise), you will only want to configure a firewall on the machine that connects directly to the Internet. Assume the computer in this lab is the machine connected to the Internet.

Step 1 In Windows XP, return to Network Connections. Right-click the Local Area Connections icon of the external connection (the one connected to the Internet) and select Properties. Click the Advanced tab, and then click the Settings button in the Windows Firewall box. This opens the Windows Firewall dialog box (see Figure 24-4).

In Windows Vista/7, open the Control Panel, then open Windows Firewall. In Windows Vista, select *Change settings*. In Windows 7, select *Turn Windows Firewall on or off*.

Step 2 Turn on the firewall to protect the PC from unwanted access through the Internet connection.

Step 3 In Windows XP, select the Advanced tab of the Windows Firewall dialog box and click the Settings button for the Network Connection Settings (see Figure 24-5).

→ **Note**

The following advanced options have been removed from the Windows Firewall settings in Windows Vista/7 in an attempt to make the OS more secure; thus, the following steps will only work in Windows XP. There are still methods for setting up exceptions (see the Exceptions tab in the Windows Firewall dialog box, specifically the Add Port button), but most of the advanced features have been moved to Administrative Tools. Windows 7 uses the *Allow a program or feature through Windows Firewall* link to enable you to set firewall settings for each installed application.

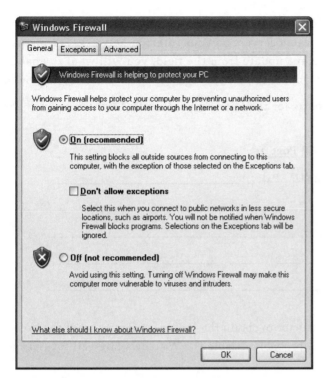

FIGURE 24-4 The Windows Firewall dialog box

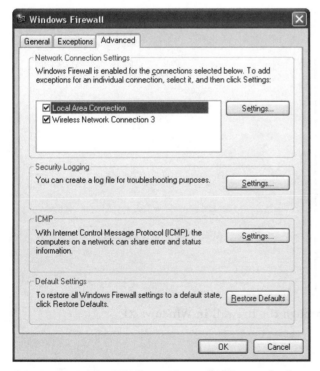

FIGURE 24-5 The Windows Firewall Advanced tab

Step 4   This opens the Advanced Settings dialog box, where you can allow various services to pass through the Internet connection and access dedicated servers on your internal network. For instance, if you have an FTP server that you have technicians update from the field, you will want to enable external communication by allowing TCP service port 21 to pass through the firewall (see Figure 24-6).

Using the Edit button, identify the service ports for the following protocols (I have completed the first one for you; see Figure 24-7):

    a.   File Transfer Protocol (FTP Server): **TCP Port 21**_____

    b.   Internet Mail Access Protocol version 4 (IMAP4): _____

    c.   Simple Mail Transfer Protocol (SMTP): _____

    d.   Post Office Protocol version 3 (POP3): _____

    e.   Secure Sockets Layer (HTTPS): _____

    f.   Hypertext Transfer Protocol (HTTP): _____

Step 5   To complete this lab, check with your instructor to obtain the proper configuration of the firewall to allow the completion of further labs. You will probably disable the Windows Firewall for normal classroom use.

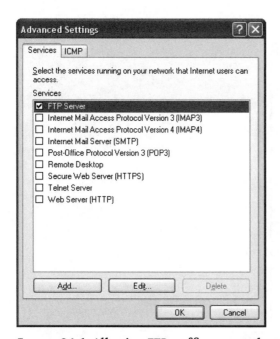

Figure 24-6 Allowing FTP traffic to pass through the firewall in Windows XP

FIGURE 24-7 Service Settings showing the TCP port number for the FTP server in Windows XP

 30 MINUTES

Lab Exercise 24.04: Configuring Windows Internet Connection Sharing

Now that the main PC is secure from external threats and attacks, it's time to configure this machine so that all of the PCs can take advantage of the secure Internet connection. Welcome Internet Connection Sharing (ICS)! With ICS, you will be able to set up a small LAN that allows all the client machines to access the Internet through the ICS host computer (this PC).

Learning Objectives

In this lab, you will implement the steps to use ICS. It will take some extra hardware to actually test the configuration, but you can still learn the basic concepts through the configuration exercise.

At the end of this lab, you'll be able to

- Configure Internet Connection Sharing

✔ **Cross-Reference**

To further explore ICS, refer to "Windows Internet Connection Sharing" in Chapter 24 of *Mike Meyers' CompTIA A+ Guide to Managing and Troubleshooting PCs.*

Lab Materials and Setup

The materials you need for this lab are

- A working computer running Windows

- An additional network interface card for the ICS host computer

- A network switch
- A second computer running Windows to be configured as the client
- Optional: A machine connected to the Internet

Getting Down to Business

ICS allows a small workgroup of computers to connect to the Internet through one of the workgroup computers acting as an ICS host computer. There are a few items that need to be configured on both the ICS host computer and the clients. The host will have two communication devices installed (in this case, two NICs). The network will need a switch to allow multiple computers to communicate. Finally, the client machines will have to be configured to obtain their TCP/IP settings automatically.

→ **Note**

It may seem convoluted to connect an Ethernet cable coming from your Internet source to your computer just so you can connect another Ethernet cable to a switch—why not just connect the switch to the Internet source? But ICS is perhaps at its most beneficial when dealing with dial-up connections. In that case, you'd use a single NIC and a modem. Since most dial-up modems don't offer an Ethernet output, the only way to share the Internet connection would be with ICS!

Step 1 To use ICS, you will need two communication devices installed in the computer: either a modem connected to the Internet and an NIC connected to the internal network, or an NIC connected to a broadband interface and an NIC connected to the internal network. (If you need to install a second NIC to facilitate this lab exercise, perform Lab Exercise 24.02, Steps 1–3.)

Step 2 Open the Local Area Connection Properties dialog box for the network device connected to the Internet, as you did in previous lab exercises. Click the Advanced tab in Windows XP and the Sharing tab in Windows Vista/7 (see Figure 24-8). Under Internet Connection Sharing, check the *Allow other network users to connect through this computer's Internet connection* checkbox. Click OK.

Step 3 Once you've clicked OK, a hand icon (representing sharing) should appear under the Local Area Connection that has just been configured with ICS (see Figure 24-9).

Step 4 Test the ICS feature by following these steps:

a. Verify that the ICS host computer is capable of communicating with the Internet. Connect the external Local Area Connection NIC to the broadband interface (DSL or cable).

b. Power up the switch, and connect the internal interface from the ICS host computer to the switch.

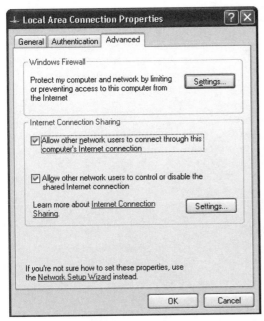

FIGURE 24-8 The Advanced tab of the Local Area Connection Properties dialog box showing Internet Connection Sharing in Windows XP

c. Connect the network interface card of the client PC to the switch.

d. Open the Local Area Connection Properties dialog box, as you did in previous lab exercises. On the General/Networking tab, select Internet Protocol Version 4 (TCP/IPv4) and click Properties. In the Properties dialog box, verify that *Obtain an IP address automatically* and *Obtain DNS server address automatically* are selected (see Figure 24-10).

FIGURE 24-9 A shared Local Area Connection

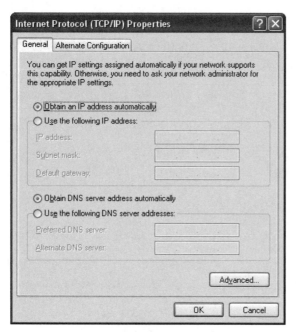

FIGURE 24-10 Internet Protocol (TCP/IP) Properties dialog box

Launch Internet Explorer on the client machine; verify that the connection is set up to use the LAN connection. Type **www.comptia.org** in the address bar and press ENTER. If there are any problems, shut down both machines and check all of the connections. Boot the ICS host computer first (allow all of the services to start), then boot the client machine.

 20 MINUTES

Lab Exercise 24.05: Upgrading and Tweaking Internet Explorer

Now that you have improved and protected your client's Internet connectivity, you will want to make sure that the method they use to interact with the Internet is the most current. Mozilla Firefox, Google Chrome, and Microsoft Internet Explorer are currently the three most popular browsers. The following steps will help you upgrade your client to the latest version of IE (version 9 as of this writing) and introduce you to some of the configuration areas that you should be aware of.

Learning Objectives

When it comes to applications—and this includes Internet Explorer—the computer technician is looked to as the Master or Mistress of All Things Computer. For this reason, a knowledge and awareness of applications, in addition to learning and practicing your craft as an IT technician, will enhance your reputation as an expert. In this lab, you'll briefly explore the upkeep of a networking application.

At the end of this lab, you'll be able to

- Evaluate and upgrade the IE application
- Fine-tune IE settings

Lab Materials and Setup

The materials you need for this lab are

- A working computer running Windows XP (at least SP2), Windows Vista, or Windows 7
- Internet access, preferably high-speed to facilitate downloads

Getting Down to Business

Internet Explorer is one of the most popular browser applications. You and your client may launch an Internet search engine such as Google or Yahoo! to locate and visit manufacturers' Web sites to research and, in some cases, purchase new hardware and software. You'll want to make sure that IE is up to date and working efficiently to make your client's browsing more pleasant.

✖ Warning

The following lab steps have you update Internet Explorer and change some of the configuration settings. If you are in an instructor-led class, or performing these operations on machines in your organization, verify you have permission to perform the upgrades.

Step 1 Open your current browser and navigate to the Microsoft Windows Internet Explorer page (http://windows.microsoft.com/en-US/internet-explorer/products/ie/home) as of this writing. Examine the new features and requirements. Near the large download link, find a separate link for downloading other versions of IE9. Does IE9 work with all versions of Windows? _____

Verify that your system and OS meet the requirements, and then download Internet Explorer 9.

Step 2 When the download has finished, open Internet Explorer. It looks very different from Internet Explorer 8. Microsoft has changed a lot of the old labeled buttons to just icons. Click on the cog wheel in the upper-right corner and select Internet Options.

On the General tab (see Figure 24-11), you can set the home page (or home pages), set browser history settings, change search defaults, and adjust tab settings. There are also options to set the appearance of Web pages displayed by the browser.

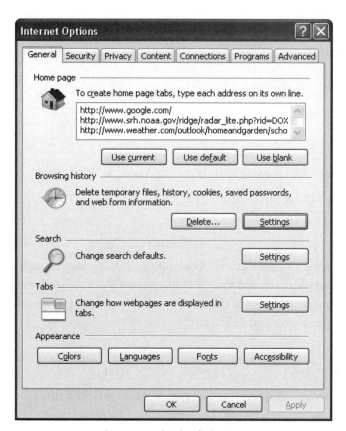

FIGURE 24-11 The General tab of the Internet Options dialog box in Internet Explorer 9

Step 3 Click the Advanced tab and explore the many settings that can be configured to modify how the browser deals with components and content. Navigate down to the Security heading and locate *Empty Temporary Internet Files Folder when browser is closed*. I like to enable this setting.

Explore some of the other tabs available in Internet Options and experiment with the different items you can configure. Microsoft has done a good job of setting the browser up with default setting that will work in most installations, but as the expert, you will want to be familiar with customizing the browser.

Lab Analysis Test

1. Tanner wants to configure his wireless network so that if Andrew just happens by with a laptop and a wireless card, he will not be able to gain access to the network without Tanner's approval. What component(s) does Tanner need to configure?

2. Brandon is using his school's computer to do some research for a term paper. He attempts to surf to a Web site he has found on Google, only to receive an *Access Denied* message from the browser. What could cause this to happen?

3. Andrew has configured his four-computer network to use Internet Connection Sharing. He has double-checked the ICS host computer, and it can access the Internet. All of the physical connections between the computers and the switch seem to be in good shape. Yet, he still cannot access the Internet from a client machine. What might he have missed?

4. Mary has stated that when she used the CNET Bandwidth Meter Online Speed Test, she achieved Internet transfer speeds around 7.5 Mbps. What type of Internet access do you think Mary has?

5. Cindy is installing a high-speed connection to the Internet. What are the four components she will need to verify and have on hand?

Key Term Quiz

Use the following terms to complete the following sentences. Not all terms will be used.

analog

dial-up

digital

drivers

HTTP

ICS

ISP

PnP

POP3

RJ-11

RJ-45

SSID

transceiver

Windows Firewall

1. When connecting to the Internet using a high-speed digital subscriber line, the DSL _____ is often referred to as a DSL modem.

2. The protocol that is synonymous with the World Wide Web is _____.

3. If the NIC isn't detected automatically, you'll need to install _____ manually.

4. Every wireless network has a network name that all of the machines accessing it must configure. This network name is known as a(n) _____.

5. The slowest means of accessing the Internet still in use today is _____.

Chapter 25
Multimedia

Lab Exercises

You have been hired as an entry-level tech for a public school district. Your first day on the job, the technology manager asks how familiar you are with the recording, storing, and playback of audio files on computer systems. It turns out that the history department wants the students to be able to record audio documentaries on historical events, store the files on the network, and produce podcasts of the documentaries. Demonstrating your enthusiasm, you respond that you are somewhat familiar with sound and will tackle the project. You are tasked with researching the sound card, building the prototype system, and providing some basic audio recording and storage training to the history instructors.

As a competent PC tech, you need to understand not just the tasks of installing the physical sound card and associated drivers, but also the applications that take advantage of the PC's sound capabilities. As such, the CompTIA A+ certification exams expect you to know about sound cards and their workings. The following lab exercises introduce you to sound card hardware and drivers, as well as the basic use of some of the popular Windows audio applications.

 30 MINUTES

Lab Exercise 25.01: Installing Sound

The first task on the agenda is to do a little research on sound cards and choose a few that meet the needs of this project. There are a number of different sound chips, and the "card" can be anything from the onboard sound capability of a mid-priced system to professional multichannel (input/output) devices used in recording studios. After you assemble a few candidates, you will select a sound card and then install, configure, and test that card. For the purpose of completing this lab, it is perfectly acceptable to use any working card, or an onboard sound device if that's what you have available.

Learning Objectives

This lab teaches you the basics of installing and configuring a sound card.

At the end of this lab, you'll be able to

- Identify features of sound cards
- Remove and install a sound card and associated devices (speakers and microphone)
- Configure a sound card

Lab Materials and Setup

The materials you need for this lab are

- A working computer system running Windows

- A removable sound card, microphone, and speakers properly installed and functioning (the sound drivers must either be part of the operating system in use or be available on disc or online)

✖ Warning

Different versions of Windows handle the drivers differently, to say the least. You should have a current driver for your sound card handy, just in case Windows decides it cannot remember your sound card when you go to reinstall!

Getting Down to Business

This lab will step you through removing, researching specifications for, installing, and configuring a sound card.

✔ Cross-Reference

For more information on sound cards, review the "Getting the Right Sound Hardware" section in Chapter 25 of *Mike Meyers' CompTIA A+ Guide to Managing and Troubleshooting PCs*.

Step 1   Take a moment and look up the specifications of your current sound card online. Identify the following:

Resolution _____

Sampling rate _____

Dynamic range _____

Signal-to-noise ratio _____

Now see if you can find this information online for some other cards—try M-Audio Audiophile 192, Creative Sound Blaster X-Fi Xtreme, and Turtle Beach Audio Advantage Amigo II.

Step 2   Now that you've seen some of the relevant specifications, the next step is to practice removing and reinstalling the sound card.

✔ **Hint**

This lab assumes that you have a removable sound card, not onboard sound. If all you have to work with is a system with onboard sound, go into the CMOS setup utility and turn off the onboard sound. Make what observations you can and resume the exercise with Step 3. When the time comes in the second half of Step 3 to reinstall the sound card, just go back into CMOS and enable the onboard sound again.

a. Shut down your system properly. Unplug the power cord.

b. Remove the case cover from your system and locate the sound card (see Figure 25-1).

What type of slot does the card use? _____

c. Disconnect any cables that are attached to the sound card (both internal and external), take out the screw that secures the sound card to the case, and then carefully remove the card. Make sure you're properly grounded before you touch the card!

What sort of internal connectors does the card have? _____

d. What sort of external connectors does it have? _____

e. Does the card have jumpers? What are they used for? Again, look on the Internet for the answers. Find the name of the card manufacturer and search that company's Web site for information on your specific model. This information is also available in the documentation for the card, if you still have it around.

_____

_____

FIGURE 25-1 A typical sound card

f.   What is the brand name of the sound-processing chip?

_____

g.   Is the name on the chip different from the name of the manufacturer of the card? (For example, the chip might have *ESS* printed on it, while the board is marked *Creative Labs*.)

_____

Step 3   With the card out of your system, turn on the machine and let it boot to the Windows desktop. Then go to Device Manager and see if your sound card is still listed.

Did Windows automatically remove the device when the card was removed? _____

If the sound card is still listed, highlight its icon, right-click, and select Uninstall. (Am I sure? Yes, I'm sure!)

Save your changes and shut your system off properly.

The next steps will confirm that the device has been removed:

a.   Reboot your system, go to Device Manager, and confirm that the sound device is no longer listed.

b.   Shut down your system and disconnect the power cord. Insert the sound card in the slot where you originally found it, secure the card to the case using the screw you removed, and reconnect all the cables.

c.   Reboot the system. When plug and play (PnP) kicks in, your system should recognize that you have added a card.

Windows will now locate the software drivers for the new hardware you installed. In fact, unless you uninstalled them, the drivers should still be on your system.

Step 4   Return to Device Manager. Find your device and open the Drivers tab and confirm that Windows installed the same drivers in the system. If necessary, use the driver disc to reinstall the correct drivers.

Step 5   To confirm that sound is working properly, start by ensuring that the speakers are powered and connected, and that the volume is set at a comfortable level.

Make sure your speakers are plugged into the proper jack on the sound card.

Is the speaker pair plugged into a working AC outlet, or does it have good batteries?

_____

Is there a volume adjustment knob on your speakers? _____

If you have a volume knob, adjust it to the middle position, and then access the Control Panel.

Now place a Volume icon in the taskbar's system tray/notification area so that volume adjustments will be more convenient. Follow the procedure that matches your operating system.

- In Windows XP, open the Sounds and Audio Devices Control Panel applet, and check the *Place volume icon in the taskbar* box.

- In Windows Vista, right-click the taskbar and select Properties. Then, click the Notification Area tab and make sure Volume is checked under *Select which system icons to always show*.

- In Windows 7, right-click on the taskbar and select Properties. Under Notification area on the Taskbar tab, click on Customize. Next to Volume, select *Show icon and notifications*.

Once you have the Volume icon in the taskbar's system tray/notification area, right-click it and select Open Volume Mixer, then follow these steps:

a.   In Windows XP, check to be sure that the *Mute all* or *Mute <device name>* option is not selected (see Figure 25-2). In Windows Vista/7, make sure the speaker icon beneath each audio device is not covered by a red circle with a line through it (the symbol for mute).

b.   Adjust the slider(s) to the center position.

You now have a good starting point to play sounds. Once you have ensured that the speakers are successfully putting out sound, you can go back and customize the levels to your liking.

Step 6   Test the speakers, and adjust the sound volume to a comfortable level. A good tool to use to test your sound card is the DirectX Diagnostic Tool. In Windows XP, click Start | Run and type **dxdiag** to launch the DirectX Diagnostic Tool (see Figure 25-3). In Windows Vista/7, go to the Start Search bar and type **dxdiag**. Press ENTER.

a.   Click the Sound tab, and examine the information displayed about your sound card and drivers.

b.   Click the Test DirectSound button (Windows XP only). This steps you through a series of tests to confirm the operation of your sound system.

c.   Switch to the Music tab and click the Test DirectMusic button (Windows XP only). This tests whether your system supports the DirectMusic component of DirectX.

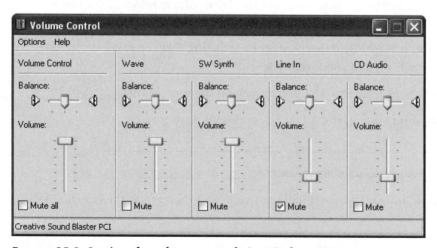

FIGURE 25-2 Setting the volume controls in Windows XP

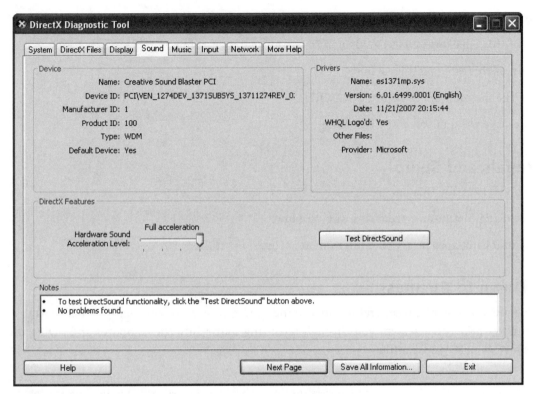

FIGURE 25-3 Using the DirectX Diagnostic Tool in Windows XP

Step 7 You've learned how to remove, install, and configure a sound card. You've also learned how to test the various parts of the sound system. Now it's time to talk about troubleshooting.

Your sound system is working, but your speakers sound a little rough. Are they "blown" out because they were overdriven with poor adjustments? You can go to Eminent Technology's Multimedia Speaker Test Web site and test the response of your speakers at different frequencies:

www.eminent-tech.com/music/multimediatest.html

These tests will help you confirm whether your speakers can still handle all the frequencies they are designed to handle.

 30 MINUTES

Lab Exercise 25.02: Recording Sound

With the sound card installed, configured, and tested, it's time to get the project really rolling with recorded sound. It is expected that each student's documentary will last from eight to ten minutes and will encompass typical current events. Each student has a microphone, sound card, and speakers. What you want to do is get the speech recorded digitally, maybe add some music, and choose the audio quality based on the expected delivery method.

Learning Objectives

The purpose of this lab exercise is to guide you in the recording of sound.

At the end of this lab, you'll be able to

- Use the microphone to record a WAV file

- Fine-tune the quality of the recording

Lab Materials and Setup

The materials you need for this lab are

- A working computer system running Windows

- A sound card, speakers, and a microphone properly installed

Getting Down to Business

Once you have installed, configured, and tested a sound card, you need to run some applications to see if this is going to work. This lab steps you through recording sound into the computer and saving the recording as a WAV or MP3 sound file.

Step 1 To check your system's ability to capture audio so that you can record the documentaries, you will use Windows Sound Recorder. Make sure your microphone is plugged into the proper connector before you proceed.

Access Sound Recorder in Windows XP by selecting Start | All Programs | Accessories | Entertainment | Sound Recorder. In Windows Vista/7, select Start | Accessories | Sound Recorder. In Windows XP, you'll see something similar to an audio cassette player. The buttons are the same—Record, Play, Fast Forward, Rewind, and Stop—but they're labeled with icons instead of words. In Windows Vista/7, however, Microsoft has stripped almost every control from the Sound Recorder, leaving only a Record button (see Figure 25-4). You can't even use Sound Recorder to listen to what you just recorded. You'll only be able to record at a single quality level, and the only format available is WMA (Windows Media Audio).

→ **Note**

To best complete this lab, use a Windows XP computer.

FIGURE 25-4 Using Windows Sound Recorder

Step 2 Using Sound Recorder from Windows XP, let's explore three different levels of recording. Open Sounder Recorder and load a sound file of any format. When working with digital audio files, the balance between sound quality and sound file size is driven by the project. If you were recording a project for CD, you would want the highest quality. For streaming audio and podcast audio, the MP3 file format is probably acceptable. Telephone quality, while achieving small file size, is not considered production quality.

    a. To set the recording quality, select File | Properties and then click the Convert Now button. In the Sound Selection dialog box, click the Name drop-down menu and select CD Quality. Click OK and then OK again to return to the Sound Recorder window.

    b. Click the red Record button and start talking into the microphone. Watch the graph to see that your voice is being recorded. If nothing seems to be happening, check your microphone connections.

    c. Record a full 60 seconds of CD-quality audio, and then click Stop (the button with a square icon, next to Record). To hear your recording, click Play (the single right arrow).

    d. To discover how much space this sound file uses, select File | Properties and observe the file's data size. Record the file size here:

    _____

    e. Create a subfolder named **podcast** in your My Music folder and save the sound file as **cdquality.wav** in the podcast folder.

✔ Hint

As you've probably figured out, our scenario for the history department would require a more sophisticated digital audio recording application. One minute is not going to be a very lengthy documentary! Sound Recorder is a good application to demonstrate the steps required to record audio, and you could use it to set up custom sound files to play during events. An example would be the infamous sound file that announces: "You've got mail." If you would like to explore digital audio recording and playback further, you can find and download the open source program called Audacity at http://audacity.sourceforge.net.

Step 3 Telephone quality is very low resolution and frequency response, meaning that it will probably sound muffled and dull. Follow these steps to convert the CD-quality sound file to a telephone-quality sound file:

    a. Select File | Properties, click Convert Now, and change the Name setting to Telephone Quality. Click OK and then OK again to return to the Sound Recorder window.

    b. Now check out the data size of the file and record it here: _____. Has the size of the sound file changed? How does it sound? _____

    c. Save the sound file in the podcast folder as **telephonequality.wav**.

Step 4 Finally, you will explore saving a recording as an MPEG Layer-3 (MP3) sound file. This is probably the best balance between audio quality and file size.

a. Launch Sound Recorder and open the cdquality.wav file.

b. To set the recording quality to the MP3 format, select File | Properties and then click Convert Now. In the Sound Selection dialog box, click the Format drop-down list and select MPEG Layer-3, then click OK.

c. Note the file's data size and record it here: _____. Has the size of the sound file changed? How does it sound? _____

d. Open the podcast folder and save the sound file as **mp3quality.mp3**.

✔ **Hint**

In the Sound Selection dialog box, you can also set more specific attributes for an MP3 file; just click the Attributes drop-down list after selecting MPEG Layer-3 and you'll see a number of options to fine-tune the quality of your recording.

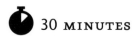 30 MINUTES

Lab Exercise 25.03: Exploring Windows Media Player

Now that you have successfully recorded the project, you will have to look at some of the methods used to play the files and create an archive of the documentary on CD. The Windows environment has used Windows Media Player since the introduction of version 6.1 in 1998. In this exercise, you will learn some of the basic navigation steps for using Windows Media Player 12, and burn your recordings to an audio CD.

Learning Objectives

In this lab exercise, you'll learn how to navigate and play audio files, and then you'll learn how to burn an audio CD using Windows Media Player 12.

At the end of this lab, you'll be able to

- Open and play sound files of various formats

- Navigate Windows Media Player 12

- Burn a CD of your recording

Lab Materials and Setup

The materials you need for this lab are

- A working computer system running Windows

- Three or more audio files to burn

- A sound card, speakers, and a microphone properly installed

- Windows Media Player 12 or newer (WMP12 is used in the lab exercise)

- A commercially produced music CD of your choice

- A blank CD-R or CD-RW

Getting Down to Business

Once you've recorded the sound and saved it as a WAV or MP3 sound file, you need a method to audition the finished product and package the sound file for distribution. You may want to make an MP3 file for portable players or streaming audio over the Internet, or you may want to distribute high-quality audio CDs.

✔ **Hint**

There are a number of paths you could take to accomplish the playback of your recordings and archive them to a CD. This lab exercise steps you through one method that explores some of the features of Windows Media Player 12. Some of the steps, windows, and icons may look different depending on the version of Windows Media Player you use.

Step 1 Launch Windows Media Player and then follow these steps:

a. Open Windows Media Player 12 (see Figure 25-5).

b. Click on the Play tab in the upper-right corner. This tab enables you to create playlists. Use the navigation tree on the left side of the program to locate your files, and then drag them to the playlist tab (labeled "Play") on the right. The first song you drag will start playing automatically. Click on the Save list button to save the selected files as a playlist (see Figure 25-6). Save the list as **Podcast**.

c. Click the Burn tab, and then drag and drop Podcast into the Burn List pane on the right side of the Windows Media Player window.

d. Insert a blank optical disc into an optical drive on your system with recording capabilities, and then click the Start Burn button.

e. Wait while the podcast audio file is burned to the optical disc, completing the task of archiving your recordings.

FIGURE 25-5 Windows Media Player

Step 2   While you have Windows Media Player open, explore the other options available to you as you work with sound files. One of the most popular uses of the computer when it comes to working with audio is to convert your CDs to MP3 sound files for use on portable MP3 players. Complete the following steps to calculate how many CDs you could fit onto a 8-GB MP3 player:

a.   Insert a music CD into the optical media drive.

b.   Click Tools | Options to open the Options dialog box for Windows Media Player. Click the Rip Music tab.

FIGURE 25-6 Creating a playlist

c. Under Rip Settings, click the Format drop-down list and select WAV (Lossless). Use the information at the bottom of the dialog box to calculate the number of CDs that would fit onto an 8-GB MP3 player at this bit rate.

_____

d. Click the Format drop-down list again and select MP3. Experiment with the Audio quality slider (which ranges from 128 Kbps to 320 Kbps), and calculate the number of CDs that would fit onto an 8-GB MP3 player at various quality settings.

_____

Lab Analysis Test

1. Suddenly and for no apparent reason, the speaker icon no longer shows up in the taskbar/notification area. In Windows Vista, where would you check to be sure it is enabled?

2. John replaced his motherboard with one that has built-in sound. He still wants to use his Creative Labs Audigy sound card. What must he do to prevent conflicts?

3. Theresa has been using her system for a long time to visit with friends in chat rooms. Lately her friends are complaining that her sound quality is getting worse. What should she check first?

4. Karl is not getting any sound from his speakers. What three things should he check?

5. John complains about annoying sounds when he opens and closes certain programs and sometimes when he clicks his mouse. He asks you if you can make them go away. Can you?

Key Term Quiz

Use the following terms to complete the following sentences. Not all terms will be used.

aux

compression

line-in

.mid

MP3

sound card

sound file

Sound Recorder

speaker

WAV

1. Joe wants to record himself singing the '50s classic "Hound Dog" to honor the birthday of Elvis Presley. He plugs a microphone into his sound card and opens _____, the recording software that comes with Windows.

2. Joshua is the keyboard player for a local band. He records some of the band's songs into a sequencer using MIDI. When he looks for the files on the computer, he can only find files with the _____ extension.

3. The MP3 format is popular because of the _____ scheme it uses.

4. The most common sound file format for portable sound players today is _____.

5. By default, the Windows XP Sound Recorder saves audio recordings as _____ files.

Chapter 26
Portable Computing

Lab Exercises

The world has gone mobile, and accomplished technicians travel right along with it. General technicians have always worked on the software side of portables, tweaking power management options to optimize battery life for the users. Working on the hardware side of portable computing devices of all stripes, however, used to be the realm of only highly specialized technicians. As portable computing devices become increasingly common and the technology inside becomes more modular, however, frontline general technicians (think CompTIA A+ certified technicians here) increasingly get the call to upgrade and repair these devices.

Most laptops and netbooks have parts that a user can easily replace. You can swap out a fading battery for a newer one, for example, or add a second battery in place of an optical drive for long airplane trips. Lurking beneath access panels on the underside or below the keyboard on some models are hardware components such as RAM, a hard drive, a network card, and a modem—just like laptop batteries, these units can be easily accessed and replaced by a technician. Some laptops even have panels for replacing the video card and CPU.

In this series of labs, you'll do four things. First, you'll use the Internet to research the upgrades available for portable computing devices so you can provide proper recommendations to employers and clients. Second, you'll open a laptop and gut it like a rainbow trout—removing and replacing RAM, the most common of all hardware upgrades. Third, you'll perform the traditional task of a portable PC technician, tweaking the power management options to optimize battery life on particular models. Finally, you'll tour a computer store to familiarize yourself with the latest and greatest portable offerings.

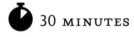 30 MINUTES

Lab Exercise 26.01: Researching Laptop Upgrade Paths

Your boss just sent word that one of your most important clients wants to extend the life of their sales force's laptop computers by upgrading rather than replacing. You've been asked to provide an upgrade track for your client. This requires you to research the laptops used by the company to determine which upgrades you can make, and to verify that the laptops themselves are not so old that the cost to upgrade them outweighs the cost of new laptops with new technology. You have to determine whether you can add RAM, replace the hard drives, or replace the aging batteries. Get to work!

Learning Objectives

Given the manufacturer and model number of a notebook computer, you'll figure out how to upgrade your client's computers.

At the end of this lab, you'll be able to

- Determine the replacement price of a battery

- Determine memory upgrades, including the quantity and type of RAM

- Determine hard drive upgrades, including the capacity and price of a hard drive

Lab Materials and Setup

The materials you need for this lab are

- A working PC with Internet access

Getting Down to Business

Limber up your surfing fingers because you're about to spend some time on the Web. Researching information about hardware and software is something technicians do all the time. The better you are at it, the better you are at your job!

When you're searching for replacement and upgrade parts and information, always take a look at the device manufacturer's Web site. Most major PC manufacturers, such as Dell and Lenovo, have comprehensive product specification sheets available to the public on their sites. You can even order replacement parts directly from them! A popular tactic for researching upgrades is to grab the upgrade specs from the manufacturer's site and then search the Internet for the best prices. Not only are you doing your job well, but you'll be saving your company money too!

In the following steps, you'll navigate the tumultuous seas of the Internet in a quest to find the Golden Fleece of laptop battery, memory, and hard drive upgrades.

Step 1　Fire up your Web browser, and surf over to the device manufacturer's Web site. Try www.dell.com, or do a Google search for **laptop battery**. Many sites sell every laptop battery imaginable. The goal of this exercise is to become familiar with using the Internet to identify parts, confirm the specifications, and purchase replacement batteries. Once you reach a suitable Web site, answer the following questions:

You need replacement batteries for several Dell Precision M4400 laptops. What's the vendor's part number and price for this battery?

_____

What's the voltage and power capacity of the battery?

_____

✔ **Hint**

Just like any other electrical power source, batteries are rated according to voltage (9.6 V, for instance), current capacity (2600 milliamps per hour, or mAh), and sometimes power capacity (72 watts per hour, or WHr). When purchasing laptop batteries from third-party vendors (that is, vendors other than the laptop manufacturer), make sure to buy a battery that matches the voltage recommended by the manufacturer. Depending on the type of battery (Ni-Cd, Ni-MH, or Li-Ion), the current or power capacity of replacement batteries may be greater than that of the original battery. This is not a problem—increased current/power capacity means longer run times for your portable PC.

Step 2   Search the manufacturer's Web site for information on memory. If that isn't available, flip your browser over to www.kahlon.com to check RAM prices and availability. If the site isn't available, perform a Google search to find other Web sites that sell **laptop memory**. Then answer the following questions.

Your client has a Dell Precision M4400 with 1 GB of RAM. How much RAM can you install? How many sticks of RAM will it take to upgrade this machine to a respectable 4 GB of memory, and how much will it cost?

_____

_____

Step 3   Stay where you landed in your search for memory upgrades. Does the vendor have replacement or additional hard drives available as well? If not, try www.kahlon.com, but now research possible hard drive upgrades for the Dell Precision M4400 the client owns. Answer this question:

The client's Dell Precision M4400 laptops have 160-GB hard drives plus a currently unused modular media bay that could be used to house a second hard drive. How much would it cost to add a second 320-GB hard drive to the Dell?

_____

 30 MINUTES

Lab Exercise 26.02: Replacing and Upgrading RAM

Your client settled on the RAM upgrades as the first step for making their laptops more usable, and you get tagged as the person to remove the old RAM and install the new. Upgrading RAM is the most common technician-performed upgrade on portable PCs and something you're likely to run into in the real world.

Learning Objectives

In this lab, you'll learn essential skills for upgrading portable PCs.

At the end of this lab, you'll be able to

- Access the RAM panel in a laptop

- Remove RAM in a laptop

- Install RAM properly in a laptop

Lab Materials and Setup

The materials you need for this lab are

- A working portable computer

- A very tiny Philips-head screwdriver

- An anti-static mat

✖ Warning

Opening a portable computer can result in a nonfunctional portable computer. Don't use the instructor's primary work laptop for this exercise!

Getting Down to Business

You're about to open the sensitive inner portions of a portable computer, but before you do, it's a great idea to refresh your memory about avoiding electrostatic discharge (ESD). The inside of a laptop looks different from the inside of a desktop or tower case, but the contents are just as sensitive to static electricity. Watch out!

Step 1   Using your handy screwdriver or other handy tool, open the access panel for the RAM. Every portable PC offers a different way to access the RAM, so I can't give you explicit directions here. Most often, you'll find a removable plate on the bottom of the laptop secured with a tiny Philips-head screw. Some laptops require you to remove the keyboard, unscrew a heat spreader, and then access the RAM. Figure 26-1 shows a typical panel, accessible from the underside of the laptop.

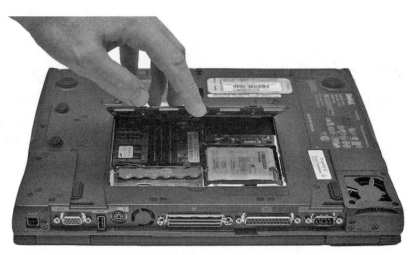

Figure 26-1 Opening the access panel to find RAM

Step 2   Once you have the panel open, push outward on the restraining clips on the RAM stick(s). This will cause the RAM to pop up partially (see Figure 26-2).

Step 3   Remove the RAM gently, gripping only at the noncontact edges. Place the stick(s) on an anti-static pad or in an anti-static bag.

Figure 26-2 Releasing the RAM

Step 4 Install the replacement RAM into the laptop, reversing the process of removal. Place the stick(s) at an angle into the RAM slots and push firmly. Once the contacts have disappeared, press the body of the RAM into the restraining clips.

✔ **Hint**

> If you don't have new RAM to install, simply install the RAM you removed in Step 3. This gives you the opportunity to practice!

Step 5 Replace the access panel.

Step 6 Power on the laptop to confirm that the new RAM is recognized and functioning properly.

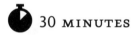 30 MINUTES

Lab Exercise 26.03: Adjusting Power Management to Optimize Battery Life

Several of your sales staff members have to attend a conference on the other side of the country. The conference came up on short notice, so everyone needs time to prepare, even while on the flight to the conference. You've been tasked with configuring power management on their laptops to optimize battery life so they can work as long as possible while on the plane.

Learning Objectives

In this lab, you'll adjust the power management features for a PC, a task that's vital to proper support of portable PCs.

At the end of this lab, you'll be able to

- Enable and disable power management in the CMOS
- Change power management settings in Windows

Lab Materials and Setup

The materials you need for this lab are

- A working computer with Windows installed
- A BIOS that supports power management

✔ **Hint**

Having a notebook computer available is a plus. Performing these steps on a notebook computer will allow you to configure the settings for the Portable/Laptop power scheme and then remove the power cord, running on battery power to experience the actual results. If you're practicing on a regular desktop PC, keep in mind that a notebook will have two options for each adjustment: one for when the notebook is using battery power, and one for when it's connected to the alternating current (AC) source.

Getting Down to Business

Windows PCs have two separate areas for power management: the CMOS setup program and the Control Panel. You'll start with CMOS and then go to the Control Panel.

Step 1   Boot your system, and enter the CMOS setup program.

✔ **Cross-Reference**

Refer to the "Power Management" section in Chapter 26 of *Mike Meyers' CompTIA A+ Guide to Managing and Troubleshooting PCs* for more information on power management on portable PCs.

Now follow these steps:

a.   Go to the Power Management Setup screen.

b.   Enable power management if it's currently disabled.

c.   Look at each option for common-sense settings. For example, when operating on battery power, the portable should be configured for maximum energy efficiency, thus increasing run time.

d.   Make sure the ACPI setting is enabled if the BIOS supports it.

e.   Save your settings, and boot the system to the Windows desktop.

✔ **Hint**

ACPI is short for Advanced Configuration and Power Interface, a power management specification developed by Intel, Microsoft, and Toshiba. ACPI enables the operating system to control the amount of power given to each device attached to the computer. With ACPI, the operating system can turn off peripheral devices, such as optical drives, when they're not in use.

Step 2   Access the Power Options applet in the Control Panel, and make a note of your current power management settings.

Check out the different power schemes available (this will depend on your specific system) and change the settings to see how they affect when the monitor and hard drives turn off. Each of these schemes has adjustable times. The tabs and settings will differ depending on which version of Windows you're running. Be sure to look at them all. To see more detailed power scheme settings in Windows Vista/7, be sure to click *Change power/plan settings* and then *Change advanced power settings*.

✔ Hint

The Windows XP Power Options Properties dialog box (on a notebook) has five tabs: Power Schemes, Alarms, Power Meter, Advanced, and Hibernate (see Figure 26-3). You can use the Alarms tab to set the time when the battery alarm is activated. The Power Meter tab shows the percent of charge remaining in the battery.

✖ Warning

Some PCs and some components don't like standby and suspend modes. They can cause your computer to lock up. Be aware of that, and if your computer locks up, turn those settings off.

Step 3 Once you've finished experimenting, enable or disable power management as you prefer.

FIGURE 26-3 Accessing the Windows XP power options on a portable computer

Open

Lab Exercise 26.04: Field Trip to Play with the Latest Portable PCs

The best way to understand portable PCs (laptops, netbooks, tablet PCs, and smartphones) is to play with one. If there isn't one available in the classroom, then this exercise is for you.

Learning Objectives

This lab will take you into the field for a little computer browsing—for educational purposes, of course!

At the end of this lab, you'll be able to

- Recognize the variations in key features among different portable PCs

Lab Materials and Setup

The materials you need for this lab are

- A local computer store or other retailer with a good selection of portable PCs you can examine

✔ Hint

If you don't have a store nearby, use the Web to browse a computer store such as CompUSA (www.compusa.com), or go to a manufacturer's Web site such as Dell's (www.dell.com) and customize a laptop to your heart's content. Be sure to explore all the options and customizations you can add to it. Just make sure you don't click Buy!

Getting Down to Business

Portable PCs are manufactured by a wide variety of companies, and no two notebooks are created equal. Some notebooks feature a slim and lightweight profile and are designed for the busy traveler; others feature a full complement of ports and rival desktop PCs in their power and features. Netbooks are smaller, compact versions of laptops that are ideal as long-term traveling companions. They can fit in a purse or backpack and thus are handy for browsing or doing e-mail on the road. Tablet PCs have pen-based interfaces that allow you to use them like a paper notepad. Smartphones are great for staying connected everywhere you go—we'll take a closer look at smartphones and their tablet relatives in Chapter 27. Take a look at all the available models and compare their features.

Step 1   Go to your local computer store or office supply store and check out the portable PCs on display. Try to find a store with a variety of brands. Bring this lab manual (or a copy of the following chart) with you to record the different specs you find.

Step 2 Pick out three portables, preferably from different manufacturers. For each portable, record the following information.

Feature	Portable 1	Portable 2	Portable 3
Size/weight			
Screen type/size			
CPU			
RAM			
Pointing device(s)			
I/O ports			
ExpressCard(s)			
Hard disk drive/solid-state drive			
Floppy/optical drive(s)			

Lab Analysis Test

1. Bill wants to upgrade his memory from 2 GB to the maximum amount of RAM his notebook can take. He has a Lenovo ThinkPad T500 notebook. How much RAM does he need to buy?

2. Teresa complains that her Windows XP notebook turns itself off without any warning. What should she adjust?

3. Maanit will be traveling from the United States to India. He'll use his laptop to watch DVDs on the way, usually on battery power. Lately, the battery seems to run out of juice well before the battery specifications indicate. What could possibly cause this recent development? Are there any recommendations you would make to Maanit to improve his laptop's performance?

4. During your research earlier in these exercises, which did you discover to be the most expensive—hard drives, memory, or batteries? Which component was the most inexpensive to replace?

5. Would the LCD screen or hard drives turn off, for energy conservation, if you set your power scheme to Always On and you walked away for a long period of time? Why or why not?

Key Term Quiz

Use the following terms to complete the following sentences. Not all terms will be used.

ACPI

battery

hard drive

hibernate

memory

netbook

notebook

Power Meter

Power Options

Power Scheme

standby

1. The amount of time the hard drive will continue to spin once it's no longer being accessed is determined by the _____ setting in Windows XP and the advanced power settings in Windows Vista/7.

2. You can use the _____ applet in the Control Panel to set the power conservation options for the notebook computer.

3. The battery, _____, and _____ are all upgradeable laptop components.

4. The amount of power remaining in a battery can be determined by looking at the _____.

5. Software can control power consumption if _____ is turned on in the CMOS setup program.

Chapter 27
Mobile Devices

Lab Exercises

The Internet-connected experience has jumped off of our desks and into our hands. Smartphones and tablets, grouped into a category called "mobile devices," enable you to consume, communicate, and create all sorts of digital goodies on the go. You don't even need to sync them with your desktop if you don't want to; they can function independently of any other device. In fact, most of today's smartphones and tablets are more powerful than the PC you had five years ago. These devices are everywhere, so you need to know something about them. As a PC tech, people will assume you know how to fix anything technical, including smartphones and tablets. The following lab exercises are meant to familiarize you with the most basic features of Apple iOS and Google Android smartphones and tablets.

 30 MINUTES

Lab Exercise 27.01: Comparing Apple iOS and Google Android

Several companies compete for mobile device dominance, but two of the biggest (and most important for the CompTIA A+ 220-802 exam) companies are Apple and Google. As much as some might hate to admit it, Apple practically invented the modern touchscreen smartphone with the first iPhone. On the other hand, there are a lot more Android devices available (in multiple form factors and prices, unlike Apple's single smartphone and tablet offerings). While other mobile device ecosystems exist (like Windows Phone 7 and BlackBerry), you'll encounter Apple iOS and Google Android devices so much more often in the field that it makes sense to focus on these two mobile OSs when doing research in this lab exercise.

Learning Objectives

In this exercise, you'll research the differences between Apple iOS and Google Android.

At the end of this lab, you'll be able to

- Differentiate between Apple iOS and Google Android

Lab Materials and Setup

The materials you need for this lab are

- An Internet-capable PC for research

- Optional: An iOS device and an Android device for comparison

Getting Down to Business

At first glance, Apple iOS and Google Android devices have a lot in common: big touchscreens, icons you can tap, Web pages you can swipe, and so on. Peek under the surface, however, and you'll see how different the two mobile operating systems really are. You need to understand how both Apple iOS and Google Android operate, what they have in common, and how they differ.

Step 1   First take a look at Apple's mobile operating system, iOS. A mobile operating system is a lot different from a desktop OS, so make sure you know all the details. Open your Web browser and search for the following topics.

a.   What is the latest version of Apple iOS?

_____

b.   What devices use iOS?

_____

c.   List five features of the latest version of Apple iOS.

_____

_____

_____

_____

_____

Step 2   Next, take a look at Google's mobile operating system, Android. Android devices don't all use the latest OS, and most device manufacturers customize the OS with a special user interface. Keep this in mind when searching for information about Google Android.

a.   What is the latest version of Google Android?

_____

b.   List a few smartphone and/or tablet manufacturers that use Android.

_____

  c. List five features of the latest version of Android.

_____

_____

_____

_____

_____

Step 3 For each feature, fill in the following table with a **Yes** or **No** response to indicate whether or not it applies to each OS. Some features are present in both Android and iOS devices.

	Android	iOS
A closed source operating system	_____	_____
An open source operating system	_____	_____
Can sync with iTunes	_____	_____
Can be used with smartphones and tablets	_____	_____
Can install apps	_____	_____
Devices use a capacitive screen	_____	_____
Devices use a resistive screen	_____	_____
Can connect to Bluetooth devices	_____	_____
Devices can expand storage through external flash memory	_____	_____
Has mouse support	_____	_____

 30 MINUTES

Lab Exercise 27.02: Installing Apps in iOS

Installing an app (a short and hip way of saying "application") is probably one of the more important skills to have when using any mobile device. In this exercise, you'll connect to a wireless access point and download an app using an Apple iOS device like the iPad, iPhone, or iPod. Remember that you can do this on Android devices as well, but with multiple app stores and sources available, the Android app ecosystem can seem a lot more confusing. Apple's closed app ecosystem means that the process is centralized and straightforward.

→ **Note**

Installing an app on an Android device can be quite different, but I encourage you to try both!

Learning Objectives

In this lab, you'll connect to a WAP, then download and install an app.

At the end of this lab, you'll be able to

- Configure an iOS device for wireless access and install a new app

Lab Materials and Setup

The materials you need for this lab are

- An iOS-compatible device with access to the Internet

- An Apple ID

Getting Down to Business

I'm sure we've all heard the line, "There's an app for that," but you're about to test that theory. Finding and installing the right app is what makes a modern smartphone smart.

Step 1   First, you will connect to a Wi-Fi network so that you can get on the Internet. If you don't have an available Wi-Fi connection, skip to Step 2.

- a.   Go to the home screen by pressing the home button on your device (the big physical button beneath the screen). Tap on the Settings icon (see Figure 27-1); you might need to swipe to another screen if you've moved the Settings icon. Tap on Wi-Fi. Make sure the Wi-Fi is set to ON. Tap on the appropriate SSID to connect.

- b.   If the Wi-Fi network is encrypted, provide the password on the next screen. Tap Join.

FIGURE 27-1 iOS Settings button

c. You should now see a checkmark next to the network you chose. Tap the small arrow button on the Wi-Fi network you joined to view the network settings. You should see all of your DHCP information (see Figure 27-2). You can also tap Forget this Network, which removes any profile information you have for that particular SSID. (Don't do that right now, though.)

d. Press the home screen button to return to the home screen. When connected to a wireless network, you should see your Wi-Fi signal strength in the status bar at the top of the screen, near the time.

Step 2 Now that you are connected to the Internet, you will download an app from the App Store.

a. Tap on the App Store icon, then tap Top 25. List the current Top 5 Free apps.

_____

_____

_____

_____

_____

b. Tap Search, then type **mactracker** in the search box. Tap the Search button.

FIGURE 27-2 Wi-Fi network settings screen

c. Tap Mactracker. (It should be the top search result.)

d. Give a short description of this app.

_____

_____

e. What is the app's version number and how big is it?

_____

f. Tap INSTALL and enter your Apple ID password.

g. The Mactracker app will download and install onto your device. Depending on your Internet connection speed, this might take a while.

Step 3 Once Mactracker has successfully downloaded, you should see the app on one of your home screens.

a. Tap the app to open it (see Figure 27-3). What you are seeing is a historical listing of every Apple product ever made.

FIGURE 27-3 Mactracker app running

b.   Swipe (scroll) down and tap on iPhone. Tap iPhone 4S. Fill in the following specifications.

Initial price for the 16-GB model: _____

Display resolution: _____

Capacities: _____

Processor type: _____

Processor speed: _____

Number of cores on processor: _____

What version of iOS was released with this device? _____

How long will the battery last while talking over a 3G network? _____

c.   Exit the app by pressing the home button. Once you are at the home screen, you might think the app has been closed because you can't see it anymore. But guess what? That app is still loaded in your device's RAM.

d.   Double-tap the home button quickly. The home screen slides up to reveal a row of apps on the bottom. This bar works a lot like the taskbar in Windows.

e.   Tap the Mactracker app and hold your finger on the screen. All of the icons should start jiggling. This is referred to, in all seriousness, as "jiggle" mode.

f.   Tap the white minus sign in the red circle on the Mactracker app. It has now been officially released from RAM! Tap on the faded top half of the screen to exit the task switcher and return to the home screen.

Step 4   Now that you've used the Mactracker app, you will uninstall it from your phone.

a.   To uninstall the Mactracker app, find it on one of the home screens. Tap and hold the Mactracker icon. The entire screen will enter jiggle mode. Tap the white × on the black circle. It will ask for a confirmation. Tap Delete.

b.   Press the home button to exit jiggle mode.

 30 MINUTES

Lab Exercise 27.03: Setting Up the Lock Screen

Just like your computer, your smartphone or tablet can contain a lot of private information. Your smartphone might have access to an e-mail account with messages that you don't want prying eyes to see, or maybe you're 16 years old and don't want your parents snooping around your text messages. In either case, it may be necessary to implement security on your mobile device.

Learning Objectives

In this exercise, you'll be setting up screen locking on an iOS device.

At the end of this lab, you'll be able to

- Lock a screen with any iOS device

- Navigate the available security settings in iOS

Lab Materials and Setup

The materials you need for this lab are

- An iOS-capable device such as an iPhone, iPad, or iPod

Getting Down to Business

You will enable the lock screen on your iOS device. Note that this lock screen only protects your iOS device when it falls asleep. Also keep in mind that touchscreens have a bad habit of revealing lock screen passcodes through the smudges left on the screen by your fingers. Clean your screen!

Step 1   First, you will enable the passcode on your iOS device.

   a.   Turn on your iOS device and go to the home screen.

   b.   Tap the Settings icon, then tap General. Tap on Passcode Lock (see Figure 27-4).

FIGURE 27-4 Passcode Lock settings

    c.   Tap Turn Passcode On.

    d.   Enter a four-digit passcode that you can remember. Re-enter your passcode.

    e.   Congratulations! You have just set up the passcode. Now take a look at how the security works and all the different configuration settings you can enable.

    f.   What will happen if you turn on Erase Data?

    g.   Look at the Require Passcode option. How long can you delay requiring a passcode to unlock the iOS device?

    h.   What happens when you turn off Simple Passcode?

Step 2   Now that you've enabled the passcode, test that it works and locks your iOS device.

    a.   Tap the home button to return to the home screen.

    b.   Tap the power button (lock button) to make your screen go dark. Tap it again to wake up your device. Swipe to unlock it, and then enter your passcode. (If you changed the Require Passcode time, you will need to wait longer to wake up your iOS device.) You should be prompted to enter the passcode. Enter it now.

    c.   Tap the power button to make the screen go dark. Tap it again to wake up your device. Swipe to unlock it. Type your passcode *incorrectly*. Do it again…and again…and again! How many times can you enter your passcode incorrectly before the device no longer accepts your attempts? How long are you prevented from entering it again?

Step 3   You can keep the passcode feature turned on if you like it, but if you don't like it, you can follow these steps to turn it off.

    a.   Return to Settings. Tap on General, then Passcode Lock. Tap in your passcode.

    b.   Tap Turn Passcode Off. Enter your passcode. The passcode is now disabled.

Lab Analysis Test

1. Piotr wants to get a new tablet so he can play games, check his e-mail, and watch his favorite TV shows. He can only afford a 16-GB model, but is concerned that he'll run out of space. Give him a good recommendation for a tablet and explain your reasoning.

2. Kitty wants to back up all of the data and apps on her iPhone to her PC. What software does she need and how would she make the backup?

3. Explain the difference between capacitive and resistive touchscreen devices.

4. Xavier wants to purchase a mobile device but isn't sure of the difference between a smartphone and a tablet. Explain the differences and similarities between the two device types.

5. What are the different ways you can get data (documents, music, and movies) onto your smartphone?

Key Term Quiz

Use the following terms to complete the following sentences. Not all terms will be used.

Android

Android Market

app

App Store

Apple

Bluetooth

capacitive

closed source

Google

Google Play

home screen

iOS

iPad

iPhone

iPod

jiggle

open source

passcode

resistive

smartphone

swipe

sync

tablet

tap

1.   All Apple smartphones and tablets use a(n) _____ screen.

2.   To download an app on an Android device, you must go to what is currently called the Android _____. This used to be called the Android _____.

3.   A(n) _____ is a mobile device that is the perfect "couch surfer." It is great for checking e-mail, reading a book, or even watching a TV show on a 10-inch screen.

4.   The three Apple devices, _____, _____, and _____, all use a(n) _____ platform.

5.   When you use an iOS device and want to delete an app, you must first enter _____ mode.

Chapter 28
Printers

Lab Exercises

Printers continue to be a major part of the day-to-day working environment, both at home and in the office, despite attempts to create a "paperless office." What this means is that the PC technician will have to understand the operation of several types of printers and be able to keep them in good working order. Many companies have service contracts for their more expensive printers (they're usually leased property anyway!), but there will always be printers that need a good technician's love and care.

This chapter's lab exercises will take you through a scenario in which your boss walks into your office and tells you five printers are being delivered to you—two impact printers using legacy parallel ports, two USB inkjet printers, and an HP LaserJet laser printer using a network interface. You need to install them and make sure they work properly so that they're accessible by anyone in the company who needs them. You'll learn about some of the key differences between the two most popular types of printers (inkjet and laser printers), and you'll load printer drivers. Finally, you'll look at some of the maintenance issues that are required to keep the printers up and running and some of the techniques to follow when they stop.

 30 MINUTES

Lab Exercise 28.01: Examining Types of Printers

There's an enormous amount of information on the Internet about printers. All of the top printer manufacturers—HP, Lexmark, Canon, and so forth—have Web sites that can provide insight about modern printers. As a PC technician, you'll need to visit these sites for information about your new printers, and to download the most current drivers for those printers.

✖ **Warning**

You must have access to the Internet for this exercise. If you don't have access, refer to Chapter 28 of *Mike Meyers' CompTIA A+ Guide to Managing and Troubleshooting PCs* for a review.

Learning Objectives

In this lab, you'll compare the features of impact, inkjet, and laser printers using the Internet.

At the end of this lab, you'll be able to

- Recognize the key differences between impact, inkjet, and laser printers

- Identify and visit Web sites on the Internet dedicated to printers and printer troubleshooting

Lab Materials and Setup

The materials you need for this lab are

- A working computer with Windows

- A connection to the Internet

- Access to either an inkjet printer or a laser printer

✔ **Hint**

A trip to your local computer store or other retailer with a good selection of printers would be beneficial for a general knowledge of printers.

Getting Down to Business

Fire up your favorite Web browser and head out on the old Information Superhighway. The Internet is just brimming with helpful information about printers.

✔ **Hint**

Web sites have the annoying tendency to either disappear or drop the information that was once relevant to a particular subject. If any of the links in this exercise are no longer active or don't seem to contain the relevant information, you may need to do a little Web research of your own. As always, practice safe surfing! There are thousands of online forums available, and they can contain questionable hyperlinks, poor-quality information, and in some cases, outright wrong information. Try to stick with legitimate manufacturer and technical Web sites, examine where that hyperlink is going to reroute your computer, and visit multiple sites to verify information you discover in the forums. Consider it excellent practice for real-world tech work!

Step 1   To find information about inkjet printers, access the following Web site to complete this step: http://computer.howstuffworks.com/inkjet-printer.htm/printable. If this link doesn't work, you can also do a Google search and look for information about how inkjet printers work.

    a.   What's the major difference between impact and non-impact printers?

        _____

        _____

    b.   What part of an inkjet printer moves the print head back and forth across the page?

        _____

    c.   List the two ways in which the droplets of ink are formed in inkjet printers.

        _____

        _____

    d.   The type of paper used in an inkjet printer greatly influences the quality of the image produced. What are the two main characteristics of inkjet printer paper that affect the image the most?

        _____

        _____

Step 2   For information about laser printers, access this site to complete this step: www.howstuffworks.com/laser-printer.htm/printable. Do a Google search or refer to the textbook if this site isn't available.

    a.   What's the primary principle at work in a laser printer?

        _____

        _____

    b.   What moves the image from the drum to the paper?

        _____

c. Printer Control Language (PCL) and PostScript are both examples of what?

    _____

    _____

d. What's toner? Is it an ink, wax, or something else?

    _____

Step 3 Put these steps in the printing process of a laser printer in the correct order (don't forget to reference the textbook as well):

Charge: _____

Clean: _____

Develop: _____

Fuse: _____

Transfer: _____

Expose: _____

Process: _____

Step 4 If you have access to a laser printer, open it and carefully examine the insides. Also read the printer manual for details on the specifications. Access the manufacturer's Web site for additional information.

If you don't have access to a laser printer, go to your local office supply or computer store and ask a salesperson to show you the differences between various impact, inkjet (black and white as well as color), and laser printers.

Look inside your laser printer.

a. What parts are easily removable and replaceable?

    _____

b. Practice removing and reinserting the toner (see Figure 28-1) and paper.

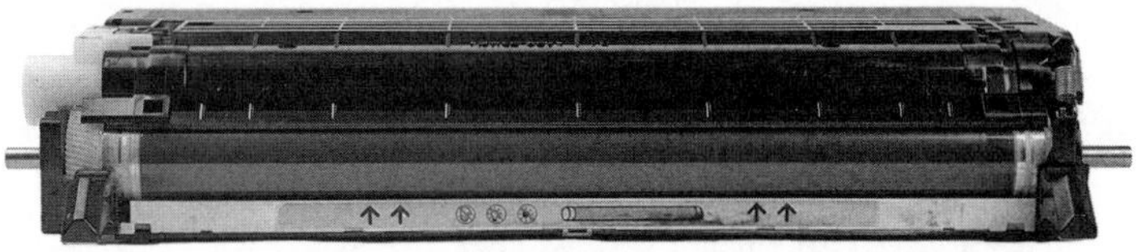

FIGURE 28-1 A toner cartridge with its photosensitive drum exposed

---

✖ **Warning**

Remember to turn the printer off before removing anything but the toner or paper. Also, be careful not to spill any toner inside the printer.

Look at the manual or the manufacturer's Web site for these specifications.

c. How much RAM can it hold? _____

d. How much effect does the amount of RAM have on the cost of a new printer?

_____

e. Are the drum and toner separate, or are they one replaceable part?

_____

f. What is the speed of the printer (pages per minute)? _____

g. What is the quality of the output (resolution)? _____

_____

h. What are the number and types of ink cartridges? _____

_____

i. What is the price of a new printer? _____

j. What is the cost per page? _____

✔ **Hint**

Most inkjet (and even laser) printers are priced very low, so they're affordable to buy initially. Using them is another question. Calculate the cost of the ink and how many pages it'll print. This calculation will amaze you. They're not so cheap after all.

---

k. What can you conclude from your research about the true total cost of printing, including consumables? _____

_____

 30 MINUTES

Lab Exercise 28.02: Installing a Printer

The key to a successful printer installation is having the correct software drivers and understanding how the printer will interface with the computer. You'll most likely need the drivers when you install those five printers your boss is having delivered to you, and you'll also have to configure the printers you are installing to use parallel, USB, and network interfaces. A common practice in multiple-user environments—companies considered to be small office/home office (SOHO)—is to use a printer with its own network interface card (NIC), so that computers from anywhere in the network can print directly to the printer through the network interface.

Learning Objectives

In this lab, you'll install a printer, first as a directly connected device, and then as a network device. You will then explore and change its settings.

At the end of this lab, you'll be able to

- Recognize the variations in key features of laser printers

- Install a laser printer in Windows

- Change laser printer settings in Windows

- Configure a TCP/IP port for a network printer

Lab Materials and Setup

The materials you need for this lab are

- A working computer with Windows installed

- An inkjet or laser printer for installation (or you can skip Step 1)

- Optional: A print device with a network interface card

Getting Down to Business

These days, installing a printer is a fairly straightforward task. This is good news, because you'll probably do your fair share of it as a computer technician.

Step 1 To install a plug-and-play printer:

  a. Connect the printer to your system via a parallel or USB port.

  b. Turn on the printer, and then turn on the PC.

  c. As the boot sequence progresses, the plug-and-play feature will locate the printer and install it for you. Follow the instructions on the screen.

✔ **Hint**

Here's the twist. If your printer is older than your operating system, the OS should install the printer drivers with little interaction on your part. If the printer is newer than your OS, then you'll need to have the driver disc handy because the system will stop and ask you for it. Some printer manufacturers actually require you to start their own printer installation programs even before connecting the printer to a system. As always, consult the manufacturer's instructions first.

Step 2 To install a printer that is not plug and play:

a. Access the Printer applet. In Windows XP, select Start | Printers and Faxes. For Windows Vista, select Start | Control Panel | Printers. In Windows 7, go to Start | Devices and Printers.

b. Click the Add a Printer button or link. A wizard should pop up on the screen. Click Next to proceed (Windows XP only).

c. You want to install a printer attached to your PC, so select the local printer option (see Figure 28-2). In Windows Vista/7, clicking on the option will advance the wizard automatically. In Windows XP, select the local printer option and click Next.

d. Follow the steps through the Add Printer Wizard by selecting LPT1 and then a printer from the list of printers or your driver disc. Finish the installation by printing a test page.

✖ **Warning**

If you weren't able to install an actual print device for this exercise, don't print a test page when it asks. You'll receive some interesting messages if you do.

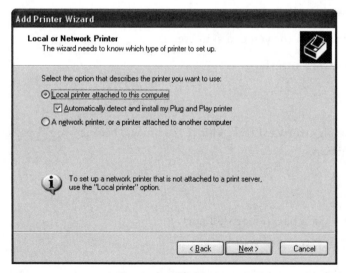

Figure 28-2 Installing a local printer

Step 3 In the following steps, you will set up a TCP/IP printer interface port for a Hewlett-Packard LaserJet printer with a built-in NIC (a technology Hewlett-Packard calls JetDirect). If you have access to a printer with a network interface, or your classroom is equipped with one, use the IP address or printer name of the printer when configuring the port. This will allow you to actually test the installation.

 a. In Windows XP, open the Printer & Faxes folder by way of Start | Control Panel | Printers & Faxes and launch the Add Printer Wizard by clicking *Add a printer* under Printer Tasks. On the welcome screen, click Next. In Windows Vista, go to Start | Control Panel | Printers. Right-click in the window and select Add Printer. In Windows 7, go to Start | Devices and Printers and click on *Add a printer*.

 b. While it may seem counterintuitive, select the local printer installation option again. Windows considers installing a printer via IP address as installing a "local" printer because it uses a "local" port.

 c. Click the *Create a new port* radio button and select Standard TCP/IP Port from the drop-down menu.

 d. In Windows XP, this launches the Add Standard TCP/IP Printer Port Wizard (see Figure 28-3). You'll see the same options in Windows Vista/7, but without the extra wizard. Click Next.

 e. In the Add Port dialog box, enter the IP address of the network printer. The Add Standard TCP/IP Printer Port Wizard (XP)/Add Printer Wizard (Vista/7) automatically creates the port name (see Figure 28-4). Click Next.

 f. If the IP address is fictitious, for the purpose of completing the lab steps, the Add Standard TCP/IP Printer Port Wizard (XP)/Add Printer Wizard (Vista/7) will be unable to identify the printing device. In the Additional Port Information Required dialog box, click the drop-down menu for Standard and select (in this case) Hewlett Packard JetDirect (see Figure 28-5). Click Next.

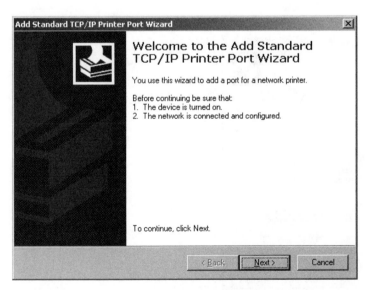

Figure 28-3 The Add Standard TCP/IP Printer Port Wizard

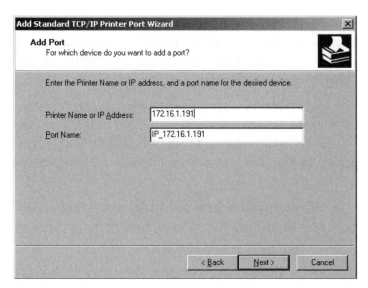

FIGURE 28-4 The TCP/IP address and port name of a network printer

    g.   Review the port characteristics and click Finish (see Figure 28-6).

    h.   You will now follow the steps through the Add Printer Wizard by selecting a printer from the list of printers or your driver disc as you did when directly connecting to the printer in Step 2.

✖ Warning

Again, if you are unable to install an actual print device for this exercise, don't print a test page. You'll receive some interesting messages if you try.

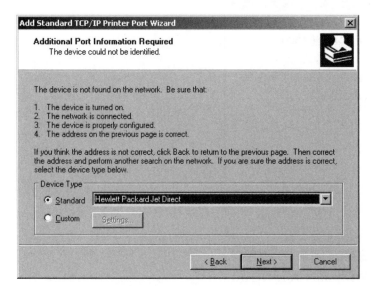

FIGURE 28-5 Selecting the Standard HP JetDirect device type

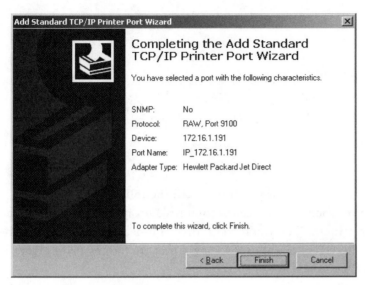

FIGURE 28-6 Port characteristics

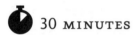 30 MINUTES

Lab Exercise 28.03: Maintaining and Troubleshooting Printers

It is estimated that technicians, especially those working for the help desk or desktop support group for a small- to medium-sized organization, spend approximately 30 percent of their time on printer issues. If you think about it, of all the components used in computing technology, printers have the highest percentage of moving parts. Moving parts are more likely to need maintenance than are static components.

Printers also like to be finicky and stop printing, usually resulting in a phone call from the client to the help desk for quick resolution. The following exercises will help you develop some understanding of laser printer and inkjet printer maintenance, and what steps to take when they stop printing.

Learning Objectives

In this lab, you'll research laser printer maintenance kits, clean dirty inkjet nozzles, and troubleshoot a failed print job.

At the end of this lab, you'll be able to

- Select a proper maintenance kit for various laser printers

- Clean and verify operation of inkjet nozzles

- Manage print jobs in Windows

- Restart a stalled print spooler

Lab Materials and Setup

The materials you need for this lab are

- A working computer with Windows installed

- A connection to the Internet

- Access to an inkjet printer

Getting Down to Business

The following exercises will round out your activities as you finish with the rollout of the five new printers in your office. You will want to get your Internet connection fired up again and research the maintenance kit available for your laser printer. Then you'll check the print-head nozzles of the inkjet printers and run the cleaning routine if necessary. Finally, you should prepare for any print errors so that you can correct them quickly and efficiently.

Step 1 Laser printers are, by design, highly precise machines. They typically move thousands of sheets of paper per month through the printing mechanism, placing 1200–1600 dots per inch (DPI) of toner on each page. As such, toner cartridges need to be replaced from time to time and parts that wear out need to be refurbished. Most manufacturers offer a maintenance kit for the printer to assist in the upkeep of the printer when these common parts age or fail. It would be a good idea to have a maintenance kit on hand for each model of laser printer in your organization.

✔ **Hint**

Most of the current manufacturers of laser printers—HP, Lexmark, Kyocera, Canon, and so forth—offer some form of maintenance kit for their printers. You should be able to find via an Internet search the available kits, their contents, and competitive pricing. Don't be surprised to find the maintenance kits somewhat costly, though they should still be only a fraction of the cost of replacing the printer.

Select a laser printer make and model, and perform an Internet search to identify the appropriate maintenance kit, its contents, and the average cost of the kit. Use this information to fill in the following items:

Printer model: _____

Maintenance kit: _____

Contents: _____

_____

Price: _____

Step 2 Though you have just installed new inkjet printers, if the printer sits idle for an extended period of time (a few weeks or months), or the ink cartridges have been replaced, you may need to check the print quality and clean the nozzles. The following steps were performed on an Epson Stylus PHOTO 890 in Windows XP but are similar to the steps required on HP and Lexmark inkjet printers. Consult the manual for specific instructions. Note that available maintenance options vary widely from printer to printer, so you will need to read the documentation that came with your printer.

✖ Warning

The nozzle cleaning process uses a fair amount of the expensive ink. If you are working on a personal inkjet printer, or one in the classroom, after printing the nozzle check page, run the nozzle cleaning process only if required.

a. Open the printer applet (whatever your version of Windows happens to call it) and select your inkjet printer.

b. In Windows XP, right-click the printer and select Properties. In Windows Vista/7, right-click the printer and select Printing Preferences.

c. In Windows XP, click the Printing Preferences button (see Figure 28-7).

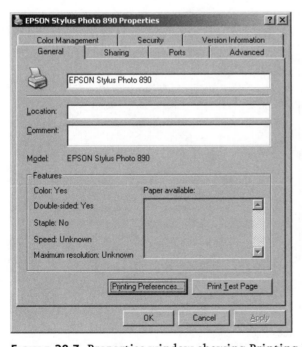

FIGURE 28-7 Properties window showing Printing Preferences button

d. Select the Utility tab (see Figure 28-8) and click Nozzle Check. This will print a test pattern using the cyan, yellow, magenta, and black ink nozzles.

e. If the printout is not clear or there are dropouts, click Head Cleaning to clear the nozzles and then return to the Nozzle Check to verify performance.

Step 3 When you are called upon to troubleshoot a failed print job, you should follow a logical step-by-step process to make sure that no obvious, possibly simple failure has occurred. If the power cord has been kicked out or the paper tray is open, troubleshooting the network connectivity or the printer driver would waste valuable time. Once you know the print device is online and ready and there are no paper jams or mechanical errors, it might be time to open the Print Manager and attempt to restart the document.

The following steps are meant to be a rough guideline to troubleshoot and diagnose a failed print job:

a. First, check the physical print device:

- Is the printer plugged in, and is the power turned on?

- Is the printer out of paper or is there a paper jam?

- Is the toner low or in need of replacement?

FIGURE 28-8 Utility tab under Printing Preferences

- Are there any error messages on the printer's LCD readout or any error indicator lights flashing?

- Is the printer online and ready to print?

    If you examine all of these areas and find everything appears to be in working condition, then you may have a problem with the connectivity between the computer and the printer, or there may be problems with the document or drivers.

b. Make sure that the connections between the computer and the printer are in good condition and securely fastened. These may be USB, Firewire, parallel, or UTP using RJ-45 connectors.

✔ Hint

To create a failed print job, disconnect the printer cable, shut the power off on the printer, or open the printer paper tray. If you do not have a physical printer, create a printer, following the steps in Lab Exercise 28.02. Send a print job to the printer; the printer icon should appear in the system tray and indicate that the print job has failed. Then continue with Step 3.

---

c. After checking all of the physical components, try to resend the document. Open the Print Manager by clicking the icon in the system tray/notification area.

    In the Print Manager, select the failed print job by highlighting the job with *Error* in the Status column (see Figure 28-9).

    Select Documents | Restart. If you are creating the printer problem, the printer icon in the system tray/notification area indicates that the print job has failed once again.

d. Highlight the document once again, and then select Documents | Cancel to delete the document.

If this were a real scenario, you would verify that the print drivers were installed and are the correct drivers for the operating system. You would then perform Step 4 to see if the problem is related to the print spooler.

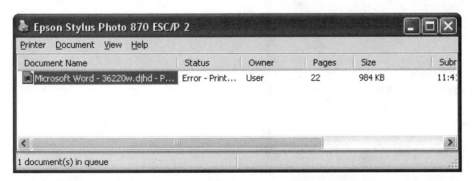

FIGURE 28-9 Print Manager showing error status on a Word file

Step 4   If the print device is online and ready, there are no paper jams or mechanical errors, and restarting the document is of no help, you can check to see if the print spooler is stalled. The print spooler is a holding area for print jobs and is especially important for network printers. If the print device runs out of paper while printing a document, you may have to stop and start the print spooler before the print device will receive jobs again.

In Chapter 18, you accomplished this task using the command line. Now you will use the Services snap-in for the Microsoft Management Console (MMC) to do the same thing, only more quickly and in a GUI.

   a.   Launch the Services console by opening Administrative Tools in the Control Panel and then double-clicking Services.

   b.   Scroll down and highlight Print Spooler. Select Action | Properties. You should see that the print spooler is started and running (see Figure 28-10).

   c.   Click the Stop button. The print spooler indicates that it has stopped.

   d.   Click the Start button. The print spooler indicates that it has started.

   e.   Alternatively, you can highlight Print Spooler in the Services console and select Action | Restart. You'll see a message stating that the print spooler is stopping, and then another message indicating that the print spooler is starting.

In the real-world scenario, your print spooler service would be restarted, and you should have a healthy, functioning print server once again.

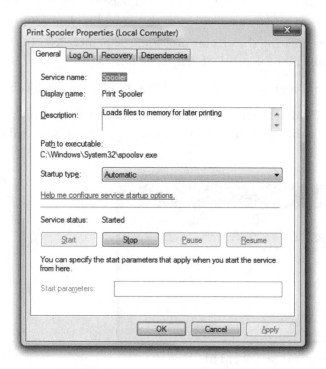

FIGURE 28-10 Print Spooler Properties dialog box

Lab Analysis Test

1. Patrick and Erik are having a small disagreement. Patrick says that printers can use numerous different interfaces, while Erik says that there are only two: parallel and USB. Who is correct? List the interfaces you are aware of and a typical use of each interface.

2. Theresa is using Windows and just purchased a printer from a friend. When she installs it using the original driver disc that came with the printer, it won't install properly. Why?

3. Danyelle has just joined a large organization as a level II tech and is tasked with the evaluation of all the laser printers in use. The business managers are concerned that all of the units will need to be replaced because of frequent paper jams and poor print quality. Danyelle makes her recommendations, and is actually awarded a bonus for saving the company money. What is her recommendation?

4. Brandon has sent a document to the printer, but the document never actually prints. Where can Brandon check to see the status of the document?

5. Why are laser toner cartridges so expensive?

Key Term Quiz

Use the following terms to complete the following sentences. Not all terms will be used.

dpi

ECP

IEEE 1284

impact

inkjet

laser

primary charge roller

primary corona

TCP/IP port

toner

transfer corona

transfer roller

USB

1. The part of the laser printer that actually causes the toner image to be created on the paper is the
_____ or _____.

2. To use a printer that's attached to the network with its own NIC, you must configure a(n)
_____.

3. The resolution of a printer is measured in _____.

4. The printer that spits ink onto the paper is a(n) _____ printer.

5. Printers with platens are _____ printers.

Chapter 29
Securing Computers

Lab Exercises

Obviously, keeping your computer secure is important. Several chapters have already been devoted to securing Windows and networks. But there are still a few more helpful tools you should know about to keep things running smoothly. Local Security Settings (also labeled Local Security Policy, sometimes in the same version of Windows) enables you to set a variety of rules about using the system; Event Viewer shows you information about events you didn't even know were happening; and Microsoft Security Essentials is a free tool that enables you to clean your system of, and protect your system against, viruses and other malicious software. Each of these tools increases the power you have over your own security and the security of your computer. You'll also learn how to handle a computer that has illegal materials on it or is part of a criminal investigation.

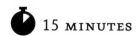 15 MINUTES

Lab Exercise 29.01: Configuring Local Policies

NTFS permissions are powerful tools to control with great detail what users and groups can do to folders and files. However, NTFS does not cover a number of important security issues that don't directly involve the file system. For example, what if you don't want a particular user group to shut down the computer? What if you want to make sure all accounts use a password of at least eight characters? What if you want to prevent certain users from reformatting the hard drive? These types of security settings are all controlled under the umbrella term of *local policies*.

✔ **Hint**

There are hundreds of different policies that you may configure for a system. This lab only covers a few of the most basic policies!

Learning Objectives

At the end of this lab, you'll be able to

- Locate and open the Local Security Policy/Settings utility

- Create, modify, and delete local policies with Windows

Lab Materials and Setup

The materials you need for this lab are

- A Windows PC with the C: drive formatted as NTFS

- Access to the local administrator password

Getting Down to Business

Local Security Settings is a very powerful applet that enables you to adjust all sorts of settings for and details about your system. Simply put, it is a series of rules you define, ranging from how many attempts to log on a user is allowed, to who can change the time on the clock!

Step 1   Log on using an account with administrator rights. From the Control Panel, open Administrative Tools. Double-click Local Security Policy. When opened, it should look something like Figure 29-1.

Double-click (or single-click in Windows Vista/7) the Account Policies icon to expand its contents: Password Policy and Account Lockout Policy. Click Password Policy in the left column, right-click *Password must meet complexity requirements* in the right column, and select Properties. Enable this policy, as shown in Figure 29-2, and click OK.

Create a normal user account and call it **Janet**. Try making a simple password like **janet** and see what happens. Keep trying to make a password until you get one that is accepted. What do you need to do to make an acceptable password? Hint: Use the help in the User Accounts Control Panel applet to get some ideas as to what you need to do.

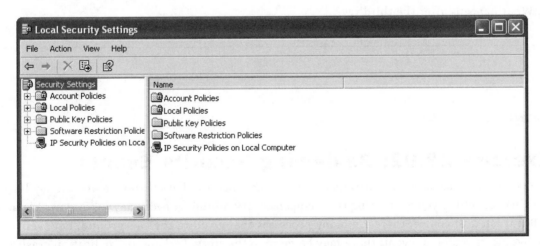

FIGURE 29-1 Local Security Settings in Windows XP

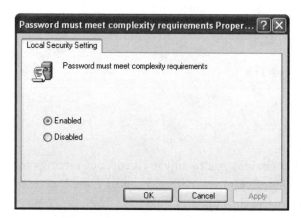

FIGURE 29-2 Enabling password complexity

Step 2 Head back to the Password Policy in Local Security Settings and enable Enforce Password History. Open the User Accounts applet from the Control Panel and try to change a password to the same password you already have. What happens?

_____

Step 3 In Local Security Settings, click Account Lockout Policy under Account Policies in the left column. An account lockout is when the operating system no longer allows a certain account the right even to try to log on. Try to change the properties on the *Account lockout duration* setting—it is disabled until you set the *Account lockout threshold* to something other than the default of 0. Try changing the *Account lockout threshold* to 3 attempts. Note that Windows now automatically sets the *Account lockout duration* and the *Reset account lockout counter after* settings to 30 minutes.

Log off the computer. Use the Janet account and intentionally attempt to log on using incorrect passwords. What happens after the third try?

_____

 20 MINUTES

Lab Exercise 29.02: Reviewing Security Events

With all the pop-ups, dialog boxes, and little message bubbles that Windows throws at you all day long, you would think it's telling you everything that happens every minute of every day—Windows Vista, doubly so. But it isn't. Of course, there are many processes that go on in the background, but even when Windows alerts you of an event, there may be more to the story. Perhaps an application crashes unexpectedly and Windows provides little or no feedback. It's possible that one tool in Administrative Tools took notice and can help—Event Viewer.

→ **Note**

You learned about Event Viewer in Chapter 19 as a troubleshooting tool. This lab shows you how it can also be used as a security awareness tool.

Learning Objectives

In this lab, you'll practice using Event Viewer.

At the end of this lab, you'll be able to

- Work with Event Viewer to track events on your system

Lab Materials and Setup

The materials you will need for this lab are

- A PC with Windows

Getting Down to Business

Think about your actions on a computer as a series of events: you log on, you open an application, you close it, you log off, and so forth. This is how Event Viewer sees things, but in a lot more detail. If something goes wrong, Event Viewer usually records it. It also records a lot of things that are perfectly normal—the trick is being able to sort through all the information, which Windows makes fairly simple.

Step 1 Access Event Viewer by going to the Control Panel and opening Administrative Tools. Double-click Event Viewer to open it (see Figure 29-3).

Step 2 Windows Vista/7 adds the extra step of expanding the Windows Logs folder in the left column and adding an Actions panel on the right side, but otherwise Event Viewer is very similar in each version of Windows. Four or five logs should be listed. The important one for now is Application; the events in this log all concern the operation of applications on your system. Click it in the left column and a long list of events should appear on the right.

Step 3 Scroll through the list and look at the different levels used by Windows to describe events (the Type column in Windows XP; the Level column in Windows Vista/7). Click the column label at the top of the list to sort the events by level. You should see a lot of events labeled Information. These are your everyday events—any successful operation, such as proper use of a driver, is marked as Information.

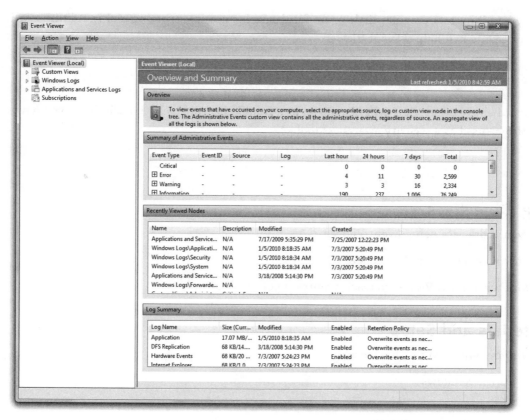

FIGURE 29-3 Event Viewer

Step 4 There might also be a few events labeled Warning or Error. Warnings do not indicate that something bad *is* happening but rather that something bad *will* happen. An example of a Warning event is when Windows is low on resources, such as disk space. Errors are more serious. These events occur when there is a failure or loss of functionality, such as when an application crashes.

Go through the list and see if you can find any Warnings or Errors. Double-click one and look at the Event Properties dialog box that pops up for more information on what happened. A lot of Event Viewer's reports can be very cryptic, which is why Windows Vista/7 now has a handy Event Log Online Help link built into Event Viewer. Clicking the link opens a dialog box asking for permission to send information about the event over the Internet. Your browser will open and take you to the Microsoft TechNet database. There isn't information available on every single event, but it can be very useful in tracking down problems.

If you don't have Windows Vista or Windows 7, you can always record the Event ID number that is listed with the event and search for it on the Internet. For example, if it is Event ID 1002, simply search for **"Event Viewer ID 1002"** and see what comes up. You're likely to find out at least a little more than you knew before.

Step 5 Search through the Security and System logs to see what sorts of events they record. In the Security logs, use the Task Category detail to see what each event records. Write down three Task Categories recorded by the Security log.

_____

_____

_____

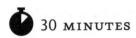 30 MINUTES

Lab Exercise 29.03: Cleaning and Protecting a Client's Computer

Geek Squad, the popular PC repair arm of Best Buy, reports that over 75 percent of their service calls involve cleaning malware off of a computer and then showing customers how to protect their PCs from malware and other attacks.

Windows comes with many programs and features to protect your computer, but these tools are useless if they are not used properly. In this lab exercise, you will check the computer for malware, clean the malware from the computer, and then go through the steps to reduce the likelihood of another attack.

Learning Objectives

At the end of this lab, you'll be able to

- Remove malware from a Windows system

- Configure Internet security software (antivirus/antimalware)

Lab Materials and Setup

The materials you need for this lab are

- A Windows XP (SP2 or later), Windows Vista, or Windows 7 PC

- Microsoft Security Essentials (or another Internet security suite)

✔ **Hint**

This is a great lab for students who want to bring a PC from home—or one that belongs to a friend—for testing and cleaning.

Getting Down to Business

A new system brings with it new problems. You've set up user accounts with passwords and activated firewalls, but there is still one more important piece of protection required. Antivirus and antimalware software can actively and passively protect you from unwanted malicious activity. Actively, you can usually scan entire computers for any issues. Passively, many tools are available that will constantly monitor your PC as you use it and watch out for viruses and other problems you may encounter on the Internet.

This lab will walk you through setting up Microsoft Security Essentials software, compatible with Windows XP (SP2 or later), Windows Vista, and Windows 7, available at www.microsoft.com/Security_Essentials/. There are, of course, other software solutions available, some of them free, but Microsoft's tool is fairly complete and multifunctional (and yes, free).

Step 1 The first step is to download the software (if you haven't already done so). When you open the executable, it will extract itself and begin the installation. Follow the instructions. Then it will run itself, update itself, and scan itself—it's all quite impressive to watch (see Figure 29-4).

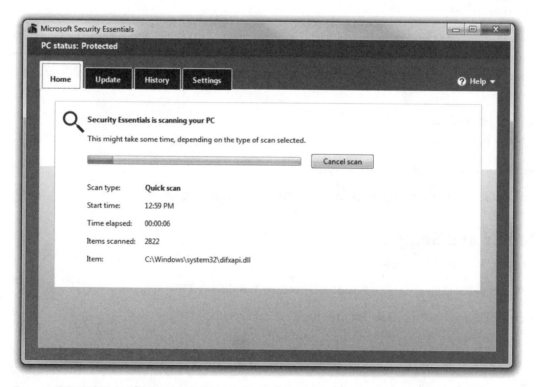

FIGURE 29-4 Microsoft Security Essentials performing a scan

Step 2 Microsoft Security Essentials will finish the scan and report its findings. It will give you the option to clean your computer or perform another action, but the defaults are usually correct. If a malicious file is found, the file can be quarantined or destroyed, and Microsoft Security Essentials will alert you when it has finished.

Step 3 Now that you've completed your initial scan, there are other options available to you. You can pick between running a Quick scan or a Full scan. A Full scan performs the same actions as the Quick scan, but also goes through the Registry. You can also set up a Custom scan to scan only certain directories.

The Update tab allows you to update virus and spyware definitions, although Microsoft Security Essentials also does this automatically. The History tab keeps track of all the potentially harmful items the software finds and what actions it performed. The Settings tab allows you to set up the program as you wish, including scheduling regular scans, setting what files and locations to exclude from scans, and adding removable drives to the scan (see Figure 29-5).

To add removable drives to the scan, under the Settings tab, click Advanced in the left column. Check the box for *Scan removable drives*. Microsoft Security Essentials will now scan the contents of each removable drive, such as USB thumb drives.

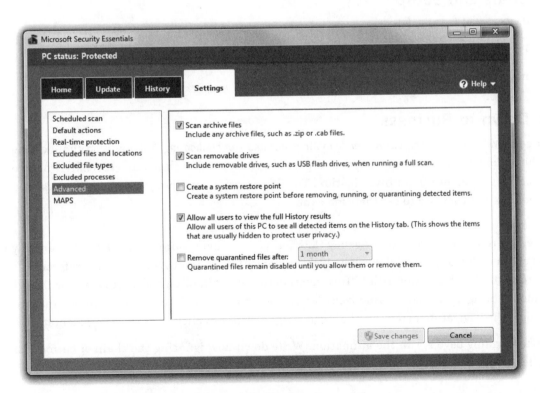

FIGURE 29-5 The Settings tab of Microsoft Security Essentials

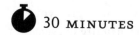 30 MINUTES

Lab Exercise 29.04: Protecting the Chain of Custody

When dealing with computers and electronics, any device you work on could have illegal or prohibited content on it. As a technician, you need to be able to identify any such material and then report it to the proper channels. One method of dealing with this sort of content is by following the chain of custody (CoC).

Learning Objectives

In this lab, you will identify the fundamentals of dealing with prohibited content and/or activity.

At the end of this lab, you will be able to

- Define the chain of custody

- Explain why you use the chain of custody

Lab Materials and Setup

The materials you need for this lab are

- A PC with Internet access

- A notepad and pen

Getting Down to Business

In Chapter 29 of *Mike Meyers' CompTIA A+ Guide to Managing and Troubleshooting PCs*, you read that dealing with prohibited content can be a very important part of your job as a technician, especially when your equipment becomes evidence in an investigation. This lab exercise will give you a better understanding of the procedures that they use to get their job done.

Step 1   The Environmental Protection Agency (EPA), as part of their training materials, has an easy-to-understand chain of custody tutorial on their Web site (www.epa.gov/apti/coc/) that I'll reference for this lab exercise. Under the section titled "Introduction to the Chain of Custody," click on the Overview link. This should bring up a smaller window, titled Introduction to Chain of Custody. Time for some reading! Follow the navigation arrows in the bottom-right corner to click through the presentation.

a.   After reading page 2, run the animation. Write down how ignoring the chain of custody has affected the court case.

_____

_____

b. Using your own words, define chain of custody.

_____

_____

c. In what four situations are samples and data legally considered to be in your custody?

_____

_____

_____

_____

d. The presentation lists quite a few guidelines for how to conduct chain-of-custody procedures. List the three you feel are the most important from the guidelines given.

_____

_____

_____

Step 2 After going through the presentation on chain-of-custody procedures, answer the following questions.

a. When should you follow chain-of-custody procedures?

_____

b. Why should you follow chain-of-custody procedures?

_____

Lab Analysis Test

1. While browsing the Internet, Maxel has been getting a lot more pop-ups lately. He assumes he has some kind of adware on his system. What should he do to fix this?

2. Jason is working on a document when Word crashes. Which log in Event Viewer will give him more information? Which level would it be most likely identified as?

3. In the Local Security Policy/Settings applet, what does *Account lockout threshold* control?

4. What is the path used in Windows 7 to access the Security log in Event Viewer?

5. What are two methods of learning more about a particular event in Event Viewer?

Key Term Quiz

Use the following terms to complete the following sentences. Not all terms will be used.

adware

antivirus program

chain of custody

definition file

event auditing

Event Viewer

incidence reporting

Local Security Policy/Settings

object access auditing

phishing

polymorph virus

pop-up

spam

spyware

Trojan

virus

worm

1. _____ is a type of unsolicited e-mail that usually contains hoaxes and get-rich-quick schemes.

2. A(n) _____ appears as a new window in front of whatever application you are using.

3. It is necessary to have a(n) _____ to protect your computer from malicious programs and other malware.

4. _____ keeps track of every event that occurs on your system and assigns it a level, such as Information or Warning.

5. A piece of malicious software that gets passed from computer to computer is known most generically as a(n) _____.

Chapter 30
Virtualization

Lab Exercises

Virtualization is the latest big trend in computing. Using virtual machines, you can run an entire virtual operating system on top of your existing OS. If you have Windows 7 installed, for example, you can download a virtualization application like VMware Player or Oracle VM VirtualBox, install Ubuntu Linux on it, and run Ubuntu inside Windows! The difference between software and hardware gets confusing when you realize that the virtual OS uses virtual hardware to re-create virtually everything in the system case beneath your desk.

Virtualization promotes efficient use of hardware and energy resources, and also enables you to easily create images of the virtual machine, providing excellent fault tolerance and disaster recovery options.

In this chapter, you'll explore some of the features of common virtual machine technologies, install a virtual machine on your PC, and then use Windows Virtual PC to set up a special virtual machine called Windows XP Mode.

In Lab Exercises 30.02 and 30.03, you will be using virtualization software to create virtual machines. Virtual machines are exactly like physical computers in that they need operating systems to work. Prior to beginning the lab exercises, you will want to prepare the operating system installation media. Lab Exercise 30.02 requires a copy of Ubuntu Linux and Lab Exercise 30.03 uses Windows XP Mode, which requires Windows 7 Professional, Ultimate, or Enterprise. Ubuntu 10.04 LTS (Long-Term Support) will be supported for five years, from April 2010 to April 2015, and is a free Linux distribution. It can be downloaded at www.ubuntu.com. Create an installation disc or copy the installation disc image (.iso) to a flash drive for use in the lab exercises. You can find instructions for this procedure on the Ubuntu Web site.

 20 MINUTES

Lab Exercise 30.01: Identifying Virtualization Technologies

As discussed in the introduction to this chapter, virtualization takes on many aspects of the physical devices used every day in the computing environment. Organizations may choose to install multiple virtual servers on one physical machine to handle Web services, e-mail services, file sharing, and print services, to name a few. Before you work with the actual virtualization programs and before you take the CompTIA A+ certification exams, you will want to explore all of the technologies associated with virtualization.

Time to explore!

Learning Objectives

At the end of this lab, you'll be able to

- Define virtual desktop technologies
- Define virtual server technologies

Lab Materials and Setup

The materials you need for this lab are

- A PC with Internet access

Getting Down to Business

You will actually install and configure a number of virtualization technologies and operating systems in the next few lab exercises. Before you do, it is important that you understand the underlying solutions that virtualization technology provides. In this lab, you will use your textbook and the Internet to develop a brief description and summary of the characteristics of the virtualization technologies.

Step 1 Start by researching virtual desktop technology. There's plenty of information to be found using Google. Use keywords like "virtualization" or "VMware" (a popular brand) to locate good information. What are they key features of most virtual desktops?

_____

_____

_____

_____

Step 2 Virtual servers are similar to virtual desktops but provide some advanced features and support for applications not found in the virtual desktop offerings. Describe the differences between a virtual desktop and a virtual server.

_____

_____

_____

_____

 45 MINUTES

Lab Exercise 30.02: Installing and Configuring VMware Player

VMware is arguably one of the leading developers of virtualization applications. To introduce you to VMware, you will download VMware Player and install it on a Windows 7 machine, and then you will run Ubuntu Linux in the virtual machine. You'll see what it's like running a second OS inside your native OS.

Learning Objectives

In this lab exercise, you will use VMware Player virtualization software to install a virtual Ubuntu machine on a Windows 7 PC. You will then navigate a few of the Ubuntu programs and commands.

At the end of this lab, you'll be able to

- Install and configure VMware Player on a Windows 7 host system

- Install and run Ubuntu 10.04 LTS as a virtual operating system in VMware Player

Lab Materials and Setup

The materials you need for this lab are

- A system connected to the Internet or access to VMware Player

- Ubuntu installation media

- A Windows 7 system

Getting Down to Business

You will be working with the VMware Player application to install a virtual operating system.

Step 1 Launch your browser and navigate to www.vmware.com, the home of VMware. Move your pointer over the Support & Downloads tab at the top of the page. Go to the Product Downloads menu and select All Downloads. Click on VMware Player, listed under the Desktop & End-User Computing category. On the VMware Player page, click the Download button as shown in Figure 30-1. To download VMware Player, you will have to register using your e-mail address. Complete the registration and download the latest version of VMware Player for Windows. Once downloaded, proceed to launch the setup file to install the application.

Step 2 At the Welcome to the installation wizard for VMware Player screen, click Next (see Figure 30-2).

The next screen is the Destination Folder screen, where you may choose the default location or select Change to install in a different folder. Choose the default location or change the folder where the VMware Player program will be installed.

Click Next once again, choose the checkbox to *Check for product updates on startup*, and click Next. Now uncheck the checkbox to *Help improve VMware Player* and click Next. Select where you would like to create shortcuts for VMware Player, and click Next.

Now you will see the window Ready to Perform the Requested Operations. Click Continue to begin the process. VMware Player setup will perform the installation. This may take several minutes.

You will now be instructed that the setup wizard needs to restart your system. Click Restart Now to reboot the Windows machine.

FIGURE 30-1 The VMware Player download page on the VMware Web site

FIGURE 30-2 VMware Player 4 welcome screen

Step 3 Now you will launch the VMware Player, create a new virtual machine, and use Easy Install to automatically install Ubuntu on the new virtual machine. Perform the tasks in the following instructions to create a new virtual machine.

a. Double-click the VMware Player icon and accept the VMware End User License Agreement.

b. At the Welcome to VMware Player screen, click the Create a New Virtual Machine icon to create a new virtual machine. This will launch the New Virtual Machine Wizard (see Figure 30-3).

c. At this screen, you will choose where to install the operating system from. You are going to use the Easy Install method, installing the operating system as you build the virtual machine. Using your Ubuntu installation media, either insert the optical disc into the system, choose the *Installer*

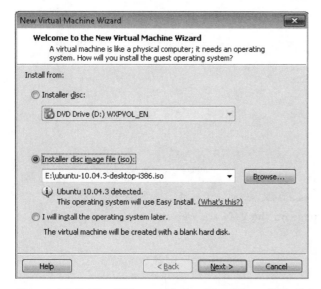

FIGURE 30-3 The VMware Player New Virtual Machine Wizard

disc radio button, and select the optical drive from the drop-down menu, or choose the *Installer disc image file (iso:)* option and browse to the disc image. Click Next.

d.   Now you will set up a user name and password for the Ubuntu virtual operating system. Enter the full name **Student** in the dialog box. Then enter the user name **student** in lowercase and enter a password of your choosing. Click Next.

e.   You will now name the virtual machine and choose the location for the virtual machine folder. You may use the defaults or change the name and location. Click Next.

f.   Specify the disk capacity. The recommended size for Ubuntu is 20 GB. Leave the default setting for *Split virtual disk into multiple files* and click Next, splitting the virtual disk (vmdk) into multiple, smaller files. This helps facilitate copying the virtual machine to other media such as a flash drive.

g.   Now you are ready to create the virtual machine. Review the virtual machine settings as shown in Figure 30-4, check the box *Power on this virtual machine after creation*, and then click Finish to begin building the virtual machine.

h.   Depending on your physical hardware, you will receive several hints:

   •   VMware Player requires a 64-bit processor to run a 64-bit virtual operating system. Click OK.

   •   Removable media, such as flash drives, cannot be mounted to both the host operating system and the guest operating system simultaneously. You may mount the removable media at a later time. Click OK to accept the default.

i.   If your machine is connected to the Internet, you may choose to install VMware Tools for Ubuntu. VMware Tools is a suite of utilities that enhances the performance of the virtual machine's operating system and improves management of the virtual machine.

   If you choose to install the tools at a later time, you will receive an error message at the bottom of the VMware Player window when the system boots. You may ignore this for the lab exercise.

FIGURE 30-4 VMware Player new virtual machine summary page

Step 4 When the VMware Ubuntu virtual machine reboots, you will be prompted for your user name and password. After entering your information, you will now have a fully functioning installation of Ubuntu as a virtual operating system on top of the host operating system. To explore some of the features of VMware Player, complete the following steps:

a. Insert a flash drive into the physical host machine.

b. At the top of the VMware Ubuntu virtual machine window, click on the Virtual Machine tab item to open a drop-down menu.

c. Click on Removable Devices and, from the expanded menu, choose the flash drive (it may identify the manufacturer, such as SanDisk Cruzer) and select Connect (Disconnect from host). You will receive the message "A USB device is about to be unplugged from the host and connected to this virtual machine." Click OK.

d. Now in the Ubuntu system, click Places and navigate down to the Computer icon. Click Computer to open the window. Do you see the icon for the flash drive? (See Figure 30-5.)

FIGURE 30-5 Ubuntu running in a VMware Player virtual machine on Windows 7. Note the flash drive icon.

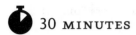 30 MINUTES

Lab Exercise 30.03: Installing and Configuring Windows XP Mode and Windows Virtual PC

As is fairly typical with Microsoft, if there is a technology related to computer applications or operating systems, they have probably designed a product to compete in the market. This is the case with virtualization. To this end, Microsoft offers Windows Virtual PC.

Microsoft has continued to offer their Virtual PC virtualization software with the inclusion of Windows XP Mode in Windows 7 to facilitate running legacy programs on a virtual machine running Windows XP, rather than in a "compatibility mode."

✔ **Tech Tip**

Microsoft is very particular with the distribution of Windows XP Mode and Windows Virtual PC. These products will only install on the following systems: Windows 7 Professional, Windows 7 Ultimate, or Windows 7 Enterprise. In addition, you will have to download and install a Windows Activation Update, which is automatically launched when you begin the steps to download Windows XP Mode and Windows Virtual PC.

Learning Objectives

In this lab exercise, you will install Windows Virtual PC and then install Windows XP Mode (a preconfigured Windows XP Professional virtual machine).

At the end of this lab, you'll be able to

- Install Windows Virtual PC
- Install and configure Windows XP Mode on a Windows 7 system

Lab Materials and Setup

The materials you need for this lab are

- Windows 7 Professional, Enterprise, or Ultimate
- Internet connectivity

Getting Down to Business

To facilitate legacy applications in Windows 7, Microsoft introduced the Windows XP Mode virtual machine. Windows XP Mode (XPM) is a virtual machine package for Windows Virtual PC containing a preinstalled, licensed copy of Windows XP Professional with Service Pack 3 as its virtual operating system.

The Windows XP Mode virtual machine is seamlessly integrated into Windows 7 and offers "one-click launch of Windows XP Mode applications."

In this lab, you will install Windows XP Mode and Windows Virtual PC and evaluate their functionality.

Step 1   Boot a Windows 7 Professional, Ultimate, or Enterprise system, launch your browser, and navigate to www.microsoft.com/windows/virtual-pc/default.aspx. Click on *Get Windows XP Mode and Windows Virtual PC now*, then select your system and language as shown in Figure 30-6. After you have entered your operating system and language information, a list of four steps will be displayed.

Use the following instructions to complete the four steps:

a.   In Step 1, it is recommended that you either e-mail or print the instructions before restarting your computer.

b.   In Step 2, click the Windows XP Mode Download button to begin the download. Microsoft will install an Activation Update and run a Windows validation process. Once the validation process completes successfully, click Continue and save the file WindowsXPMode_en-us.exe.

c.   In Step 3, click the Windows Virtual PC Download button and save the file Windows6.1KB958559-x86-RefreshPkg.msu.

d.   You will only need to perform Step 4 if you are running Windows 7 without Service Pack 1 (SP1) installed. If you are not running SP1, click on the Windows XP Mode Update button. Verify that all of the required files are in the Download folder and close the browser window.

✔ Hint

Earlier versions of Windows 7 and Windows Virtual PC required Hardware Assisted Virtualization Technology. Step 4 enables Windows XP Mode for PCs without Hardware Assisted Virtualization Technology. If you are running Windows 7 with Service Pack 1 (SP1), you will not be required to run Step 4.

Step 2   Click Start | Computer | Downloads and launch the Windows6.1-KB958559-x86-RefreshPkg.msu installation file located in the Downloads folder, as shown in Figure 30-7.

Depending on the version of Windows 7, you will either install the x86 (32-bit) or the x64 (64-bit) Windows Virtual PC Update installation file. Some versions of Windows 7 also ship with Windows Virtual PC preinstalled. If your system displays the message "The update is not applicable to your computer," as shown in Figure 30-8, then check your Start | All Programs menu to see if Windows Virtual PC is already installed. What are your results?

FIGURE 30-6 The Windows Virtual PC page

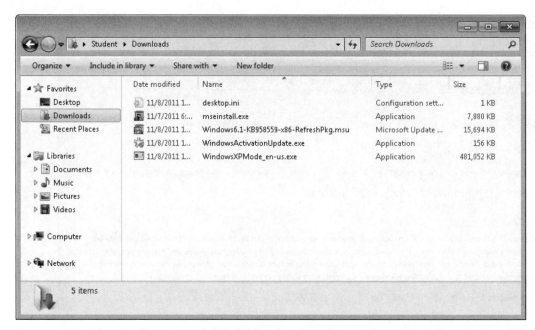

FIGURE 30-7 The Windows Downloads folder showing the Windows Virtual PC Update file and the Windows XP Mode file

If Windows Update KB958559 (Windows Virtual PC) was not previously installed, follow these directions to install it:

a. Select Yes to install the Update for Windows (KB958559).

b. Read and accept the license terms to begin the installation.

c. When the installation has completed, you will be instructed to restart your computer for the updates to take effect. Click Restart Now.

Step 3 After your computer reboots, you will install the Windows XP Mode virtual machine. Open Start | Computer | Downloads and double-click the WindowsXPMode_en-us.exe file located in the Downloads folder, as shown earlier in Figure 30-7. Perform the installation directions as follows:

a. Select Run when you receive the Open File – Security Warning.

b. In the Welcome to Setup for Windows XP Mode screen, click Next.

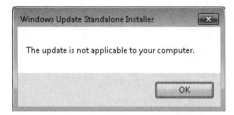

FIGURE 30-8 Windows Update Standalone Installer message

c. Select the default location of C:\Program Files\Windows XP Mode\ and click Next.

d. When the setup completes, uncheck Launch Windows XP Mode and click Finish.

Step 4   You will now install and configure Windows XP in the Windows XP Mode virtual machine.

a. Click Start | All Programs | Windows Virtual PC | Windows XP Mode to begin the Windows XP Mode Setup wizard.

b. Accept the license terms and click Next.

c. Select the installation folder and enter a password for the XPMUser, as shown in Figure 30-9, and click Next.

d. Next, you can choose to activate Automatic Updates, which will help protect your computer. Choose either *Help protect my computer by turning on Automatic Updates now (recommended)* or *Not right now* and then click Next.

e. Click Start Setup to start the Windows XP Mode setup. This will take a few minutes, and while setting up, the wizard will display some features of Window XP Mode and the steps that are being performed.

f. When the setup completes, check the box to launch the Windows XP Mode virtual machine, and then click Finish. The Windows XP Mode virtual machine will launch, as shown in Figure 30-10.

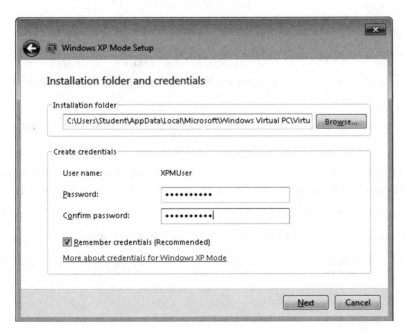

Figure 30-9 Installation folder and credentials window in the Windows XP Mode Setup

FIGURE 30-10 Windows XP Mode – Windows Virtual PC

Lab Analysis Test

1. Matthew has worked through the lab exercises in this chapter, but he is still unclear about the exact differences between a virtual desktop and a virtual server. Detail some of the characteristics of each to help Matthew with his studies.

2. Create three short examples that help to explain why someone might use virtualization in the workplace.

3. While downloading VMware Player, Jonathan notices some of the other free products that VMware offers. He asks if you know the differences between the various offerings. Using the Web site www.vmware.com, write a short description of each of the free products that VMware offers.

4. What are some of the hardware requirements for running virtual machines on a PC?

5. What are the primary differences between VMware's products and Microsoft's Windows Virtual PC/ Windows XP Mode packages?

Key Term Quiz

Use the following terms to complete the following sentences. Not all terms will be used.

bare-metal virtual machine

hosted virtual machine

hypervisor

snapshot

virtual desktop

virtual machine manager (VMM)

virtual server

VMware Player

Windows Virtual PC

1. The two terms typically used to describe virtualization software are _____ and _____.

2. VMware has established itself as one of the leaders in the virtualization software market. It currently offers two free products. One of these is called _____.

3. When working with virtual machines, one of the convenience features is to be able to take a(n) _____ to capture the current configuration of the machine.

4. Typically, when building a virtual server, the virtualization software is going to be of the _____ variety. This is also known as a "native" virtual machine.

5. Windows XP Mode uses _____ to run a virtual version of Windows XP.

Chapter 31

The Right PC for You

Lab Exercises

Picking the right PC is a very personal choice, but the number of PCs available can make the search overwhelming. CompTIA, in their infinite wisdom, has decided to break down and categorize the different types of computers that users can choose from. Depending on the type of work that a user does, you need to be able to point them to a PC that can fill that role. Think of it as being similar to picking out an automobile. Some people need a truck with four-wheel drive and a huge bed for hauling equipment, while others need a small, compact car for city driving. In this chapter, we'll research a few different types of computers using the Internet and explore their differences.

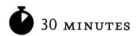 30 MINUTES

Lab Exercise 31.01: Building a Thick Client

The thick client is a strange beast, mostly because techs rarely use the term "thick client." Techs only refer to a thick client when comparing it to its smaller sibling, the thin client. Both thin and thick clients exist in a client/server network environment, where PCs connect to a central server to access resources. Depending on the workload, you may want to let your local workstation bear some of the burden of processing, keeping your applications locally stored on your thick client. On the other hand, the thin client can be very light on processing capability. It relies heavily on the server to store the applications and, in some cases, even process the data. In reality, a thick client is just the good old-fashioned PC we all love. It can run the Windows operating system and just about any standard desktop application you throw at it.

Learning Objective

In this exercise, you'll research what it takes to create a standard thick client.

At the end of this lab, you'll be able to

• Find parts for a standard thick client by using the Internet

Lab Materials and Setup

The materials you need for this lab are

• An Internet-capable PC for research

Getting Down to Business

By Chapter 31, you've had quite an adventure, learning about all the different aspects of computing. You've seen everything from microprocessors to power supplies, from Microsoft Windows to video cards. Now it's time to put all that experience to the test. You will research the parts for a fully functional thick client. Here is the list of criteria your PC must meet to qualify as a thick client:

- Runs the latest Windows operating system

- Runs standard desktop applications such as Microsoft Office and Internet Explorer

- Network connectivity

- Storage (SSD or HDD)

- Monitor

- Keyboard and mouse

Step 1   Open a Web browser and visit a Web site from which you can purchase computer parts. Suggestions include:

- www.newegg.com

- www.tigerdirect.com

- www.cdw.com

Your instructor will set a price limit for you. You don't want to make a high-end gaming machine—at least not yet! If this is a self-guided course, then set a limit of $650. That should keep you in the realm of the thick client.

Step 2   Shop for the parts listed in the following table and complete the other columns for each component you choose.

Part	Model/Version	Web Site	Price
Motherboard			
CPU			
RAM			
Hard drive			
Optical drive			
Power supply			
Case			
Mouse			
Keyboard			
Monitor			
Windows OS			
Video card (optional)			

Step 3   Add up all the prices for your parts.

Grand total: _____

If you went over budget, find less expensive parts for your components and try to cut some corners to make that perfect thick client computer.

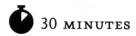 30 MINUTES

Lab Exercise 31.02: Building a Gaming PC

In Lab Exercise 31.01, you priced the parts for a standard thick client computer. Now let's have a little more fun and see what we need to build a gaming PC. Everything will be very similar to the previous exercise when picking out your parts, but with a special twist: your PC will need to be able to handle some of the most hardware-intensive applications on the market.

Learning Objective

In this exercise, you'll research what it takes to create a gaming PC.

At the end of this lab, you'll be able to

- Find components for a gaming PC by using the Internet

Lab Materials and Setup

The materials you need for this lab are

- An Internet-capable PC for research

Getting Down to Business

Creating a gaming computer takes all the knowledge you gained from creating a thick client, plus the following additional requirements to make it a gaming PC:

- Runs the latest Windows operating system
- Powerful CPU (high clock speed and multiple cores)
- Network connectivity
- Storage (SSD or HDD)
- 22-inch monitor
- Keyboard and mouse

- High-capacity RAM

- High-end graphics card

- High-end sound card

- High-end cooling system

Step 1 Open a Web browser and visit a Web site from which you can purchase computer parts. Suggestions include:

- www.newegg.com

- www.tigerdirect.com

- www.cdw.com

Just like in the previous lab exercise, the instructor will set a price limit for you. If this is a self-guided course, then set a limit of $1500. In a perfect world, I would give you an unlimited budget to get all the highest-end components in the world, and while it's always fun to be a dreamer, I want to show you a realistic, everyday gaming machine.

Step 2 Shop for the parts listed in the following table and complete the other columns for each component you choose.

Part	Model/Version	Web Site	Price
Motherboard			
CPU			
After-market CPU cooler			
RAM			
Hard drive			
Optical drive			
Power supply			
Case			
Mouse			
Keyboard			
Monitor			
Windows OS			
Video card(s)			
Sound card			
Speaker/headphones			

Step 3   Fill in the following table with any additional parts you might need to purchase, such as fans, lights, or fans with lights!

Model	Web Site	Price	Qty.

Step 4   Now, add up all the prices for your parts.

Grand total: _____

Did you go over the price limit of $1500 or the price set by your instructor? If you went over your budget, maybe you need to get some lower-capacity RAM or let go of a graphics card, if you went with an SLI or CrossFire setup. Do what you need to do to fall within the price limit.

Step 5   Now, let's take a look and see if the power supply you chose will actually power your computer. There are many power supply calculators online that will show you how much wattage you need to power your components. Open your Web browser, go to your favorite search engine, and search for "power supply calculator." You can also just go to this Web site, which I use all the time: http://extreme.outervision. com/psucalculatorlite.jsp. Fill in the calculator with your gaming PC's specifications.

Does the power supply you chose supply enough wattage for your gaming rig? If so, how much wattage do you have left over?

_____

→ **Note**

When building your gaming PC, you'll need a power supply that can properly power all of your high-end components.

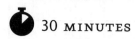 30 MINUTES

Lab Exercise 31.03: Building a Home Theater PC

These days, computers are used not only to check e-mail, create documents, and play video games, but also to view pictures, listen to music, and watch TV shows and movies. To really take advantage of your media collection, you need a PC that can integrate with your home theater setup (if you have one).

The market for home theater boxes is still young, but there are a lot of options. Apple TV, Roku, Windows Media Center, and XBMC are all designed to take your media and put it on your television. With so many options, your client might need help picking out the right parts. This lab exercise explores the criteria of what comprises a home theater PC.

Learning Objective

In this exercise, you'll research what it takes to create a home theater PC.

At the end of this lab, you'll be able to

- Find components for a home theater PC using the Internet
- Use Windows Media Center and XBMC

Lab Materials and Setup

The materials you need for this lab are

- An Internet-capable PC for research
- A Windows operating system with Media Center installed

Getting Down to Business

To create a home theater PC, you will use many of the components that you used in the previous lab exercises in this chapter. I am not going to list all of those parts again here, but rather just list the specific components necessary to build a home theater PC:

- Sufficiently powerful CPU and RAM to run your operating system
- Enough storage for your OS and media
- Network connectivity
- Wireless keyboard/mouse combo
- Graphics with HDMI output
- HTPC case (ATX, microATX, ITX)
- TV tuner card
- Blu-ray Disc drive

Step 1 Open a Web browser and visit a Web site from which you can purchase computer parts. Suggestions include:

- www.newegg.com
- www.tigerdirect.com
- www.cdw.com

Step 2 Shop for the parts listed in the following table and complete the other columns for each component you choose.

Part	Model/Version	Web Site	Price
HTPC case			
Motherboard with built-in HDMI			
TV tuner			
Surround sound speakers with receiver			
Blu-ray drive			
Wireless keyboard			
Wireless mouse			
Video card with HDMI (optional)			

Step 3 Now that you have found the components for your home theater PC, you need a way of getting your media onto that 70-inch flat screen TV you own (right?)! I want to show you two different options. One is included with some versions and editions of Windows, while the other is a free download that works with any copy of Windows. Let's first take a quick tour of Windows Media Center.

→ **Note**

Don't confuse Windows Media Center with Windows Media Player. They are entirely different.

To use Windows Media Center, you need one of the following operating systems:

- Windows XP Media Center Edition
- Windows Vista Home Premium or Ultimate
- Windows 7 Home Premium, Professional, Enterprise, or Ultimate

→ **Note**

Microsoft has announced that they will drop built-in DVD playback in Windows 8 and that Media Center will only be available as a paid add-on.

a. Using the appropriate version of Windows, open Windows Media Center. When you open it for the first time, you are given the choice of an Express or Custom installation (see Figure 31-1). Click on Custom.

b. Click Next at the Windows Media Center setup screen.

FIGURE 31-1 The Windows Media Center Get Started screen

c. Choose whether or not you want to join the Customer Experience Improvement Program. This sends data back to Microsoft so that they can improve Media Center. Click Next.

d. The next screen asks if you want to download periodic updates to your cover art collection and TV listings. Click Yes, and then click Next.

e. Media Center will tell you that you have finished installing the required components. Click Next.

f. Media Center will prompt you with a choice to set up several features further. You can configure these options later, so click the option to finish, and then click Next.

g. You have now configured Windows Media Center. You can visit the Settings area to configure additional options, such as where your media libraries are located, and to configure your TV tuner to get a signal to watch what is on TV. Media Center guides you through it all.

Step 4   Another popular option for how to present your media is called XBMC (unofficially known as the Xbox Media Center). Some crafty people modified the original Xbox to add a media center, hence the name. It has since grown into an open source project that can be run on just about any operating system available. (It can even run as a live CD.) To get XBMC, visit www.xbmc.org and follow these steps:

a. Move your mouse pointer over the Downloads link then click Get XBMC.

b. Choose the operating system on which you are installing XBMC and wait for the download to finish. It's a pretty big file. Depending on your Internet connection speed, it might take a while.

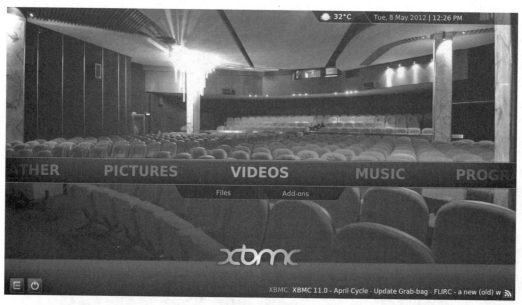

FIGURE 31-2 XBMC running with the default skin

c.   Once it has finished downloading, run the setup file and follow through the installation instructions. Then run XBMC (see Figure 31-2).

d.   At first glance, XBMC looks overwhelming—you can change just about anything in XBMC. Take some time to get acquainted with the interface. I don't use the mouse in XBMC. Using the keyboard feels more like using a remote control as you would in a traditional home theater. Highlight SYSTEM using the arrow keys and press ENTER.

e.   The System menu hides the real power of XBMC. It has so many configurable options, I could write an entire book on just this menu! Go to Add-ons and press ENTER (see Figure 31-3).

FIGURE 31-3 The Add-ons screen in XBMC

f.   Add-ons are exactly what they sound like. They add extra functionality to XBMC, such as watching YouTube or Hulu within the media center. Select Enabled Add-ons and press ENTER.

g.   Select Skin and press ENTER. What is the name of the default skin in XBMC?

_____

h.   Press BACKSPACE twice to return the Add-ons screen. Select Get Add-ons and press ENTER. Press ENTER again for XBMC.org Add-ons.

i.   Go to Skin and press ENTER to view the choices (see Figure 31-4).

j.   Look at all the skins available! And these are just the ones that are built into the default add-on packages. There are countless users out there who are making skins that might suit your personal taste. This, right here, is where XBMC shines. Find a skin that fits your style, press ENTER, then select Install. Press ENTER again. XBMC will download and install the skin.

k.   Once the skin has downloaded, answer the prompt by selecting Yes to switch the skin. Press the BACKSPACE key as many times as needed to return to the main screen.

l.   If you don't like the skin you chose, go back to Step 4d and try again.

m.   Which skin did you like the most?

_____

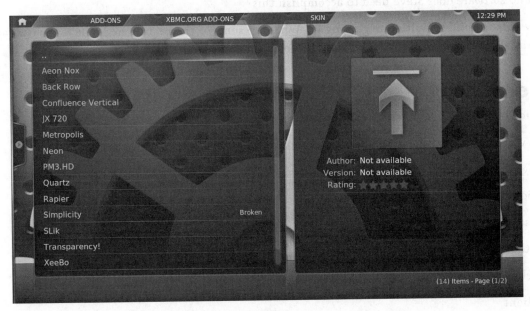

FIGURE 31-4 The list of available skins in XBMC

n. Once you have found your skin, take some time to experiment and explore by adding folders to the VIDEOS and MUSIC menus.

o. Remember, XBMC is an open source project. You can find documentation and walkthroughs for this application with a quick search in your favorite search engine. Have fun with it!

→ **Note**

The creators of XBMC release regular updates for the media center software. The steps outlined in this lab exercise may not lead to the same options in future updates.

Lab Analysis Test

1. Bruce wants to build a computer that specializes in audio/video editing. What can you tell him about that type of workstation that makes it unique?

2. Tony wants to build a home server PC. What features will it need to have in order to be a good home server?

3. Natasha is trying to decide if she should have thin clients or thick clients attached to the network. Explain the similarities and differences between thin and thick clients.

4. Steve wants to watch TV, broadcast over the air, on his computer in his living room. What hardware and software does Steve need to accomplish this?

5. Clint wants to build the ultimate gaming PC. What are some of the requirements he'll need as far as hardware is concerned for have the gaming PC of his dreams?

Key Term Quiz

Use the following terms to complete the following sentences. Not all terms will be used.

audio/video editing workstation

gaming PC

graphics workstation

home server PC

home theater PC

thick client

thin client

TV tuner

virtualization workstation

Windows Media Center

XBMC

1. A(n) _____ is a type of computer that connects to a server on a network. It offloads much of the processing to the server. In many situations, this computer doesn't even have a hard drive.

2. A(n) _____ is a powerful computer that is used with applications like Adobe Photoshop, Adobe Premiere, and Autodesk SketchBook Pro.

3. A(n) _____ is a computer that can run a second "guest" operating system on top of another operating system, sharing the hardware resources of one computer.

4. A computer that has RAID functionality along with the ability to stream media to other workstations on the network is most likely a(n) _____.

5. By installing a(n) _____, you will have the ability to watch over-the-air television on your computer.

Chapter 32
The Complete PC Tech

Lab Exercises

At this point you're well on your path to becoming a CompTIA A+ certified technician. You have an excellent understanding of the major technical aspects of computer systems: hardware, software, networking, and the Internet.

When a client launches an application, that person isn't thinking about what happens behind the scenes: "Hey, look at me! I'm using the keyboard and mouse to input data! The processor is calculating all of the information to produce the desired results and present the output on the screen or in hard copy form on a printer. This is only possible because the operating system, applications, and data were successfully stored on the hard drive." You, as the tech, *do* have to think about all of this, but you also need the user's perspective. When you look at the computer system as a whole—that is, as a practical tool that can create and process everything from your résumé to the latest Hollywood thriller—you'll have a better understanding of how your clients envision the computer.

In the real world of PC tech, you also have to work with people: customers, clients, supervisors, coworkers, family members, maybe even spouses. You have to develop the skills for calmly gathering information about the state the computer is in and how it arrived there. Usually, your clients won't use the most technical language to explain the situation, and they may be frustrated or even a little on the defensive, so you need to be understanding and patient. You want them to see you as an ally, and to ensure that they do, you'll need to treat them with respect and kindness. You also need to develop the skills that will enable you to get a job—you might be the best tech in the world, but you need to know how to communicate that to a potential employer.

Bear in mind that someone who doesn't understand computers can still be quite intelligent and capable in other areas; talking down to a client is a bad idea! The client also trusts in your integrity to solve the problem in the most efficient and cost-effective manner possible, and to return their machine and data uncompromised.

Finally, and most importantly, you should cultivate a good troubleshooting methodology. It's difficult to give you a specific checklist, but the following guidelines should help:

- Identify the problem.

  - Question the user and identify user changes to the computer and perform backups before making changes.

- Establish a theory of probable cause (question the obvious).

- Test the theory to determine the cause.

  - Once the theory is confirmed, determine the next steps to resolve the problem.

  - If the theory is not confirmed, reestablish a new theory or escalate the problem.

- Establish a plan of action to resolve the problem and implement the solution.

- Verify full system functionality and, if applicable, implement preventative measures.

- Document findings, actions, and outcomes.

→ Note

You should be familiar with the six steps of the troubleshooting theory for both real-world application and the CompTIA A+ exams.

Don't forget that often the client will be there with you, hanging on your every word. Explain the steps you are taking to configure a new system, or to repair damage and recover data from hardware failure or malicious software. When backing up data prior to working on a system, err on the side of caution; make your best effort to determine which data is vital to your client and to their business, even if they are vague about what data needs to be protected. Try to give them realistic expectations of what you likely can or cannot do so that the outcome is a pleasant surprise rather than a bitter disappointment.

The scenarios presented in this chapter will make you think about how to act as a gainfully employed PC technician and show you some of the situations you'll encounter out in the field. You can also think about the scenarios from a job seeker's perspective—chances are good that a prospective employer will ask you how to deal with situations like the ones described in this chapter. First, however, let's look at how to handle the interview itself.

✔ Hint

Ideally, for the lab exercises in this chapter, you should have a partner play the role of the client while you play the role of the PC tech (or the interviewer and job seeker for the first lab exercise). Work through the scenarios in a live, person-to-person role-playing of each situation, just as if it were real. If you are working in a classroom setting, try to work with different classmates through each of the different scenarios.

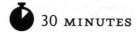 30 MINUTES

Lab Exercise 32.01: Preparing for the Technical Interview

Sitting for an interview and selling yourself to complete strangers is the stuff of many a PC tech's nightmares. Trust me! You might think it sounds easy, but once you're in the hot seat and actually doing it, everything changes. So buckle down and pay attention during this lab because it could make or break your chance of landing that job!

Before we get started in earnest, here are some tips to keep in mind when interviewing for a job:

- No chewing gum.

- Turn your cell phone off and keep it out of sight. No texting!

- Comb your hair and keep it out of your eyes (if you have to swing your hair to the side every minute, get a haircut). Messy hair looks very unprofessional and reflects poor self-image.

- Brush your teeth.

- Males—Tuck in your shirt, pull up your pants, and wear a belt.

- Females—No miniskirts or low tops, and keep your stomach covered.

- Shake hands firmly.

- Maintain good eye contact at all times.

- No sneakers allowed!

- Do not offer information that is not pertinent to the interview. Think before speaking and always tell the truth.

For more tips on job interviewing, see "10 Killer Job Interview Questions and Answers," by Carole Martin, available at www.bspcn.com/2007/08/24/10-killer-job-interview-questions-and-answers/.

Learning Objectives

In this lab exercise, you will practice role-playing as an interviewee (if no interviewers are present, you may also have to role-play as an interviewer). You will be critiqued as you are probed to say and do the right thing at all times. So get ready for some fun in preparing for the interview process.

At the end of this lab, you'll be able to

- Speak clearly, professionally, and technically

- Describe how IT affects the workplace

- Effectively communicate what you know

- Know what to bring and wear to the interview

Lab Materials and Setup

The materials you need for this lab are

- An updated résumé that lists all your skills; technology courses that you're currently taking or have completed; and reliable references, other than family—preferably customers or people who know your skill level and character, and have worked with you for a period of a minimum of six months.

- A digital portfolio (a CD) that includes an updated copy of your résumé; pictures or short video clips of you working on computers, possibly building a computer; any presentations or technology-related projects you've been involved in implementing; a log of customers you've supported; and any Web sites you've created that demonstrate your skills—not MySpace or Facebook! By the way, you will leave this CD with your interviewer, so make it good.

Instructors: For the setup, enlist or bring in at least four volunteers from the technology industry, such as local PC repair shop managers, Geek Squad reps, and so forth, to help you interview your students. Use people from the business world as much as possible, but if you're under tight timelines, just ask your school's principal, guidance personnel, media specialists, or other teachers to assist you. They make great interviewers because your students most likely do not know them as well as they know you and thus will take this exercise more seriously.

Getting Down to Business

This is a work-in-progress lab that will be beneficial to you for life. Once you've started the process of learning to present yourself effectively, you will be surprised at how many opportunities you'll get to use these skills.

Step 1 Type your résumé and save it to multiple places. Have your instructor guide you as to what to include and what not to include. Run a spell check! Print and proof it yourself first and then allow your instructor to critique it.

✔ Hint

The Web offers many places for the serious job seeker to post a completed résumé electronically, such as www.monster.com, but it is wise to have properly formatted paper copies as well to turn in with your application.

Step 2 Type a list of personal and professional references on a separate document. Contact each reference and ask him or her if they will be a reference for you. Make your references aware they may get a call about your potential interview.

Step 3 On the day of the interview, "dress for success"; evaluation of your appearance comprises 50 percent of your grade. As a class, set up a room with at least four tables/stations, one for each volunteer interviewer, with at least three chairs at each station.

Step 4 Enter the interview area quietly. Make sure to have your printed résumé, references, and digital portfolio ready to turn in. Interviews should last no more than 10 minutes. Ideally, the interviewers will ask everyone the same questions, but you never know what you'll be asked.

Step 5 Once you have been interviewed, the interviewers will compare their thoughts and choose two or three top students to be interviewed by the entire group of interviewers. This is called a panel interview and is the type of interview students will most likely encounter when being interviewed for various jobs.

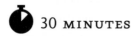 30 MINUTES

Lab Exercise 32.02: Scenario #1: Computer Obsolescence and Expense of Replacement

An independent salesperson for a multiline musical instrument dealer walks into your shop carrying a weathered laptop case. He lays the case on the counter and asks simply, "Is there anything you can do?" You open the case to find an early-2000s model IBM ThinkPad. You open the lid on the ThinkPad and see a semicircle indentation and spider-web cracks all across the screen. The LCD panel has been completely smashed!

As the expert in this situation, you have to make some decisions about what would ultimately be the most timely and cost-effective solution. You then have to explain your recommendations to the client carefully and respectfully because either solution will most likely be costly and therefore stressful for him.

✔ Cross-Reference

Before you work through the role-playing scenarios, go back and reread Chapter 32 in *Mike Meyers' CompTIA A+ Guide to Managing and Troubleshooting PCs*.

Learning Objectives

This exercise will test your ability to stay cool in the face of a concerned client, even as you may have to deliver news that the client doesn't want to hear.

At the end of this lab, you'll be able to

- Assess the damage and back up the client's data

- Convey the options available to the client

- Provide a recommended solution to the client

Lab Materials and Setup

The materials you need for this lab are

- A partner or classmate to play the role of the client (if you don't have a partner, you can still work through the scenario and complete the Lab Analysis Test at the end of the chapter)

- A notepad or computer-generated "trouble ticket" to simulate the practice followed in many computer support organizations

- Optional: A demo machine and/or Internet access, to re-create the scenario and research options on vendor Web sites and tech forums

Getting Down to Business

To begin, have your partner read the Client section that follows. You will then read the PC Tech section and use the specifics to analyze the situation and recommend the best course of action. Sit down and work through the scenario with your partner. If possible, use the Internet or demo machines to make the role-playing scenario more valid.

CLIENT:

You are an independent salesperson for a multiline musical instrument dealer and spend about 20 days a month on the road. You use the laptop to keep all of your customer data and product information up to date. You were finishing up a particularly busy week when you fell asleep with the laptop on your lap. You placed the laptop next to your bed in the hotel only to step on it in the middle of the evening. Your entire business relies on the information contained in the computer, and having it down, even for a short time, is going to create problems.

Along with the time-critical issues, you are also an independent salesperson and self-employed—you pay your own travel and lodging expenses, health benefits, and life insurance. A costly repair or replacement was not in your planned budget.

PC TECH:

As the technician, you are going to analyze the laptop and quickly recommend that the hard drive be backed up immediately. Using a laptop IDE harness and duplicating the hard drive to a volume on the shop data server, you can alleviate the customer's concern that all his data will be lost.

You know that the machine is over 10 years old, and that the replacement screen and labor to install it are probably going to cost a fair amount. You use the Internet to research replacement LCD screens and try to estimate the overall cost of the repair. Not only is it expensive, the availability of the screen is backlogged over three weeks. It is also a good bet that other components in the machine will begin to age and fail even if the screen repair is warranted.

Your job is laid out before you. You need to discuss the options of repairing the current machine, warts and all, or having the client upgrade to a more modern laptop.

 30 MINUTES

Lab Exercise 32.03: Scenario #2: Hardware Failure, or I Can't See Anything!

One of the marketing analysts in your company calls the help desk and complains that he's unable to get his monitor to work. He arrived this morning and the computer just never booted. There's a mission-critical presentation on this system that is due to be presented today at 2:00 P.M. It's now 1:00 P.M. and nobody has returned his call, even to say that his initial request was received! The analyst storms into the IT department and demands some assistance. You look up from your screen just in time to see your supervisor and the analyst barreling toward your cubicle. Your supervisor asks if you will accompany the analyst to his department and see if you can figure this out.

In cases such as this, the tech's job is not only to troubleshoot the problem and provide a solution, but also to provide customer service and present a good image of the IT department to other employees. As the expert in this situation, you not only have to solve the issue—you must also make your best effort to diffuse the agitation of the anxious analyst.

Learning Objectives

The plan is to have a classmate play the role of the client, and you to play the role of the PC tech. This exercise will give you a great opportunity to display not only your tech skills, but also your professionalism in a tough, time-crunch situation.

At the end of this lab, you'll be able to

- Analyze the problem with input from the client

- Diffuse the frustration of the client

- Provide a complete solution

Lab Materials and Setup

The materials you need for this lab are

- A partner or classmate to play the role of the client (optionally, if you do not have a partner, work through the scenario and complete the Lab Analysis Test at the end of the chapter)

- A notepad or computer-generated "trouble ticket" to simulate the practice followed in many computer support organizations

- Optional: A demo machine or Internet access to re-create the scenario and research options on vendor Web sites and tech forums

Getting Down to Business

To begin, have your partner read the Client section that follows. You will then read the PC Tech section and use the specifics to analyze the situation and recommend the best course of action. Now sit down and work through the scenario with your partner. If possible, use the Internet or demo machines to make the role-playing scenario more valid.

CLIENT:

You arrived this morning and started your normal routine: You dropped your briefcase in the corner of your cube, carefully placed your coffee on the file cabinet (away from the computer), and pressed the power button on the computer. You exchanged a few pleasantries with your fellow workers and sat down to make the finishing touches on the presentation you will be delivering at 2:00 P.M. today, only to find a completely blank screen. You attempted to reboot the computer, and verified that the power light was lit on the monitor (you do know *that* much about computers). But it was still a no-go!

You placed a call with the help desk and tried not to panic. Some friends invited you to lunch, and you joined them with the hope that the IT department would visit while you were gone so that you could return to a working machine. When you returned, nothing had been done!

You are a little tense, but you know that you are at the mercy of the IT group. You head on down to the IT department and visit directly with the support supervisor. He introduces you to one of the techs, who is now traveling to your desk with you. The only thing you can remember doing differently was authorizing an Automatic Windows Update last night as you were leaving.

PC TECH:

Well, you've certainly been here before—a critical situation with severe time constraints, but now it's 1:20 P.M. and the analyst is very tense. You arrive at the analyst's desk and have him run through the routine that he followed when he arrived this morning. You ask if anything has changed since yesterday when the machine worked. You then run a check of the obvious diagnoses and troubleshooting steps.

> ✔ **Hint**
>
> It is imperative that you keep detailed records of the diagnosing and troubleshooting steps. If you have set items that you check first (remember: simple to complex), then you will perform a quick check of the power lights, power cord connections, monitor connections, and whether the monitor settings menu is accessible, enabling you to rule out simple items that may have been overlooked in a time of stress.

If none of the simple solutions appears to work, you have two issues on your hands. One is that you need to get the system back up and running, and the other is that your client has a big presentation due in 30 minutes (yes, it took 10 minutes to check the simple items, so it's now 1:30 P.M.). You know that your organization has all of the employees save their documents to Documents, which is mapped to the server to facilitate backups. You have the analyst log on to a coworker's machine, access his Documents folder, and fine-tune his presentation with 10 minutes to spare.

You send a calmer analyst to the meeting, complete the analysis of the system, and perform the required repairs. Record the additional steps you would take to complete this trouble ticket. How would you communicate your findings with the analyst? Share the results with your instructor.

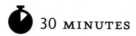 30 MINUTES

Lab Exercise 32.04: Scenario #3: What Do You Mean, a Virus?

You're just finishing up lunch when one of your neighbors walks into your shop with her family computer under her arm. She knows you from the neighborhood, and has heard that you know a fair amount about computer systems (I hope so, since you are working in a computer shop!). She asks if you can take a look at her system.

You ask what seems to be the problem, to which she responds, "It seems to be running really slow. We can't find some of the documents and pictures we used to have, and every time we try to access the Internet, it kicks us off!"

You recommend that she return to whatever she was doing and leave the machine with you; it just so happens that your schedule is open this afternoon, so you should be able to take a quick look at the system. You ask if there are any passwords you'll need, and the client responds, "No, we don't worry about passwords." You fill out a trouble ticket with the contact information and let her know you'll be in touch with her shortly.

Learning Objectives

Viruses are a simple fact of life in today's computing landscape, and any tech should be able to both remediate existing virus infections and take preventative measures against future infections. It's sometimes tempting to treat customers as though their virus infection serves them right, but you have to maintain your professional demeanor in these situations, as you'll come across a lot of them.

At the end of this lab, you'll be able to

- Analyze the machine to determine if it exhibits the symptoms the customer has indicated

- Perform routine maintenance and optimization

- Make recommendations to the client for the upkeep of her machine

Lab Materials and Setup

The materials you need for this lab are

- A partner or classmate to play the role of the client (optionally, if you do not have a partner, work through the scenario and complete the Lab Analysis Test at the end of the chapter)

- A notepad or computer-generated "trouble ticket" to simulate the practice followed in many computer support organizations

- Optional: A demo machine or Internet access to re-create the scenario and research options on vendor Web sites and tech forums

Getting Down to Business

To begin, have your partner read the Client section that follows. You will then read the PC Tech section and use the specifics to analyze the situation and recommend the best course of action. Now sit down and work through the scenario with your partner. If possible, use the Internet or demo machines to make the role-playing scenario more valid.

CLIENT:

The computer you are dropping off to the shop is the family computer and is used by all the family members—two teenagers, you, and your spouse. The machine is constantly online, using a high-speed cable Internet connection, and there are tons of music files, pictures, and games stored on the hard drive.

You are not completely computer savvy, so if asked by the tech, you respond that you do not know if there is any antispyware or antivirus software installed, although it's possible that the kids have installed something. All you know is that the machine is running slowly, you have lost some documents and pictures that you wanted, and the machine will no longer connect to the Internet.

When you drop the machine off at the repair shop, the tech attempts to send you on your way, but you would like to see what he is doing and possibly learn how to make the system run better. You are fairly insistent, and finally work out that the tech will walk you through everything when you return.

PC Tech:

You set the system up on your test bench and boot into Windows 7. The system does take an inappropriate amount of time to boot and load all of the programs (you notice there are a large number of items in the system tray, but it is surprisingly devoid of an antivirus icon). You take a quick note of the version of Windows 7 and notice that no service packs are installed, so it's a good bet that Windows Update has not been running either.

You check Device Manager and Event Viewer to verify that there are no specific hardware issues; everything seems to check out there. You then run Disk Cleanup—which uncovers over 4 GB of temporary Internet files. It is a 500-GB hard drive that is almost filled to capacity. Finally, you double-check whether any antivirus/antiadware/antispyware programs are installed, and find nothing.

✔ **Cross-Reference**

Refer to Lab Exercise 29.03, "Cleaning and Protecting a Client's Computer," for more information on how to clean up a machine that appears to have no specific hardware problems causing issues, but merely an accumulation of junk files, adware, spyware, and viruses.

You contact the customer and recommend that she stop back by the shop to discuss your recommendations for the machine. You still do not know if the lost files are recoverable, but you know you'll have to work through the other problems before you get there.

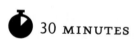 30 MINUTES

Lab Exercise 32.05: Scenario #4: No Documents, No E-Mail, and I Can't Print!

You arrive at work bright and early at 7:00 A.M. to find several voice mail messages blinking on your phone. You are one of the desktop support specialists at a large financial institution, and you usually make a point of arriving early to catch up on some of the studying you have been doing to pass your next IT certification exam. However, it looks like you will have to put this on the back burner for today. You check the messages, and it appears that the entire proposals department is in already, working on an investment proposal for a prominent client. The messages are frantic requests to fix the computer systems in the proposals department. Apparently, none of the computers are able to access the documents the team has been working with all week; they could not e-mail their concerns and the network printer is down!

You have an idea of what might be happening, but you are going to drop by the proposals department and check some of the individual machines before you make a rash decision. You close your textbook and walk over to the proposals department.

Learning Objectives

Staying cool in high-stakes situations is the hallmark of a true tech, so look at this lab as an opportunity to improve your troubleshooting skills in the face of pressure. At the end of this lab, you'll be able to

- Verify that this is not an isolated problem with one or two machines

- Diagnose and troubleshoot from simple to complex, and record your findings

- Follow proper procedures to escalate the trouble ticket

Lab Materials and Setup

The materials you need for this lab are

- A partner or classmate to play the role of the client (optionally, if you do not have a partner, work through the scenario and complete the Lab Analysis Test at the end of the chapter)

- A notepad or computer-generated "trouble ticket" to simulate the practice followed in many computer support organizations

- Optional: A demo machine or Internet access to re-create the scenario and research options on vendor Web sites and tech forums

Getting Down to Business

To begin, have your partner read the Client section that follows. You will then read the PC Tech section and use the specifics to analyze the situation and recommend the best course of action. Now sit down and work through the scenario with your partner. If possible, use the Internet or demo machines to make the role-playing scenario more valid.

Client:

You are the Chief Financial Officer (CFO) for this large financial institution. You have asked your entire team to come in today at 6:00 A.M. to finish up an investment proposal for a high-profile client. Everybody is on point, but as soon as things begin rolling, a number of your staff appear at your door: "The network is down!"

They inform you that they have left numerous messages with the IT department, but you do not expect anybody to be there until 8:30 A.M. or so. Just as you are preparing to call the Chief Information Officer (CIO) at home, one of the desktop support specialists arrives on the scene.

You ask the desktop support specialist if he is up to the challenge of determining the cause of the outage and, if so, whether he has the authority to complete the tasks involved to get the network up and running again. The specialist seems like a sincere individual, so you ask him to perform the initial investigation and report to you as soon as he has a handle on the situation.

PC Tech:

This issue is going to challenge you on a professionalism level more than it will challenge you as a technologist. You should run through some quick checks of the various computers in the proposals department. Check the physical connections and log on to a few of the machines to verify that the network connectivity is down.

As soon as you can verify that the entire department is down, make sure you communicate with the CFO to apprise him of the situation. This is a case of escalation—you need to get your network administrators online and have them troubleshoot the network. You have checked a few machines in other departments to verify that there is network connectivity in the building, and it is only the proposals department that is down.

You assure the CFO that you're on the issue and will him them when the network admin is onsite. You then make a call to your friend, who just happens to be one of the network administrators; she is only a few minutes from the office, and tells you to hang tight and plan on joining her in the switch room. You're going to have an opportunity to work the issues through to the resolution. Don't forget to update the CFO!

Lab Analysis Test

1. Write a short essay summarizing the problem, discussion, and solution of the smashed laptop screen from Scenario #1.

2. Write a short essay summarizing the problem, discussion, and solution of the nonfunctioning monitor from Scenario #2. Be sure to include details on handling the analyst's stress level and frustration with the IT department.

3. Write a short essay summarizing the problem, discussion, and solution of the slow machine and Internet connection problems from Scenario #3. Be sure to include details on the steps and updates you would recommend that the client authorize.

4. Write a short essay summarizing the problem, discussion, and solution of the network outage in Scenario #4. Be sure to include details on the steps you would take to escalate the issue to the proper individual, the documentation paper path, and communication with the CFO.

5. Write a short essay describing the six steps included in the troubleshooting theory. List these steps in order and discuss the importance of each.

Key Term Quiz

Use the following terms to complete the following sentences. Not all terms will be used.

    CFO

    document

    obsolescence

    question

    theory of probable cause

    trouble ticket

    troubleshooting theory

    verify

1. There are six steps to the _____.

2. You should always _____ the repair after you verify full system functionality.

3. The limited lifetime of a PC is referred to as _____.

4. After you establish a(n) _____, you should always test.

5. A(n) _____ is a computer-generated report that usually includes contact information, the problem description, and the problem solution.

Index

Symbols and Numbers